Larousse
Greek and Roman Mythology

Larousse
Greek and Roman
Mythology

Joël Schmidt

Edited by Dr. Seth Benardete
Classicist, New York University

McGraw-Hill Book Company
New York   London   St. Louis   San Francisco
Toronto   Hamburg   Mexico

DICTIONNAIRE DE LA MYTHOLOGIE GRECQUE ET ROMAINE

English translation © 1980 by Larousse, U.S.A., Inc.
Copyright © 1965 by Librairie Larousse, S.A., Paris

Library of Congress Cataloging in Publication Data

Schmidt, Joël.
  Larousse Greek and Roman Mythology.

  Translation of Dictionnaire de la mythologie
grecque et romaine.
  Includes index.
  1. Mythology, Classical—Dictionaries.
I. Benardete, Seth. II. Title.
BL715.S313   292'.13'0321   80-15046

Editorial: Philip M. Rideout with Inez M. Krech and Jeanette Mall

Translator: Sheilah O'Halloran, M.A.

Design: BOOKGRAPHICS

Typography: Rocappi

1234-DON-83210

And it was ultimately in the form of paideia, "culture," that the Greeks bequeathed the whole achievement of the Hellenic mind to the other nations of antiquity. Augustus envisaged the task of the Roman empire in terms of Greek culture. Without Greek cultural ideals, Greco-Roman civilization would not have been a historical unity, and the culture of the western world would never have existed.

Paideia: the Ideals of Greek Culture
Werner Jaeger, trans. by Gilbert Highet
Oxford University Press, 1939

EUROPA, photo Anderson-Giraudon

Introduction

The mythology of the Greeks and Romans remains alive today because it is very close to human reality. The major Greek and Roman gods, of which this book attempts to give as complete an overview as possible, are not abstract entities but beings imbued with life and possessing qualities and faults that are all too similar to those of humans. Their very immortality, rather than lifting them above the realm of mortals, bestows upon them the importance of examples and makes them continual references even for us today. Through the anthropomorphism of the gods of Antiquity, through these divinities incarnate, the intangible sacred may be more easily understood.

Mythology continues to live because it sets the stage for heroes whose moral and physical trials, whose metaphysical doubts and anxiety in the face of Death, Love and Fate, strike a familiar chord in humans and continue to concern modern man. The work presents the lives of major heroes of mythology—their journeys, their meanderings and the dangers they encountered and somehow overcame. It describes the outburst of passions of these extraordinary beings which, very often, have a divine origin. Through the story of these heroes, the reader can participate fully in the exaltation of courage, that classical "virtue" that continues more or less to shape Western consciousness. All of these gods and all of these heroes are representations of very ancient myths that recount, in the form of legends and tales, the history of inventions (Talos and the saw); of early cultivation (Triptolemus and Demeter for wheat, Dionysus for wine); and of the first discoveries. They offer a colorful and captivating explanation for all the natural phenomena that were often acted out in ancient Greece and Italy.

Thus, in a way, Greek and Roman mythology established the themes that were subsequently reexplored and developed by literature, morality, the humanities and even the sciences. For this reason, this dictionary includes such words as *friendship, birth, death, deluge,* etc. Also included are the names of major countries, cities, rivers, springs and mountains as mythological legends assume an even more effective and lifelike importance when they are seen in terms of geography and history.

That mythology is a moving, changing, complex thing is indisputable. The table of the principal literary sources of mythology included in this dictionary illustrates how much mythology owes to the development of Greek and Latin literature. More than eight centuries elapsed between Homer's *Iliad* and *Odyssey,* written in the 8th century B.C., and Ovid and Seneca. Thus mythology was constantly reworked, modified and adapted to the tastes and customs of successive periods in history by poets, dramatists and historians. Homer, whose work is brimming with life, was succeeded by Hesiod who introduced some order in the genealogies of the gods and in the expression and classification of the myths. Then, at the end of the 6th century, Greek tragedy emerged; in the choice of subjects and language, this was largely inspired by mythology. Dramatists like Aeschylus, Sophocles and Euripides revived many a timeworn myth. They rejuvenated and transformed the gods and heroes of the great legendary royal families of Greece and gave them a persuasive life force in the new versions to which, generally speaking, this dictionary has conformed in both the bodies of the articles and the genealogical charts. It should be pointed out that, to avoid weighing down the text, cross-references have been omitted. However, an extensive index provides cross-references among important entries for ease in reading about a subject at length.

With the decline of Greece in the 2nd century and the ever-increasing predominance of Rome, Greek mythology was Latinized. Naturally the Romans continued to worship their local gods under their original names—in fact, the reader will find specific articles on the major Italic divinities—but they finally likened their major gods to those of the Greeks. In the *Aeneid,* Virgil recounted the adventures of Aeneas, the Romans' national hero, just as Homer, eight centuries before, had related the adventures of Ulysses, the national hero of Greece. Ovid, in the *Metamorphoses,* and many other Latin poets adapted numerous Greek legends to purely Latin ethics and aesthetics. This dictionary has yielded, in part, to their tradition. Seneca, finally, borrowed the subjects for his tragedies from the main mythological narratives while freely adapting them to evoke the effects of practical morality.

This simple and all too short bird's-eye view of ancient Greek and Roman literatures strives to prove that mythology is not established once and for all; every effort has been made to present the different Greek and Latin versions of the same legend. Furthermore, it is impossible to neglect to mention the influence of mythological themes on the literary thought of the 16th and 17th centuries, on poets such as Chénier, Leconte de Lisle or Valéry and, even more recently, on Cocteau (the myth of Orpheus). It is to be hoped that the reader will recognize the disturbing analogies that exist between certain ancient legends and Western legends or tales: for instance, Hero and Leander, an ancient foreshadowing of Tristan and Isolde; or Cupid and Psyche and their influence on the myths of Prince Charming, Beauty and the Beast and Cinderella; or Pyramus and Thisbe, precursors of Romeo and Juliet. Finally, it would be a grave disservice to deny the effect of mythology on the fine arts, both in ancient times as well as today. However, for the sake of conformity between image and text, this dictionary uses as illustrations mainly ancient masterpieces of Greek and Roman art. Let the reader discover in this dictionary that mythology is the everlasting and constantly renewed translation of the major collective principles that govern humanity beyond the contingencies of time and space.

ABAS. **1.** Grandson of Danaus, son of Lynceus and Hypermnestra, and grandfather of Danaë who was the mother of Perseus; Abas, the twelfth king of Argos, has many a famous hero among both his ancestors and his descendants.

2. There is another **Abas,** the eponym of the Abantes, the people of Euboea. He was believed to have been born of the love of Poseidon and Arethusa.

ABEONA and ADEONA. Roman divinities presiding over travels. According to St. Augustine, Abeona is invoked upon the departure *(abire)* of children; Adeona is invoked upon the approach *(adire)* of newcomers.

ABSYRTUS. Son of Aeetes, the king of Colchis, and brother of Medea, Absyrtus met with an unfortunate fate. When Medea left home with Jason, she took her brother along. But when she discovered that Aeetes was pursuing her, she killed Absyrtus, cut up his body, and scattered his limbs along the road, in order that Aeetes would be overcome with horror and abandon the pursuit. Her plan succeeded.

ACADINA. It was customary to throw tablets on which oaths had been inscribed into this fountain in Sicily dedicated to the Palici. Depending on whether the tablets sank or floated, the oaths were sincere or insincere.

ACAMAS. Three heroes bear this name. One, the son of Theseus and Phaedra,. was dispatched to Troy to rescue Helen, who had been carried off by Paris. During the negotiations, which proved fruitless, Acamas seduced Laodice, one of Priam's daughters. Shortly before the fall of Troy, Acamas was one of the eight heroes who hid in the famous wooden horse and were thus able to enter the city secretly.

A second **Acamas,** the son of Antenor and Theano, also made a name for himself during the same war but was finally killed.

The third **Acamas,** who hailed from Thrace, met a similar fate; he perished at the hands of Ajax.

ACARNAN. This son of Alcmaeon and the nymph Callirhoë was the grandson of the celebrated Theban seer Amphiaraus. His father was killed by Phegeus. With the protection of Zeus, Acarnan was able to grow at an astonishing pace and reach adult size within but a few months. Thus, he quickly avenged his father's death by killing the murderer, his wife and his children. He then took refuge in Epirus where, according to Ovid, he founded the State of Acarnania.

ACASTUS. One of the heroes of the Argonauts' expedition, Acastus succeeded his father Pelias, the king of Iolcus, who had been killed by his daughters on the perfidious advice of Medea. To honor the spirit of his departed father, Acastus wanted to sacrifice one of the parricides, but Heracles stole her from him. Afterwards, Peleus, who had come to the court of Acastus to be purified of the accidental murder of the king of Phthia, scorned the love of Astydamia, the wife of Acastus. Unable to seduce Peleus, Astydamia took revenge by accusing him of trying to compromise her honor. Acastus wished to uphold the sacred rules of hospitality, so did not kill him. After having disarmed him, he left him sleeping in a forest, thinking that he would be devoured by ferocious beasts. Chiron, a Centaur, managed to awaken Peleus and warn him of the danger to which his host had exposed him. Overcome with vengeful anger, Peleus returned to Iolcus and killed both Acastus and his wife.

ACCA LARENTIA. The Romans used this name to refer to two women whose legends were gradually confused with one another. The first was the wife of the shepherd Faustulus. This woman raised Remus and Romulus, the twins who had been found by her husband.

The second **Acca Larentia** enjoyed the favors of Hercules, who had won her in a game of dice with the guardian of his temple. She later married Tarutius, the proprietor of the future site of Rome. She in turn inherited the site and at her death bequeathed it to its new settlers. Her name seems to mean "Mother of the Lares." Her festival, the Larentalia or Larentinalia, was on December 23.

ACHATES.   1. After the fall and burning of Troy, Aeneas managed to escape with his father and son, first to Mount Ida and later to Italy. Achates, one of his friends, did not hesitate to accompany him on these perilous journeys: since then, his loyalty has become legendary.

2. Achates is also the name of a river in Sicily where the stone known as "agate" was found for the first time.

ACHELOÜS. The longest river in Greece, the Acheloüs marks the borders of Aetolia and Acarnania. The god of the river played a prominent role in many legends. The son of Oceanus and Tethys, he was the brother of more than three thousand rivers which he held in his sway. He appears in the twelve labors of Heracles, with whom he battled for Deianira. Conquered by the hero in their first struggle, Acheloüs returned to fight in the form of an enormous serpent and then, about to be strangled, in the form of a raging bull; but he was vanquished a second time by Heracles, who broke one of his horns, which later became the symbol of the horn of plenty. Some ancient authors interpreted this myth as the symbol of the fertility of a river that had been revered above all others by the ancients and to whom sacrifices were always offered on the advice of the oracle of Dodona. Four nymphs who, on his

The god Acheloüs, his body covered with scales and uncoiled like the meanderings of a river, seems to want to entangle Heracles. But the hero manages to overwhelm him by seizing him by the horn, which has since become the symbol of the horn of plenty. Detail of a vase, 4th cent. B.C., British Museum.

banks, had neglected to invoke him in their prayers, were carried off by his waters, as they swelled in anger, and changed into islands (the Echidnas).

ACHERON. The Acheron flows in Epirus, terminating in a deep crevasse. Considering its sinister appearance and the etymology of its name ("the river of woe") as well as its descent into the belly of the Earth, the Ancients believed that it was one of the rivers of the Underworld which the souls of the dead had to cross, on Charon's barge, before embarking on their final sojourn. To account for the origin of this river that was of such capital importance, the Greeks invented a legend naming Helios as his father and Gaia as his mother. Acheron had been banished to the Underworld by Zeus because he had given water to the Titans in their struggle with the Olympians. In Latin literature, Acheron refers most often to the very depths of the Underworld itself.

ACHILLES. The greatest of all Greek heroes, Achilles' praises were sung at length by Homer in the *Iliad*. His glory has been handed down over the centuries; his legend has been embellished with thousands of details. For the sake of simplification, a distinction is generally made between the Achilles of Homeric tradition and the Achilles of post-Homeric traditions. The son of Thetis and Peleus, the king of Phthia in Thessaly, Achilles was entrusted to the scholar Phoenix from whom he learned the art of eloquence and the handling of arms. It is also said

Achilles and Ajax have temporarily abandoned the labors of the Trojan war for a game of dice. Ajax (right) has removed his shield and helmet. The two heroes express the idea, cherished by the Ancients, of friendship built upon the same martial ideas. Athenian amphora, 6th cent. B.C., Vatican Museum, photo Alinari-Giraudon.

that he received lessons in medicine from the centaur Chiron. Hungering for glory and adventure and accompanied by his closest friend Patroclus, he followed the two Greek heroes Nestor and Ulysses, who took part in the siege of Troy. Despite the warnings of Thetis, he preferred a short but glorious life to a longer yet obscure existence. His beauty, his bravura, his strength of spirit, and the precious protection of Hera and Athena all contributed to his renown. However, the hero was not without weaknesses. Touchy, excessive in his passions and his grudges, he abandoned the struggle

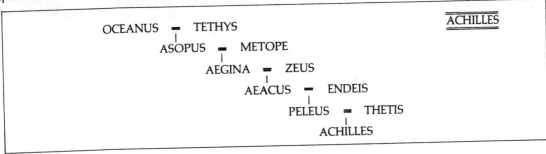

ACHILLES

OCEANUS ▬ TETHYS
|
ASOPUS ▬ METOPE
|
AEGINA ▬ ZEUS
|
AEACUS ▬ ENDEIS
|
PELEUS ▬ THETIS
|
ACHILLES

Here Achilles has assumed the appearance of Apollo. The hero is closely related to the gods. Antique bronze, Louvre.

In an attitude of despair, Achilles and his companions mourn over the body of Patroclus whom Hector has just slain. Silver oenochoe from the Bernay Treasures, Bibl. Nat., photo Giraudon.

when Agamemnon stole Briseis, the beautiful captive with whom he was in love. Deprived of his support, the Greeks suffered defeat upon defeat. But at the news of the death of his beloved friend Patroclus, who had been slain by Hector, Achilles emerged from his depression and donned a magic armor forged by Hephaestus at Thetis's request. He once again joined the battle. He slew Hector after a single battle and dragged his enemy's body around the city of Troy for all the terror-stricken Trojans to see. Then, once appeased, he piously agreed to return Hector's remains to King Priam, his father. However, the hero's days were numbered. Achilles was not destined to see the final victory of the Greeks. He fell beside the Scaean gates at the foot of the wall of Troy, stricken by the hand of Paris, guided by Apollo. He was buried on the banks of the Hellespont amid tears and wailing.

According to later traditions, Thetis tried on several occasions to procure immortality for her son Achilles. To do this, she rubbed him with ambrosia during the day and dipped him into fire at night. Finally, she dipped him into the waters of the Styx. The body of Achilles became invulnerable except for his heel by which his mother had held him. When the Trojan War broke out, Thetis recommended that her son disguise himself as a woman and, under the name of Pyrrha, mingle with the daughters of King Lycomedes to avoid the warriors' pressure. But Ulysses, having learned from the seer Calchas that Achilles' presence in the Greek ranks was essential for victory, tricked Achilles into following him. Later, during the siege of Troy, he was about to betray his allies for the love of Polyxena, the daughter of Priam, when an arrow pierced his heel, killing him. Surely these later accounts, although they add nothing to the glory of Achilles, do not detract from the Greeks' adoration for their favorite hero who, according to popular tradition, was to spend a happy eternity either on the White Isle at the mouth of the Danube or in the Elysian Fields.

Much more than a mere hero, Achilles was regarded in Antiquity as a demigod and revered in many regions of Greece. Temples and cults were dedicated to him, particularly in Sparta and Elis. It was imagined that he was enjoying a radiant afterlife, surrounded by divinities whose existence and pleasures he shared in eternal joy, punctuated by countless festivities and battles.

ACIS. A young Sicilian shepherd, Acis was the son of Faunus and the nymph Symaethis. His youthful beauty seduced the Nereid Galatea, who fell in love with him. But one day, as the two lovers were locked in a tender embrace, the giant Polyphemus surprised them. In his jealousy he threw a huge rock at Acis, who was crushed. The blood that gushed from his body produced a river which, ever since, has flowed at the foot of Aetna.

ACONTIUS. This handsome young man from the Isle of Ceos arrived one day in Delos for the festival of Artemis. On the way, he met Cydippe, a beautiful young Athenian of noble family with whom he fell instantly in love. To win her hand in marriage, Acontius, because of his inferiority in birth, devised this stratagem: he wrote on a quince the following words: "I swear by the temple of Artemis to marry Acontius." Then he tossed the fruit at her feet. Intrigued, Cydippe picked up the quince and read the inscription aloud. Suddenly, she realized the meaning of the words and wanted to stop, but it was too late. Artemis, the witness and guarantor of oaths, permitted no false oaths. Three times the young woman was engaged to marry someone other than Acontius. Three times Artemis afflicted her with an illness. Then her father consulted the Delphic oracle and discovered the truth about Acontius's scheme. Upon his return to Athens, he offered his daughter's hand in marriage to this persevering lover.

ACRISIUS. This son of Abas fought with his twin brother Proetus even in the womb of their mother Aglaïa, and later to ensure himself possession of the kingdom of Argos, which their father had left them. They are said to have been the inventors of the shield. Victorious in the early stages of the war, Acrisius was later defeated and obliged to accept an agreement that divided the kingdom: Tiryns went to Proetus while Acrisius took over Argos. This king's life was marked by fatality. An oracle had predicted that he would be killed by the son of his daughter Danaë, so Acrisius locked her up. But Zeus managed to join her and of their union a son, Perseus, was born. Later, the hero involuntarily killed Acrisius while throwing a discus, thereby fulfilling the prophecy.

acropolis. The upper part of an ancient city, as opposed to the lower part, was generally known as the "acropolis." Originally, the acropolis was a place of refuge for the rural or urban populations when they were threatened by enemy invasions or natural plagues. The idea of protection that the Greeks found on the

The Acropolis at Athens. Middle to second half of the 5th cent. B.C., photo Alison Frantz.

rocks high above their city was naturally transformed into the concept of a sacred place. In fact, the gods are supposed to sanctify these privileged places from which all danger seems to be dispelled. The kings, nobility and tyrants also established residence on the Acropolis, seeking on these peaks a sort of direct communion with the gods to whom they drew nearer, this communion working to the advantage of their government. In Italy, it was on the acropolis that the flight of the birds was examined and the entrails of victims were examined in elevated temples to enlist the tutelary assistance of the divinities. These gods often indicated their presence on the acropolis by means of signs: thus, at a relatively late period people revered on the Acropolis in Athens both the hole that Poseidon made in a rock with a thrust of his trident and the stumps of the olive tree that Athena caused to emerge from the arid earth. Each acropolis in Greece, in the Hellenistic countries and in Italy has its own particular aspects, its own personality and its local gods. Among the most famous spots are Corinth, Athens, Tiryns and Mycenae; in Asia, there is Troy, and the Hellenistic acropolis of Pergamum; the Capitol in Rome and all the hills that surround the Etruscan cities of Tuscany.

ACTAEON. This young Theban, the son of the shepherd Aristaeus and his wife Autonoë, became one of the finest hunters in the country thanks to the enlightened guidance of the centaur Chiron. But one day his vanity proved fatal. In fact, he prided himself on being able to surpass Artemis, the goddess of hunting, and on being more skillful than she. While pursuing game in the mountains of Cithaeron, he surprised Artemis as she was bathing. Already irritated by his impertinence, she did not forgive this last fault and, after changing him into a stag, she had him devoured by the fifty dogs accompanying him. His dogs were inconsolable until Chiron made for them a likeness of Ac-

The dogs, on the order of the goddess Artemis, devouring Actaeon. Behind the raised arm of the unfortunate victim can be seen the head of the animal whose form he is assuming. Artemis appears both firm and unpardoning. Detail of the Selinus metope, National Archaeological Museum, Palermo, photo Anderson.

taeon. According to certain mythographers, the dogs represent the fifty days during which there is absolutely no vegetation, of which Actaeon is one of the symbols.

ACTOR. The grandfather of Patroclus, Actor was, according to one version of his legend, king of Pherae where he received and purified Peleus, the murderer of Phocus, the son of Aeacus.

ADMETUS. King of Pherae, in Thessaly, Admetus took part in the Calydonian Boar Hunt and the expedition of the Argonauts, and welcomed Apollo who was exiled from Olympus for killing the Cyclopes. He made the god the guardian of his flocks. Admetus was in love

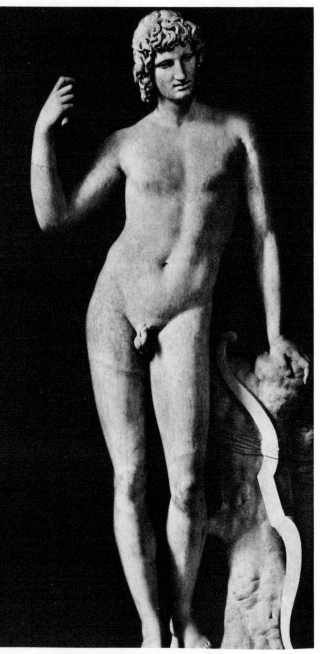

Adonis, the protégé of Aphrodite. National Archaeological Museum, Naples, photo Anderson-Giraudon.

with Alcestis. In order to marry her, he was obliged to yoke a lion and a boar to his chariot; in this task, he relied on Apollo's advice. The god, in recognition of his host's hospitality, helped him tame the two wild beasts and thus win the hand of the young woman. However, in his delight, he forgot the traditional sacrifice to Artemis on his wedding day. The goddess decided to punish him. When he entered his nuptial room he saw, in the place of his beloved spouse, a pile of hissing snakes. Apollo managed to appease his sister and the gods agreed that Admetus would escape death when his hour arrived if a member of his family would agree voluntarily to take his place in the land of the Shades. He even plied the Moirae with liquor so that the fatal thread would not be cut. For his part, Admetus begged his parents to die in his place but they refused. Only Alcestis, in her love, decided to sacrifice herself but, as some say, thanks to Heracles, and others, thanks to Persephone, she was reunited with the king and their happy union continued for many years afterwards.

ADONIS. The myth of Adonis originated in Syria. Before arriving in Greece, it underwent a number of changes in Egypt and Cyprus. The son of Cinyras, the king of Cyprus, and his daughter Myrrha, who was changed into a myrrh tree, Adonis was taken in hand by Aphrodite, who entrusted him to Persephone. The Queen of the Underworld was smitten with the young boy and refused to give him back. Aphrodite, who herself was not untouched by Adonis, complained to Zeus; the god of gods decided that Adonis would spend one third of the year with Persephone, one third of the year with the goddess Aphrodite, and the other third would be spent as Adonis himself chose. But the passion of the goddess of love incited the jealousy of her lover, Ares (or Apollo, or Artemis, according to other mythographers). Adonis was attacked by a wild boar, sent by one of these gods, and suffered a mortal wound to the groin. Artists and poets have tried to outdo one another in describing this death so mourned by Aphrodite, indeed giving free rein to imagination and lyricism. It is said that each drop of Adonis's blood gave rise to an anemone, spring's first short-lived blossom, while the blood of Aphrodite that flowed from the scratches she suffered from the bramblebushes as she hurried to nurse her wounded lover changed the roses from white to crimson. Never has the symbolism in a myth been so obvious. Adonis represents the plants that retreat to the realm of the dead to join Persephone in winter and return to earth in springtime, reunited in love only to blossom and bear fruit alone in summer. Adonis, which may well be the Semitic title "Adon" (Lord), is related to Tammuz, the Babylonian consort of Ishtar.

ADRASTUS. The legend of this king is linked to the expedition of the Seven against Thebes, during which he played a major role. Still young, he was forced to flee Argos and join King Polybus of Sicyon whom he succeeded to the throne. He wasted no time making amends, at least for the sake of appearance, with Amphiaraus who had murdered his father and to whom he offered his sister Eriphyle in marriage. He then regained sovereignty over Argolis. He subsequently married off his two other sisters Argeia and Deipyle, the former to Polynices, who had just been exiled from the throne of Thebes by his brother Eteocles, and the latter to Tydeus, who had been forced to flee Calydon after having committed a murder. Besieged by his guest's complaints, Adrastus decided to restore to Polynices his sovereign rights over Thebes, and he led the way in the war of the Seven Leaders, ignoring a prediction by Amphiaraus which foretold the death of all those who took part in the war, except Adrastus himself. The prediction proved correct: Polynices, Tydeus, Amphiaraus, Capaneus,

Hippomedon and Parthenopaeus all perished in the course of the struggle. Adrastus was able to get back to his territories thanks to the swiftness of his horse Arion, a gift from Heracles. Tradition has it that the king took part in the second expedition against Thebes, that of the Epigoni, with the sons of the six dead heroes. This time victory was complete for the Argive, but his son Aegialeus was killed in battle and Adrastus, brokenhearted, died soon after.

AEACUS. This legendary king, born of the love of Zeus and Aegina, reigned on the island that bore the name of his mother. His subjects having been decimated by a plague, he begged his divine father to repopulate his kingdom. Zeus obliged. He transformed all of the ants of Aegina into men and women. Thus, according to legend, the Myrmidons were born and these people were later led by Achilles, the grandson of Aeacus, to the ramparts of Troy. Particularly beloved of the gods, Aeacus was asked by the Greeks to raise a solemn prayer to the heavens to beg Zeus to put an end to a drought that was destroying their countries. Once again, he saw his divine father oblige him. But his piety was soon put to a severe test when he learned that his two sons, Telamon and Peleus, jealous of the exploits of their half-brother Phocus, had killed him by throwing a discus at his head. Aeacus was obliged to banish them from the island. At his death, because of his uprightness and his sense of fairness, he became an assistant to Rhadamanthys and Minos as a judge in the Underworld, where he was responsible especially for judging the dead who hailed from Europa.

AËDON. Homer related that Aëdon was the daughter of Pandareos and the wife of the Theban king Zethus. She had only one son, Itylus, while her sister-in-law Niobe had given birth to six sons and six daughters. Overcome with morbid jealousy, Aëdon plotted the murder of one of her nephews. However, she killed her own son by mistake. In response to her request that she cease to be of human form, Zeus changed her into a nightingale.

AEETES. Son of the Sun and of Perseis, this king reigned first over Corinth and later in Colchis over the city of Aia. He was known to have several wives, the most famous of whom was Idya, Medea's mother. At the beginning of his reign, Aeetes welcomed to his court Phrixus, to whom he gave the famous ram whose Golden Fleece was dedicated to the god Ares. Some time after, the king saw Jason and the Argonauts arrive in Colchis in search of the celebrated trophy on the order of Pelias. To obtain it, Jason, assisted by Medea, performed a certain number of formidable feats imposed by Aeetes. But, in the end, the king went back on his word and Jason was obliged to seize the Golden Fleece by force, then fleeing with Medea. Medea, in order to wreak horror upon her father who followed them in hot pursuit, cut up her brother Absyrtus and scattered the pieces along her route. Aeetes gathered up and buried his son's remains and returned home. But during his absence, his brother, Perses, had seized power and Aeetes was not able to claim his legitimate sovereignty until many years later when he became reconciled with Medea.

AEGESTES. Also known by the name of "Acestes," Aegestes was the son of the river-god Crimisus who, in the form of a bear or a dog, had relations with the Trojan woman Egesta, whose father had sent her to Sicily so that she would not be sacrificed to Poseidon. Aegestes founded on the island of Sicily a city which he called Segesta in honor of his mother. Another tradition recounts that he was the friend of Aeneas and that he fought in the ranks of King Priam and the Trojans. According to a third version, Aegestes, already settled in Sicily, welcomed Aeneas there upon his return from Troy and even buried Anchises, the father of his guest, on Mount Eryx.

AEGEUS. The son of Pandion, Aegeus was banished from Athens with his father. Later, with the help of his brothers—Nisus, Pallas and Lycus—he seized power once again. His first two marriages were sterile. Then, desperate because he did not have a son to succeed him, he had relations with Aethra, the daughter of the king of Troezen, and asked her, in the event a son was born, not to expose him but to raise him with care, without revealing to him the name of his father; Theseus was to be this son. The hero left for Greece to fight against his cousins, the fifty sons of Pallas, who had usurped the sovereignty. After revealing himself to his father, he reestablished him on the throne. Later, Aegeus killed Androgeus; for this murder, he was forced to submit to the terrible demands of Minos. When the Minotaur demanded his yearly tribute of seven young women and seven young men, Theseus went to Crete to combat him. Aegeus instructed his son to hoist a white sail if he returned victorious from this expedition. Upon his return, Theseus, in his joy at having conquered the monster, forgot his father's instructions. Aegeus, seeing the ship's black sails, believed that his son had perished. In despair, he threw himself on the rocks in the sea that, since then, has borne his name, the Aegean.

AEGINA. Carried away by Zeus, the nymph Aegina, daughter of the river-god Asopus, was transported by her divine lover to the island of Oenone where she gave birth to Aeacus. She later married Actor and became the mother of Menoetius, father of Patroclus. Aeacus returned several years later to his place of birth with a colony of Pelasgians and named the island after his mother.

aegis. Though associated with the Greek word *aigis,* meaning "goatskin," the aegis probably was a storm cloud (*kataigis*, "hurricane") originally. Conceived of as a sort of breastplate/shield, it was, according to legend, invented for the first time by Zeus. The god, in fact, just before he fought against the Titans, took the skin of Amalthea, the goat that had suckled him, and used it as protection against the blows of the Titans. For quite some time the goatskin, fringed most often with serpents, was the basic symbol of Zeus and Athena. But soon the aegis of Athena was depicted as a breastplate made of flakes of skin, which was not only a defensive weapon but also became an offensive weapon, on the center of which was placed the head of the Gorgon Medusa that petrified everyone who laid eyes on it.

AEGISTHUS. On the faith of an oracle that ensured him that if he had a son he could take revenge on his brother Atreus, Thyestes had incestuous relations with his sister Pelopia. A son, Aegisthus, was born of this union. Exposed at birth by his mother, he was recovered and suckled by a goat. Having discovered him, Atreus raised him as his own son and then instructed him to do away with Thyestes. But Aegisthus discovered that Thyestes was his real father and killed his uncle. From that point on he reigned with Thyestes over the kingdom of the Mycenae until he was dethroned by Agamemnon. During the absence of Agamemnon, who had left for the war on Troy, he managed to seduce Clytemnestra. When Agamemnon returned, Aegisthus had him assassinated during a banquet or else, according to another version, while he was bathing. Aegisthus was to perish in the same way at the hand of Orestes, his stepson.

AEGYPTUS. The son of Belus and Anchinoë, and grandson of Poseidon, Aegyptus conquered the country to which his name was given, namely *Egypt*. He made his mark in Antiquity, along with his fifty sons, through the violent persecution he inflicted on his brother Danaus, who was forced to flee with his fifty daughters and seek refuge in Argos. In tragic circumstances, the daughters of Danaus killed the sons of Aegyptus. Without assistance and stripped of his support, Aegyptus died brokenhearted shortly afterwards.

AENEAS. A descendant of the royal house of Dardanus and a relative of Priam, king of Troy, whose daughter Creusa he married, Aeneas was the son of Anchises and Aphrodite. Raised in the woods by nymphs and the Centaur Chiron, Aeneas did not take part in the early stages of the Trojan War; however, one day while he was watching his herds, he was attacked by Achilles, who stole part of his cattle. Aeneas, therefore, took refuge in Lyrnessus. Pursued by Achilles, he was forced to leave the city, under the protection of Zeus, and headed

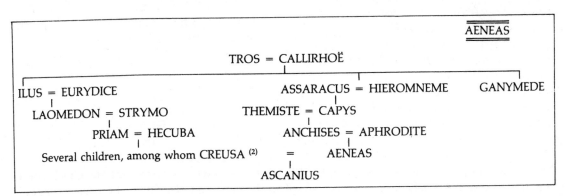

Aeneas fleeing Troy. To shelter his aged paralyzed father Anchises from the Greeks, the hero carried him on his back. He thus reveals his filial piety, a principal quality of this ancient hero. Detail of a Greek vase, Louvre, photo Giraudon.

for Troy where he joined the ranks of the Trojan warriors. During this long war, Aeneas was a brave, wise and pious hero; he did indeed put his life on the line, but in extremely perilous situations he often resorted to the protection of the gods, particularly when he came up against Achilles. Seeing Aeneas in danger of death, Poseidon snatched him away in a cloud right before the very eyes of his enemy. During the destruction of Troy and the extinction of Priam's race, Aeneas, according to one of the most ancient traditions, retired to Mount Ida with his father, his son and a few loyal followers, and there he founded a new kingdom of Troas.

However, according to later versions, which were made universal by Virgil in the *Aeneid*, Aeneas fled from Troy, carrying his blind and paralyzed father Anchises on his back, leading his son Ascanius behind him with one hand, and holding in the other hand the gods of the city—the Penates—as well as the Palladium.

He gathered together a few comrades on Mount Ida and set off for the Hesperides, the unknown West. During a somewhat eventful journey, he established solid bonds of friendship with the pilot of his ship, Palinurus; with Achates, whose loyalty became legendary; and with many other Trojans. He stopped in Thrace, passed by way of Delos, then arrived in Crete. For more then seven years, he wandered on the seas seeking a shore, braving tempests and the wrath of the gods, especially Hera's. Just as he was about to reach the shores of Italy, after stopping in Sicily, in Drepanum where the aged Anchises died, the ships of Aeneas were suddenly thrown onto the African coast, near Carthage, by a storm. Queen Dido, who had founded Carthage, welcomed the hero and proceeded to fall in love with him. But the gods did not will a marriage between Dido and Aeneas; Zeus ordered Aeneas to return to Sicily where he received the hospitality of King Aegestes. When he finally arrived on the coast of Italy, in Cumae, he descended to the Underworld, guided by the Sibyl, then returning among the living, he headed for Latium. There, after concluding a treaty with Evander, he fought and killed Turnus, the leader of the Rutuli, in order to win the hand of Lavinia, the daughter of King Latinus. Virgil's poem ends with this victory. Roman historians described the founding of Lavinium by Aeneas, that of Alba Longa by Ascanius, and the legendary birth of a small nation called upon, as predicted by the god Faunus, to dominate the world.

AEOLUS. Several gods and heroes are known by this name. One, the son of Hellen and the nymph Orseis, is regarded as the father of the Aeolians who formed one of the branches of the Greek nation. His children, it is said, were many. However, the most ancient legend mentions only four of his sons—Sisyphus, Athamas, Cretheus and Salmoneus. Another **Aeolus** is the grandson of Hellen.

The most famous **Aeolus** is none other than the god of the Winds, the son of Poseidon. He reigns over his tumultuous subjects, locked in a cave on the Aeolian islands or held captive in goatskin bottles. He only grants them leave on the order of Zeus. If he happens to disobey the supreme master and frees the winds, without having been so instructed, he unleashes disasters, tempests and shipwrecks. Moreover, he plays a role in the Homeric cycle. He kindly receives Ulysses and hands over the bottles that have been entrusted to him. One of them contained the wind that was to propel the hero toward his native land. But on the open sea, the companions of Ulysses opened all the bottles and provoked a monstrous storm which threw the ship of Ulysses onto neighboring shores. Considering him damned by the gods, Aeolus abandoned the hero to his fate.

AËROPE. The daughter of Catreus, the king of Crete, and the wife of Plisthenes, legend has retained the name of Aërope because she was the mother of Menelaus and Agamemnon. Remarried, she perished in the course of the struggle between Atreus and Thyestes.

AESCULAPIUS. The god of Medicine, Aesculapius was revered by the Greeks under the name of *Asclepius.*

AESON. The son of Tyro and Cretheus, who founded the kingdom of Iolcus, Aeson succeeded his father to the throne. He married Alcimede and had a son, Jason. However, Aeson's half-brother Pelias expelled him from the throne, held him prisoner, and sent Jason to capture the Golden Fleece, thinking this formidable heir to the throne would never return alive from such a perilous mission. Indeed, Jason's death was soon announced and Pelias wasted no time disposing of Aeson. He did, however, allow him to kill himself by drinking bull's blood. Upon learning this tragic news, Alcimede hanged herself. But Jason had not been killed, in fact, and some say that Aeson was revived by Medea who also restored his youth with a magic potion.

AETHER. The son of Erebus and the Night, according to Hesiod, Aether corresponds in cosmogeny to the upper part of the sky, that which touches the most brilliant and purest light of the Sun and remains the favorite abode of Zeus. United with Day, his sister, Aether begat a certain number of essential elements of the universe, of life and its disorders such as the Earth, the Sky, the Sea and the Oceans.

AETHRA. The wife of Aegeus, Aethra also married Poseidon. Her son, Theseus, claimed as his father both the king of Athens and the god. Aethra lived in Attica but several years after her husband's death she was carried away by the Dioscuri, who enslaved her and made her a servant to Helen. After the Greeks' victory in Troy, Aethra was freed by her grandsons, Demophon and Acamas.

Poseidon prepares to seduce Aethra, the wife of Aegeus. Here the artist has used a version of the legend that considers Theseus to be the son of Poseidon. Attic hydria, 5th cent. B.C., Vatican Museum, photo Alinari.

Agamemnon, the commander-in-chief of the Greek expedition against Troy, had an argument with Achilles. Athena, the goddess of War but also of Harmony and Reason, tries to reconcile the enemies and mediate in their conflict. But Agamemnon and Achilles draw back in an attitude indicating enormous pride and disdain. Agamemnon grips his royal cloak in his raging hand. Tanagra terra-cotta, private coll., photo Giraudon.

AETNA. This volcano bears the name of a nymph, the daughter of Uranus and Gaia, who intervened in the quarrel between Demeter and Hephaestus over possession of Sicily. Aetna, which rises above the city of Catania, served as a prison for Typhon and Enceladus after their defeat at the hands of the gods of Olympus. The smoke and fire that escaped from the crater of this volcano came, according to common belief, from the blazing breath of the giants.

A Latin version of the legend of Aetna contended that it was the dwelling place of Vulcan and his assistants. There he forged the armors of the gods and heroes.

AETOLUS. Endymion, the king of Elis, had many sons. In order to ensure his successor to the throne, he proclaimed that the throne would be handed down to the winner of a certain chariot race. Epeios was the winner and was proclaimed king. His brothers all fled, with the exception of Aetolus, who rightfully succeeded Epeios on the throne. However, during the famous games in honor of Azan, the son of Arcas, the chariot of Aetolus accidentally overturned that of Apis, the son of Phoroneus, and Apis was killed. Banished from Elis for this involuntary murder, Aetolus sought refuge in the land of the Curetes, in Corinthian territory, and there he became king, naming the country Aetolia in his honor.

AGAMEDES. Along with his brother-in-law Trophonius, Agamedes was one of the most celebrated of the legendary architects of ancient Greece. He was responsible, in particular, for numerous temples that were the pride of Delphi and Thebes. He was summoned to Boeotia by King Hyrieus who requested that he build a residence where he could hide his treasures. Attracted by the prospect of profit, Agamedes arranged with Trophonius to construct the building in such a way that one stone could be easily removed; in this way, each night, they had little trouble stealing from the treasures, unbeknownst to the king. Hyrieus, who saw his riches diminishing, enlisted the help of the architect Daedalus. Daedalus set a trap in which Agamedes was soon caught. Fearful that Agamedes would betray him, Trophonius cut off his head and fled. The story found in Pindar and Plutarch is quite different. According to these writers, Apollo advised Agamedes to enjoy himself to the hilt for six days, upon completion of a temple at Delphi. On the seventh day, he was to be rewarded for his work. Indeed, on the seventh day, Apollo granted him a peaceful death, believed to be one of the greatest rewards that might be granted to a mortal.

AGAMEMNON. The legends differ on the origin and genealogy of this king. Homer recounted that he was the son of Atreus and the grandson of Pelops. Like Menelaus, his brother, he was raised with Aegisthus and Thyestes in the house of Atreus. After Atreus was murdered by Aegisthus and Thyestes, who acceded to the throne of Argos, Agamemnon and Menelaus were exiled to Sparta. But there they mobilized an army and were able to drive away the two usurpers. Agamemnon became the king of Argos and one of the most powerful rulers in all of Peloponnesus. He married Clytemnestra, the daughter of Tyndareos, who bore him three daughters—Iphigenia, Chrysothemis and Laodice (Electra appeared in the legend only much later)—and one son, Orestes. When Paris abducted Helen, the wife of Menelaus and sister of Clytemnestra, Agamemnon resolved to avenge his brother. He was chosen above everyone else, after a great deal of bargaining, as commander-in-chief of the expedition against Troy. Two years were spent building the fleet and mobilizing the armies that joined forces in Aulis, the port of Boeotia.

Unfortunately, just as they were about to raise anchor, Agamemnon boasted of having slain a deer with such incredible skill that not even the goddess Artemis could equal his feat. To avenge this impious pride, the goddess forbade the winds to fill the sails of the Greek ships, thus preventing their embarking on the expedition to punish Troy. The armies consulted the seer Calchas, who declared that only the sacrifice of Iphigenia, Agamemnon's most beautiful daughter, would appease the wrath of Artemis. Despite his sorrow and loathing, but driven by political ambition, the king yielded to

the will of the goddess and summoned his daughter on the false pretext that he wished her to marry Achilles. He prepared the altar where she was to be slaughtered when, it is said, Artemis, finally appeased, lifted Iphigenia up and carried her away to the land of the Taurians, substituting a doe which was slaughtered instead. The winds picked up and the fleet set sail for Troy. But victory was still beyond the grasp of the Greeks. In the tenth year of the war, Agamemnon bickered with Achilles over Briseis, a young captive whom both wished to possess. Achilles, forced to yield, withdrew to his tent and refused to take part in the battle. Agamemnon soon realized that final victory was impossible as long as Achilles refused to participate. Through the death of Achilles' comrade Patroclus, the king became reconciled with Achilles and sent Briseis to him.

When the gods, having abandoned the Trojans, permitted the Greeks to sack the city, Cassandra, the daughter of Priam, was given to King Agamemnon. Cassandra, who had been blessed with a particularly remarkable gift of prophecy yet condemned to disbelief of her predictions, begged her royal lover not to return to his homeland: She foresaw the deadly designs of Clytemnestra. Agamemnon did not believe her and, having had two children by her, namely Teledamus and Pelops, he returned home. Clytemnestra and her lover Aegisthus greeted him warmly, hypocritically hiding their intentions, prepared a bath for him to soothe his weary limbs and, when he had removed his armor and weapons, they killed him. Cassandra and her two infants met the same fate. Later, Orestes avenged his father's death.

Among the Greek characters in the Trojan War, Agamemnon stands out not so much for his bravery, cunning or chivalry, the eminent qualities most often attributed to Achilles or Ajax, but for his majesty, his dignity and, according to Homer, for his eyes and head that resembled those of Zeus and for his chest, similar to that of Poseidon.

AGANIPPE. Located in Boeotia, at the foot of the Helicon, the spring of Aganippe gushed forth one day beneath the hoof of Pegasus, the winged horse. The dwelling place of a nymph, the daughter of Permessus, the river of Boeotia, Aganippe was a favorite spot of the Muses.

AGAVE. Daughter of Cadmus and Harmonia and wife of Echion, Agave was punished by Dionysus for having denied that Dionysus was the son of Zeus by Semele. Suddenly crazed, she tore her son Pentheus to pieces.

AGENOR. The son of Poseidon and Libya, this brother of Belus, the king of Egypt, held sway in Phoenicia. He sent his sons—Cadmus, Phoenix and Cilix—to look for his daughter Europa, who had been abducted by Zeus. They were not to return before they found their sister; none of them was ever heard from again.

ages. The Greeks and Romans believed that man had lived for many a long century under the reign of Cronus, free from suffering, and in a constant state of joy and bliss. During this golden age, mortals knew nothing of hate and war; they were forever young, loving and respecting one another, and they delighted in the most virtuous of games and festivities. Death took them by surprise, peacefully, and they greeted slumber fearlessly, secure in their hopes for happy and eternal rest. But Zeus dethroned Cronus and the silver age replaced the golden age. Although fertile, the earth yielded its riches more parsimoniously. Work became obligatory and men began to know suffering. Territories and wealth were shared and men began jealously to hem themselves in, staying within the confines of their own land. Then finally came the bronze and iron ages and with them came the age of crime, hate, wars, revolutions and invasions. Vice triumphed over virtue

all too often. Unhappiness, illness, famine and epidemics plagued men relentlessly. Fear of the gods welled up in the hearts of all mortals.

This myth of humanity blissful in primordial times and gradually decayed by corruption was extolled above all by the Romans, who worshiped Saturn (Cronus), the first king of the Latins, whose reign, it is said, was supremely beneficial to the prosperity of Rome.

Hesiod complicated this picture of degeneration by inserting between the bronze and iron ages the age of heroes, "better and more just" than the one before.

AGLAUROS. Athena entrusted to this daughter of Cecrops the wicker cradle of Erichthonius, instructing her to watch over it and not to open it. With her sisters Herse and Pandrosos, she yielded to her overwhelming curiosity and opened the cradle. There she saw a newborn baby, enveloped in snakes, and driven mad by the sight, she and her sisters threw themselves from the top of the Acropolis. According to Ovid, however, they escaped death, and he gave Aglauros a role in the love of Herse and Hermes. Moreover, Aglauros married Ares and bore him a daughter, Alcippe, whom Halirrhotius, one of Poseidon's sons, violated. Ares killed him in revenge.

agriculture. The Greeks believed that agriculture had originated in the Nile Valley in Egypt and that Isis should be credited with inventing the practice, especially the cultivation of grain, while cultivation of the vine was a gift from Osiris. According to the Greeks, agriculture was brought to Greece by fugitives who, at the same time, initiated worship of the two great Egyptian gods. Soon, the Greeks identified Isis with Demeter and Osiris with Dionysus; furthermore, they believed that Demeter had given the first grains of wheat to Celeus of Eleusis, and had instructed Buzyges ("he who yokes the oxen") in the art of working the land

and Triptolemus in the art of sowing. Dionysus, meanwhile, received with every honor by King Icarius, gave him the first vine as a symbol of his gratitude.

AIUS LOCUTIUS. When the Gauls of the Senon tribe, under the leadership of Brennus, marched on Rome in 390 B.C., a voice emerged from the center of the heavens announcing the invasion of the city by alien hordes. However, no one heeded the warning. Rome was actually burned and pillaged. After the invaders retreated, the Romans personified and deified this prophetic voice whose warning they had unfortunately ignored and gave it the name of "Aius Locutius." Each part of the name is derived from a different verb with the common meaning "speak," "declare."

AJAX (the Greater). Too old to take part in the Trojan War on the Greek side, Telamon, king of Salamis, sent his two sons Teucer and Ajax. In the *Iliad*, Ajax is considered to be one of the most valiant warriors, second only to Achilles: he singlehandedly turned back a Trojan counterattack that threatened to set the Greek ships ablaze. He made his mark during single combats and even wounded Hector. After the death of Achilles, Ajax and Ulysses quarreled over the hero's arms and Ulysses prevailed. Suddenly driven mad, Ajax left his tent that night and slit the throats of the cattle, thinking he had slaughtered warriors. When he came back to his senses, he was the laughingstock of his fellow warriors; unable to bear this dishonor, he threw himself on his sword and killed himself. Always one to embellish mythical narratives with changes and metaphors, Ovid related that the blood of Ajax gave birth to a flower, the hyacinth, the first letters of which are also the first letters of Ajax (Aias in Greek). Telamon avenged his son's death by drawing the vessels of Ulysses against the reefs on the coast of his kingdom. The tomb of Ajax

Ajax, son of Telamon, armed with a long lance, withstanding a single combat with Hector who, with his sword and due to the suppleness of his body, manages to ward off the blows. Apollo can be seen at the extreme right. Greek vase, late 6th cent., early 5th cent. B.C., Louvre, photo Giraudon.

was erected at Cape Rethea. A cult was dedicated to the hero at Salamis and a temple was set aside especially in his honor.

AJAX (the Lesser). Ajax, the son of Oileus, the king of Locris, was known as "Ajax the Lesser" not only because of his size but also to distinguish him from Ajax the Greater, son of Telamon. He armed some forty ships and battled valiantly, though cruelly, against the Trojans. His story, related by Homer and Virgil, shows him pursuing Cassandra, the daughter of Priam, to the temple of Athena where he would have taken her by force even though she was clasping the statue of the goddess. Outraged by this sacrilege, the Achaeans themselves wanted to stone him to death. But he escaped by sea with his fleet. The raging Athena provoked a storm which he escaped by taking refuge on a reef. There, he solemnly braved the gods. Poseidon, who until then had protected him, was overcome with anger and cracked open the reef with a thrust of his trident and the impious Ajax was swallowed up by the waves. Still not appeased by this punishment, Athena sent a plague and a famine to Locris which threatened

Helmeted, his sword in his right hand and his shield in his left, Ajax, the son of Oileus, prepares to defy the Trojan warriors. Opuntian coin, 4th cent. B.C., Bibl. Nat., Cabinet des Médailles.

to annihilate all of its inhabitants. The oracle of Delphi was consulted and it was declared that the goddess would be appeased if, every year for a thousand years, two young Greek girls were sent to Troy. If the girls managed to escape the Trojans and reach the temple of Athena, their lives would be saved and they would become priestesses of the temple. It is said that this custom was indeed respected.

ALBA LONGA. This Italian city, located not too far from Rome, was founded by Ascanius, the only son of Aeneas. This king had several legendary successors, among whom were Tiberinus who drowned in the Albula River, henceforth called the Tiber, and Silvius Procas, the father of Numitor and Amulius and the grandfather of Romulus and Remus. In Antiquity, Alba was considered to be one of the founding cities of Rome.

ALBUNEA. Owing to her gifts of prophecy, this nymph, who is considered to be one of Italy's most famous sibyls, delivered her oracles in a forest, near Tibur where the Anio River (today the Teverone) forms a lovely waterfall and cascades into the Tiber with a sound that resembles thunder and at one time was considered to be the very voice of Jupiter. Since elsewhere in the surrounding area there were sulfurous waters and a lake from which poisonous vapors rose, the Romans believed that these spots were directly inspired by the gods.

ALCATHOUS. Son of Pelops and Hippodameia, Alcathous won the hand of Evaechme, the daughter of Megareus, by killing on Mount Cithaeron a monstrous lion that was wreaking terror. He used its tongue, which he cut out, to refute other claimants. He then settled in Boeotia where he acceded to the throne of Onchestus. His reign was characterized, above all, by the reconstruction of the Megara walls, destroyed by the Cretans of Minos, and by the construction of one of the city's citadels. For this formidable undertaking, Alcathous received Apollo's help; the stone on which the god had placed his lyre retained a very particular property for quite some time afterwards: it emitted sounds whenever it was struck.

ALCESTIS. This daughter of King Pelias had many suitors who vied for her hand. Her father had decreed that he would give her in marriage to whoever would be able to harness ferocious beasts to the royal chariot. Admetus, the king of Thessaly, succeeded and married Alcestis. She offered her life in exchange for that of her husband, who had offended Artemis. She took poison and her soul descended to Tartarus. According to one legend, Persephone was so moved by this boundless love that she restored her to life. According to another tradition, Heracles, a guest of Admetus, confronted Thanatos, Death, at the grave site and stole Alcestis away from him. Alcestis remains for all a model of marital tenderness.

ALCINOUS. The grandson of Poseidon, Alcinous was the most famous king of the Phaeacians, a mythical people who lived on the Isle of Scheria, identified with Corcyra. With his wife Arete and his daughter Nausicaa, Alcinous was constantly welcoming strangers into his home, particularly castaways. The Argonauts stopped at his palace for a rest, and his most famous guest, Ulysses, took refuge there after a storm had tossed him, stripped of everything, onto the banks of the island. Alcinous wished him to marry Nausicaa, but after his refusal he had Ulysses brought to the shores of his land and left him sleeping in the sand. Poseidon, irritated by the attention showered upon the hero, changed Alcinous' ship to stone and destroyed the Phaeacian port.

ALCITHOË. This daughter of Minyas was changed into a bat because she refused to take part in a procession in honor of Dionysus. Her sisters, Leucippe and Arsippe, were driven mad for following her example. Leucippe devoured her own son, before fleeing with Arsippe to the mountains, where Hermes changed one of them into an owl and the other into a screech owl.

ALCMAEON. The brother of Amphilochus and the son of the Argive soothsayer Amphiaraus and his wife Eriphyle, Alcmaeon was chosen to lead the campaign of the Epigoni against Thebes. Eriphyle, having received as a gift the necklace of Harmonia that had been given to her by Thersander, drove her son to leave just as she had instructed her husband to take part in the first war against Thebes, where he was to perish. But Alcmaeon's fate, during the war, was to be less tragic. Victorious, Alcmaeon himself slew Laodamas, the son of Eteocles, and returned to his own land to kill his mother who had forced him and his father to take part in wars from which she secretly hoped they would never return. This matricide invoked the wrath of the Erinyes: Alcmaeon hastily left his fatherland and found help and purification in the palace of King Phegeus of Psophis. There he married Arsinoë, his protector's daughter, to whom he gave the mantle and necklace of Harmonia. When a terrible drought beset the country that had dared to welcome someone who had killed his mother, Alcmaeon resumed his wandering until he reached the River Acheloüs which purified him again and gave him his daughter Callirhoë in marriage. Callirhoë, in turn, requested the attributes of Harmonia. Therefore, Alcmaeon returned to the court of Phegeus to claim the precious objects, declaring that he wished to offer them to the god Apollo. But Phegeus soon learned the truth and realized the lie of which his daughter Arsinoë had been made a victim. He then killed his hypocritical guest. Alcmaeon had sons, Acarnan and Amphoterus.

ALCMENE. The daughter of Electryon, king of Mycenae, Alcmene agreed to marry Amphitryon, even though he had murdered her father, provided he would avenge the deaths of her brothers. In his absence she was seduced by Zeus, who had assumed her husband's appearance. When her husband returned from battle victorious, he learned of his wife's involuntary infidelity and wanted to burn her at the stake. Zeus saved the unfortunate woman by sending a sudden downpour that extinguished the flames. At Amphitryon's death, Alcmene followed her two sons, Iphicles, son of her husband, and Heracles, son of Zeus, to escape the hate of Eurystheus. When Eurystheus perished, Alcmene gouged out his eyes. She then returned to Thebes where she lived for many years. When she died, Zeus carried her away to the Island of the Blest where she married

Rhadamanthys, one of the judges in the Underworld.

ALCYONE. The daughter of Aeolus, king of the Winds, Alcyone married Ceyx, son of the Morning Star. Such a union could bring nothing but happiness, and indeed it did, so much so that it invoked the jealousy of Zeus and Hera, to whom the couple would compare themselves. They were, therefore, changed into halcyons. According to another version of the myth, Ceyx had to leave Alcyone one day to consult an oracle. His vessel was shipwrecked during a storm that had risen through the anger of Zeus. The unfortunate Ceyx drowned. Warned by a dream sent by Morpheus, the god of Sleep, during which she heard Ceyx tell her of his decease, Alcyone rushed to the shore and discovered her husband's body which had been tossed up on the beach by the waves. In despair, she threw herself into the sea. She was immediately changed into a halcyon, with its plaintive cries. Her beloved husband underwent the same transformation. Henceforth, they never left one another's side and the couple has become the symbol of marital fidelity. To assure the brood and posterity of the halcyon, the kindly gods ordered Aeolus to calm the winds for seven days preceding the winter solstice and seven days following it.

Mythology also tells of another **Alcyone,** with whom Poseidon was smitten, and who was accorded a considerable posterity by the god of the seas. This Alcyone is one of the seven Pleiades.

ALCYONEUS. **1.** One of the Giants who rebelled against the gods of Olympus, Alcyoneus battled Heracles in Phlegra in Macedonia. But each time the Giant fell to the ground from which he had sprung, he immediately got up again. Heracles carried him on his shoulders to another country where he killed him with an arrow.

2. According to another legend, **Alcyoneus** was a handsome young man from Delphi who was chosen by fate to be fed to Lamia, an atrocious monster that was ravaging the country. While on his way to be sacrificed, Alcyoneus met another young man, Eurybatus, who, overcome with love for him, offered to be sacrificed in his place. As he arrived at the monster's lair, Eurybatus managed to seize Lamia and smash his head. In the monster's place, a spring gushed forth and took the name of *Sybaris.*

allegories. With no genealogy and myths, allegories are the deified representations of moral abstractions such as Virtue, political abstractions such as Peace or Victory, social abstractions such as Poverty, and physical abstractions such as Health. Unknown for most of the Greeks, allegories appeared late for the Romans who gradually multiplied them, raised statues in their honor, worshiped them and sometimes even dedicated temples to them, emphasizing their respective characters and attributes.

ALOADAE. This name refers to Ephialtes and Otus, the sons of Poseidon and Iphimedeia. At the age of nine, they were nine fathoms tall and nine cubits broad. Full of inordinate boldness, they undertook to pile Ossa on Olympus and Pelion on Ossa, so as to chase the gods from heaven and steal the goddesses, Hera and Artemis, with whom they were in love. They began by chaining Ares in a bronze pot from which the god of War was freed by Hermes only some thirteen months later. But the Aloadae were unable to execute their plan. Irritated by their presumptuousness, Apollo pierced them with his arrows. Mythographers also claim that Artemis, in the form of a doe, passed rapidly between the two of them; Ephialtes and Otus each threw his javelin, missing the animal but killing one another. An exemplary punishment was dealt them in the Underworld. They were tied with serpents to a column around which an owl hooted dolefully.

ALOPE. The king of Eleusis in Arcadia, Cercyon, the son of Hephaestus, had a daughter, Alope, who was seduced by Poseidon. Not daring to own up to her fault, the poor girl gave birth to a child that she immediately abandoned. The newborn was suckled by a mare and later found by shepherds who noticed that he was clad in royal garments. This news reached the palace of Cercyon who thus discovered what his daughter had done. He had her killed by burying her alive but the gods took pity on her and changed her into a spring.

ALPHEUS. This river-god of Elis, the son of Oceanus and Tethys, one day spotted the nymph Arethusa who, relaxing after the hunt, was bathing in his waters. Wild with love, he set about pursuing her to the island of Ortygia, where he was about to join her when Artemis took pity on the nymph and changed her into a spring. However, the god did not relent and, crossing the sea, he mingled his waters with the beloved waves of the spring-nymph. Another legend is often added to this one: Artemis, herself pursued by Alpheus, covered her face with mud as did her companions. The god, unable to recognize her, turned back amid the mocking laughter of the nymphs.

ALTHAEA. Married to Oeneus, the king of Calydon, Althaea was the mother of a great number of children, the most famous of whom were Meleager and Deianira. But it is also said that Deianira was begotten by Dionysus who had fallen in love with Althaea and had asked Oeneus to lend him his wife. In return, Dionysus would give Oeneus the vine, unknown in his kingdom until that time. After the Calydonian Boar Hunt, Althaea hanged herself for having voluntarily caused the death of Meleager.

AMALTHEA. According to some traditions, Amalthea was the nymph who cared for Zeus when Rhea protected him from the voracity of his father Cronus. Amalthea took the child to Mount Ida where she nourished him with the milk of a goat whose hide Zeus later used to fashion a shield. But according to other versions of the same legend, Amalthea is the name of the goat that suckled the divine child when the nymphs of Ida adopted him. The divine nursling was already blessed with such vigor that one day he broke one of the horns of the devoted animal. He gave it to the compassionate nymphs, promising them that it would be filled with everything their hearts desired. This is one of the mythical origins of the famous "horn of plenty," the other being connected to the legend of the river-god Acheloüs.

AMATA. The wife of Latinus, king of Latium, Amata gave birth to a son who died at an early age, and to Lavinia, whom she planned to marry to her nephew Turnus, the king of the Rutuli. But the oracles decreed otherwise: King Latinus gave his daughter to Aeneas who had just landed on the coast of his territories. Hostile to the Trojan hero and his companions, Amata incited Turnus to declare war on them. But the outcome of the war was favorable to the strangers and fatal to Turnus who perished during a battle. When she learned of the defeat and death of Turnus, Amata killed herself.

AMAZONS. The Amazons belonged to a fabulous breed of warrior women who, according to ancient mythographers, lived in the Caucasus and in Asia Minor, on the shores of the Thermodon River where they founded the city of Themiscyra. Governed by a queen, the Amazons would permit the presence of a man but once a year to perpetuate their race. It is said they would kill their newborn sons. On horseback, armed with bow and shield (some-

Fierce and determined, their faces revealing a sort of dignified cruelty, the Amazons prepare to finish off a Greek warrior who has already been wounded in the thigh. Greco-Italian amphora, 4th cent. B.C., photo Giraudon.

times axe or spear), they would scour the provinces of Asia Minor, plundering and pillaging. The right breast of these magnificent beings was burned off, so that they could better handle their bows and arrows and to facilitate movement in combat. Numerous heroes battled these women who were not only strange but cruel as well. Heracles was given the task by Admeta, daughter of Eurystheus, of stealing from Hippolyta, their queen, the enchanted belt that Ares had given her as a present. She agreed to give the object to the hero when Hera, herself changed into an Amazon, traveled through Asia Minor claiming that Heracles wanted to abduct the queen. Immediately, all of the Amazons took up their arms and, in the course of the struggle, Heracles killed Hippolyta. Under the reign of Theseus, the Amazons invaded Attica and besieged Athens to avenge the abduction of their queen Antiope. But the Athenians managed to repel them. When they ventured into Lycia, they were also conquered by Bellerophon. Pausanias links their legend to that of the Trojan War. Led by their queen Penthesileia, the Amazons came to the aid of Priam, who was about to be defeated by the Greeks. But once their queen met her demise at the hand of Achilles, they relinquished the battle. Fond of hunting and vigorous exercise, the Amazons worshiped, above all, the Artemis of Ephesus, the goddess with many breasts, in whose honor they were the first to institute a cult.

ambrosia. Homer considered ambrosia to be the food of the gods. Honey-based, it was used in numerous preparations, from the most pleasant perfumes to the most flavorful liquors. It possessed magical properties that made the gods invulnerable and ensured perfect happiness and immortality to men who were among the ranks of heroes. Ambrosia was often served with nectar, a sweet drink made from a refined distilling of certain plants.

AMPELUS. The son of a satyr and a nymph, the personification of the vine, Ampelus, a companion of Dionysus, died very young when he was killed by a bull. Other versions of his legend claim that he fell from an elm tree, covered with branches, on which he had climbed to gather grapes. At the request of Dionysus, he was placed in the sky as one of the constellations.

AMPHIARAUS. The son of Oecles and Hypermnestra, Amphiaraus was the great-grandson of the soothsayer Melampus and inherited his ancestor's gift of prophecy. But he also possessed the solid qualities of courage and endurance which placed him in the ranks of heroes. Having driven Adrastus from the throne of Argos, he finally became reconciled with him and married his sister Eriphyle who gave birth to Alcmaeon and Amphilochus as well as two daughters. After taking part in the Calydonian Boar Hunt and the expedition of the Argonauts, his help was enlisted in the campaign against Thebes with six other leaders. Amphiaraus refused to go, seeing the unfortunate outcome of the expedition and his own impending death. However, an agreement had been reached between him and Adrastus, and one stipulation was that Eriphyle would serve as mediator in case of dispute. Polynices, well aware of this woman's love of finery, gave her the necklace that the gods had brought to Harmonia when she married Cadmus. Lured by the necklace, Eriphyle ordered Amphiaraus to leave immediately for the struggle against Thebes. Amphiaraus yielded to her wishes and instructed his sons to avenge him later. As Amphiaraus had predicted, the Argives were conquered and left Thebes hastily. During their flight, Zeus struck the Earth open with a bolt of thunder and Amphiaraus disappeared. However, the god of gods granted him immortality as well as the power to continue his oracles at Argos and Attica.

AMPHICTYON. This second son of Deucalion and Pyrrha was not as famous as his brother Hellen, the father of all Greeks, but he did play an important part in the myth of the founding of Athens. As the king of Attica, he gave the city its name and dedicated it to the goddess Athena. He created as well the Amphictyonic League which assembled, in a community more religious than political, the twelve great cities of Greece. A very pious king, he received Dionysus in his court. According to one version of the legend, he was the first to initiate the prudent practice of mixing water with wine.

AMPHILOCHUS. With Alcmaeon, Amphilochus, one of the two sons of the soothsayer Amphiaraus, the husband of Eriphyle, took part in the expedition of the Epigoni and, on his return, may have helped his brother kill their mother. However, the Erinyes who hounded Alcmaeon left Amphilochus alone. Possessing, like his father, the gift of prophecy, he battled against Troy and assisted Calchas, the official soothsayer of the Greeks. Later, in Cilicia, he founded Mallus but disputed the sovereignty of the city with another seer, Mopsus. In a single combat, both perished. However, their souls became reconciled and their oracles continued. The questions of those who consulted their oracles were inscribed on tablets and the answers were given to them in dreams.

AMPHION. The son of Zeus and Antiope, twin brother of Zethus, Amphion was abandoned at birth by his mother, who feared her father's wrath, and entrusted to the shepherds of Mount Cithaeron who raised the twins. Amphion was blessed with musical talent and was noticed by Apollo, who offered him a lyre. Zethus preferred vigorous exercise such as combat and work in the fields. Their mother, enchained by her uncle Lycus, was miraculously freed from her bonds and managed to join her sons. Revealing their origin to them, she incited them to commit murder. Amphion and Zethus set out for Thebes. On their arrival, they killed Lycus and tied his wife, Dirce, by the hair to the horns of a wild bull, which dragged her over the rocks until she finally died. On this spot arose a spring that bore her name. Masters of Thebes, the two brothers ruled the city with great care and built ramparts to protect it. All Amphion needed to do was play his lyre and the enchanted stones piled themselves up and formed walls, a symbol perhaps of the kinship between architecture and music. While Zethus married Thebe, the eponymous heroine of the city which had formerly been known as Cadmea, Amphion took as his wife Niobe, the daughter of Tantalus. But all their children perished for having insulted Leto, the mother of Apollo and Artemis. Amphion, it is said, was killed through divine retribution by the two gods and plunged into Tartarus for having begotten an insolent race.

AMPHITRITE. As Hera is the legitimate spouse of Zeus, Persephone the wife of Hades,

A beautiful young woman with Roman features, Amphitrite accompanying her husband Neptune on his chariot. Roman mosaic, Louvre, photo Giraudon.

Amphitrite, the daughter of Nereus and Doris, was bound to Poseidon in matrimony. Poseidon, in fact, first noticed her as she was playing on the beach with her sisters, the Nereids, and wished to have her as his wife. She escaped and sought refuge with Atlas, as far away from the sea as possible. But a dolphin abducted her and brought her back to the god of the Sea, who made her the mother of Triton.

AMPHITRYON. This son of Alcaeus, the king of Tiryns, accidentally killed his uncle Electryon, the father of Alcmene. Banished from the city, he sought refuge in Thebes where he was purified of the murder by King Creon. He then requested the hand of Alcmene, who had followed him. But before submitting, Alcmene demanded that he avenge the death of her brothers who had been killed by the sons of King Pterelaus. Creon agreed to help, provided his kingdom was rid of the uncatchable Teumessian fox sent by Dionysus. Accompanied by the hound Laelaps, which no quarry could evade, he pursued the uncatchable fox until Zeus resolved the difficulty by turning both fox and hound to stone. Creon and Amphitryon then embarked on their punitive journey to the isle of Taphos, the capital of which was impregnable: in fact, Pterelaus was blessed with a golden hair that made him invulnerable. His daughter Comaetho, out of love for Amphitryon, cut the fatal hair and her father's death spelled victory for Amphitryon. But the hero showed the girl no gratitude and had her put to death while he offered the kingdom of Taphos to Cephalus. He finally returned to Alcmene and begat Iphicles, who was born one day before Heracles, his half-brother. Amphitryon died shortly afterward, during a battle against the Minyans led by Erginus.

AMPSANCTUS LACUS. A small lake between Apulia and Samnium, not far from Aeculanum, the capital of the Hirpini people.

Toxic and nauseating vapors rose from its waters and these were considered by the Ancients to be a sign that the Underworld was near.

AMYCUS. This king of the Bithynian Bebryces, the son of Poseidon, used to force strangers who passed through his territories to fight him with their bare fists. Following these competitions, Amycus, who was always the victor, would most often kill his adversaries. However, when the Argonauts landed in his domain, Polydeuces accepted the king's challenge, and during a close struggle, he managed by his skill to reduce the formidable giant to his mercy and made him promise to leave strangers in peace from then on.

AMYMONE. When Danaus, the father of the Danaids, arrived in Argos, he found the land devastated by a drought, sent by Poseidon. He sent his fifty daughters, especially Amymone, to look for sources of water. As she was taking a nap, a satyr accosted her and wanted to seduce her. She cried to Poseidon for help. With his trident, he chased the satyr away and then pierced a rock from which flowed the spring, called Danaide. The god also coveted Amymone, and from their union came Nauplius, the founder of the city of Nauplia.

AMYNTOR. King of the Dolopians, Amyntor, husband of Cleobule, had a son, Phoenix. A mistress of the king's accused Phoenix of trying to seduce her. Outraged, the king struck his son blind and put the curse of childlessness on him. Phoenix subsequently became one of Achilles' companions in the war against Troy. Later Amyntor refused to give the hand of his daughter Astydameia to Heracles and also opposed the hero's entry into his kingdom. Heracles slew the recalcitrant king and carried off his daughter.

ANAXARETE. This young woman from Cyprus, loved by the shepherd Iphis, felt nothing but great disdain for her suitor. In despair, the young man hanged himself on the doorpost of his beloved. Several days later, Anaxarete leaned out her window to watch the funeral procession of Iphis. This show of insensitivity displeased the goddess Aphrodite who changed the young woman into stone.

ANCAEUS. The son of Lycurgus and father of Agapenor, and commander of the Arcadian contingent in the Greek expedition against Troy, Ancaeus succeeded Tiphys as pilot of the *Argo* during the journey of the Argonauts.

ANCHISES. Anchises was the father of Aeneas, the fruit of his love affair with Aphrodite, who had instructed him not to speak to anyone of their union. Anchises, having freely imbibed one day, committed the indiscretion of bragging about his good fortune. Zeus, to punish him, struck him with a bolt of thunder. According to some mythographers, he received but a minor wound. According to others, he was stricken blind and lame. Of the house of Priam, Anchises happened to be in Troy with his son when the city was taken. Old and feeble, he surely would have been killed if Aeneas had not carried him on his shoulders to a ship aboard which they both set out for the open sea. But Anchises never lived to see the shores of Latium. He died off the coast of Sicily and was buried near Mount Eryx.

ANDROGEUS. The son of Minos and Pasiphaë, this magnificently athletic Cretan beat all competition at the Panathenaean Games. However, since his victories overshadowed the glory of Athens, Androgeus, at the instigation of Aegeus, the king of Athens, was killed by jealous competitors. With the help of Zeus, who plagued Athens with famine and pestilence, Minos avenged his son's death by waging a campaign against Attica. To end the calamities that were devastating their land, the Athenians questioned the oracle and were forced to send seven youths and seven maidens to Crete each year to be devoured by the Minotaur.

ANDROMACHE. Andromache, the daughter of Eëtion, the king of Thebes of Mysia, was the wife of Hector and mother of Astyanax. Destiny was against this woman whose marital fidelity and dignity are held up as examples by all ancient writers. Indeed, she saw her father and seven brothers perish at the hand of Achilles during the Trojan War and perhaps, according to one tradition, even her son who was thrown from the heights of the city's ramparts. Spared during the sack and burning of the city, she was given to Neoptolemus, the son of Achilles. Thus, she was forced to marry, against her wishes, the son of the man who had murdered her entire family. She bore three children from this second marriage: Pielus, Molossus and Pergamus. When Neoptolemus died, she remarried, this time marrying Helenus, Hector's younger brother, in memory of her first husband from whose death she never managed to recover. She died in Asia where she had followed her son Pergamus who founded, according to legend, the city that bears his name.

ANDROMEDA. Cassiopeia, the wife of Cepheus, king of Ethiopia, one day acted quite imprudently, boasting of the beauty of her daughter Andromeda and claiming that her beauty surpassed that of the Nereids. Poseidon, irritated at this show of disdain for his daughters, sent a sea monster to ravage the country. When Cepheus consulted the oracle of Ammon, he was told that his kingdom would be delivered from this scourge if Andromeda were sacrificed to the god. She was, therefore, tied to a rock on the shore and waited to be devoured. But Perseus, meanwhile, landed in Ethiopia at just that moment. He rescued Andromeda by killing the monster. Then he married her. Chagrined, Phineus, a brother of Cepheus to whom Andromeda had been promised, mobilized his followers and attacked the hero during his wedding festivities. Thanks to the head of the Gorgon that Perseus was holding, all the assailants turned to stone. Andromeda followed her husband to Greece. She had several children, among whom were Sthenelus and Electryon. After her death, she was placed among the northern constellations, near those of Perseus, Cepheus and Cassiopeia.

ANGERONA. This Roman goddess, whose name is probably Etruscan (Ancaru), has her feast day on December 21. The Romans depict her with a finger on her lips or a gag on her mouth. A statue of this kind stood on an altar in the Curia Acculeia or the sacellum Volupiae (the open-air sanctuary of Pleasure).

ANGITIA. Legend is unclear on the exact attributes of this Roman divinity revered by the Marsi in the Lake Fucinus region. An expert in the art of preparing poisons and antidotes, able to charm snakes, she knew the magic words to dispel demons. In Hellenistic legends, she is often identified with Circe and Medea.

ANIGRUS. This river in Elis, which empties into the Ionian Sea, was known in Antiquity because of its waters' unpleasant taste. To explain this peculiar characteristic, people used to say that the centaurs, wounded by Heracles, bathed there, leaving behind their beastly odor.

ANNA PERENNA. A Roman goddess worshiped on March 15. Ovid tells two stories. In one she is said to have been deified for having made cakes that saved the plebs from famine when they sought refuge on the Sacred Mount during the Secession. According to the other, after the death of Dido, her sister Anna fled from Carthage to Italy, where Aeneas welcomed her with a kindness that seemed suspicious. Lavinia, the wife of Aeneas, devised a plan to have Anna disposed of. Anna, warned of the plan by her sister Dido in a dream, took

flight and plunged into the river Numicius where she was transformed into a nymph. Her name is thought to come from a prayer to live in the year (annare) and through the year (perennare) in the way one wishes.

ANTAEUS. This monstrous giant, the son of Gaia and Poseidon, lived in the desert of Libya and fed on lions. He attacked all travelers indiscriminately and killed them mercilessly because he had promised his father Poseidon to build him a temple with human skulls. Heracles, in search of the Golden Apples of the Hesperides, met him along the way and overwhelmed him three times. But each time the giant hit the ground, Gaia endowed him with renewed strength. Once he discovered the secret of this miraculous vigor, Heracles lifted his opponent off the ground and suffocated him with his powerful hands.

ANTENOR. The brother-in-law of Priam and the spouse of Theano, the sister of Hecuba, Antenor belonged to the council of Troy and was known for his wise and peaceful spirit. Several times he tried to calm the dissensions between the Greeks and Trojans to avoid a confrontation between the two peoples. He received the Greek contingent, led by Ulysses and Menelaus, that came to claim Helen from the Trojans. During the same war, he tried several times to reach a truce. Accused of treason because of his prudence and his reservations about a conflict that he felt harmful to the cause and the existence of Troy, he owed his salvation to the arrival of the Greeks who, grateful for his efforts, spared him, his wife and children both physically as well as materially. He was able to leave his burning city freely and landed on the Adriatic coast where he founded the colony of Padua in the territory of the Veneti.

ANTEROS. This Greek god is the brother of Eros. Born of the same mother, Aphrodite, he possesses, depending on the case, two powers: Anteros avenges his brother when mortals resist love or betray it; but he also opposes him because, in mortals' hearts, he replaces passion with antipathy and unfeelingness. Hindering monstrous unions, preventing the return of primitive chaos, he is, in the disorder of love, an organizing and weighting factor.

ANTICLEA. The wife of Laertes, Anticlea could not bear the absence of her son Ulysses and, having no word from him for many long years, she died of a broken heart. Before her marriage, she had lived intimately with Sisyphus, whom one version of the legend considered to be the real father of Ulysses.

ANTIGONE. **1.** The daughter of Oedipus and Jocasta, sister of Ismene, Eteocles and Polynices, Antigone had a sorrowful life and an atrocious death but never gave up a devotion and grandeur of spirit that are unequaled in mythology. When her father was chased from Thebes by her brothers and when, his eyes gouged out, he had to beg for food along the roadside, Antigone served as his guide and cared for him until the end of his days, comforting him and helping him until his final moment in Colonus. Then she returned to Thebes; but there a new and cruel trial awaited her. Her brothers were arguing over power and Polynices, who had gone to seek help from Adrastus, the king of Argos, returned with a foreign army to besiege the city and battle against his brother Eteocles like an enemy. After the death of the two brothers, Creon, their uncle, assumed power in Thebes. He held solemn funeral rites for Eteocles, but refused to have a burial for Polynices because, aided by strangers, he had borne arms against his country. Thus, the soul of Polynices would never know eternal rest. However, Antigone, who considered it a sacred duty to bury the dead, went out to her brother's body one night and, according to rite, threw a few handfuls of earth on his body. Surprised by a guard and taken to Creon, she was condemned to death and buried alive in a tomb of the Labdacids. Rather than die of hunger, she chose to hang herself. Haemon, Creon's son and Antigone's betrothed, killed himself in despair. Eurydice, the wife of Creon, could not bear the death of her son whom she loved above all else and she killed herself as well.

2. Legend also speaks of another **Antigone,** the daughter of Eurytion, the king of Phthia, who married Peleus.

ANTILOCHUS. Exposed at birth on Mount Ida, this hero was found by his father Nestor, the king of Pylos, and accompanied him to Troy. During a battle, according to the most common tradition, he was slain by the Ethiopian Memnon. His ashes were entombed next to those of his two friends, Achilles and Patroclus. The three heroes met again in the abode of the blest on White Island where, in the midst of complete happiness, they continued their exploits and festivities forever.

ANTINOUS. Son of Eupeithes of Ithaca, he appears in the *Odyssey* as Penelope's chief suitor. Proud and brutal, he multiplied the misdeeds in the palace of Ulysses, tried to kill Telemachus whose presence bothered him, squandered Penelope's wealth, and insulted the swineherd Eumaeus, who had brought a beggar into the room where he was dining with his friends. Ulysses was hiding behind this humble disguise: he killed Antinous as he raised a cup to his lips.

ANTIOPE. Her beauty was fatal to this daughter of the river-god Asopus or Nycteus, the king of Thebes. Zeus, who was in love with her, seduced her in the form of a satyr; frightened and fearing her father's wrath, Antiope fled and sought refuge with Epopeus, the king of Sicyon, who married her. But Lycus, the brother of Nycteus, seized Sicyon, killed the king and took his niece back to Thebes. En route, Antiope gave birth to twins, Amphion and Zethus, whom she abandoned and who were found by shepherds. Persecuted by Dirce, the wife of Lycus, she was treated to the grace of the gods, was delivered, and was reunited with her children who avenged her for the unworthy treatment to which she had been subjected. Lycus and Dirce were killed. But Dionysus would not let the perpetrators of these murders escape unpunished and he drove Antiope mad; she wandered throughout Greece until Phocus, the grandson of Sisyphus, cured her and married her.

APHRODITE. Her powers are immense: a kindly goddess, she protects marriages, promotes loving harmony between spouses, blesses couples with fertility, presides over births. She also fertilizes fields. But she may also be a dreaded divinity because she often symbolizes passion that nothing can stop, a goddess who drives mad with love those whom she wishes to destroy. She even ravages legitimate unions, driving husbands to adultery, as she encourages fertility in illicit love affairs and incites mortals to revel in every sensual pleasure and vice. Thus, Aphrodite becomes a fatal goddess whose magic belt endows those it encircles with a strange power of perpetual desires. Fruits with numerous seeds, the symbols of fertilizing strength, such as the pomegranate, the poppy and the apple, are usually dedicated to her. Among the birds that pull her chariot or surround her are the dove, the swan and the pigeon, all symbols of marital fidelity. Aphrodite is usually depicted nude or seminude, in voluptuous poses, draped in a thin veil that clings to the full yet harmonious shapes of her body. Because of her sensuality, she is often identified with the Phoenician goddess Astarte.

Consecrated by Paris as the most beautiful of all goddesses, Aphrodite, in return, offers the hero the young and beautiful Helen. Private coll., photo Giraudon.

There are two versions of the legend concerning the origin of Aphrodite, goddess of Love and Beauty. According to the first, she is the daughter of Zeus and Dione; according to the second, she was born of the blood that dripped into the sea when Cronus castrated Uranus. This blood fertilized the water and Aphrodite arose from deep within a wave, as white and as beautiful as foam. From that point on, love, of which she was the divine incarnation, was to reign over gods, men and all living creatures. The wife of Hephaestus, she frequently deceived the god and, in particular, developed a passionate love for Ares, whom she bore famous children such as Eros and Anteros. But she was surprised by her husband, who imprisoned the two lovers in a net. Ashamed,

Aphrodite left Olympus for a time. However, she was to betray Hephaestus again by sharing the beds of Dionysus, Hermes and Poseidon. Nonetheless, the goddess was not satisfied fully by the love of the gods of Olympus. Mortals, such as Anchises of Troy, also succumbed to her beauty and grace; thus she gave birth to Aeneas, the ancestor of the Julians, from whom Caesar claimed to have descended. Finally, she passionately loved Adonis, a symbol of vegetation as it is reborn each year to life and love. Having received from Paris the famous golden apple as a sign of her surpassing beauty, she showed her gratitude to the Trojan hero by creating between him and Helen a love that was to prove supremely fatal to the city of Troy.

APOLLO.   One of the twelve major divinities of Olympus, Apollo was born in Delos where his mother Leto, seduced by Zeus, sought refuge to escape Hera's jealous fury. Apollo had a twin sister, Artemis, in whose company legends often depict him.

When Zeus learned of the birth of Apollo, he gave him a golden miter, a lyre and a swan-drawn chariot. Suckled on nectar by the goddess Themis, the newborn became, in just a few days, a magnificent adolescent who left in his chariot, equipped with a quiver and arrows, for the land of the Hyperboreans. After a year there, he arrived in Delphi where he began his life's work. He first made his mark not far from the city by killing the serpent Python, which lived in a cave on Mount Parnassus. But his love affairs are even more famous. Radiantly handsome, beautifully built, he seduced countless nymphs, including Coronis who bore him a son, Asclepius, whom Zeus struck by lightning in anger. Apollo, to take revenge on the sovereign god, pierced and killed with arrows the Cyclopes who had fashioned thunderbolts for Zeus. Irritated by this show of presumptuousness, Zeus banished Apollo from Olympus.

"Apollo Belvedere," the incarnation of masculine beauty, Vatican Museum, photo Anderson-Giraudon.

This god had other well-known loves: he loved the nymph Daphne, who, to escape him, was transformed into a laurel tree; he seduced the nymph Clytia, the daughter of Oceanus, and changed her into a sunflower when, having been abandoned by Apollo, she revealed to the father of Leucothea, her rival, her divine par-his powers and sometimes attribute a deadly nature to him. This is why he is often regarded as the god of Thundering Punishment. All sudden deaths result from wounds that he inflicts. Sometimes he condemns humanity to a slower, more excruciating death by sending a plague. However, in the eyes of the Greeks, Apollo is, above all, a kindly god and the leader of prophecies and deification: the pythoness speaks in his name; as the inspiration for musicians and poets, he is sometimes called *Apollo Musagetes*, the patron god of all the arts.

ARACHNE. This young girl from Lydia, the daughter of Idmon of Colophon, a city famous for its purple dyes, excelled in the art of weaving. She even boasted of being a better weaver than Athena, the official spinner of Olympus. The goddess took up the challenge. But Arachne wove a piece of fabric depicting the love of the Olympian gods with such skill, that Athena could find no fault with it. Her anger knew no bounds. She tore up the work of her rival and struck her, so that the poor creature, terror-stricken and mortified, hanged herself with a rope. Thus, Athena changed her into a spider.

ARCAS. The son of Zeus and Callisto, Arcas was killed by Lycaon and served at a banquet to his father, who hastened to revive him. Proclaimed king of the Arcadians, he married Leanira, the daughter of Amyclas, king of Sparta. He had two sons, Elatus and Aphidas, and a third, Azan, born of the nymph Erato. He taught his subjects the arts of spinning yarn and sowing wheat. Along with his mother, he was changed into a bear and placed among the constellations. His three sons divided up his kingdom.

ARES. The son of Zeus and Hera, Ares belongs to the generation of the twelve great gods of Olympus. However, he never occupied an

The patron of Music, Apollo Musagetes accompanies the dance of the Muses who use castanets to set the rhythm of their dance. Lekythos with figures on white background, Louvre, photo Giraudon.

amour's new loves. During his stay on Earth, Apollo found accommodating hospitality in the court of King Admetus, whose flock he tended. For this reason, the god is often considered to be the patron of livestock. When his exile on Earth came to an end, he received permission to return to Olympus. The Greeks multiplied important place in Greek worship. The god of War and Combat, his brutal appearance, his violent and aggressive behavior, and his love of slaughter and battles make him likeable to neither mortals nor gods. Moreover, legends have often depicted him during combats in perilous situations from which he did not always emerge victorious. During the Trojan War, he generally sided with the Trojans; he was often forced to measure up to the bravura of certain heroes and to the calculating and reasonable intelligence of the goddess Athena. Thus, legend shows Ares, wounded by the hero Diomedes with the help of Athena, retreating to Olympus howling. The god was scarcely more successful with Heracles, who pierced his thigh with an arrow. The Aloadae held him captive in a bronze vase for many years while the gods, his brothers, took pleasure in humiliating him by calling a trial and convicting him of murder. Ares' love affairs with mortals were numerous because, despite his barbaric nature, the god is not without a certain mature and virile beauty. But his offspring are rough creatures, ruffians, violent beings, like the bandit Cycnus, Diomedes of Thrace, Lycaon or Oenomaus. Among the immortals, only Aphrodite conceived a passionate love for Ares, who symbolized in all his power passionate and sensual strength. Possibly imported from Thrace, he was not worshiped on a large scale in Greece. It is understandable that the Greeks, whose spirits were drawn to the subtleties of reason and the fine points of intelligence, would exhibit a certain amount of repugnance for a god who was somewhat foreign to them because of both his origin as well as his nature and powers. However, the Romans held him in high esteem and identified him with their god Mars.

ARETHUSA. A follower of Artemis, this Nereid was changed into a spring to escape the advances of the river-god Alpheus.

ARGONAUTS. These were the heroes who set sail for Colchis with Jason at the helm in order to bring back to Pelias, the king of Iolcus, who wished to banish his nephew from the throne, the Golden Fleece of the ram consecrated to Ares by Aeetes, the king of Colchis. Some fifty strong, the illustrious Argonauts, among whom were Jason, Admetus, Amphion, Tydeus, Theseus, Heracles, the Dioscuri, Orpheus and a host of other heroes, set sail in the *Argo*, built out of Dodona wood under the direction of Athena. Apollonius of Rhodes charts the course of the famous sailors. Their journey took them first to the island of Lemnos, then to Samothrace where, on the advice of Orpheus,

A helmeted Ares during the battle of the Gods and Giants. Detail from the frieze of the Treasury of the Siphnians at Delphi, 6th cent. B.C., Delphi Museum, photo Alison Frantz.

they learned the mysteries. Having crossed the Hellespont, the Argonauts dropped anchor off the coast of the island of Cyzicus, the country of the Doliones, governed by Cyzicus who welcomed them hospitably with every honor. But after leaving the island, they were caught in an immense storm and thrown onto the territory of Cyzicus one dark and gloomy night. The inhabitants of Cyzicus did not recognize their guests from the night before and, taking them for pirates, they waged a merciless battle against the intruders, during which their king was killed by Jason. In the morning, both sides realized their mistake and, through funerary games and vigils, they honored the mortal remains of the king and his warriors. After leaving the island, the *Argo* put into port off the coast of Mysia where Hylas was dragged into the sea by nymphs who were smitten with him. Heracles and Polyphemus, who set out to look for him, were abandoned by their companions who raised anchor and set sail for the country of the Bebryces where they killed King Amycus and many of his subjects. Upon their arrival in Thrace, the Argonauts, with the help of the Boreads Calais and Zetes, helped to rid the soothsayer Phineus of the Harpies that were tormenting him incessantly. As a sign of his gratitude, the soothsayer gave his guests advice on the ways to avoid the dangers they would face during their journey. Thus the Argonauts were able to pass, without too much trouble, among the Symplegades, or Clashing Rocks, which, pushed against one another by opposing currents, were crushing the ships. After reaching the Black Sea, they approached, in Colchis, the palace of King Aeetes, who possessed the Golden Fleece. With the help of Medea, the daughter of the king, Jason took hold of the Golden Fleece and set sail again. Medea, who fled with the Argonauts, killed her brother Absyrtus and scattered his limbs in her wake, thereby preventing Aeetes from following

Athena, left, contributes her skill and knowledge to the building of the *Argo*. She helps one of the workers fasten a sail to a mast, while another worker constructs the ship's bow. Ancient relief, Villa Albani, Rome, photo Alinari.

them as he set about gathering up his son's remains. However, this criminal act displeased Zeus who sent a mighty tornado to engulf the *Argo*. A seer declared that only Circe could purify the criminal heroes. Therefore the *Argo* sailed up the Eridanus (the Po) and the Rhone, then down toward the Mediterranean until they reached Sardinia and the island of Aeaea, where Circe dwelled and where they dropped anchor. The sorceress purified the Argonauts and they were able to set sail once again. They resisted the melodious chants of the Sirens with the help of Orpheus who, with his lyre, surpassed the dangerous witches. They then passed unharmed between Charybdis and Scylla and reached the land of the Phaeacians, Corcyra. King Alcinous, a friend of Aeetes, demanded that they return Medea, but only if she was a virgin. So Jason hastened to marry this woman who had followed him so faithfully. Afterwards, the ship set sail for Libya and Crete where the giant Talos, who killed all strangers, succumbed to the spell of Medea while tearing a vein in his foot, which caused his death. When the Argonauts left Crete, opaque darkness suddenly enveloped them. They begged Phoebus to light their way. The god granted their wish and the sailors managed to reach the small island of the Sporades. At that point, their journey ended. After disembarking at Aegina, they reached Iolcus with the precious Golden Fleece.

According to some mythographers, this immense voyage is no more than the image of a colonization venture in the Pontus Euxinus (Black Sea) and in Asia Minor, or the symbol of the discovery of marvelous gold mines in the Caucasus (the ancient Colchis).

ARGOS. 1. The son of Zeus and Niobe, Argos was one of the kings of the city of Argos.

2. Also known by the name of **Argos** is a Thespian who built the *Argo,* the ship on which the Argonauts embarked.

3. Still another **Argos,** the son of Phrixus and Chalciope of Colchis, after being shipwrecked, was embraced by the Argonauts and joined their expedition.

4. The most famous **Argos** bore the surname *Panoptes* ("he who sees all"). A giant with one hundred eyes and formidable strength, he dabbled in various exploits and, most notably, he killed a wild bull that was ravaging Arcadia. He also slew the monster Echidna. Confident in his abilities, Hera instructed Argos to keep a constant watch over Io, the lover of Zeus, whom she had changed into a heifer. Indeed the giant slept with only fifty eyes closed while the other fifty remained open. However, Hermes, on the order of Zeus, and thanks to the enchanting sound of his flute, managed to plunge the fearsome guardian into a deep sleep and thereby chop off his head. In memory of her deceased servant, Hera placed the one hundred eyes of Argos on the plumage of the peacock, her sacred animal.

ARGOS. In Greek mythology, several cities are known by this name. The most famous was founded by the river-god Inachus or, according to another tradition, by his son Phoroneus or by his grandson Argos. But this first royal race was dethroned by Danaus, and his descendants were dethroned, in turn, by Pelops. Soon, the kingdom was divided into two independent states: Mycenae, which was governed by Atreus and his son Agamemnon, and Argos, which found renewed splendor under the reign of Orestes. During the Dorian invasion, the Peloponnesus, and Argos in particular, fell to Temenus and his descendants.

ARIADNE. This daughter of Minos and Pasiphaë fell in love with Theseus, who had come to Crete, and provided him with a thread that kept the Athenian hero from losing his way in the winding corridors of the Labyrinth and enabled him to kill the Minotaur. Carried away by Theseus, Ariadne was, according to the most current tradition, abandoned on the island of Naxos, one of the Cyclades. Dionysus discovered her sleeping there and married her, giving her for their wedding a golden crown, which he later placed among the constellations.

ARION. This poet of Lesbos undoubtedly lived at the end of the 7th century B.C. He was considered to have invented dithyrambic poetry. He played the cithara to perfection. He obtained from his friend Periander, tyrant of Corinth, permission to leave for Sicily where a song and poetry competition was being held. He took first prize there. Laden with gifts, he boarded a ship and headed home. But the sailors coveted his riches and decided to kill him. Apollo, therefore, appeared in a dream to Arion, told him of the danger in store for him, and promised him his protection. When the sailors attacked him, Arion asked them to grant him a supreme favor: to allow him to play the cithara and to sing one last time. A host of dolphins, drawn by the tender yet melancholy melody, gathered around the ship. When Arion, after finishing his lament, flung himself into the sea, one of them carried him on its back to Cape Taenarum, from which point the hero was able to return to Corinth and confound the sailors who were executed on Periander's orders.

ARISTAEUS. Seduced by Apollo, the Nereid Cyrene gave birth to a son, Aristaeus, among whose ancestors was the river-god Peneius. His education was entrusted to the centaur Chiron and the Nymphs, who taught him how to cultivate the olive tree, how to prepare milk and, above all, how to raise bees. His wife Autonoë, daughter of Cadmus, bore him a son, Actaeon, who was to be changed into a stag and devoured by his dogs. Aristaeus was not always faithful to Autonoë; he enjoyed pursuing the Nymphs, the Dryads and, in particular, Eurydice, whom he loved. Fleeing from him one day, Eurydice stepped on a viper and died from its sting. The Dryads avenged their sister by killing all of Aristaeus' bees. Aristaeus, in tears, went to his mother for advice. Cyrene sent him to the seer Proteus who delivered oracles, but with such bad grace that he had to be chained so he would not escape. Proteus finally let himself be subdued and advised Aristaeus to sacrifice four bulls and four heifers to appease the spirits of Eurydice. When he returned, nine days after the sacrifice, Aristaeus saw thousands of bees swarming from the animals' entrails: the gods had pardoned him. It is understandable that Aristaeus, a pupil of the Nereids and well versed in farming techniques, should rank among the rustic divinities in various provinces of Greece, particularly in Thessaly, Boeotia and Arcadia.

ARISTEAS. Aristeas was an epic poet who lived, it is believed, around the 6th century B.C., but whose biography has been reduced to a series of fantastic tales. Half magician, Aristeas had the power to disappear in his own way and reappear in various eras and places. For several years, he was one of Apollo's companions and in the form of a raven followed this god in his journeys to the country of the Hyperboreans.

ARISTODEMUS. One of the Heraclidae, the son of Aristomachus, prepared with his brothers, Temenus and Cresphontes, to conquer the Peloponnesus. But he neglected to consult the oracle of Apollo. He was struck by thunder and died. He was the father of Eurysthenes and Procles, to whom he bequeathed his kingdom of Laconia for them to share.

ARTEMIS. Known to the Romans as *Diana*, Artemis is the daughter of Zeus and Leto. She is both the protectress of virginity and the helper of women in the travail of childbirth. Artemis was born on the island of Delos the same day as Apollo, her twin brother, whom she often resembles both in nature and powers. Armed with arrows, she mercilessly kills those who, one way or another, have dared to insult her divine person and that of her mother, particularly the children of Niobe, and Orion, who tried to seduce her. Generally speaking, she is responsible for sudden deaths: her arrows are

One of the most classical representations of Artemis, with arrow-laden quiver and short tunic. "Artemis of Versailles," Hellenistic art, Louvre.

stag and having him devoured by his dogs. In the ancient world, however, several Artemises were known. Thus, the Taurians adored an Artemis, a cruel goddess atop a chariot drawn by bulls. She carried a torch in her hand and her forehead bore a crescent of the moon. Strangers were sacrificed to her; thanks to his sister Iphigenia, Orestes was able to flee and escape this savage custom.

Another **Artemis,** that of Ephesus, differed from the traditional goddess: in fact, rather than refuse love, she surrendered to it without restraint and nourished men and the Earth with her many breasts that swelled with milk. However, despite all this confusion, the Greek Artemis remains the huntress and the chaste, and it is with these features and attributes that she is depicted in most legends.

ASCALAPHUS. 1. The son of Ares and Astyoche, Ascalaphus led a body of Orchomenus Minyans to Troy and perished at the hand of Deiphobus, one of King Priam's sons.

2. When Hades permitted Persephone to return to the world of the living, provided she had eaten nothing during her stay in the Underworld, **Ascalaphus,** one of her guardians, claimed that the goddess had eaten a pomegranate, despite the warning she had been given. Demeter, Persephone's mother, punished the tattletale by changing him into an owl.

ASCANIUS. The most current tradition considers Ascanius to be the son of Aeneas and Creusa. According to the other versions of his legend, he was the son of Aeneas and Lavinia. After the fall of Troy, a flame was supposed to have whirled above his head. Aeneas perceived in this phenomenon a favorable omen to the search for a new establishment, and decided to found a colony in Italy. Mythographers agree in crediting the son of Aeneas with the construction of Alba Longa. He is considered to

always precise, thunderingly rapid and deadly. Like Apollo, she sided with the Trojans against the Greeks and obliged Agamemnon, guilty of boasting that he surpassed her with a bow and arrow, to sacrifice Iphigenia, whom she saved at the very last moment. Beautiful, chaste and virginal, stormy and jealous of her talents as a huntress, she punished Actaeon, who claimed to have surpassed her, by changing him into a have borne the surname of Iulus and he is regarded as the ancestor of the famous Julian family of Rome.

ASCLEPIUS. Hesiod and Pindar related the story of this god of Medicine, who was so famous in Antiquity that the Romans themselves adopted him and revered him under the name of Aesculapius. Seduced by Apollo, his mother, Coronis, daughter of Phlegyas, king of Thessaly, was destined never to know her son. If legend is to be believed, she was unfaithful to her divine lover with a mortal, Ischys. Apollo, informed of his lover's infidelity, killed her. But when the body of Coronis began to be consumed on the funeral pyre, Apollo, stricken with remorse, snatched his living son from the belly of his dead mother and entrusted him to Chiron. Asclepius learned from this wise and learned centaur the art of making up medicinal herbs and preparing remedies. Soon he acquired such skill that he succeeded not only in curing the ill, but in reviving the dead as well; Glaucus, Tyndareos and Hippolytus, in particular, owe their return to life to Asclepius. In response to the complaints of Hades, who feared that he would have to close his kingdom's gates for lack of subjects, and who also feared that the order of nature would be disturbed by miraculous cures, Zeus struck the overzealous Asclepius with a bolt of thunder. To avenge the death of his son, Apollo killed the Cyclopes who had forged the thunder and was condemned by the gods to a short exile on earth as punishment.

Despite his tragic death, Asclepius was entitled in Antiquity to divine honors. Many feeble, blind and sick people came to his sanctuaries, especially in Epidaurus, to ask for a cure or relief from their suffering. Asclepius, therefore, appeared to them in dreams and revealed the remedy that would restore their health. His main symbol was the serpent, a Chthonian symbol and the image of renewal as well, since

His face serene, Asclepius holds his traveling staff entwined with serpents that his daughter Hygieia, the goddess of Health, is feeding. Ancient marble, Vatican Museum, photo Alinari-Giraudon.

this animal changes skin each year. Asclepius transmitted his miraculous gifts to his children Machaon and Podalirius, the physicians of the

Greek army in its battle against Troy, to his daughter Hygieia, the goddess of Health, and to his descendants, the Asclepiads, who formed a sacerdotal brotherhood in which the "secrets" of their illustrious ancestors were handed down from father to son.

ASOPUS.   This river of the Peloponnesus which empties into the Corinthian Sea was deified. Like all Greek rivers, it had been begotten by Oceanus and Tethys. Asopus himself had two sons and twenty daughters by one of the daughters of the River Ladon, Metope. One of his daughters, Aegina, was abducted by Zeus who had changed himself into an eagle. Sisyphus, the king of Corinth, hurried to share the news with the river-god who, in a fit of fury, caused his waters to swell and devastated the country. Zeus cast the informer into the Underworld and blasted the indignant father with thunder so that his waters rushed back to their bed.

ASTERIA.   Daughter of the Titan Coeus and Phoebe, wife of Perses and mother of Hecate, Asteria changed herself into a quail to escape the amorous advances of Zeus, then threw herself into the sea and was changed into a rocky island that took the name of *Ortygia* (Greek *ortux*, quail) before being renamed Delos when her sister Leto gave birth to Apollo and Artemis there.

ASTEROPE.   The entire progeny of this Pleiad is generally overlooked. The only known fact is that she married a Titan.

ASTRAEA.   Just and virtuous, this daughter of Zeus and Themis lived among mortals in the happy moments of the golden age. But, when the human spirit became perverse, she withdrew, along with her sister Modesty (*Pudicitia*), from her stay among the living, and under the name of *Virgo* settled in among the heavens' stars.

ASTYANAX.   Fearing a possible restoration of the kingdom of Troy, the Greeks killed the heir to the throne, Astyanax, son of Hector (who called him Scamandrius) and Andromache, by hurling him from atop the city's ramparts.

ATALANTA.   Boeotian and Arcadian legends attribute to this heroine the character of Artemis, of whom she may be a local representation. Exposed at birth by her father Iasus (or Iasius), who wanted only male children, Atalanta was suckled on the milk of a she-bear and taken in by shepherds, who raised her. She loved hunting and strenuous exercise; she shot arrows into Rhoecus and Hylaeus, two centaurs who tried to attack her, and, during the Caly-

Atalanta wears the same short tunic as Artemis, whose hunting companion she often is. Antique marble, Louvre, photo Giraudon.

			ATHAMAS	
NEPHELE = ATHAMAS = INO = THEMISTO				
			SCHOENIUS	
PHRIXUS HELLE		LEARCHUS MELICERTES	ATALANTA	

donian Boar Hunt, she was the first to wound the beast. But the goddess Aphrodite saw her chastity as a challenge. To avoid marriage, Atalanta devised a strategy. All suitors would be obliged to compete against her in a race. If anyone defeated her, which seemed impossible, since she was considered to be the swiftest of all mortals, he would win her hand. If a suitor were defeated, his head would be chopped off. Thus, many a suitor perished until Hippomenes, through trickery (he cast golden apples before her), outran Atalanta and married her. Some time after the wedding, the couple entered a sanctuary that was consecrated to Zeus, or to Demeter according to another version of the story, and were locked in fond embraces. Outraged at this act of profanity, the god turned them into lions.

ATE. One of the many allegorical divinities of mythology, Ate, the daughter of Eris (Discord), and Zeus, personifies men's fatal deviation. She drives mortals to error and destruction. The goddess had lost the privilege of living with the gods of Olympus. Indeed, Zeus had promised to give his future son Heracles supremacy over Mycenae. Urged on by Ate, Hera first gave birth to Eurystheus who was also a descendant of Perseus and thus deprived his half-brother of the empire Zeus had intended him to have. Vexed by her evil-mindedness, Zeus took Ate by the hair and threw her to Earth, forbidding her ever to return to the company of the gods. Since then, she has never left mortals, whom she throws into confusion and leads astray.

ATHAMAS. The son of Aeolus, this king of Boeotia married, in Orchomenus, Nephele who

bore him two children, Phrixus and Helle. But the first marriage, concluded without the couple's consent, was not a happy one and Athamas shared his tenderness with Ino, the daughter of Cadmus, who bore him two sons, Learchus and Melicertes. Hera, who had conceived a deep aversion for the couple, drove Athamas mad. In a frenzy, he killed Learchus. Banished from Boeotia, he went, in his misery, to consult the Delphic oracle who advised him to settle in a spot where wild animals would invite him to dine with them. Upon his arrival in Thessaly, Athamas came across a pack of wolves devouring a lamb and which fled as he approached. He immediately realized that, according to the prediction of the oracle, he had arrived at the end of his misery and founded, on the very site of the miracle, the city of Alus, overlooking the surrounding area, which came to be known as *Athamantia*.

ATHENA. When she was pregnant with Athena, the goddess Metis (wisdom or guile) was swallowed by Zeus, her lover, who feared that the child she was carrying would dethrone him. But the god soon felt the pains of a violent headache. Hephaestus split his skull with an axe and out sprang Athena, armed and helmeted, uttering an immense war cry. The goddess, one of the twelve divinities of Olympus, was to be involved, either directly or remotely, in most of the major cosmogonical tales. Blessed with noble reason, having acquired a sense of wisdom from her mother, she indeed became for the gods a precious counselor and helped them especially to conquer the Giants. However, she did not hesitate to quarrel with Poseidon over possession of Attica. While the god struck the

Athena Parthenos. Roman copy of the 5th cent. B.C. gold and ivory statue by Phidias which stood in the Parthenon. National Archaeological Museum, Athens, photo Alison Frantz.

Acropolis with his trident and caused a splendid steed or, according to other versions, a saltwater lake to arise, the goddess offered the inhabitants of the country an olive tree, a symbol of peace as well as wealth. The inhabitants de-

cided that the tree would be more useful than the horse and finally chose Athena as their patron. The goddess provided constant protection for the great heroes of Attica and most of the Greek commanders during the Trojan War. Soon, Athena's powers developed and multiplied. She was no longer simply the chaste goddess who stripped Tiresias of his sight because the soothsayer had dared to watch her bathe, or who had Hephaestus banished from Olympus for having tried to compromise her honor. She was no longer just the goddess of War wearing a breastplate and armor, carrying a golden lance and a shield on which was embossed the head of Medusa, as she is depicted by the Palladium: she became the protectress of the State, the goddess ensuring the impartiality of laws and their just application both in the tribunals as well as in the assemblies. But law alone cannot ensure the perpetuity of a State and its people: that must also come from the country's prosperity. Athena watches over agriculture

The owl, one of Athena's sacred animals. Bronze coin of Athens, Bibl. Nat., Cabinet des Médailles.

Seated on his throne and holding a thunderbolt in one hand, Zeus welcomes the birth of Athena who, armed and helmeted, springs from his forehead, cloven with the help of Hephaestus. The owl, the new goddess's favorite animal, is perched on the back of the throne while a winged spirit, or perhaps even Eileithyia, the goddess of childbirth, hidden under the throne, lends a helping hand on this happy occasion. Poseidon, armed with his trident, stands behind Zeus. Greek amphora, Louvre.

with particular benevolence. She invented, for man's convenience, farming implements that enabled the land in Attica to supply a better yield. She is also the goddess of weavers and potters. Furthermore, the goddess protects all families, protects the harmony and chastity of couples, the honor of the household and everyone's health ("Athena Hygieia"). Through the favorable influence of her reason and her subtle, reflective thought, Athena endows literature and the arts. It is only fitting that this divinity appears as the divine symbol of Greek civilization who, by her warrior strength, her intelligence, her wisdom, the moderation in her habits and the studied beauty of her artistic

A familiar attitude of Athena's: helmet raised, forehead leaning on her spear, body supported by one foot and bent slightly forward, the goddess of Arts and Intelligence reflecting. Greek art, circa 450 B.C., Acropolis Museum, Athens, photo Alinari-Giraudon.

Atlas, his body bent, his muscles swelling, supporting the world on which the signs of the Zodiac are inscribed. Ancient sculpture, National Archaeological Museum, Naples, photo Alinari.

and literary monuments, was able to impose her dominance on the world. Later, the Romans identified her with Minerva.

ATHENS. This city in Attica is supposed to have received its name from the goddess Athena, who one day quarreled with Poseidon over who was to possess it. She had given the city an olive tree and was thereby chosen as protectress by Cecrops, one of the first mythical kings of Athens. Other legendary princes succeeded him to the throne, among whom were Aegeus and his son Theseus. This hero accomplished in the city important political and social reforms of a democratic nature. He reunited the twelve independent boroughs of Attica and made Athens their capital. He sealed this union by introducing festivals: the Panathenaea festival and the Synoikismos, which all inhabitants of Attica celebrated. During the classical era, people claimed to have found the ashes of this monarch and to have buried them, with much ado, in a temple whose location has not, to this day, been discovered.

ATLANTIS. According to Plato in the *Critias*, when the gods divided up the world, Athena received the city of Athens and Poseidon received Atlantis, an immense island located to the west of the pillars of Hercules. The god lived there with a young woman named Clito who bore him ten children. The eldest, Atlas, divided the island into ten States and took possession of the central mountain. The kings of Atlantis, vassals of the king, descendants of Atlas, exploited nature's riches—copper, iron, gold, founded cities and settled in enchanting palaces, building walls and canals around their city that were useful for both defense and trade. About 9000 years before Plato, they tried to dominate Africa and Europe but were repelled by the Athenians and their allies. The island of Atlantis, in punishment for the vices and pride of its inhabitants, was swallowed up

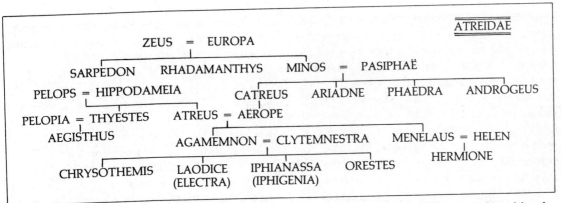

ATREIDAE

by Oceanus. It is possible that Atlantis, the fabled country, was confused by the Ancients with the Azores, about which the Phoenicians recounted marvelous tales. Even today, many authors still uphold the validity of Plato's story and seek to identify and locate this island whose existence remains, despite everything, hypothetical.

ATLAS. The son of Iapetus and the Oceanid Clymene, this Giant belongs to the first generation of gods. With his brothers, he fought against Zeus. In punishment for this crime, Atlas was condemned to bear the sky on his shoulders. It is also told that Perseus asked for his hospitality, but met with a refusal. Vexed, the hero showed him the head of Medusa and the Giant, petrified, was turned into a mountain named "Atlas" upon which, according to the Ancients, the heavens rested. His many children included the Pleiades, the Hyades, and the Hesperides.

ATREIDAE. The Atreidae, a family that includes many of mythology's famous characters, derive their name from Atreus, who descended from Tantalus and Pelops. This family is characterized by the cruelty of a fate that was against each of its members and drove them to inexpiable crimes and hatred. Therefore, the great writers of tragedy found in their legends choice subjects to illustrate the cruel confusion of souls that are damned or abandoned by the gods and by hope. There are Atreus and Thyestes, two brothers who were enemies until death; King Agamemnon murdered by his cousin Aegisthus; Orestes, Agamemnon's son, who murdered his mother Clytemnestra and was pursued by the Furies.

ATREUS. Like Eteocles and Polynices and numerous brothers in mythology, Atreus and Thyestes, sons of Pelops and Hippodameia, hated each other with inexpiable passion. After murdering his half-brother Chrysippus, Atreus was forced to flee with his brother to Mycenae where he was taken in by King Sthenelus. Since the succession to the throne was an open issue, the two brothers quarreled over the power, each devising the most cowardly swindles to do away with the other. Thus Thyestes, with the help of his sister-in-law Aërope, stole the Golden Fleece of a lamb that his brother possessed and demanded that the holder of the Golden Fleece be made king. Atreus, unaware of the theft and certain to win, gladly accepted the proposal. But Hermes alerted him in a dream to the treachery of Thyestes; he followed the advice of the god and, when he awakened, he declared that if the sun reversed its course, he, Atreus, would be proclaimed king. Indeed the sun set in the east and thus Atreus became king of Mycenae. Confident of his rights and of divine protection, he therefore plotted the cruelest of ways to persecute his brother. Not content with having massacred his nephews, he served them to his brother as a meal. He even urged Aegisthus to kill Thyestes but Aegisthus realized that Thyestes was his father and turned the sword on his uncle. Married twice, Atreus had a certain number of children made famous by legends: by Cleola, the granddaughter of Pelops, Plisthenes; by Aërope, the widow of Plisthenes, Agamemnon and Menelaus, according to one of the traditions. Atreus had no children by a third marriage to Pelopia.

ATTIS. The name of this Phrygian divinity cannot be separated from the name and legend of Cybele. According to Ovid, the goddess developed for Attis, a handsome young Phrygian shepherd, a violent but platonic love. She entrusted him with the leadership of her cult and instructed him to remain chaste. But Attis betrayed his promise: he fell in love with the nymph Sagaritis and married her. Angry, Cybele killed her rival and drove the unfortunate shepherd mad until one day, in a frenzy, he mutilated himself. Legend has it that the goddess later repented and revived Attis in the form of a pine.

AUGE. Aleos, the king of Tegea, married Neere, by whom he had three sons and one daughter, Auge. In Delphi, having learned from the oracle of Apollo that the son of his daughter would kill his uncles, Aleos, upon his return home, made Auge a priestess of Athena, thus consecrating her to perpetual chastity. Some time later, Heracles, visiting the king's court, became drunk and raped Auge. She bore a son named Telephus. When Aleos learned of the birth, he sold both mother and infant as slaves. The young woman was taken to Mysia where she married King Teuthras. Telephus did indeed finally kill his uncles one day by accident.

AUGEAS. Most often considered to be one of the sons of Helios and the brother of Actor, Augeas, king of Elis, accompanied his brother on the expedition of the Argonauts. He is known especially for the role he played in the legend of Heracles. He possessed a rich and enormous herd of cattle, but was extremely negligent and never cleaned the stables. Augeas, therefore, assigned this task to Heracles. In return, the hero asked the king for one tenth of his herd, assuring him that the work would be accomplished in a single day. Heracles opened a gap in the walls of the stables and flooded them with the waters of the rivers Alpheus and Peneus. That evening, everything was clean. Heracles came to collect the compensation for his work. Augeas, breaking his vow, refused. Phyleus, the king's own son, took Heracles' side before the tribunal charged with settling the dispute; they were condemned and both were banished from Elis. But they returned with an army and, after uncertain battles, Heracles took control of the city, killed Augeas, and replaced him on the throne with Phyleus, who had remained his faithful companion.

AUTOLYCUS. Son of Hermes and Chione, Autolycus is the father of Anticlea and the grandfather of Ulysses. During his life, he taught Heracles the art of using his fists to fell his adversaries. He took part in the expedition of the Argonauts but he is known above all as a thief without peers because he was able to alter or camouflage the appearance of animals that he was stealing. Thus, he was able to steal the oxen of Eurytus, king of Euboea. It is also said that he stole a helmet and gave it to Ulysses as a present and that this helmet enabled the hero to steal imperceptibly into Troy. Finally, Autolycus pilfered part of the herd of Sisyphus; but Sisyphus, who had taken the precaution of branding his cattle, easily realized that he had been robbed. One version of the legend claims that Sisyphus, in his anger, seduced Anticlea, the daughter of Autolycus and fiancée of Laertes, and that he was the real father of Ulysses.

AUTOMEDON. Driver of the chariot of Achilles, Automedon hailed from the island of Scyros in the Aegean Sea. He left this territory, leading a contingent of his countrymen, to assist the Greeks in their war against Troy. He was famous for his gentleness and, above all, for his fidelity. When Achilles died, Automedon dedicated his services to Neoptolemus, the son of the famous hero. The name of Automedon has, through the ages, come to signify a skillful and loyal coachman.

AVERNUS LACUS. Like the Lerna swamps or Lake Ampsanctus, Lake Avernus, bordering on the cape not far from Cumae, was formed in the crater of an extinct volcano. From its stagnant water noxious vapors rose, killing the birds. "Avernus" is fancifully derived from the Greek *Aornis* (without birds). Believing that the lake communicated with the Underworld, the Romans dedicated it to Pluto, god of the Underworld. The lake was surrounded by immense trees whose crowns, bending over the water, formed an arch that the rays of the sun could not penetrate; not far from these forsaken shores, people consulted an oracle of the Shades. Ulysses turned to this oracle upon his return from Troy.

B

BACCHANTES. Followers of Dionysus, the Bacchantes accompanied the god on his journeys and especially on his long voyage to India. Though not priestesses, they hold an important position in the religion and worship and appear significantly during the mysteries and festivals celebrated in honor of their master. Dressed in lion skins, often bare-chested, they carry the thyrsus, a staff entwined with a vine branch and ivy, and participate in a frenzied dance which plunges them into a mystical ecstasy and endows them with an extraordinary and dreaded strength, of which certain heroes were the unfortunate victims. They are, therefore, called the *Maenads* ("the Frenzied"). However, like Apollo's servants, the Muses, the Bacchantes can inspire poets with their enchanting powers.

BACCHUS. Roman divinity of Wine and the Vine, of Debauchery and Licentiousness, Bacchus, identified with Dionysus, did not originally play an important part in the Roman religion. But his worship spread, and its initiates succumbed, during the *Bacchanalia*, to orgies which prompted the Senate in 186 B.C. to attempt to combat the disorder they produced.

BATTUS. Hermes was driving a herd of cattle that he had stolen from Apollo when he encountered an old man named Battus. Fearing

Raised by the nymphs and divinities of the woods, the god Bacchus plays with a faun, carrying his symbol, the cluster of grapes. Roman art, Vatican Museum, photo, Alinari-Giraudon.

that his theft had been discovered, he promised him a heifer if he agreed not to reveal the secret. Then to test him, the plundering god changed his appearance, pretending to be looking for a lost herd and asked Battus whether he had seen the perpetrator; he promised him a reward at the same time. Battus immediately betrayed his secret. Hermes, indignant, changed him into a rock.

BAUCIS. Because of her purity and the gentleness of her hospitality, Baucis, the wife of Philemon, attracted the favors of Zeus and Hermes. When she died at an extremely old age, she was changed into a linden tree and given a place near her husband who had been changed into an oak.

BELLEROPHON. Son of Glaucus and grandson of Sisyphus, Bellerophon in his youth killed Belleros, tyrant of Corinth. Banished from the city for this crime, he took refuge with Proetus, king of Tiryns, who purified him of his murder. But Stheneboea, the wife of Proetus, fell in love with the hero, who rejected her with disdain. Vexed, the queen accused him of having tried to rape her. The king believed her. However, not wishing to kill his guest himself because of the sacred laws of hospitality, he assigned the task to his father-in-law Iobates, king of Lycia, and he sent Bellerophon to him with the order to kill him. Iobates, like Proetus, did not wish to strike the hero, and for the same reason. He asked Bellerophon to perform a certain number of tasks and each one was more dangerous than the next. Bellerophon zealously accomplished all that was asked of him. He succeeded in breaking in Pegasus, the winged horse, with the help of magical reins given to him by Athena. He

Having extracted him from the body of Semele, Jupiter placed the young Bacchus in his thigh for three months. Here the god can be seen being born. Mercury, wearing a large petasus, prepares to welcome him while the three Parcae watch over the destiny of the newborn divinity. Ancient relief, Vatican Museum, photo Anderson-Giraudon.

slew the Chimaera. He conquered the savage Solymi and their allies, the Amazons. Finally, he put an end to the activities of a band of pirates that was ravaging the Carian coasts by killing them all. Showing no gratitude for these victories, Iobates lay an ambush for the hero, but every last Lycian was killed in the process. Finally realizing that Bellerophon was protected by the gods and believing that he was of divine origin, Iobates honorably made amends,

granted him the hand of his daughter Philonoë and, at his death, bequeathed him the throne of Lycia. But the hero, intoxicated by his exploits, was not able to restrain himself to the limits of decency imposed by the gods on humans. Mounted on Pegasus, he wanted to be accepted in Olympus and become immortal. Stricken by Zeus and thrown from his horse, he fell back to Earth and killed himself; according to another version, he did not die, but roamed the world over, lame, blind and lonely.

BELLONA. This divinity of Sabine origin, nurse, sister or spouse of Mars, depending on the tradition, was gradually identified with the Greek goddess Enyo. Like Enyo, Bellona accompanied Mars, the god of War, in the midst of the slaughter on the battlefields. A helmet on her head, a spear in her hand, she drove the god's chariot.

BELUS. In addition to the king of Tyre who bore this name and was the father of Dido and Pygmalion, legend has retained the story of another Belus, twin brother of Agenor and son of the nymph Libya and Poseidon. Belus, who was proclaimed king of Egypt, married Anchinoë, daughter of the Nile. Of this marriage, Danaus, father of the Danaids, and Aegyptus were born.

BERENICE. This Egyptian princess (born 273 B.C.), whose name belongs to both legend and history, was the wife of Ptolemy III Euergetes. When her husband left to wage war against Syria, Berenice promised to dedicate her hair to the gods if they would protect the king. Ptolemy returned home safe and sound. But later when the votive hair disappeared, it was given a place among the constellations. She was murdered in 221 B.C. by her own son Ptolemy IV.

birds. In Greek and Roman worship, birds were either sacrificial animals or the symbols of certain gods of whom they recalled a legend or

The hero Bellerophon managed to capture the winged horse Pegasus near the spring Pirene where he was drinking. He finally broke Pegasus, whose name means spring, by putting reins on him. Thanks to this fabulous animal that was swifter than the Wind, Bellerophon was always able to accomplish famous feats victoriously. Relief, 1st cent. A.D., Palazzo Spada, Rome, photo Anderson-Giraudon.

a particular attribute. Thus, the majestic and formidable eagle is the incarnation of Zeus; the white dove, consecrated to Aphrodite, represents love in peace in the hearts of men; the peacock, the sacred animal of Hera, owes the particular nature of its plumage to the goddess who adorned it with the one hundred eyes of Argos; the owl is the prophetic bird dedicated to Athena. Sometimes, too, in legends certain characters are changed into birds; they are thus subjected to the wrath of a god or to his care; or else this metamorphosis may be a sign of the gods' pity, but most often it is a sure sign of their anger. Picus was changed into a woodpecker because he failed to succumb to the charms of the enchantress Circe; Coronis was changed into a crow by Athena to escape the advances of Poseidon; Aëdon, the unconsolable mother who inadvertently killed her son Itylus, was changed into a nightingale; Perdix, thrown from the top of the Acropolis by his uncle Daedalus, assumed the appearance of a partridge at the last minute. Finally, certain birds have their own legends, such as Phoenix who, unable to perpetuate his race, was burned and reborn from his ashes.

birth. Women in labor could enlist the aid of a certain number of divinities. Thus, they would ask Eileithyia and Mater Matuta to soothe the pains of childbirth and dispel all threats that could be detrimental, at the moment of birth, to the health of mother and child. They also implored Juno, the goddess of Woman, and requested a beautiful and healthy newborn, the symbol of the felicitous fertility of marriage.

BITON. The legend of Biton cannot be separated from that of his twin brother Cleobis. These two young Argians were the children of Cydippe, a priestess of Hera. As the time for offering sacrifices to the gods approached, and since the white oxen who were supposed to pull the sacred chariot were still in the pasture,

Biton and Cleobis harnessed themselves to the chariot and pulled it over a very long distance to the temple. Moved by their piety and their brotherly love, their mother asked Hera to grant them the most magnificent gift that may be bestowed on mortals. Hera, tender-hearted, plunged the two children into everlasting slumber.

blindness. Among the characters in ancient legends who are stricken blind, blindness generally represents blindness of the soul or reason, the source of criminal tendencies or impiety. Sometimes, like Oedipus, homicidal heroes work justice themselves: they cannot bear a light capable of illuminating their fault in all its significance and horror. But if these sinners have acquired a spirit of contrition or found wise sorcerers such as Asclepius or Chiron, they can recover their sight by exposing their dimmed eyes to the sun, the symbol *par excellence* of light that restores to a soul its purity and warmth and rids the soul of all impurity.

BONA DEA. An ancient divinity of Latium, sometimes called *Fauna,* and wife of Faunus, the "Good Goddess" was famous in Rome because of her rites which only matrons were permitted to attend. She delivered oracles and made woman fertile.

BOREAS. The North Wind, chilly and harsh, Boreas is an old man who is bearded, winged, and dressed in a short tunic. He blows from Thrace where he lives in a cave on Mount Haemus. Like his brothers Zephyrus and Notus, he is the son of Eos and Astraeus. It is told that he carried away Oreithyia, the daughter of Erechtheus, king of Athens, in a whirlwind of dust and forced her to marry him. They had many children, among whom were Zetes, Calais, Cleopatra and Chione. Oreithyia became the cool breeze that soothes the heat of summer. According to another tradition, Boreas assumed

Boreas embodies the fearful North Wind, with his fierce appearance, his wings and his winged ankles, and his tunic, with folds in the shape of feathers. Here he can be seen abducting Oreithyia, one of the daughters of Erechtheus, king of Athens. She was to bear him two sons, Calais and Zetes. Attic vessel, 5th cent. B.C., Vatican Museum, photo Alinari-Giraudon.

the form of a horse to marry the mares of Erichthonius. These gave birth to twelve colts which trod so lightly that, when they passed, the heads of wheat did not break and the sea showed not a ripple. Renowned particularly in Athens, Boreas helped to defend the city during the Persian wars by sending a storm that destroyed the Persian vessels.

BRISEIS. During the Trojan War, the city of Lyrnessus was seized and pillaged by the Greeks. Briseis, the daughter of Brises, the priest of Apollo, was reduced to slavery and became the servant of Achilles. Achilles, for his part, refused to take part in the combat after he was forced to hand over his captive to King Agamemnon. Upon the death of Patroclus, the hero resumed fighting under the leadership of Agamemnon, who gave Briseis back to Achilles.

BRITOMARTIS. A companion of Artemis, this chaste Cretan nymph, daughter of Zeus, was pursued for nine months by Minos, who was smitten with her and followed her over hill and dale. After nine months, just as he was about to catch her, she threw herself off a cliff into the sea where fishermen miraculously caught her in their nets.

BUSIRIS. This king of Egypt, a true tyrant, sent an expedition to steal the Hesperides, the daughters of Atlas who were famous for their beauty. Heracles met the messengers of Busiris en route and killed them all. During this time, a fearful drought and famine were ravaging Egypt. A Cyprian seer, Phrasius, declared that all strangers had to be sacrificed to appease the wrath of Zeus; Busiris applied the advice of Phrasius to the letter and sacrificed the seer himself. When Heracles arrived in Egypt, Busiris imprisoned him and was preparing to sacrifice him, but the hero tore off his bonds and killed the bloodthirsty tyrant, his son Amphidamas, as well as all his servants and assistants.

BYBLOS. This Phoenician city was known in Antiquity for the importance of its temple, introduced in honor of Adonis. According to legend, the city received its name from Biblis, the great-granddaughter of Minos who, to escape the incessant love of her brother Caunus, hanged herself in horror and despair.

C

CABEIRI. These divinities, who were worshiped in the archaic times of Greece, remain a mystery because almost nothing is known about their characters, their nature and their origin. The most common tradition considers Hephaestus to be their father. The god of Fire is supposed to have granted his sons extensive powers over metals and, more generally, over the development of metallurgical techniques. The Cabeiri were invoked particularly in Samothrace, Lemnos and Imbros to watch over the prosperity of the fields and to protect mariners against shipwrecks in those regions that were surrounded by rocks and where navigation was especially dangerous. Later, Rome began to worship the Cabeiri without, however, giving them a name, calling them instead simply "powerful gods" and associating them with the triad of Jupiter, Minerva and Mercury. There are two known ancient representations of a Cabeirus, one Greek, the other Roman, each symbolizing the powers of this divinity: a Thessalonican coin shows him holding a hammer; a Trajanic medal shows him wearing a pointed hat, holding in one hand a cypress branch, a symbol of the hereafter.

CACUS. This son of Volcanus, an enormous giant with three heads that breathed fire, lived in a cave on Mount Aventin and pillaged the surrounding regions. When Hercules arrived in Italy, after having slain Geryon and stolen his oxen, he stopped on the bank of the Tiber and fell asleep. Cacus stole some of the beasts while the hero was sleeping and dragged the animals by the tail into his cave, making them walk backwards to mix up the footprints. When the hero awakened, he realized that he had been robbed. Alerted by the bellowing of the captive animals, or according to another version of the legend, informed by Cacus's own sister, Hercules entered the cave. Wringing the neck of his adversary who vomited flames and smoke, Hercules strangled him.

CADMUS. The son of Agenor and Telephassa, Cadmus was instructed by his father to search for Europa, his sister and not to return without her. Unable to find her, he stopped in Thrace and consulted the Delphic oracle. The god instructed him to follow a cow whose flanks would bear a disc similar to that of the moon. Cadmus found the animal in Phocis and followed it to Boeotia. Exhausted, the cow finally lay down at the very place where the future city of Thebes was to be built. As a sign of his gratitude, Cadmus wanted to sacrifice the cow but he realized that the spring where he was going to fetch the water for the sacrifice was guarded by a dragon. He killed it and, on the advice of Athena, sowed the monster's

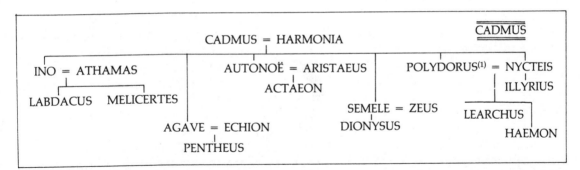

teeth which gave rise to a multitude of giants. These killed one another until only five remained and these five helped the hero build his city. Zeus entrusted him with the government of Thebes and he married Harmonia, a daughter of Ares and Aphrodite. He governed his people wisely and taught his subjects the Phoenician alphabet. His wife bore him many children, such as Agave, Semele, Ino, Polydorus, Autonoë. At their death, the couple was changed into serpents and welcomed by the gods in the Elysian Fields.

CAECULUS. This son of Volcanus is credited with having founded the city of Praeneste, today Palestrina. Two shepherds, the Depidii, had found a newborn, conceived in the breast of their sister by a spark that escaped from the hearth. They named him Caeculus, for after their sister had exposed him, he was found near a fire temporarily blind (*Caecus*). When he reached adulthood, during the ceremony preceding the founding of the city of Praeneste, he invoked Volcanus, his father. The god surrounded those attending with a circle of flames that he immediately extinguished on his son's orders. After this miracle, Caeculus was deified and many people came to settle in Praeneste to benefit from his protection.

CAENIS. The daughter of the Lapith Elatus, Caenis one day asked her lover Poseidon to change her into an invulnerable warrior. Having changed sex along with her name (Cae-

neus), she fought side by side with her compatriots against the Centaurs who, unable to kill her, buried her alive by beating her with a tree trunk. Transformed into a bird after her death, she later returned to her female state, it is said.

CALAIS. Son of Boreas and Oreithyia, Calais and his brother Zetes were two winged beings who never left one another's side and were named, because of their parentage, the "Boreads." Their sister was Cleopatra, who married Phineus, king of Thrace, and bore him two children. Phineus soon repudiated Cleopa-

Cadmus appears here with the features of a winged spirit and the body of a dragon, doubtless in memory of the animal he killed at the site of the future city of Thebes, where he became a legendary king. Greek vase, photo Camera.

tra and married Idaea, a Scythian princess. Jealous of her two stepsons, Idaea claimed that they had tried to seduce her. On this false accusation, the unfortunate pair had their eyes gouged out and were thrown into prison. During the expedition of the Argonauts, the Boreads went to Thrace to free their nephews; they also forced Phineus to send his second wife back to her native land. Other versions claim that Calais and Zetes gouged out the eyes of Phineus. It is also said that the two brothers showed their brother-in-law a great deal of tenderness and rid him of the Harpies who tormented him incessantly. Finally, one tradition states that the Boreads were among those who urged Jason to abandon Heracles and Polyphemus on the shores of Mysia and to set sail without them. Later, in revenge, Heracles shot arrows into Calais and Zetes on the island of Tenos.

Calliope gives Homer the tablets on which the poet will engrave his works with the direct inspiration of this Muse of epic poetry. Sarcophagus of the Muses, Louvre, photo Giraudon.

CALCHAS. A descendant of Apollo through his father Thestor, Calchas received the gift of prophecy from his divine ancestor. He was one of the most famous soothsayers of Greek mythology, more skilled than anyone else in the art of foretelling the future from the flight of birds. He was chosen by the Greeks as their official seer in their war against Troy. He announced the total duration of the expedition; he recommended the sacrifice of Iphigenia to calm the wrath of Artemis; he revealed that Troy would not be taken without the help of Achilles and Philoctetes, who possessed the bow of Heracles. He also put an end to the plague ravaging the Greek army by asking Agamemnon to return Chryseis to her father, Chryses, priest of Apollo. He also inspired the Greeks to build the famous Trojan horse. On his return, tossed on the coast of Ionia, Calchas met another seer, Mopsus, who proved to be even more of an expert than he and, as he had learned from an oracle, he died of sorrow.

CALLIOPE. First of the nine Muses, an assistant to *Apollo Musagetes,* of whom she is one of the wives, Calliope is the goddess of epic poetry. Her majestic air, her forehead encircled by a golden crown, indicate, according to Hesiod, her supremacy over the other Muses. She holds a stylus and tablets, sometimes a trumpet. The poets often consider her to be the mother of Orpheus.

CALLIRHOË. 1. This daughter of the river Acheloüs was married to Alcmaeon whom her father had just purified of a murder. Soon, she refused to let her husband near her until he gave her the necklace and mantle of Harmonia. Alcmaeon was killed trying to retrieve the two objects from his first wife, Arsinoë. Callirhoë instructed her two sons Amphoterus and Acarnan, whom Zeus, at her request, had caused to grow in a single day, to avenge their father. They killed Phegeus, the father of Arsinoë, and his two sons, the perpetrators of Alcmaeon's murder.

2. Married to Chrysaor, **Callirhoë**, the daughter of Oceanus, mothered the monsters Echidna and Geryon.

3. Daughter of the river-god Scamander, another **Callirhoë** was the wife of Tros, one of the founders of Troy, for whom the city is named, and the mother of Ilus and Ganymede.

CALLISTO. Callisto was the daughter of Lycaon, or according to another version, a nymph in the entourage of Artemis. Wishing to seduce her, Zeus assumed the form of Apollo and made her the mother of Arcas. To protect her from the jealous fury of Hera, the god turned her into a bear. It is also said that this metamorphosis was the work of Hera, or Artemis, who, while bathing, realized her companion's pregnancy. Arcas grew up to become king of Arcadia. One day while hunting in the mountains, he came across a bear that was actually his mother. In his ignorance, he prepared to kill her, but Zeus, to avoid this crime, changed him into a bear as well and lifted both mother and son into the sky where they were given a place among the constellations as the Great Bear (the Big Dipper) and the Little Bear (the Little Dipper). But, in deference to one last plea from Hera, Poseidon forbade them to set on Ocean's horizon.

CALYDON. **1.** This son of Thestius was killed by his father who found him by surprise in his mother's bed and believed he had committed an act of incest. Realizing his mistake, Thestius killed himself by throwing himself into the river Axenus, which bore his name before being renamed the Acheloüs.

2. An ancient city, the capital of Aetolia in the land of the Curetes, **Calydon** is rarely mentioned in historical narratives, but mythological accounts grant it its rightful stature, particularly in telling of the Calydonian Boar Hunt.

The city was governed by a line of legendary kings, among whom Oeneus and Diomedes were particularly famous.

Calydonian Boar. Sent in revenge by Aphrodite, to whom King Oeneus had neglected to make a sacrifice, this monstrous beast ravaged the Calydonian region, killing cattle and terrifying the inhabitants. The son of King Meleager enlisted the services of the bravest heroes in all of Greece to combat this scourge. Atalanta, the only woman to take part in the hunt, dealt the first deadly wound and Meleager finished off the beast. Meleager offered the huntress the boar's hide as a sign of his respect and gratitude, thereby provoking the anger of the other hunters.

CALYPSO. Nymph and queen of the island of Ogygia, Calypso welcomed Ulysses who had just been shipwrecked. In love with the hero, she spent seven years trying to make the hero forget his native land in her enchanted grotto, that was hemmed in by poplars and cypresses and abounded in vines that were laden with grapes. She even offered him immortality. But his love for Ithaca and Penelope burned in the heart of Ulysses and he spent his days contemplating the shore and the sea, his eyes brimming with tears. Touched, Zeus dispatched Hermes to Calypso: Ulysses was to leave the island. Despite her sorrow, Calypso obeyed. She helped the hero build a raft and gave him the supplies he needed for his voyage. Ulysses left her, his heart filled with hope as he headed back to his beloved fatherland.

CAMENAE. Nymphs of the springs and woods in the ancient Roman religion, the Camenae were soon identified with the Greek Muses. Their name is possibly Etruscan.

CANENS. This Roman divinity of song was the wife of King Picus. After her husband was changed into a boar and then a woodpecker by the enchantress Circe, Canens, grief-stricken, set out in search of him. At the end of the sixth day, Canens collapsed, exhausted, on the banks of the Tiber and sang one last time of her love before fading into the air.

CAPANEUS.   Aeschylus portrayed the son of Hipponous, Capaneus, one of the "Seven against Thebes," as an arrogant man whose brutality equaled his impiety. He scaled the walls of Thebes but Zeus struck him down with a thunderbolt since he was irritated by his blasphemy. At his funeral, his wife Evadne threw herself onto the funeral pyre where the body was customarily burned. Capaneus left behind a son, Sthenelus who, ten years after his father's death, took part in the second expedition against Thebes, that of the Epigoni.

capitol.   The three great Roman gods, Jupiter Optimus Maximus, Juno and Minerva, were worshiped as a sort of trinity on one of the hills in Rome, called the "Capitol." These three deities were considered to protect the city and state from possible disintegration and ruin. Furthermore, when generals celebrated their victories, they would always go to the Capitol to offer a sacrifice to whichever god of the trinity had made victory possible. In ancient Italy, each large city possessed a capitol.

CAPYS.   The husband of Themiste and father of Anchises, this Phrygian was considered to be one of the ancestors of Aeneas and the founder of the city of Capua in southern Italy.

CARMENTA.   Four traditions attribute various origins to this Camena. The first, related by Virgil, regarded her as a nymph of the Springs, daughter of the river Ladon. The second bestows on her the gift of prophecy, which she practiced in Arcadia, delivering oracles in verse (*carmen*). A third tradition identifies her as a goddess who protects women in childbirth. For this reason, she was worshiped by Roman matrons. Finally, after the Hellenization of the Roman gods, she was given a place in Greek mythology. She was thus called Nicostrate, the wife of the god Mercury and mother of Evander, with whom she left Arcadia to seek refuge with Faunus, king of Latium. At her death, she was placed among the deities who were indigenous to Rome. She has the features of a young woman crowned with beans, a food often mentioned in myths of the Underworld. She holds a harp, symbolic of her prophetic powers.

CARNA.   Ovid recounts the story of this nymph who lived on the banks of the Tiber and vowed to remain chaste. She submitted to the violation of the god Janus who offered her, in return, all power over door hinges. Certain mythologists linked Carna to Caro (flesh) and attributed to the goddess supreme power over the physical well-being of mortals. She also protected newborns. Today, mythographers place Carna among the gods of the Underworld because people would offer her beans, the symbolic vegetable of the Underworld.

CASSANDRA.   The daughter of Priam and Hecuba, the twin sister of Helenus, this Trojan woman of royal blood was infallible in her prophecies. She had received this gift from Apollo who asked her to yield to his advances. She pretended to accept but, once she was endowed with the power, she refused to keep her promise. The god, indignant, ordained that Cassandra's prophecies would never be taken seriously. Thus, Cassandra was powerless as she witnessed the preparations for the Trojan War, which she had predicted. She vainly opposed the entry into Troy of the famous wooden horse. When the city fell, she was pursued and held captive by Ajax, son of Oileus. After the sack of Troy, she was handed over to King Agamemnon, who developed a real love for her and made her the mother of two children. In vain, she begged her master and lover not to return home. Agamemnon was killed in Argos by his wife, Clytemnestra, and Cassandra and her two children shared the same fate.

CASSIOPEIA. According to the best-known tradition, Cassiopeia was the wife of Cepheus, the king of Ethiopia. One day, she claimed that she and her daughter, Andromeda, were as beautiful as the Nereids. Vexed, the nymphs asked Poseidon to avenge them for this insult. The god sent the country a sea monster which, according to the oracle, would not be appeased unless Andromeda, chained on the shore of the Ocean, were given to him as food. Perseus was able to kill the monster and free Andromeda. After her death, Cassiopeia became a constellation.

CASTALIA. Apollo, smitten, one day pursued this simple yet beautiful young woman of Delphi near his temple. To escape him, she threw herself into a spring, which then bore her name. The spring, which flows at the foot of Mount Parnassus, abounds in fresh, crystal clear water. Her banks were frequented by the Muses who are known as Castalides.

CASTOR. One of the Dioscuri, brother of Pollux, son of Leda and Tyndareos.

caverns. In the eyes of the Greeks, caverns were the most highly regarded of sacred places because of their darkness and the unexplored nooks where divinities hid. There are also many myths that tell of heroes and gods being born in caverns. This is why it was customary to set up small altars in grottoes where sacrifices were offered and oaths were sworn. Indeed, these underground places were believed to be in touch with Chthonian deities from whom the earth draws its fertility. In certain caverns where volcanic activity was seen, due to the presence of mephitic vapors or carbonic gas, the Pythiae dwelled and delivered the oracles of the gods that had been invoked.

CECROPS. The first mythical king of Athens, Cecrops, born of the Earth, was a mixed creature: half man and half serpent. He married Aglauros who bore him a son, Erysichthon, and three daughters, Aglauros, Herse and Pandrosos, who played a tragic role in the legend of Erichthonius. During the reign of Cecrops the dispute took place that pitted Athena against Poseidon for the patronage of Attica. Because of his wisdom, the king was selected as a mediator. Poseidon caused a salted sea to gush forth on the Acropolis. Athena gave rise to an olive tree. The king gave preference to the goddess. Irritated, Poseidon unleashed a tidal wave on Attica. The reign of Cecrops ended happily. He commissioned the first citadel of Athens which was named for him (Cecropia). He taught his subjects the art of writing. He promulgated the first laws on the organization of his territory into twelve tribes. In addition, he established marriage rites. Abolishing human sacrifices, he organized the worship of gods. Some contend that Cecrops hailed from Sais in Egypt and that he had brought to Attica an Egyptian colony, thus importing the first elements of civilization into Greece.

CELAENO. This Pleiad, seduced by Poseidon, mothered Lycus, king of the Mariandynians, who played a certain role in the expedition of the Argonauts.

CELEUS. The first king of Eleusis, spouse of Metaneira, Celeus offered his hospitality to Demeter who was wandering through Greece in search of her daughter Persephone. To thank him for his act of piety and charity, the goddess wanted to grant immortality to Demophon, the king's son. But this well-meaning intention ended tragically with the death of Demophon. To console Celeus, Demeter bestowed on him a certain number of gifts as well as the honor of being her first priest.

Despite their strange form, the Centaurs appear here to be formidable opponents. One of them has just taken hold of the foot of a faun to make him stumble and he prepares to trample on his victim with his hooves. Detail of a Roman relief, Vatican Museum.

CENTAURS. Ixion married a cloud that Zeus had shaped to resemble Hera, and of this union the Centaurs were born. They had the monstrous appearance of a man's bust and a horse's body. They fed on raw flesh and lived like beasts in the forests of Thessaly. Their brutal customs and their immoderate love of wine and women inspired fear in mortals. Only two of them, Pholus and Chiron, distinguished themselves from their peers by exemplary goodness and wisdom. They are portrayed in special legends. As for their congeners, they sometimes play a role in the heroic cycles. They crop up particularly in the legend of Theseus: Pirithous, the king of the Lapiths, his companion in arms, had the unlucky idea of inviting the Centaurs to his wedding. The Centaurs became intoxicated and wanted to rape the young bride, Hippodamia. Mass bedlam ensued, pitting the Centaurs, armed with tree trunks and flaming logs, against the Lapiths. The Lapiths managed to repel the Centaurs, who were forced to retreat to the outskirts of Pindus. There, Heracles pursued them. He involuntarily wounded the generous Centaur Chiron who, to be relieved of his suffering, begged to be permitted to die. He passed to the other world by yielding his immortality to Prometheus. Heracles also strangled the Centaur Nessus who fought with him over one of his wives, Deianira. All these myths, which afford the Centaurs the features of men-horses, undoubtedly arise from the fact that the Thessalians, skilled in the art of equitation, seemed, in the eyes of the Greeks, to identify with their mounts.

CEPHALUS. The son of Deion and Diomede according to some, and of Hermes and Herse according to others. Cephalus married Procris; their happiness seemed perfect when Cephalus came up with the idea of testing his wife's fidelity. He, therefore, disguised himself as a stranger and tried to seduce her with lavish gifts. Procris finally succumbed and Cephalus revealed his identity. In shame, she left for Crete where Artemis gave her a dog and a magical spear. In turn, Procris returned home disguised as a seductive young woman who offered herself to Cephalus in exchange for the two gifts from the goddess. Cephalus accepted and Procris revealed her identity. The husband and wife were then reconciled. However, jealousy plagued the young woman; she imagined that Cephalus, during his hunting outings, joined Eos, the Dawn. One night, she surreptitiously followed her husband; inadvertently, she stirred a branch. Thinking that there was an animal in the bushes, Cephalus hurled his spear and killed the unfortunate creature. The court of the Areopagus at Athens sentenced the murderer to a lifetime of exile. After many adventures, and constantly haunted by the ghost of Procris, he threw himself into the sea.

CEPHEUS. **1.** Aleus and his son Cepheus both took part in the expedition of the Argonauts. At his father's death, Cepheus received the kingdom of Tegea in Arcadia. He instructed his daughter Sterope to watch over his kingdom and she did this with the help of a lock of Medusa's hair, enabling her to repel all possible enemies. Then Cepheus left with Heracles against Lacedaemon where he was to perish along with his sons.

2. Legend tells of another **Cepheus,** the son of Belus, king of the Cephians, who hailed from Ethiopia. He was the husband of Cassiopeia and the father of Andromeda. After his death, he was placed among the stars.

CERBERUS. From the union of the two monsters, Typhon and Echidna, Cerberus was born, and he was assigned to guard the entrance to the Underworld. This dog had three heads, a neck encircled with serpents, and teeth whose bite was as poisonous as that of a viper. This tricephalous monster, who stayed in front of a cave on the banks of the Styx, permitted the shadows of the dead to enter the Underworld but forbade them to leave. Foolhardy mortals who tried to venture into the kingdom of the dead were mercilessly torn to shreds. Sometimes Cerberus was not as merciless as his reputation had made him out to be and certain mortals or heroes managed to tame him. Psyche, sent by Aphrodite to fetch Persephone, gave Cerberus a cake and managed to coax him. The Sibyl of Cumae, Diophobe, also gave him a kind of soporific cake when she brought Aeneas to the Underworld. It is also known that Orpheus was able to charm the inexorable monster with his lyre and his songs. Finally,

The creator of the vase has painted Cerberus with two heads topped by a hissing serpent. He is standing at the entrance to the Underworld, depicted here by the columns of a portico. Heracles, who has prudently laid down his club, approaches the ferocious animal in order to fetter him. To the rear, Athena watches over the hero. Detail of a Greek vase with red figures on a black background, photo Giraudon.

The two Cercopes were tied to a pole by Heracles and hung upside down. Selinus metope, National Archaeological Museum, Palermo, photo Anderson-Giraudon.

with Heracles, Cerberus met with a humiliating defeat. Assigned to take hold of the dog and bring him back to Earth on the simple and difficult condition that he did not resort to weapons, Heracles barehandedly half strangled him and thus brought him to Eurystheus, who, out of fear, had him returned to the realm of the dead.

CERCOPES. These gnomes, both malicious and evil-minded, the children of Theia, lived by pillage and even dared one day to attack Heracles in order to rob him. But the hero had no difficulty catching them and attaching them upside down on a stick. In this position, they realized that the buttocks of Heracles were black. They began to laugh and, in so doing, provoked the hero to laugh as well. Heracles, amused, agreed to release such congenial companions. But, persistent in their evil actions, the Cercopes ended up irritating Zeus, who turned them into monkeys.

CERES. Identified with the Greek goddess Demeter, Ceres is a very ancient Latin divinity. Her name, derived from the verb *crescere*, bespeaks the functions of the goddess. She is the sap gushing from the soil—Ceres is one of the Chthonian deities—that rises and swells young shoots. She ripens wheat and yellows the crops.

CERYX. Aglauros, one of the daughters of Cecrops, was loved by Hermes who, according to legend, begat Ceryx whose name means "herald." Another version contends that Ceryx is the younger son of Eumolpus. But, generally speaking, Ceryx is regarded in Antiquity as the herald of the mysteries of Eleusis, introduced by his father, and as the mythical ancestor of the sacerdotal dynasty of the Ceryces, who played a major role in the celebration of the mysteries.

CETO. The daughter of Pontus and Gaia, Ceto married her own brother, Phorcys, and gave birth to the Gorgons, the Graiae, the dragon that guarded the apples of the Hesperides, and the Hesperides themselves.

CEYX. 1. Through his love for Alcyone, his wife, Ceyx was transformed into a seabird.

2. Having inadvertently killed Eunomus, a child who provided him with water, Heracles decided to leave his wife Deianira and his son Hyllus and exile himself in Trachis, placing himself under the protection of **Ceyx,** the nephew of Amphitryon and king of the city. But the fate of this king was far from happy. Indeed, he lost his son Hippasus who had followed Heracles on an expedition against the city of Oechalia. However, he welcomed, with no malice, the sons of Heracles who were being pursued by Eurystheus; but, fearing for the

peace of his kingdom, he was obliged to send them away.

chaos. Chaos is not a god but a principle, that of the confused beginning of all things, the image of what existed before the gods, before mortals, the source of all things. Chaos begat Erebus and the Night. Then, from its jumbled mass, sprang the Day and Aether with the first burst of light crucial to the blossoming of life.

chariot. A vehicle of war and transportation, the chariot is, in mythology, reserved for the gods and heroes. Both Zeus and Poseidon are mounted on chariots drawn by four high-spirited horses. Hades burst through the Earth on a chariot to abduct Persephone. Helios drove his solar chariot through the skies. The chariot is, therefore, the symbol of strength and sovereignty since it rapidly transports the gods from one end of the universe to the other, and the shattering noise of its wheels, rubbing against metal axles, inspires terror and silence in souls. Moreover, in Homeric combats, it is the essential instrument of victory. But only the great heroes, the kings and leaders possessed chariots. Finally, there are numerous legends in which heroes, such as Pelops, were obliged to win the hand of a king's daughter by participating in chariot races from which they were bound to emerge victorious.

CHARITES. Called *Graces* by the Romans, the three Charites—Aglaia, Euphrosyne and Thalia, formed, according to Hesiod, a triad personifying both charm and beauty. Ancient texts and traditions differ on their family background and origin. They were believed to be the daughters of Zeus and Aphrodite, and the Greeks often associated the worship of the goddess of Beauty with that of the Charites. However, they are also often considered to be the daughters of Zeus and Eurynome, the most beautiful Oceanid. They focus on the Earth the rays of the sun, they warm the hearts of men,

The goddess Ceres holds in one hand the staff of the voyager and the plate for offerings to the divinities of the Underworld. Vatican Museum, photo Anderson-Giraudon.

embellish their lives with much enjoyment, preside over the pleasures of conversation and, more generally, good social relations. Poetry is particularly cherished by them. For this reason, they live on Olympus, joined by friendship with the Muses. Artists amused themselves as they depicted them with seductive features. They appeared as three naked young women of whom one looks in one direction, the other two in the opposite. A group of their statues in Elis gives some idea about their respective attributes: one holds a rose, another a playing die, and the third a myrtle branch.

CHARON.   The immortal son of Erebus and the Night, this poorly dressed old man, with his somber and sinister air, was assigned to transport the souls of the dead over the rivers separating them from the Underworld. Hard and unbending, the ferryman of the Underworld would not allow any living being to enter his barge even for the shortest crossing. Greedy, besides, he demanded an obolus of his passengers. Thus, a small coin was always placed in the mouths of the deceased before they were placed on the funeral pyre. But for the deceased who remained on Earth with no burial, Charon showed no mercy. Brutally repelled, their souls were forced to wander for one hundred years before their fate was decided. According to Homer and Hesiod, souls crossed the muddy and swampy waters of the Underworld themselves, guided, admittedly, by Hermes. But Roman speculation, drawing on the winged demon that leads the dead in the Etruscan religion, fashioned the character of Charon, somewhat uncertain in Greek mythology. Aeneas, for instance, managed to move him to pity by giving him a golden bough, previously offered by the Sibyl of Cumae and dedicated to Proserpina. He was able to cross the first river of the Underworld without hindrance. As for Heracles who descended to the Underworld while still alive, he assailed Charon with a shower of punches and forced him to take him in his barge. The old man was punished for this infraction of the law of the Underworld: he was banished from his task for a year.

CHARYBDIS.   The daughter of Poseidon and Gaia, Charybdis, prompted by a ravenous appetite, stole several head of cattle from Heracles and prepared to devour them. Zeus struck her with thunder and threw her into an abyss in the Strait of Messina with the monster Scylla. An image, rather than a myth or legend, of the furies of the sea, Charybdis swallowed enormous amounts of water three times a day and drew ships into her whirlwinds, spitting them out three times a day with a terrifying roar. Sailors who chose another cape to avoid Charybdis ran immediately into Scylla, who lost no time devouring them.

CHIMAERA.   Like Cerberus and many other monsters, Chimaera is the deformed offspring of the monster Echidna and Typhon. She has

With an air of severity, the incorruptible Charon prepares to transport on his barge a soul, portrayed by a Woman. Drawing from a painting on a Greek vase, photo Didier.

Chimaera has three heads: one of a lion, one of a goat and one of a poisonous serpent at the tip of her tail. Obverse of a Greek coin from Sicyon, Peloponnesus.

the head of a lion or goat and the tail of a dragon. Raised by Amisodarus, king of Caria, she terrorized the surrounding region, vomiting flames and devouring all human creatures who had the misfortune to cross her path. As he feared that the monster would attack his subjects, the king of Lycia asked Bellerophon to deliver him from this scourge. Bellerophon, mounted on Pegasus, pierced Chimaera with leaded arrows, the metal of which melted in the heat of the flames she emitted: thus she was burned to death.

CHIONE. 1. The daughter of Boreas and Oreithyia, Chione married Poseidon and produced Eumolpus. But she threw this son into the sea to escape her father's wrath. The god of the Oceans retrieved his son and entrusted him

to a daughter of Amphitrite.

2. Another **Chione,** the daughter of Daedalion, gave birth to twins: one, Philammon, was the son of Apollo while the other, Autolycus, was the son of Hermes. Proud of having been the lover of the two gods, Chione dared to compare her beauty to that of Artemis. The goddess, revolted by such brazenness, pierced the insolent woman with her arrows.

CHIRON. Among the centaurs, Chiron indeed stood out. As brutal and as uncultivated as his brothers were, he was equally remarkable, but because of his wisdom and knowledge. A product of the love of Cronus and the nymph Philyra, he had the strange form of a man-horse because his father had had to change himself into a horse to beget him. It is said that his mother, out of despair at having

The knowledgeable centaur Chiron is surrounded by a crowd of pupils who have come to listen to him or to present their children to him so that he might educate them. Against his flank, a little faun is playing with one of the children. Roman relief, Palazzo Medici-Riccardi, Florence, photo Alinari-Brogi-Giraudon.

created such a monster, asked the gods to transform her: she was changed into a linden tree. Chiron received the most valuable education from Apollo and Artemis and learned from these divine teachers the arts of medicine and hunting. Soon, patients flocked to consult the centaur, who received them in a grotto, located at the foot of Mount Pelion in Thessaly. Many were the heroes who were granted the privilege of being his disciples: Castor and Pollux, Amphiaraus, Peleus, Achilles, Nestor, Ulysses, Actaeon, Diomedes and the Argonauts, for whom he drew up a maritime chart. Immortal, he was promised an existence overflowing with various benefits. But Heracles, during a battle pitting the Centaurs against the Lapiths, inadvertently wounded Chiron in the thigh with an arrow dipped in the poisonous blood of Hydra and Lerna. Experiencing atrocious pain, Chiron, with the approval of the gods, offered his immortality to Prometheus and breathed his last breath. Zeus placed the blameless centaur among the stars, where he became the constellation Sagittarius.

CHLORIS. This daughter of Amphion and Niobe was, along with her brother Amyclas, spared by Apollo and Artemis when the irritated gods cruelly took revenge on their brothers and sisters to punish Niobe. Chloris was later to marry Neleus, the father of Nestor.

CHRYSEIS. Chryses was the priest of Apollo in Chryse. When this city of Troas was taken by the Greeks, Chryseis, his daughter, was given to Agamemnon. Smitten with this new slave, the king refused to give her back to her father, although he offered him a handsome ransom. Apollo, annoyed at this offense against one of his servants, sent the Greek army a terrible plague. To appease the god, Agamemnon was obliged to return Chryseis but as compensation he took Briseis, the captive of Achilles.

This gave rise to the long dispute between the two heroes.

CHTHONIA. **1.** By his wife Praxithea, Erechtheus had four sons and six daughters, one of whom, Chthonia, married her uncle, Butes, son of Pandion.

2. However, the daughter of Phoroneus is more famous. With her sister, Clymene, she had a temple built in honor of Demeter.

CILIX. The mythical founder of Cilicia, Cilix was one of the sons of Agenor who left for Egypt in search of his sister Europa. Unable to track her down, he decided to stop on the coast of Asia Minor among the Hypacheans. He gradually populated the plain of Cilicia with his offspring. He formed a friendship with Sarpedon and placed him on the throne of Lycia after having fought side by side with him to conquer the Mylians.

CIMMERIANS. According to Homer, this mythical people lived on the bank of the unknown Ocean which surrounds the known limits of the Earth, in those fog-covered regions where the sun never rises and night and slumber reign eternally. Later, however, attempts were made to determine the geographical boundaries of the countries in which the Cimmerians chose to live. Certain authors located them at the north of the Black Sea where, it is said, one of the entrances to the Underworld was found. Latin writers, on the other hand, considered that these people inhabited the cantons around Lake Avernus. No one knew for sure whether they lived in the north, south, east or west, and the aura of mystery surrounding them was sufficient proof of the somber fear they inspired.

CINYRAS. The king of the island of Cyprus and the high priest of Aphrodite, Cinyras gave the priesthood of the goddess special importance. The son of Apollo, according to one version, he was one of the great civilizing influences in his kingdom, introducing agriculture, music, art and domestic arts. Disdaining war, he refused to participate in the Trojan expedition, but he gave the Greeks a single boat and Agamemnon some armor. Because he had involuntary incestuous relations with his daughter Smyrna, or Myrrha, mother of Adonis, he was forced into exile. According to another legend, Adonis was born of the union of Cinyras and the daughter of a king of Cyprus.

CIRCE. One of the rare enchantresses portrayed in Greek mythology, and doubtless the most famous of all, Circe was the daughter of Helios and the Oceanid Perseis. Gifted with extraordinary powers, capable, among other things, of coaxing the stars from the skies, she excelled in the preparation of love potions, poisons and various drinks designed to change human beings into animals. She practiced her evil art on her husband, the king of Sarmates, and poisoned him. Hateful to his subjects, she was forced to flee. Mounted in the chariot of the Sun, her father, she sought refuge in Etruria. Residing in an enchanted palace there, she continued to perfect her magical techniques and changed the young and beautiful Scylla into a monster because the god Glaucus was in love with her. Picus, a king who shunned her advances, was changed into a woodpecker. However, she did not succeed in making Ulysses share the fate of some of his companions, whom she transformed into swine. The hero, on the advice of Hermes, had neutralized the brew Circe offered him by adding bits of an herb called "moly." Thereby saved from the charms of the enchantress, he forced her to restore his fellow sailors to their original human form. However, Circe, who had none of the hideous features generally attributed to sorceresses, seduced the hero. She kept him with her for over a year and had several children by him, including Telegonus, the mythical found-

Her arms raised in a magical incantation, Circe has changed one of Ulysses' comrades into a swine. Furious, the hero threatens Circe with his sword. Detail of a Greek amphora, Museum of Parma, photo Pisseri.

er of Tusculum; Latinus, the eponymous king of the Latins; and a daughter, Cassiphone. When Ulysses decided to resume his journey, she advised him to go to the Underworld to consult the shadow of the seer Tiresias, who would tell him the easiest and safest route to Ithaca, his native land. Because of her evil-mindedness, regardless of the many miracles she worked, the gods refused the gift of immortality to Circe. She perished at the hand of Telemachus, the son of Ulysses and Penelope.

CITHAERON. This chain of wooded mountains that separates Boeotia from Megara and Attica is the subject of a legend. Cithaeron was a king of Plataea who lent his name to the neighboring mountain. But some also claim that Cithaeron was a handsome young man

Her face contemplative, the goddess Clio holds in one hand a scroll where she is recording the events of epic history while her other hand counts the beat of the lines of verse. Vatican Museum, photo Anderson-Giraudon.

who shunned the love of Tisiphone, one of the the three Erinyes. One of the hairs of Tisiphone turned into a serpent that stung him and mortally poisoned him at the foot of the mountain which henceforth bore his name. It was also on Mount Cithaeron that, according to legend, Pentheus and Actaeon died. During the classical era, Mount Cithaeron was consecrated to Dionysus and the Muses.

CLEOBIS. The brother of Biton, son of Cydippe, the priestess of Hera in Argos, had his piety rewarded with eternal slumber.

CLIO. The name of this Muse is derived from a Greek word meaning "to celebrate," for she sings the praises of warriors and tells of a peo-

ple's renown. Because of this, she was quickly attributed the role of patron of history. She holds in her right hand either a trumpet to proclaim major occurrences or a cithara to sing of the exploits of a hero, or else a water clock, the symbol of the chronological order of events.

CLYMENE. Several Clymenes appear in Greek mythology: one is the daughter of Tethys and the legitimate wife of the Titan Iapetus; her posterity was glorious because she gave birth to Prometheus, Menoetius, Atlas and Epimetheus. She was also supposed to have married Helios and mothered Phaethon and the Heliades.

Another **Clymene** belonged to the Minyades. She was the daughter of Minyas, king of Orchomenus.

CLYTEMNESTRA. One of the most famous heroines of Greek tragedy, Clytemnestra, of royal blood, was the daughter of Tyndareos and Leda and, by her mother, the sister of the Dioscuri and Helen. She first married Tantalus, then Agamemnon, the very murderer of her husband. Agamemnon left shortly afterwards for Troy. In Aulis, he was obliged, on the advice of Calchas, to sacrifice his daughter Iphigenia to the goddess Artemis, who was preventing the sailing of the Greek fleet for Troas. Agamemnon hid his sinister plan from Clytemnestra. But she soon learned the news in Argos; despairing over her daughter's tragic demise (in fact, Iphigenia had escaped the sacrificer's knife) and, according to another version, deceived by her husband who was smitten with Chryseis, she took Aegisthus as her lover and with him plotted the death of Agamemnon upon his return to his fatherland. Electra and Orestes decided to avenge their father's death and killed Clytemnestra, their mother, seven years after her crime.

CLYTIA. This nymph was the daughter of Oceanus. The Sun fell in love with her, but the god soon abandoned her for Leucothea. Desperate and jealous, she took revenge by revealing to her rival's father the many loves of his daughter. Apollo was to change the informer into a heliotrope.

CNOSSUS. This ancient Cretan city was the capital of King Minos. It was made famous by its labyrinth, where the Minotaur was imprisoned. With the help of Ariadne's thread, Theseus was able to slay the Minotaur.

COCALUS. The founding king of Camicus in Sicily, Cocalus received Daedalus who had fled from Crete. In hot pursuit of him, Minos arrived shortly afterwards in Camicus. He promised a handsome reward to whoever could pass a thread through the spirals of a snail's shell. Cocalus took up the challenge and secretly asked for the advice of Daedalus who immediately found the solution. He fastened a thread to the leg of an ant who entered the shell and followed its spiral all the way to the other end: thus, Cocalus won. But Minos, knowing that Daedalus alone was capable of such ingenuity, demanded that Cocalus return the prisoner to him. Rather than hand over their guest, Cocalus and his daughters plotted the destruction of Minos and ended up by scalding him to death.

COCYTUS. The waters of this river, a tributary of the Acheron in Epirus, also communicated with the Underworld. The waters swelled as they received the tears of the wretched. On the banks of the Cocytus roamed the souls of the dead that were deprived of burials and waited to know the decision of the judges regarding what fate held in store for them.

colonies. When the Greeks, for various reasons, wished to leave their country, they went to Dodona or to Delphi to consult the oracles of the gods who would tell them where they had permission to settle. Then they chose a leader, the founder of the colony who, before leaving his native land, lit a torch in the sacred hearth of his city and carried it with him to the new city. Finally, each colonist took with him the statues of his national or family gods. Thus the Greeks, despite their dispersion throughout the Mediterranean basin, never lost the sense of belonging to a mother city and never forgot the religion and gods of their first fatherland which remained a certain guarantee of their solidarity and cohesiveness.

commerce. The Greeks had placed commerce, one of the essential activities of their economy, under the protection of a certain number of gods, but especially that of Hermes. This god of Voyagers extended his kindly powers over paths and roads where merchandise was transported. Confident in his protection, merchants could travel unharmed and without fear from one city or region to another, thereby ensuring supplies and exchanges throughout Greece. The Romans imitated the Greeks and gave their god Mercury identical powers, bestowing on him, in addition, surnames such as *Negotiator* and *Nundinator*. When barter disappeared and was replaced by money, the Romans placed the minting of coins in the temple and under the authority of the goddess Moneta.

COMUS. This god appeared only in the later times of Greek antiquity when customs were degenerating. He presided at public feasts and libations. Usually preceded by Silenus or Momos, god of revelry, he was followed by a group of merry drinkers.

CONCORDIA. One of the numerous allegorical divinities of the Roman religion, Concordia personifies harmony among families, citizens and spouses; moreover, she is often confused with the goddess of Peace, her sister, with whose symbols she is often portrayed, namely the pomegranate, the symbol of a fertile marriage, and the olive branch, the symbol of harmony in peace.

Triptolemus and Core. Persephone does not appear here with the features of the dreaded queen of the Underworld. She appears to be a radiant young woman, the beloved child of Demeter, who contributes heads of wheat to the riches of the earth. Greek krater, Louvre, photo Giraudon.

CONSUS. This god with ancient and mysterious origins was regarded as one of the divinities of the Underworld, because his altar was buried in the middle of the Great Amphitheater in Rome. He was responsible, above all, for protecting against cold, bad weather and parasites all seeds sown or buried in the ground during the intemperate season. During his festival, the Consualia, in which draft animals were exempt from work, the rape of the Sabine women occurred.

CORE. In Greek, this name means "young woman." It was given to the daughter of Demeter before her abduction and disappearance to the Underworld where she became the wife of Hades and took the name *Persephone*.

CORINTH. One of the principal centers of worship for Aphrodite, Corinth, referred to as "Ephyre" by Homer, owes its fame and its importance to its position on an isthmus. Like all Greek cities, it possessed a king and an eponymous hero, Corinthus, the son of Marathon. Assassinated by his subjects, he was succeeded by Sisyphus.

CORONIDES. This name refers to the two daughters of Orion, Metioche and Menippe, who were sacrificed to stop a plague, but the gods of the Underworld transformed them into two comets or stars.

CORONIS. The daughter of Phlegyas, king of the Lapiths, Coronis attracted the fancy of Apollo one day while she was bathing in a lake in Thessaly. But in the god's absence, the young woman developed a violent passion for Ischys, the son of Elatus, king of Arcadia, and she married him. Wishing to avenge her brother, Artemis pierced the unfaithful girl with her arrows. In despair, Apollo conducted funeral rites for his unfortunate lover and snatched the living Asclepius, whom he had begotten, from her womb.

Legend tells of another **Coronis** who, pursued by the amorous Poseidon, was changed into a crow by the compassionate Athena.

CORYBANTES. These Cretan tutelary divinities, who were to lend their name to the priestesses of Cybele, sang, it is said, around the cradle of Zeus to cover the wailing of the newborn and prevent Cronus, his father, from devouring him.

CRANAUS. This king succeeded Cecrops on the throne of Athens but was expelled by Amphictyon, one of his sons-in-law, who assumed power in his stead. Cranaus had married Pedias who gave birth to three daughters—Cranae, Cranaichme, and Atthis who gave her name to Attica.

creation. The oldest theory on the formation of the universe and the birth of the gods is provided by Hesiod in his *Theogony.* Three elements reigned at the beginning. Chaos represented the primordial state of the world, its eternal fate and the space that had always existed. Gaia, for her part, symbolized the earth, unpredictable, full of floods and upheavals. In order to have creation and birth, life and form, it was necessary for these two primordial elements to unite. Then appeared Eros, not the god of love as viewed in the classic period, but the force that permitted beings and things to draw near, touch and intermingle. Thus could be born, in the midst of darkness, the first generation of gods and vegetation. The appearance of life in the world was powerfully stimulated by Oceanus and his wife Tethys. Together they were the symbol of the complex, immense and fertile original waters that produced rivers, springs and seas and continually give life to nature.

According to a current interpretation, man came to people the world through Prometheus, who created the first man from clay. Another legend says that after the flood had destroyed all forms of life on earth, when the waters receded, Pyrrha and her husband Deucalion, son of Prometheus, miraculously escaped death. They threw rocks behind themselves and the rocks were transformed into men and women.

CREON. **1.** The king of Corinth, Creon welcomed to his court Jason and Medea who were being pursued by Iolcus. He lived for quite some time in peace with his guests until Jason fell in love with Glauce (or Creusa), the daughter of Creon, and, betraying Medea, married her. In revenge, Medea gave her rival a garment that had received a magical preparation and burst into flames on the body of the unfortunate victim. Creon died as he tried to save her.

2. Also known by this name is **Creon,** the son of Menoeceus and brother of Jocasta. He governed Thebes after the death of his brother-in-law Laius, then entrusted the kingdom to Oedipus who had delivered the country from the Sphinx; he even gave him Jocasta's hand in marriage. However, when he later learned that this union was incestuous, Creon chased the unfortunate Oedipus from Thebes, keeping his two sons Eteocles and Polynices, who wasted no time fighting openly for the throne. Having sided wholeheartedly with Eteocles, Creon was forced to sacrifice his son Menoeceus to Ares to obtain victory for his protégé. At the death of the two brothers and enemies, Creon again took control of Thebes and exhibited merciless cruelty, burying Antigone alive because she had dared to defy his order not to bury Polynices. Then, after trying to abduct Oedipus, he was killed, supposedly by Theseus.

CRESPHONTES. With his brothers Temenus and Aristodemus, of the race of the Heraclidae, and his nephews Procles and Eurysthenes, Cresphontes regained the Peloponnesus and took the territory of Messenia for himself. Married to Merope, the daughter of Cypselus, king of Arcadia, he was assassinated along with two of his sons during an outbreak provoked by the Messenians who opposed his democratic reforms. His third son Aepytus, who had escaped death, avenged his father several years later with the help of Merope, by killing Polyphontes, the usurper of his father's kingdom.

CRETE. One of the largest Mediterranean islands, Crete was famous in Antiquity for its production of wheat. It is, therefore, understandable that the worship of Demeter, the goddess of the Harvest, assumed particular importance on this island. According to Homer, Crete had some one hundred cities, all of which were more or less legendary. Moreover, its importance is exhibited in the many myths originating there. Zeus was born there, married Hera, and joined with Europa. All the legends in which King Minos appears take place in Crete, such as the legend of Pasiphaë, the Minotaur, Daedalus, the Labyrinth and Theseus. The religious center of Greek civilization, Crete was, in a sense, to Greece what Etruria was to Rome.

CRETHEUS. The founder of the kingdom of Iolcus, Cretheus married Tyro, his niece, and had three children, Aeson, the father of Jason, Pheres and Amythaon. In addition, he adopted Pelias and Neleus whom his wife had had by Poseidon. All these children played a part in the Thessalian legends.

CREUSA. 1. One of the seven daughters of Erechtheus and Praxithea, Creusa married Xuthus by whom she had Achaeus and Diomedes. However, still a young woman, she was seduced by Apollo in a cave not far from the Acropolis where she abandoned the child she had by him, a son named Ion. Hermes rescued him and raised him in the temple of Apollo in Delphi.

2. Another **Creusa** is the daughter of Priam and Hecuba; she married Aeneas and bore him a son, Ascanius. During the fall of Troy, in the confusion and general mayhem, she was separated from her husband and carried away by Aphrodite. However, she appeared to Aeneas, who was searching all over the city for her, and told him of the long journey that lay ahead of him in his search for a new territory, Italy.

3. A third **Creusa**, the daughter of Creon, king of Corinth, perished, a victim of the vengeance of Medea. She also bears the name of Glauce.

CROCUS. This beautiful mortal developed for the nymph Smilax a love that she refused to share. The gods changed him into a saffron crocus and her into bindweed.

CRONUS. This Titan, the youngest son of Uranus and Gaia, governed the Universe before the reign of Zeus and the gods of Olympus. In order to obtain almighty power, he did not hesitate to mutilate his father and take his sister Rhea as his consort. Rhea bore him many children who were destined to become the famous gods of Greece, such as Hestia, Demeter, Hera, Hades, Poseidon and Zeus himself. However, to retain the throne, he was forced to live in harmony with the other Titans, who asked him to do away with his progeny. Cronus therefore devoured his children, except Zeus for whom his mother substituted a stone wrapped in swaddling clothes, which Cronus swallowed without even noticing the swindle. But once he reached adulthood, Zeus rebelled against his father and forced him to restore his brothers and sisters. With their help, he fought the Titans who were loyal to Cronus and seized the divine power forever. Later, the Romans identified Cronus with Saturn. The legend, under the influence of orphism, was transformed to such an extent that the merciless Titan became a good and just king of the golden age.

crown. In many legends found in Greek and Roman religions, crowns were the sign of consecration to the gods. They encircled the foreheads of statues of the gods and adorned the heads of both sacrificers and victims. To each divinity corresponded a crown braided with plants, fruits or flowers. The oak supplied Zeus with a crown; the laurel supplied Apollo; the myrtle, Aphrodite; the vine, Dionysus. The forehead of the Sun was haloed with a crown of solar rays. Certain gods or goddesses, such as Cybele, who protected cities, were depicted with their foreheads adorned with a mural crown, made up of several towers.

CTIMENE. The sister of Ulysses, Ctimene was the wife of Eurylochus, a companion in adversity of the hero during his return to

Ithaca. Ctimene was never to see her husband again because, having eaten the sacred cows of Helios, he was struck by a thunderbolt.

CUMAE. One of the most ancient colonies of Greece, this city of Campania was especially famous in Antiquity because of the oracles that were delivered by the Sibyl, directly inspired by Apollo. Not far from this city there was a grotto which was believed to communicate with the Underworld. Guided by the Sibyl, Aeneas took this route in his descent to the kingdom of Shadows.

CUPID. Even more than the Greek Eros, with whom he was gradually confused, Cupid, Venus's assistant, is the personification of the keenest amorous desire.

CURETES. Often confused with the other tutelary divinities (the Corybantes, the Dactyli), the Curetes played an important role in the circumstances surrounding the infancy of Zeus: they made a great deal of noise around Amalthea while she suckled the divine infant in order to prevent Cronus' discovering where his son was hidden. The exact number of Curetes is unknown. However, they have given rise to myriad legends. The best-known recounts that, on the order of Hera, they stole from Io the young Epaphus, the child of her love affair with Zeus. Vexed by this abduction, the god struck them down.

CYBELE. This Phrygian divinity is doubtless one of the greatest goddesses of the ancient Near East. Imported to Greece and Rome, she personifies, under various names—Great Mother, Mother of the gods, Great Goddess—the vegetative and wild strength of nature. In addition, she ranks among the divinities of Fertility and shares with Jupiter, in the Roman religion, sovereign power over the reproduction of plants, animals, gods and men. Ensconced in a chariot drawn by lions, the

Wearing a sort of mural crown, Cybele sits majestically on the throne guarded by two lions, each placing a paw on the throne as a sign of possession. The chariot of the goddess is generally drawn by lions; they are characteristic of her Eastern origin. National Archaeological Museum, Naples, photo Alinari-Giraudon.

symbol of strength, she holds the key which opens the door to the Earth where all riches are locked; her head, at least in the Roman iconography, supports small towers that represent the cities she protects. There is no legend connected with her except the legend that relates her love affair with Attis; this is the origin or transposition of the orgiastic and Orphic mysteries of resurrection.

CYCLOPES. These fabulous creatures, which had a single eye in the center of their foreheads, appear in many Greek and Latin legends. They can be grouped into four classes: the Uranian Cyclopes, the blacksmith Cyclopes, the builder Cyclopes and the shepherd Cyclopes.

The Uranian Cyclopes were born of the monstrous union of Gaia (Earth) and Uranus (Sky). As there were three brothers, Uranus

The Acropolis of Tiryns, Argolis, is built of enormous stones, piled high without cement, one on top of the other. The Ancients credited the Cyclopes with this gigantic task. Photo H. Roger-Viollet.

feared seeing them rebel against him and seize power, so he had them thrown into Tartarus. Later, with the help of their brothers the Titans, and Cronus in particular, and of their indignant mother, they rebelled and mutilated their father. But Cronus also saw them as a threat to his supremacy and had them thrown once again into the Underworld. Zeus freed them from their imprisonment. As a sign of their gratitude, they fashioned thunder and lightning for Zeus and these enabled him to conquer Cronus and take control of the celestial throne. The three Cyclopes, to commemorate their role in this revolution, assumed, respectively, the names of Arges ("the bright one"), Steropes ("lightning"), and Brontes ("thunder"). To Hades they gave a helmet; to Poseidon they gave the trident, thanks to which he raises or calms the seas. Afterwards, the three Cyclopes were put to death by Apollo: the god would not forgive them for having given Zeus the lightning with which he struck and killed Asclepius, his son.

These three helpers of Zeus were assisted by the blacksmiths of Hephaestus who lived in the bellies of volcanoes, where they worked bronze to fashion the armors of the gods and heroes. Pyracmon ("the anvil") and Acamas ("the untiring") were among the most famous of these Cyclopes. Even later yet, the name of "Cyclopian walls" was given to the walls made of enormous blocks of stone, the remains of which may still be seen in Mycenae and Tiryns. Certain of the builder Cyclopes were supposed to have constructed them.

But the most famous Cyclopes of all were those described by Homer. Brutal giants, with neither faith nor laws, they raised herds of sheep, and harvested what the earth yielded spontaneously, using no agricultural techniques. They were not even afraid to devour an occasional human being who ventured into their territory and into their caves. In the eyes of the Greeks, they represent the type of savage, uncultivated race, devoid of any idea whatsoever of civilization. During their travels, Ulysses and his comrades came up against Polyphemus, the most dreaded Cyclops of all.

CYCNUS. 1. The most ancient of the many Cycnuses found in mythology appears during the Trojan War. He was considered to be invulnerable because he had been begotten by Poseidon. Achilles, however, managed to put him to death. His father changed him into a swan.

2. Another **Cycnus,** king of the Ligurians, shed so many tears over the death of his friend Phaethon, who had been struck down by Zeus, that Apollo, moved, changed him into a swan. The swan's plaintive cry is reminiscent of the wailing of the unconsolable hero.

3. The most famous **Cycnus** is the son of Apollo. He was in the habit of subjecting his friends to various tests to ensure their loyalty. Many became discouraged, rejecting the friendship of such a strange and demanding person. Only Phylius, out of love for Cycnus, succeeded, with the help of Heracles, to slay several monsters and tame a raging bull. But soon weary, he went away from his friend. Cycnus was in such a state of despair over this desertion that he threw himself into a lake along with his mother. Apollo changed them both into swans.

4. The son of Ares and Pelopia, another **Cycnus** attacked travelers who came to Delphi and stole the offerings that they had brought for Apollo. He was killed by Heracles in single combat.

CYRENE. Granddaughter of the river-god Peneus and the naiad Creusa, this nymph-huntress would run through the forests of Pindus and kill all the ferocious beasts to protect the herd of her father Hypseus, king of the Lapiths. One day, Apollo was overwhelmed by the sight of Cyrene grappling with a lion, which she managed to vanquish; he carried her away on his chariot and took her to Libya where she gave birth to a son, Aristaeus. Other traditions add that the king of Libya, Eurypylus, offered her the kingdom of Cyrene for having rid the country of a lion that was wreaking terror everywhere. Later, Virgil transformed her into a nymph who lived in the deep waters of the river Peneus.

CYTHEREA. This island, located near the coast of Laconia, was colonized by the Phoenicians who instituted the worship of Aphrodite there. The Greeks considered it to be one of the probable birthsites of the goddess, born of the foam of the waves. The epithet "Cytherean" is often given to her.

D

DACTYLI. Like the Corybantes and the Curetes, these tutelary divinities first resided on Mount Ida where their mother Rhea gave birth to them. According to legend, the Dactyli were supposed to have taken this name, which means "fingers," because their mother, in the pains of childbirth, clenched her fingers on the ground. According to another tradition, they were born of the dust that the nurses of Zeus threw behind them to erase any trace of their footsteps, thus protecting Zeus from the gluttonous fury of his father Cronus.

DAEDALUS. The origins of Daedalus are somewhat uncertain. However, almost all the versions of his legend agree that he was undoubtedly a member of Athenian royalty.

A smithy, an inventor with an inexhaustibly fertile mind, an architect and sculptor, he stimulated, according to the Athenians, the advancement of Attic art. At the beginning of his career, he was assisted by an apprentice, his nephew Talos (Perdix). One day Talos found the jaw of a dead serpent. He chiseled a facsimile in iron and thus produced the first saw. Daedalus was jealous of this pupil who did not hesitate to give him lessons, and killed him by throwing him from atop the Acropolis. The Areopagus convened to judge him. He was sentenced to exile. Daedalus took refuge in Crete where he charmed King Minos with his competence, talent and ingenuity. He was assigned the task of laying out a plan for the Labyrinth where the Minotaur was imprisoned. But for having betrayed his master by favoring the love of Ariadne and Theseus, he himself was locked up there. However, he did not get discouraged. He fashioned a pair of wings and flew away with his son, arriving alone in Cumae, safe and sound. He dedicated to Apollo the flying machine that had saved him. Then, repairing to Sicily, he was welcomed most warmly by King Cocalus, who made him his chief architect.

DANAË. Threatened by an oracle to give birth to a son who would kill his grandfather, Danaë was imprisoned by her father Acrisius, king of Argos, in a bronze tower. Zeus, who secretly loved her, entered the cell by changing himself into a golden shower and seduced the young girl. Of this enchanted union the hero Perseus was born. Incensed, Acrisius exposed his daughter and the child in a chest which he flung into the sea. Both ran aground on the island of Seriphos where Polydectes reigned; this tyrant tried to obtain the favors of the woman he had retrieved, but Perseus delivered his mother and returned to live in Argos.

DANAIDS. The fifty daughters of King Danaus followed their father when he settled in Argos, having left Egypt for fear of the fifty sons of King Aegyptus, his brother. Later, the fifty young men came to their uncle and asked him for his fifty daughters in marriage. They agreed and the marriages were celebrated. But that very evening, on the advice of their father, they took daggers and killed their husbands. Only Hypermnestra spared Lynceus. Shortly afterwards, the Danaids married the young Argives who had competed in games to win their favor. Their happiness was short-lived, however, because Lynceus killed them all. Having

Imprisoned with his son Icarus in the Labyrinth of King Minos in Crete, Daedalus fashions the wings that will permit him to flee from his prison. Icarus has already fastened his to his back and he is admiring his father's extraordinary work. Villa Albani, photo Alinari-Giraudon.

descended into the Underworld, they were finally punished for their crimes and condemned to an endless task of filling a barrel, the bottom of which had a hole in it. The Ancients claimed that this punishment was but a symbol. The Danaids were indeed supposed to have brought from Egypt to Greece the art of digging wells and irrigating the earth; until the end of time, they draw fertilizing water.

DANAUS. The son of Belus and Anchinoë, the twin brother of Aegyptus, Danaus received Libya as his lot. But, fearing the ambition of his brothers and nephews, he fled with his fifty daughters, crossed the Mediterranean and took refuge in the Peloponnesus, in Argos, where Gelanor reigned. He told the king of his intention to dethrone him. Gelanor protested but a miracle took place; a wolf suddenly appeared, attacked a herd and devoured a bull. Impressed, the Argives compared Danaus to the wolf and Gelanor to the bull, and chose the stranger as king. To thank the gods, the new sovereign erected a temple to *Apollo-Lycian* ("Apollo the Wolf"). Danaus was later killed by Lynceus, the husband of one of his daughters, Hypermnestra, and the murderer succeeded him on the throne.

DAPHNE. The daughter of the Thessalian river-god Peneus, and the nymph-priestess of Gaia, Daphne ("laurel") was pursued by Apollo who saw her changed into a laurel just as he was about to catch her. With the leaves of this tree, which afterwards was consecrated to him, Apollo fashioned a crown. Another legend is attached to this young woman: Daphne had fallen in love with a young man, Leucippus, who disguised himself as a woman to be near her. Apollo, jealous, gave Daphne and her companions the idea of undressing and bathing. The unfortunate young man was obliged to do likewise; the nymphs, discovering the hoax, were preparing to kill him when the gods snatched him away. Daphne, in her confusion, was about to be grasped by Apollo but she was able, at the last minute, to change herself into a laurel which henceforth was the god's favorite tree.

DAPHNIS. Promoted, after his death, to the ranks of the rustic demigods of Sicily, Daphnis was the son of Hermes and a nymph who abandoned the child in a laurel grove. Rescued by the nymphs, raised by a group of pastoral divinities, living as a shepherd, Daphnis invented bucolic poetry. He was so beautiful that Apollo was smitten with him and taught him to play the flute while Artemis taught him the tricks of hunting. The nymph Nomia, a shepherdess in his region, developed such a passion for Daphnis that she threatened him with blindness if he succumbed to other women. But Chimaeria, her rival, one day plied the trusting shepherd with wine: he ended up yielding to her desires. Immediately stricken blind, he roamed the countryside playing melancholic tunes on his flute until one day he went astray and fell into an abyss. Hermes changed him into a rock or, according to another tradition, carried him away to the heavens.

DARDANUS. The legendary ancestor of the Trojans, Dardanus, the son of Zeus and Electra, hailed from Samothrace from which he emigrated to the coasts of Asia Minor at the death of his brother Iasion. He was welcomed there by Teucer who gave him his daughter, Batia, and some land. He founded several cities, among which were Dardania and perhaps Troy, and left behind many children including Ilus, Erichthonius, Zacynthus and a daughter, Idaea. According to Italic traditions, Dardanus was the son of Corythus, Etruscan prince of Cortona. He was believed to have emigrated to Phrygia, symbolically uniting Italy and Troas, as the Roman legends later did.

death. In the religion of the Greeks and Romans, death is rarely personified. Certainly,

legend spoke of Persephone and Hades, who ruled the realm of the dead; but, despite their ferocious and implacable natures, neither is really identified with death. Even the god Thanatos is not a personification of death but he who grants death. Of death itself, there are no images, no allegorical representations. The worship of death among the Greeks and Romans, in the form of offerings, is a necessary homage rendered to the souls that have crossed the limits of the known and have entered into direct communication with the gods; however, this worship is not the expression of fearful veneration of a divinity who went by the name of Death.

DEIANIRA. When he descended to the Underworld, Heracles met the shadow of Meleager who advised him to marry his sister Deianira, the daughter of Oeneus and Althaea, or of Dionysus, according to another version of the legend. Having returned to Earth, Heracles was forced to conquer, during a desperate struggle, the River Acheloüs, one of the other suitors, to win the hand of Deianira. After their wedding, he left with her on an expedition against the Calydonians. On his return, his wife was abducted by the Centaur Nessus, who then tried to rape her. She called Heracles to help her; mortally wounded, the centaur bestowed upon the hero's wife a poisoned tunic, assuring her that it would bring happiness and marital fidelity forever. When Heracles fell in love with Iole, Deianira sent him the tunic to bring him back to her: once he put it on, his entire body was burned and he preferred to kill himself. In despair, Deianira killed herself, leaving behind a son, Hyllus, who became the leader of the Heraclidae.

DEIDAMEIA. This daughter of Lycomedes, king of the Dolopians, lived on the island of Scyros. When Achilles took refuge in the kingdom disguised as a woman, he seduced Deidameia by surprise. According to certain legends,

In this dry and uncultivated valley of Orissa, Apollo accomplished his first feats and, in particular, killed the serpent Python. Delphi thus became one of the most sacred places in Greece. In the foreground, the temple of Apollo and part of the amphitheater. Photo Alison Frantz.

she became the mother of Pyrrhus, better known in the Trojan War as *Neoptolemus.*

DEIPHOBUS. One of the sons of Priam and Hecuba, Deiphobus in the Trojan War was the instrument of divine fatality. He recognized his brother Paris, who had at one time been abandoned by his father, and who, under the name of "Alexander," proved to be a formidable opponent for him as he triumphed over him during the stadium games. It was also by assuming the form of Deiphobus that Athena urged Hector to fight with Achilles. At the death of Paris, despite the protests of his brother Helenus, Deiphobus married Helen, who embodied the misfortune of a Troy delivered to the order and actions of the gods. He died, killed and mutilated by Menelaus during the sack of the city. Aeneas was later to conduct funeral rites for his remains and to erect a tomb for him on Cape Rhoeteum, not far from the Hellespont.

DELOS. This island rose up from the sea at the thrust of Poseidon's trident. It welcomed Leto, who gave birth on its soil to Apollo and Artemis. To thank the island for having agreed to shelter the divine infants, Zeus set it at the center of the Cycladic archipelago. It later became the center of worship for Apollo. It was the site, among other things, of the games, the *Delia,* introduced, it is said, by Theseus. Finally, every four years, an Athenian delegation journeyed to the island to worship the god who had been born there.

DELPHI. A small city in Phocis, known as Pytho in Homer's time, Delphi, located at the foot of Mount Parnassus, rapidly acquired considerable importance in classical Greece and was considered to be the center of the earthly globe, the navel of the world, the *omphalos.* The temple of Apollo, for which the city was famous, was a place where kings and wealthy citizens hid their treasures and where the Pythia, seated on a tripod above a hole exuding

vapors, delivered oracles. It was in honor of Apollo that the Pythian games were held in Delphi because the god, not far from there, had killed the serpent Python.

deluge. The concept of deluge is common to all religions, both Eastern and Western. It is found in the Bible, during the time of Gilgamesh, and also in Greek and Roman mythology. It is highly probable that this idea of a flooding of the earth with waters originated after a catastrophic inundation by the Tigris and Euphrates as they swelled from their beds. A consequence of divine wrath, the deluge was sent by Zeus to punish men during the Bronze Age. The god allowed only Pyrrha, the daughter of Epimetheus and Pandora, and Deucalion to escape this disaster. Indeed, they found refuge in a chest which ran aground on Mount Parnassus when the waters subsided. From the deluge and from the void it left in its wake, a new race was created by Deucalion and Pyrrha from the stones they threw behind them.

DEMETER. The daughter of Cronus and Rhea, Demeter is, above all, the goddess of Corn, whose germination she stimulates, and the Harvest, whose ripening she guarantees. Moreover, all the ancient Greek regions whose economy depended for a large part on the cultivation of grain multiplied the many legends involving Demeter. In addition to her affair with Iasion, to whom she bore Ploutos, the god of wealth, and with Poseidon, who, having changed into a horse while she had turned herself into a mare to escape him, begat the steed Araeion, the best-known story about Demeter is the famous legend tracing the kidnapping of her daughter Core-Persephone (Proserpina for the Romans) by Hades. Persephone was playing with her companions in Attica, on the Eleusis plain, and was gathering flowers. Then she spotted a beautiful narcissus and, just as she was about to break its stem, the ground opened up and Hades appeared; he abducted the young girl, who let out a heartrending cry. Demeter heard this cry of terror and immediately left Olympus. For nine days and nine nights she roamed the Earth, not eating, not bathing, never resting, not even for a moment, as she searched for her daughter and the villain who had kidnapped her. On the tenth day, Helios, overcome with pity, revealed the name of the perpetrator. Then, in anger, the goddess refused to return to the land of the gods until her daughter was returned to her. She took refuge in Eleusis with King Celeus, the husband of Metaneira, who welcomed her with all respect. To thank her host, the goddess wanted to grant Demophon, the son of the king, immortality. But her magic threw Metaneira into a panic and Demeter, startled, dropped the infant into the fire. To console the parents, Demeter taught Triptolemus, their other son, the art of working the fields, sowing and harvesting grain. However, ever since the departure of Demeter, the earth had become sterile: famine and epidemics threatened mortals. Zeus, disturbed by this state of affairs, went to Hades and requested that he return Core-Persephone to Demeter. But the god of the Underworld refused because she had bitten into a pomegranate during her stay among the dead, which, magically, prohibited any return among the living. Finally, a compromise was reached. Persephone would live with her mother six months of the year and the other six months she would spend in the company of her husband Hades. The first period of Persephone's life corresponds to the springtime and the young shoots which, like the goddess, leave the earth under the watchful eye of Demeter; the second period, meanwhile, corresponds to the sowing period in autumn, like the grains of wheat nestling into the earth as Persephone returns to the realm of the dead. The mysteries of Eleusis celebrated by Demeter's worshipers also saw in this legend a perpetual symbol of death and resurrection.

The goddess Demeter seems to rise up from the Earth of which she is the fertilizing divinity. She holds a poppy, the symbol of sleep for the living and the dead, and wheat, which she protects. Two serpents, chthonian animals *par excellence*, encircle her wrists. Terra-cotta, Museo delle Terme, Rome, photo Alinari-Giraudon.

Over the centuries in Antiquity, the powers of Demeter were multiplied. The goddess was venerated as one of the main divinities of Wealth and Fertility by those initiated into the mysteries and by farmers who, at harvesttime, celebrated festivals like the Thesmophoria and the Eleusinia. Identified with Ceres by the Romans, Demeter is the symbol of ancient civilization whose perpetual economic and social blossoming she ensures by the wealth of the harvests.

demigod. Often confused with the hero, the demigod is a being who is born of a union of an immortal father with a mortal mother, or of a mortal man with an immortal woman. Condemned to perish, the demigod is not always treated like a hero after his death nor is he transported to Olympus, like Heracles, or to the country of eternal happiness, like Achilles. In fact, the concept of the demigod is the original form, simplified to the extreme, of the notion of the hero, with the notion of hero becoming increasingly complex over the ages.

demons. In certain legends, demons were occult figures, mysterious divinities from the beyond, whose influence on the actions of men could be beneficial or harmful. Hesiod characterized them as intermediaries between the gods and men. Later it was held that the deified souls of men could become demons and return to earth to torment criminals. Philosophers and poets seized on the notion of the demon and transformed it. Thus, according to Pindar, each man was torn between a demon of good and one of evil, symbolizing the destiny attributed to each life.

destiny. There is no notion that occupies a more prominent place in religion, drama and the Greek and Roman myths, both for humans and for gods, than the complex idea of Destiny. For the Greeks, Destiny is represented by Moira (the destiny or lot reserved for each person) and Tyche. For the Romans, Destiny takes the form of Fatum and Fortuna. Moira, who at first represented a single divinity, gradually assumed such importance that she was divided into three persons: Clotho, Lachesis and Atropos. But all of these representations are the expression of the inflexibility of human destiny traced beforehand and of the fatal hour of death, that no one can escape. Over the centuries, however, the Greeks modified this notion of cruel destiny and worshiped another divinity, Tyche, who was less dreaded. Tyche personified chance, both good and bad, just or unjust, intervening in the fate of men or nations when she was able to change its course.

In the Roman religion, which was more superstitious than the religion of the Greeks, destiny—Fatum—assumed a more abstract and less personal character. It came to translate the will of the gods, the oracle against which man could do nothing, total submission to supreme decisions which belonged only to immortals. Then, gradually, the idea of *fatum* became more human to a certain extent and was divided into Fatus for men, and Fata for women, rather like spirits attached to every step each mortal took and guiding the unfolding of the life bestowed upon each of them. Finally, just as the Greeks honored Tyche, the Romans invoked Fortuna who was also the image of chance, both arbitrary and capricious, with its incoherences, its injustices, and its favors.

DEUCALION. This king is the Greek hero of the Eastern tradition of the deluge, whose myth appears in all religions of Antiquity. The son of Prometheus and the Oceanid Clymene, Deucalion married Pyrrha, the daughter of Epimetheus, and settled in Thessaly over which he reigned with justice. When Zeus decided to destroy the human race, considering that the evil-mindedness of men was not only an insult to the gods but a perpetual threat as well, only Deucalion and Pyrrha were spared. Before he sent a torrential rainfall, Zeus permitted Prometheus to alert them to the danger that was imminent and to advise them to build a sort of large chest where they could take refuge during the nine days and nine nights that the deluge lasted. This was indeed done. The entire Earth was submerged and all of its inhabitants died. When the waters subsided, the two just mortals who had escaped the wrath of the god were deposited on top of Mount Parnassus. Zeus sent them his customary messenger, Hermes, who asked them to express a wish. They answered that, in their solitude, they wished to see the rebirth of the human race. "Cover your faces," Zeus instructed them, "and throw behind you the bones of your grandmother." After seeking the meaning of these words for quite some time, they realized that the bones were nothing other than the stones that covered their grandmother, the Earth, and they carried out the will of the gods. The stones thrown by Deucalion changed into men; those thrown by Pyrrha turned into women. Thus, the Earth was inhabited once again by a new

```
                                                              DEUCALION
              DEUCALION = PYRRHA
                    HELLEN = ORSEIS
                                          AEOLUS⁽¹⁾ = ENARETE
  XUTHUS = CREUSA⁽¹⁾           ATHAMAS   CRETHEUS   SISYPHUS
        ION                                                  SALMONEUS
```

race of human beings, who were more cultivated but also more courageous than their
predecessors. The sons that were born of Pyrrha were the ancestors of the conquering races
that were to build the glory of Greece.

DIANA. This ancient Italic divinity, rapidly
identified with the Greek Artemis, had been
introduced in Rome, according to some, by the
legendary king Servius Tullius. The Roman
legends of Diana were all borrowed from
Greek myths. It is said that Orestes brought to
Italy, to Nemi to be exact, the Artemis Tauro-
poulos. Near this city of Latium there was a
lake, a sacred wood and a temple dedicated to
Diana. In honor of the goddess, human sacrifices were offered. Each priest had to kill his
predecessor in order to have the right to succeed him. It is also said that Hippolytus, revived by Asclepius, had been carried away by
Artemis and transported to Italy where he assumed the name of Virbius (meaning, presumably, "he who has lived twice") in order later to
give himself over completely to the worship of
his divine abductress. However, for the Romans, Diana is not so much, like Artemis, the
huntress (although she borrowed from Artemis
the quiver and bow), as the sister of Apollo,
namely the goddess of Light.

DIDO. In her early days, this Carthaginian
heroine, revered by the Romans, was known as
Elissa; she was the daughter of Mutto, the king
of Tyre, and the sister of Pygmalion. She had
married her uncle, the rich Sicharbas, priest of
Heracles. When Mutto died, Pygmalion succeeded him but, wishing to appropriate the

wealth of his brother-in-law, assassinated him.
For quite some time, he hid the murder from
his sister as he prepared the same fate for her.
One day, Dido was alerted in a dream to these
sinister plans by the shadow of her husband
who advised her to flee as quickly as possible,
taking his treasures with her. She secretly had
her ships armed and, with a few companions,
she set sail from Tyre. During a stop in Cyprus,
she had twenty-four women abducted for the
sailors on her ship; then she continued on to
Africa. After some dealings with the natives,
she obtained as her territory a piece of land as
large as the size of a bull's hide. Foiling the
trick and exhibiting her wiliness, Dido cut the
hide into thin strips and thus took hold of a
sizeable piece of land where her comrades built
the citadel of Byrsa ("bull's hide"). All around
the citadel rose the city of Carthage which rapidly became a flourishing city. Then Iarbus, the
king of the Getulians, jealous of the city's prosperity, asked for the hand of Dido in marriage.
But Dido, who had vowed to remain faithful to
the memory of her first husband, preferred to
sacrifice herself in the flames of the funeral
pyre rather than renounce her oath. In light of
this illustrious deed, the people honored Dido
as they would a divinity.

Virgil, however, with no regard for the chro-
nology which dictates at least three hundred
years between the fall of Troy and the founding of Carthage, invented another version of
the story and introduced Aeneas into the legend of Dido. When Aeneas landed in Carthage
he was received by Dido, who gradually fell in
love with him. But the Numidian prince Iarbus

asked Jupiter to send this stranger away. Submitting to the will of the gods and without taking leave of the queen, Aeneas set sail for Italy. Desperate and incapable of surviving in the absence of her lover, Dido stabbed herself in the midst of the flames of the funeral pyre.

DIOMEDES. 1. King of the Bistonians in Thrace, Diomedes was in the habit of feeding his horses the flesh of innocent voyagers who ventured into his territory, believing that this would make his horses more alert and robust. Heracles put an end to this sinister practice by having Diomedes devoured by his own horses. He then gave the carnivorous horses to Eurystheus, who first dedicated them to Hera and then let them loose on Mount Olympus where they were torn to pieces by ferocious beasts.

2. With Achilles and Ajax, the son of Telamon, another **Diomedes,** the son of Tydeus, was considered to be one of the most valiant heroes of all Antiquity. Raised by the centaur Chiron, he succeeded his grandfather Adrastus on the throne of Argos and played an effective role in the expedition of the Epigoni in order to avenge the death of his father, one of the Seven Leaders. Later, he developed an intense friendship with Ulysses and accompanied him to Troy at the head of some twenty-four vessels. In addition to the feats he accomplished with his friend, either going out to search for Philoctetes and his arrows that were crucial to the victory at Lemnos, stealing the horses of Rhesus, or seizing from Troy the Palladium that was supposed to protect the city, Diomedes never hesitated when faced with a single combat, even against the most famous Trojan heroes such as Hector or Aeneas. And he was never conquered. Moreover, protected by Athena, he dared to attack the god Ares, whom he wounded in the side, and attacked Aphrodite as well, piercing the hand of the goddess with his spear. But this audacity displeased the goddess of Love. She inspired the wife of Dio-

medes, Aegialeia, to commit adultery. When Diomedes returned to Argos, he learned of his wife's infidelity. He then left his kingdom and journeyed to the south of Italy, to Apulia, where he met Daunus, the king of the country, who gave him his daughter in marriage. Diomedes settled in the country and founded numerous cities in southern Italy. According to some, he was killed by King Daunus; according to others, he disappeared on the orders of the gods right before the very eyes of his companions who were changed into birds. Buried on one of the islands which today bears his name, he was adored as a god.

DION. King of Laconia, Dion, the husband of Amphithea, received Apollo with such honor that the god, touched, granted the king's three daughters—Orphe, Lyco and Carya—the gift of prophecy on the condition that they not pry into things that did not concern them. But, despite the god's warnings, the first two sisters overstepped their rights by spying on the love affair of Dionysus and Carya. In punishment for their indiscretion, they were changed into rocks. Only the lover of Dionysus was changed into a nut tree.

DIONE. One of the divinities of the first generation, Dione was the daughter of Oceanus and Tethys, or else of Cronus and Gaia. She was loved by Zeus and gave birth to the goddess Aphrodite. She is also said to have been the wife of Tantalus, by whom she had Niobe and Pelops.

DIONYSUS. One of the most important and most complex gods of Greece, Dionysus, the son of Zeus and Semele, was born under somewhat strange circumstances. Semele, in fact, driven by the jealous Hera, wanted to see her divine lover in all his power. Her body was immediately consumed and Zeus had just enough time to snatch the tiny Dionysus from her belly; he sheltered him in his thigh for three

Dionysus, supported by a satyr, exhibits all the signs of fatigue and drunkenness and drops his cup of wine. Borghese vase, Neo-Attic marble, 1st cent. A.D., photo Giraudon.

months so that he would be born in due time. Disguised as a young girl and entrusted to Athamas and Ino, the young god could not escape the wrath of Hera. She drove his adoptive parents mad and forced him to flee to faraway lands where Zeus changed him into a young goat. The nymphs then assumed responsibility for his education.

But, once he reached adulthood, the god was also driven mad. He roamed the world over, introducing in each country he visited the cultivation of the vine and the way to make wine. Thus he wandered through Egypt, Syria, Phrygia, where the goddess Cybele initiated him into her mysteries. Delivered from his madness, he entered Thrace. There he went to the kingdom of King Lycurgus who opposed the introduction of the god's cult and imprisoned the Bacchantes, thus forcing Dionysus to flee to Thetis. Shortly afterwards, the god freed the Bacchantes and drove Lycurgus mad, then making the earth in Thrace sterile. To appease the god, the horrified inhabitants sacrificed their king. Having established his cult in all of the countries in the Mediterranean region, Dio-

nysus, esconced in a chariot drawn by panthers, headed to India and, accompanied by the Sileni, the Bacchantes and Satyrs, he took a mysterious voyage. Once he returned to Boeotia, he tried to introduce his cult in Thebes; but Pentheus, the king of the city, was also opposed to it. This king was torn to pieces by his mother, Agave, who had also been driven mad. The Proetides, the daughters of King Proetus, who had never agreed to welcome the god, also sank into madness and scattered themselves, wailing, throughout the country. Dionysus then took a ship to Naxos, but the crew, composed of pirates, wanted to hold him prisoner and sell him as a slave at their next stop. Dionysus immediately exhibited his power by immobilizing the ship, filling it with ivy, and evoking shrill sounds on a flute. The sailors, terrified, all threw themselves into the sea and were changed into dolphins. Before ascending to Olympus to be rightfully received into the assembly of gods, Dionysus went to the Underworld to carry his mother Semele away. He

With his beard, the face of Dionysus bears the stamp of sovereign graveness common to all gods. His hair is knotted in a bun with branches of the vine, and the leaves adorn his forehead like a crown. Greek coin from Naxos, in the likeness of Dionysus, Bibl. Nat., Cabinet des Médailles, photo Giraudon.

transported her with him into the skies where she assumed the name of *Thyone*.

Linked to wine and to drunkenness, the cult of Dionysus spread throughout Greece with the cultivation of the vine. The god thus became the symbol of the intoxicating power of nature, of sap that swells the grapes and is the very lifeblood of the plants. Often surrounded by the divinities of the fields, he was also worshiped as the god of Gardens and the Woods. Raised by nymphs, he also claimed to be adored as a god of the Water, that liquid element that is the sap and original source of all life. During the classical age, Dionysus took on the aspect of the god of joyous living, of games and festivals with which he loved to surround himself in the midst of the cries of joy of the Bacchantes. He was identified with this character especially in the Roman Empire where he went by the name of *Bacchus*. But it is also significant that the Greeks regarded him as the patron of Fine Arts, and of tragedy and comedy in particular, which both came from the performances that took place during his festivals. His role in Orphism should not be overlooked either, there he was identified with Zagreus.

In works of art, Dionysus has the features of a young man whose forehead and body are encircled with ivy, vines and clusters of grapes. He is generally accompanied by processions of Maenads, Thyiads or flutists who wear a thyrsus and abandon themselves to games, frenzied dances and reckless transports.

DIOSCURI. In mythology, this name refers to Castor and Pollux, the sons of Leda, but Castor's father was Tyndareos while Zeus was the father of Pollux. They were the brothers of Clytemnestra and Helen. Their inseparable lives and their brotherly affection are illustrated not only by the stories of their adventures but also by the works of art which portray them hand in hand; often their profiles are superimposed on a coin. Indeed, they never left one another's side and they took part in all the great legendary events. Born in Sparta, they symbolized the secular rivalry between Laconia and Attica by leading a victorious expedition against Athens in order to free their sister Helen who had been kidnapped by Theseus and hidden in the citadel of Aphidna. They took part in the Calydonian Boar Hunt; they accompanied the Argonauts on the legendary journey, each offering Jason his special talents: Pollux by a victorious boxing match against Amycus, the king of Bebryces, Castor by his equestrian skill. The Dioscuri were, however, less lucky in affairs of the heart. They abducted Phoebe and Hilaera, the two daughters of King Leucippus, who were engaged to marry Idas and Lynceus, their cousins. The latter, angered, pursued the two abductors. Castor was killed during the struggle that ensued. But Pollux, immortal, was only wounded and was carried into the heavens by his father Zeus. Pollux, however, could not get over the death of his beloved brother. Zeus therefore granted him the favor of sharing his immortality with Castor every other day.

Worship of the deified Dioscuri spread from Sparta throughout Greece, to Sicily and Italy. In Italy, they were placed among the ranks of marine gods. But this power was multiplied by countless others. The patrons of gymnastic games, they were also supposed to inspire the singer who was heard during these festivities. Their kindness sometimes changed the course of historic events. During the Peloponnesian war, the Dioscuri fluttered like two flames around the rudder of the strategist Lysander, thus confirming their protection of him. These fires, which sometimes burn during storms around ships, are well known to seamen who call them "Saint Elmo's fire," the word *Elmo* doubtless being a contraction of the word "Helen," the sister of the Dioscuri. It is also said that, mounted on steeds, they helped the Romans carry off a victory over the Italians at

The sculptor has followed the Roman legend of the Dioscuri. Castor and Pollux can be seen abducting the daughters of Leucippus—Hilaera and Phoebe—from their fiancés Idas and Lynceus. It should be noticed that the artist has taken care to give the twins identical faces and appearances. Detail of a sarcophagus, Uffizi Gallery, Florence, photo Alinari-Giraudon.

Lake Regillus and that the dictator Albinus dedicated a temple to them on the forum in Rome, facing the temple of Vesta. Finally, two examples illustrate how very important the Dioscuri were in Rome: the equestrian class regarded the Dioscuri as their patrons and honored them on July 15 each year. As for the lower classes of Rome, they were in the habit of swearing in the names of Pollux and Castor.

DIRCE. The wife of Lycus, Dirce treated Antiope with such cruelty that Zethus and Amphion, Antiope's sons, killed Dirce by tying her to the horns of a wild bull and left her, with no burial, in a place where a spring gushed forth. The spring was later known as "Dirce's spring."

divination. The ability to know the thoughts of the gods, divination, in mythology, was reserved for certain mortals who had received this talent from a god or who had been privi-leged to be born with it, having come from a family of soothsayers. In legends, the powers of the soothsayers are immense. Each State, each king, each army, each expedition had an official soothsayer. The Seven against Thebes and the Epigoni did not make any tactical decisions before consulting their soothsayer, Tiresias. During the Trojan War, the Greeks relied on the advice of Calchas. The Trojans, for their part, had a soothsayer in Cassandra who, owing to a divine curse, was neither heeded nor believed. In historical times, free divination disappeared. Colleges of priests with much more limited powers gradually assumed these functions.

divinization. In Antiquity, this favor was granted to but a limited group of mortals. In legends, certain heroes, through a special decision of the gods, were transported to Olympus where they were blessed with immortality, thus becoming divinized and adored on Earth. Gradually, divinization was conferred upon the great men of Greek and Roman history; they took a place among the gods, bearing witness for future generations to the grandeur of days past, and serving as constant models and examples, protecting the activities of men and rulers. Finally, under the Roman Empire, most emperors were the object of adoration while they were still alive, and after their deaths the Senate granted them deification. Their images were thus placed among those of the gods. The Christians were persecuted because they refused to worship the Emperor.

DODONA. One of the most ancient oracles of Greece, Dodona is located in Epirus. It is said that Dodona was given by the Pelasgians in honor of Zeus. The supreme god was asked questions and he answered through the intermediary of the branches of the oaks or beeches that rustled in the wind. The ancients even placed bronze vases on the crowns of these trees and these chinked at the slightest breeze. All these sounds were interpreted by the priests. The oracle of Dodona gradually lost some of its importance as the oracle of Delphi began to play a greater role in this sphere.

DORIS. The daughter of Oceanus, Doris had the gift of prophecy, like the divinities that live in the waters, and she owed her glory to her progeny: the wife of Nereus, she was, in fact, the mother of the Nereids. One of her daughters, Thetis, was to give birth to the most famous hero of the Trojan War, Achilles, and another daughter, Amphitrite, was to become the spouse of Poseidon.

DORUS. The legendary founder of the Dorian race, Dorus was the child of the love affair between Apollo and the nymph Phthia, according to some, and of the union of Hellen and Orseis, according to others. He was killed along with his brothers, Laodocus and Polypoetes, in the gulf of Corinth by Endymion, the conqueror of the territory which later took the name of Aetolia.

DREAMS. Greco-Roman divinities, dreams are spirits who deliver messages of the gods to sleeping mortals. Through dreams, man may know, in particular, the wishes and thoughts of Zeus and Hermes, interpreted by certain priests specialized in the art of analyzing dreams.

DRYADS. The name of these nymphs comes from the Greek word *drus* meaning "oak." Inhabiting the oak forests that were particularly sacred in the Greek religion, they protected their dwelling from sacrilegious vandals who came to deface it. Vigorous and fresh like the trees they protected, they mimicked their charges and assumed the form of a trunk and its roots up to their waists. They did indeed have the opportunity to leave the forests and to marry. Eurydice, the most famous Dryad, married Orpheus.

DRYOPE. This daughter of King Dryops was loved by Apollo. She was playing with the Hamadryads, her companions, when the god changed himself into a turtle in order to approach her. The animal, being used as a ball by the young girls, fell into the lap of Dryope and, suddenly changing itself into a serpent, he made her the mother of one of his children. Ashamed, Dryope hid this experience and later married. According to another much more pathetic version of the legend, Dryope, to amuse her son Amphissus, was gathering lotus blossoms on the banks of a lake, not knowing that the nymph Lotis had assumed this appearance to escape the advances of a suitor: blood gushed forth from the broken stems. Out of anger as well as pain, Lotis changed Dryope into a tree right before the horrified eyes of her parents.

E

ECHIDNA. Woman and serpent at one and the same time, the monster Echidna was begotten by Gaia and Pontus, or, according to another version of the legend, by Chrysaor and Callirhoë. She was considered to have given birth to the fantastic creatures that played a role of primary importance in the Greek legends: Chimaera, the dog of Geryon, Orthrus, Cerberus, the Sphinx, the Hydra of Lerna, the dragons of Colchis and of the garden of the Hesperides, Medusa, the eagle that gnawed at the liver of Prometheus, and the lion of Nemea. Evil-minded because of her very fertility and devouring innocent travelers, she was to be killed by hundred-eyed Argos, who surprised her in her sleep.

ECHION. 1. One of the five children born of the dragon teeth sown by Cadmus, the founding king of Thebes, Echion married Agave and was the father of Pentheus.

2. One of the sons of Hermes, the herald of the Argonauts, also bore the name of **Echion;** he took part in the Calydonian Boar Hunt.

ECHO. The Greeks had noticed in the mountains the echo that repeated the last words of a voice and they concocted fables in order to explain this phenomenon. The best-known relates that a nymph, named Echo, had the un-

pardonable habit of attracting the attention of Hera with incessant gossip when Zeus betrayed his legitimate wife and began to frolic with lovely mortals. One day, Hera realized the trick and punished Echo, condemning her with these words: "You will always have the last word, but you will never speak first." It just so happened that the nymph fell in love with the beautiful and lonely Narcissus. The fate dealt by the jealous goddess came to be; Narcissus called Echo and the poor creature could only repeat the last words of her beloved. The young man, weary of this situation, quickly abandoned the nymph who, in despair, lapsed into utter helplessness and grew so thin that nothing remained of her except her voice that echoes in the mountains. Another version of the legend is even more tragic. Since Echo failed to succumb to the advances of the god Pan and fled whenever he came near her, Pan grew angry and provoked the fury of the shepherds against her. They tore her to pieces and scattered her limbs all over the Earth. Since that time, Echo is everywhere and, even though she is dead, her voice is still heard.

EETION. The king of Thebes of Mysia and an ally of the Trojans, Eetion was the father of Andromache. He was killed by Achilles and buried, completely armed, by the Greek hero who, admiring his courage, granted him a sumptuous funeral. Elms were planted around his tomb by the nymphs. In Antiquity, wounds were treated with the leaves of the elm and they were considered to have the most beneficial and efficient properties if they were gathered not far from the tombs of those who had received numerous wounds.

EGERIA. A Roman nymph, Egeria may have been the wife of Numa Pompilius whom she often met secretly in a grotto not far from a spring that was later dedicated to her. She presumably instructed him in the political religion Numa established at Rome. At the death of Numa, Egeria, overcome with sadness, retired to Aricia, near the sanctuary of Diana, and shed so many tears that she was changed into a spring.

Ferocious looking, Electra, completely armed with a spear, helmet and breastplate, is followed by her brother Orestes. Both prepare to confront the Mycenaeans who want to kill them because they have assassinated their mother Clytemnestra. Greek vase, photo Camera.

EILEITHYIA. The goddess of Motherhood, the sister of Hebe, Ares and Hephaestus, Eileithyia was sent by Hera, her mother, to assist women in childbirth. In the *Iliad*, there are several Eileithyias who personify the various stages in the pains of childbirth. Eileithyia, portrayed with the features of a young woman, has one of her hands raised and, in the other, she holds a lighted torch, the symbol of life that is born in light.

ELECTRA. 1. The daughter of Oceanus and Tethys, Electra had relations with Thaumas, the son of Pontus and Gaia, and gave birth to Iris and two of the Harpies, Aello and Ocypete.

2. Legend tells of another **Electra,** the daughter of Atlas and Pleione, who, having had relations with Zeus, gave birth to Dardanus, the first king of Troy, and Iasion, the lover of Demeter and father of Ploutos. It is also said that Electra, about to be seduced by Zeus, hid behind the statue of the Palladium, which had been brought to Olympus by Athena. But the god, despite the sacrilege, had relations with Electra and, in his wrath, threw from the heavens the Palladium which was recovered by the Trojans and was considered from that point on to be the protective statue of their city. Latin tradition modified the genealogy of Electra: she was no longer the lover of Zeus but the wife of the Etruscan prince Corythus. Of the two sons that were born of the marriage, one, Iasion, emigrated to Samothrace while the other, Dardanus, settled in the Troad.

3. The most famous **Electra** is the daughter of Agamemnon and Clytemnestra. She has been immortalized by the tragedians Euripides and Sophocles. Spared by Clytemnestra and Aegisthus when they assassinated Agamemnon, she also managed to save her younger brother Orestes by hiding him under her dress and taking him away from the city of Mycenae to an old preceptor of her father's. According to one of the versions, Electra had been engaged to marry Castor shortly before her father's murder. But Aegisthus, fearing that she would give birth to a son who would one day avenge his grandfather, entrusted her to a Mycenaean peasant who allegedly never consummated the marriage. Electra lived for a long time in poverty and solitude. But one day, while she was collecting her thoughts near her father's tomb, Orestes approached her and identified himself. They decided with Pylades to kill Aegisthus and Clytemnestra. Orestes and Pylades went to the palace and announced that Orestes was dead. Having been able to enter the palace because of the rejoicing that this bit of news stirred up, they killed Clytemnestra and Aegisthus. But Electra did not abandon her brother who was ceaselessly tormented by the Erinyes; she protected him from the anger of his people who reproached him for this matricide. One day the news arrived in Mycenae that Orestes and Pylades had been sacrificed on the altar of Artemis in Tauris. Aletes, the son of Aegisthus, immediately ascended the throne and Electra went to consult the oracle to learn more. Thus, in Delphi, she met Iphigenia, her sister, who told her that she was the priestess who had sacrificed the two young men, one of whom was their brother Orestes. Electra, outraged, seized a firebrand and was about to burn her sister's eyes when Orestes appeared and the three returned joyfully to Mycenae. Orestes killed Aletes and married Hermione. Electra married Pylades and gave birth to two sons, Medon and Strophius.

ELECTRYON. The son of Perseus and Andromeda, spouse of Anaxo, Electryon was reigning over Mycenae when the sons of Pterelaus claimed the throne as their legitimate heritage and stole the cattle of the king by killing his eight sons during a skirmish. The only ones who escaped the massacre were a boy, Licymnius, and a girl, Alcmene. Amphitryon, who loved the young girl, succeeded in paying a ransom and returning the stolen herd to the king. In exchange, he received control of the kingdom and the promise of Alcmene in marriage. But the day Electryon left on an expedition against Pterelaus, he was killed; indeed, Amphitryon had thrown a club at a raging cow and it rebounded off the horns of the animal and shattered the king's head.

ELEUSIS. A city in Attica, Eleusis is known above all for its worship of Demeter and for the mysteries consecrated to the triad—Demeter, Core-Persephone, Triptolemus. These mysteries, introduced in the city by Eumolpus, traced the myth of Demeter in search of her daughter Core. They were only celebrated by those initiated into the mysteries.

ELIS. This region of Peloponnesus had as its main cities Elis, whose eponymous hero succeeded his grandfather, King Endymion, and Olympia, where every four years the famous games were held in honor of the Olympian Zeus. It was decided that Elis would be a sacred territory where no one would be permitted to enter armed and where all disputes and all wars were to be suspended.

ELPENOR. A companion to Ulysses, Elpenor was changed into a swine by Circe but regained his human form eventually. Having had too much wine, he fell from a roof and was killed. When Ulysses descended to the Underworld, he met the shadow of Elpenor and promised him a funeral that would be worthy of him.

ELYSIAN FIELDS. In Antiquity there were two different accounts, one Greek, the other Latin, about these mythical places. For Homer in the *Odyssey*, the Elysian Fields were at the very western end of World. There the climate was always mild, with no rain or snow or storms. Heroes like Menelaus were invited to spend their eternity there through the very special graces of the gods. But Virgil attributed a more precise meaning to the Elysian Fields. According to him, they were located at the very heart of the Underworld. Aeneas, who descended there to see his father, marveled at their smiling groves and their meadows, which were always green, and where the air was pleasant and the light bore shades of purple and azure. The Elysian Fields welcomed in the charm of their countryside the souls of the just and of heroes who had proven their piety.

EMPUSA. The daughter of Hecate, this demon had feet of bronze and spent her days terrifying travelers and eating human flesh. How-

Above the sleeping young shepherd Endymion, the goddess Selene, his lover, appears. She is portrayed with horns that support the crescent of the Moon, of which she is the divine incarnation. Fresco from the Casa Grande, Pompeii, photo Alinari-Giraudon.

ever, Empusa fled when people insulted her. She was able to assume all possible forms and even to change herself into a beautiful young woman to seduce her victims. It was said that she had relations at night with men and sucked their blood until they died.

ENCELADUS. The son of Tartarus and Gaia, Enceladus, the giant with a hundred arms, took part in the struggle against the gods of Olympus. He was struck down by the thunder of Zeus and perished, crushed, under the island of Sicily. According to Euripides, Silenus wanted to take full credit for the death of the giant.

ENDYMION. The son of Zeus, Endymion was the king of the Aetolians and had three sons and a daughter by one marriage. He fell in love with Selene, the moon, who bore him fifty daughters. At her request, Zeus plunged Endymion into eternal slumber, thus enabling him to remain a young and beautiful shepherd until the end of time. In love with him, the moon goes each night to join him in a cave where he rests forever and she can have relations with her beloved without ever awakening him from his slumber.

ENIPEUS. A river of Thessaly, which has its source on Mount Othrys, Enipeus was the dwelling place of a god whose form Poseidon assumed in order to have relations with Tyro and make her the mother of Pelias and Neleus.

ENVY. This allegorical divinity, who bears the name of *Phthonos* among the Greeks and *Invidia* among the Romans, has no legend attached to her. She personifies primarily the fascination of the "evil eye" that enviously looks at those that it cannot possess. An evil-minded spirit, whose heart is incessantly devoured by serpents, Envy is frightfully thin; all unsated desires gnaw at her.

ENYO. Identified with Bellona, the Roman goddess of war, Enyo, a messenger of Ares, delights in slaughter and bloodshed. In the midst of battles, she revels in war cries, shouts of pain, and the rattle of dying warriors.

EOS. This divine personification of the Dawn in Greek mythology belongs to the first generation of gods; she is the daughter of Theia and Hyperion and the sister of Helios and Selene. At the end of each night, Eos appears on the horizon on a chariot of light drawn by golden horses to announce the return of the sun. Her husbands and lovers are countless and she gave birth to a host of children. The wife of Astraeus, she preferred Orion to him, then Cephalus and finally the son of Laomedon, Tithonus, by whom she bore Memnon, the king of Egypt. The loves of Eos for young gods or mortals produced other allegories: for instance, her union with Astraeus, the dusk wind, which produced the morning star, the winds and the planets.

EPAPHUS. Io, pursued by the wrath of Hera, was changed into a heifer. She arrived in Egypt, recovered her original form of a beautiful young woman, and gave birth to Epaphus on the banks of the Nile. Hidden by the Curetes on the order of Hera, this illegitimate son of Zeus was found once again by his mother. When he reached adulthood, he reigned over Egypt. Married to Memphis, he had three daughters—Lysianassa, Thebe, and Libya who had Agenor and Bellus by Poseidon. At his death, Epaphus was revered as the very incarnation of the ox-god Apis.

EPEIUS. The son of Panopeus, Epeius left to fight against Troy at the head of thirty ships. But his reputation for cowardice became legendary in the Greek army. However, the soothsayer Prylis, the son of Hermes, enlisted his ingenuity in the construction of the wooden horse, through which the Greeks were able to invade the city of Troy. Inspired by Athena and with the enthusiastic agreement of Ulysses,

Light and airy, Eos, the divine personification of the Dawn, is carried through the air by her light wings and by the folds of her tunic which swell in the wind. With two water pitchers, she sprinkles the dew on Earth. Greek lekythos, Louvre, photo Giraudon.

Epeius assembled thousands of planks, fashioning an enormous hollow horse with a door carved into its side through which some fifty Greek heroes entered in order to hide in the belly of the horse. The animal was rolled into Troy, on the pretext of offering it to the goddess Athena, and the city, suddenly invaded by Greeks, was sacked and destroyed. Upon his return from Troy, Epeius stopped in Italy and founded the city of Metapontum. Another legend recounts that the captive Trojan women he had with him, by burning his vessels, prevented his returning to Greece and he was obliged to settle in Etruria where he ran aground. He is said to have founded Pisa, in memory of a twin city in Peloponnesus, not far from Olympia. Epeius is also credited with having made a wooden statue of Hermes at Troy which, carried out to sea, was caught in some fishermen's nets at Aenus in Thrace. When they realized that it could neither be split nor burnt they built a sanctuary for it.

EPHESUS. The major Ionian city on the coast of Asia Minor, Ephesus was known primarily for the beauty, unique in all of Antiquity, of its temple dedicated to the goddess Artemis. The goddess was portrayed in the form of a statue with many breasts, the symbol of fertility.

EPIDAURUS. This city of Argolis possessed a temple dedicated to Asclepius, where the god delivered oracles. People came from far and wide to consult the oracle. The temple was surrounded by sacred woods, in the center of which the sick who had come to obtain miraculous cures were assembled. In addition, games were celebrated there in honor of the god of Medicine.

epidemic. Generally speaking, this scourge is sent by the gods to countries guilty of crimes or sacrileges, either collectively or because of one of its inhabitants such as a hero or king. Most often, the country that is stricken by a plague does not know the reason for the wrath of the god. It must usually consult a soothsayer or an oracle like the Delphic oracle to learn the remedies for the epidemic. The gods, in their response, always demand either a sacrifice, a tribute or a banishment. Thus, Idomeneus, who sacrificed his son, provoked a terrible plague in his country that did not subside until he went into exile. Legend also shows that the Athenians were forced to send Minos seven young men and seven young women to atone for the murder of Androgeus by Aegeus and to end the epidemic that was devastating their country. Examples abound in mythology: Thebes when it was ruled by Oedipus, who killed his father and married his mother, was beset by a plague. Likewise, the kingdom of Orestes was ravaged by the same epidemic until the day that the Greeks rebuilt the temples of the city of Troy.

EPIGONI. This name was given to the sons of the Seven Leaders who had taken part in the first expedition against Thebes and had all perished, except for Adrastus, the king of Argos. To avenge their fathers' deaths, the Epigoni decided to conduct a second expedition in retaliation. The Epigoni included Alcmaeon and Amphilochus, the sons of Amphiaraus; Aegialeus, son of Adrastus; Thersander, the son of Polynices; Promachus, the son of Parthenopaeus; Sthenelus, the son of Capaneus; Diomedes, the son of Tydeus; Euryalus, the son of Mecisteus. The oracle of Delphi predicted victory for them provided they chose Alcmaeon as their leader. Alcmaeon, pressured by his mother Eriphyle, was forced to accept. The Epigoni marched on Thebes, evacuated during the night by all of its inhabitants, invaded it, and engaged in a victorious combat in which they killed Laodamas, the son of Eteocles, who, like his father before him, commanded the Theban army. The Epigoni made an offering of their booty to Apollo and proclaimed Thersander king of the nation that had finally been reconquered after more than ten years of battles. Thus Polynices was avenged for his misfortune by his son.

EPIMETHEUS. The son of Iapetus and Clymene, Epimetheus or "After-Thought" has a legend in common with that of Prometheus, his brother. The Titan who wanted to match forces with Zeus had asked Epimetheus not to accept any presents from the god. However, Epimetheus dared not refuse Pandora as his wife; all of the miseries contained in the famous box his wife opened bombarded the human race.

ERATO. The attitudes that Greek artists assign her, those signs of passion, those voluptu-

The Muse Erato, inspired by the gods who breathe into her the themes of lyric poetry, improvises on the lyre musical accompaniment for her poems. Ancient sculpture, Vatican Museum, photo Anderson-Giraudon.

ous movements, bestow on this Muse some analogies with Venus and lead mythographers to believe that she normally presides over marriages and erotic poetry. Thus, Virgil invoked her to celebrate the marriage of Aeneas and Lavinia, Apollonius of Rhodes that of Medea and Jason. Classical artists crowned her with myrtle branches and roses, placing in her left hand a lyre and in her right, a bow.

EREBUS. Originally, Erebus designated the most somber and inaccessible spot in the Underworld. Later, it was personified and became the son of Chaos and the brother of Night. But Erebus committed the crime of helping the Titans in their struggle against the gods of Olympus and was thrown into the Underworld.

ERECHTHEUS. The grandson of Erichthonius, the son of Pandion whom he succeeded as king of Athens, Erechtheus had a legend that, at a somewhat late date, disengaged itself from that of his grandfather. He had a certain number of children, including seven daughters who loved each other so tenderly that they swore that, if one of them perished, all of the others would follow her in death. It just so happened that during a battle that broke out between the Eleusinians, helped by Eumolpus, the king of Thrace, and the Athenians, the oracle of Delphi demanded that Erechtheus sacrifice one of his daughters to ensure victory. All the sisters of the victim, true to their oath, killed themselves. Erechtheus, the conqueror of Eumolpus, the son of Poseidon, was struck down by Zeus at the request of the god of the Sea.

ERGINUS. During a feast in honor of Poseidon, a Theban chariot crushed Clymenus, the king of the Minyans of Orchomenus. His son Erginus, urged on by anger, mobilized an army and marched on Thebes, which he quickly conquered. He forced the city's inhabitants to pay him a tribute of one hundred oxen every year for twenty years. Heracles, upon meeting the envoys of Erginus who had come to collect their due, cut off their ears and noses and, after attaching these bloody appendages to their necks with ropes, he sent them back to Orchomenus. Indignant, Erginus marched again on Thebes, governed by Creon, but this time he ran up against the army of young Thebans who had been mobilized and commanded by Heracles. Erginus was defeated and killed. According to another version, Erginus survived his defeat and took part in the expedition of the

Argonauts. In some versions this is another Erginus. Married, he was the father of the two famous architects, Agamedes and Trophonius.

ERICHTHONIUS. One day, while Hephaestus was pursuing Athena with amorous ardor, a bit of the god's seed fell on the thigh of the virgin goddess and fell on the ground, creating a child, Erichthonius, who was entrusted to the three daughters of Cecrops—Aglauros, Herse and Pandrosos. Erichthonius was placed in a basket that was given to Pandrosos, and Athena instructed the three sisters not to open it. Driven by feminine curiosity and impatience, they did not heed the warning of the goddess but opened the strange cradle. They saw the child, flanked by two serpents, and were so frightened at this sight that they threw themselves from the top of the citadel of Athens. Later, Erichthonius, who had become king of the city, instituted the cult of Athena in his kingdom and established the Panathenaea. His son Pandion succeeded him.

ERIGONE. When her father Icarius, an Athenian, was killed by drunken shepherds, who believed that he had poisoned them with wine, Erigone, the beloved of Dionysus and mother of the hero Staphylus, hanged herself in despair. Dionysus, grieved yet angry at the same time, drove the young girls of Athens to hang themselves from the branches of the pines, and this sort of folly continued until the oracle of Delphi claimed that the shepherds, the murderers of Icarius, had to be punished to appease Dionysus. They were hanged, therefore, and a festival was established in honor of Erigone.

ERINYES. Armed with whips and carrying torches, the three Erinyes—Alecto, Tisiphone and Megaera—with winged bodies and serpents for hair, administered the vengeance of the gods and roamed the face of the Earth to torment guilty mortals, particularly those who committed crimes against the family. According to Hesiod, they were born of the Earth fertilized by the blood of Uranus, whom Cronus had castrated. Aeschylus made them the offspring of night. Divinities of the Underworld, they incessantly pursue criminals who, through their pernicious actions, have disturbed the public and social order. They sometimes send collective punishments to an entire region in the form of an epidemic. But, most often, they pursue the criminal, inspiring in him remorse, fear of punishment, and endless anxiety. Orestes, who murdered his mother, is the type of hero who cannot escape the Erinyes. They can, on occasion, inspire inexpiable hatred, such as the hatred that pitted Eteocles against Polynices. Their demoniacal actions naturally extend to the Underworld; there they torture the souls of humans guilty of impiety and perjury; they whip them and insult them. Thus it was with respect mixed with fear that the ancients spoke of these divinities whose name of *Erinyes* was replaced, through a superstitious euphemism, by the term *Eumenides,* "the benevolent."

ERIPHYLE. In the Theban legends of the Seven Leaders and the Epigoni, Eriphyle appears as one of the symbols of the pernicious coyness of woman. The sister of Adrastus, the king of Argos, she married Amphiaraus, the soothsayer. However, as her husband and brother often quarreled, Eriphyle made them promise to use her as a mediator in the event differences arose between them. It so happened that Adrastus, at the request of Polynices, decided to send an expedition from Argos against Thebes. Amphiaraus refused to take part in these plans, seeing the unfortunate end to the war as well as his own death. To force him to accompany them, Polynices was instructed to offer Eriphyle the necklace and mantle of Harmonia, magical gifts. Delighted with these presents that flattered her feminine pride, Eriphyle forgot her love for her husband and ordered

The son of Aphrodite, Eros inherited charm and grace from the goddess of Love. Statue found in the sea, in Mahdia, Tunisia, Le Bardo National Museum, Tunis, Museum photo.

and created hatred among the warring sides. Her responsibility was, in fact, considerable with respect to the origins of the Trojan War: she offered the famous golden apple that Paris was to award to the most beautiful of all goddesses. She gave birth to a legion of evil-minded, abstract divinities such as Hunger, Pain, Oblivion and many others.

EROS. This Greek god is one of the primordial forces that governed the world before the birth of the immortals and the appearance of men. His power extends not only to beings but also to plants, minerals, liquids, fluids, in short, everything that is. He assembles, mixes and unites. He is the attractive virtue that induces things to unite and create life. He should not be confused with Cupid, the Roman god, or with Aphrodite, even though the classical era and the poets made Eros an assistant to Aphrodite and a son of Hermes and Aphrodite. Artists have portrayed him as a winged young man,

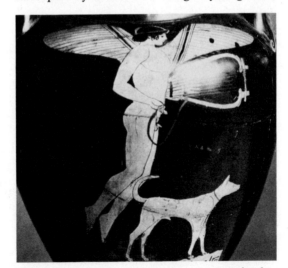

Eros, carried by his rapid wings, is sent by his mother to transmit the message of love. Here, he does not pierce men with his arrows as he does in the Roman legends, but he charms them with his lyre. Detail of a Greek amphora, Louvre, photo Giraudon.

him to join the other six against Thebes. As he had predicted, Amphiaraus perished, but his two sons, Alcmaeon and Amphilochus, avenged his death and killed their mother. The necklace of Harmonia, which was fatal to all who possessed it, subsequently was offered to the goddess Athena in the sanctuary of Delphi.

ERIS. Identified with the Roman allegorical divinity Discord, Eris was the twin sister of Ares. It is said that she was conceived when the goddess Hera touched a certain flower. She accompanied the god of war to the battlefields whose arrows pierce the hearts of men and light the flame of passion in men's souls. Eros remains, above all, before being included among the gods, an abstract entity: the desire that brings things together and induces them to reproduce.

ERYSICHTHON. Legend tells of two Erysichthons. The first was the son of Cecrops, one of the founding kings of Athens. The second, the son of a king of Thessaly, committed a sacrilege by cutting down trees in a wood that was sacred to Demeter. The goddess begged him to stop his felling but Erysichthon turned a deaf ear to her pleas. Demeter, to punish him for his misdeed, condemned him to suffer from perpetual hunger. His parents, who could not satisfy his hunger, sent him away. He ended up devouring himself despite the sacrifice of his daughter Mnestra who, selling herself as a slave, managed to provide him with food for some time.

ERYX. This hero gave his name to a mountain in Sicily at the top of which a temple was erected in honor of Aphrodite, his mother. King of the Elymi, he was blessed with formidable strength and no one ever succeeded in conquering him. By vanity, he dared to defy Heracles who was passing through his territory. Heracles agreed to fight Eryx on the condition that Eryx would agree to hand over his kingdom if he were defeated. Thus the hero took the presumptuous king in his enormous hands, threw him into the air and let him fall on the ground where he was killed. Heracles, despite his right to the kingdom, left the entire responsibility of it to its inhabitants but proclaimed that one day one of his descendants would govern it: this was Dorieus who founded a colony there.

ETEOCLES. With his brother Polynices and his sisters Ismene and Antigone, Eteocles belongs to the incestuous generation born of Oedipus and Jocasta. When Eteocles and Polynices learned of the involuntary crime of their father, they banished him from Thebes. Thus, Oedipus damned them and predicted that they would never cease to hate one another and that they would both perish in a fratricidal combat. An agreement was reached, however, between Eteocles and Polynices, each agreeing to reign over Thebes for a year, every other year. When the mandate of Eteocles was about to expire, Polynices claimed the throne but his brother refused to step down. A relentless battle known as the "Seven against Thebes" was soon to pit the two rivals against each other. Meeting in single combat, Eteocles and Polynices both perished. But Eteocles, who had defended his country, was granted sumptuous funeral rites while Polynices was denied burial.

ETHIOPIANS. According to Greek legends, the Ethiopians belonged to a mythical race. Their country had no definite borders. They lived, the ancients claimed, in the sunniest regions of the universe, near the place where Helios sets and rises at the same time, burning their skin and giving them a swarthy complexion that amazed the Ancients. In complete happiness, they led an existence dedicated to the glory of Apollo, the god of light, whose beneficial influence they appreciated each day with respect to their well-being and the fertility of their fields. The *Iliad* celebrates one of their kings, Memnon. He was the son of Eos, the Dawn, whom the Ethiopians contemplated each morning as she made her brilliant and crystal-clear appearance. Memnon led a contingent of Ethiopians who fought on the side of the Trojans.

EUMAEUS. The son of a king, Eumaeus, after being kidnapped by Phoenician pirates, became the slave and swineherd of Laertes, the king of Ithaca. He was one of the rare servants to remain faithful to his absent master and to welcome him with all the marks of joy and affection. With his help, Ulysses, disguised as a beggar, was able to approach Penelope's suitors and kill them mercilessly.

EUMENIDES. This word, which means "Benevolent," sometimes refers euphemistically to the Erinyes. In the tragedy of Aeschylus which bears their name, they are persuaded to become the goddesses of Fertility of the earth, while personifying the moral laws and sanctions connected with them.

EUMOLPUS. Thrown into the Ocean by his mother Chione, Eumolpus was recovered by his father Poseidon, who brought him to the shores of Ethiopia where he was raised by Benthesicyme, one of the daughters of Poseidon and Amphitrite. Eumolpus married one of the daughters of his adoptive mother but he was banished for having tried to rape one of his sisters-in-law. He found refuge in Thrace; but he plotted against King Tegyrius. Banished once again, he went to Eleusis, where he became king, official bard and high priest, founder of the mysteries. He was to perish at the hand of Erechtheus during the battle that pitted his city against Athens. His youngest son, Ceryx, succeeded him as high priest, and all of his descendants enjoyed the same privilege.

EUNOMUS. A young cupbearer in the court of Oeneus, the king of Calydon, Eunomus, the son of Architeles, was one day assigned to wash the hands of Heracles. He accidentally let some water fall on the hero's feet; Heracles became angry and struck the unfortunate youth so violently that he killed him. Although he was pardoned by Architeles, Heracles decided, to punish himself, to take exile with Deianira and his son Hyllus, and he went to Trachis.

EUPHEMUS. The son of Poseidon, Euphemus took part in the expedition of the Argonauts, whom he assisted with his gifts of divination. When the *Argo* approached the Symplegades, Euphemus released a dove; the two rocks tried to close in on the bird but merely tore off its tail feathers. This was the moment that the Argonauts chose to pass through, unharmed. On another occasion, swept along the coast of Libya and arriving at Lake Tritonis, the Argonauts sought in vain for quite some time an opening through which they could reach the Mediterranean. Then the god Triton or, according to some, his human incarnation Eurypylus, appeared to them; Euphemus, the son of the sovereign god of the Sea, dared to ask him the way. Triton pointed out the route and gave him a lump of earth which would enable the descendants of Euphemus to reign over Libya.

EUPHORBUS. Euphorbus was one of the most courageous Trojan warriors. He made his mark during the battle by dealing the first blow to Patroclus, who was finished off by Hector. Killed by Menelaus, who dedicated his shield to Hera, Euphorbus was reincarnated several centuries later in the person of the philosopher and mathematician Pythagoras (6th cent. B.C.), who thus illustrated his ideas on metempsychosis and successive reincarnations.

EUROPA. Agenor, the king of Phoenicia, the son of Poseidon and the Oceanid Libya, married Telephassa. Of this union, four sons were born—Phineas, Cadmus, Phoenix and Cilix—and one daughter, Europa, was born as well. As beautiful as the day, with velvety white skin, Europa was playing one day by the sea with her companions when Zeus saw her; he fell instantly in love with her. To avoid Hera's jealousy, he changed himself into a white bull with golden horns shaped like the crescents of the moon. Europa saw him, admired him, stroked him, and even went so far as to climb up on his back. Then the divine animal threw himself into the sea and disappeared. He reached the coast of Crete where

The Roman fresco from Pompeii (left) shows Europa mounted on a bull that is being caressed by one of the followers of the heroine, who is admiring the animal's beauty. Museum of Naples, photo Alinari-Giraudon. The archaic representation of Europa and Zeus shows how old the legend really is. Greek terra-cotta, Louvre, photo Giraudon.

plane trees grew that were always green to perpetuate the union of the two lovers. Europa gave birth to three children, whose names are glorified in legends: Minos, Rhadamanthys and Sarpedon. Zeus, in exchange for these three sons, gave Europa three precious gifts: Talos, a sort of robot that prevented enemies from landing on the coasts of Crete; a dog which, owing to his shrewdness and swiftness, never missed his prey; and an infallible hunting spear. Her brothers, who had set out in search of her, founded new colonies.

EUROTAS. Originally called *Himaera*, the Eurotas, the principal river of Laconia which bathes the city of Sparta, has a legend attached to it. King Eurotas, the father of Sparte, the wife of Lacedaemon, having been conquered by the Athenians because he had not awaited

the full moon to engage in battle, threw himself into the waters of a river to which he gave his name. According to modern mythographers, this suicide proves that there were sacrifices offered to Eurotas to appease his waters. But the Ancients also said that his waters were fortifying and the children of Sparta were immersed in the river at a very early age. The Eurotas often appears in epic cycles and legends. It was on its banks that Helen was abducted by Paris, that Zeus had relations with Leda in the form of a swan, and that Castor and Pollux learned the art of combat.

EURUS. This son of Eos and Astraeus is the southwest wind.

EURYALUS. 1. This Argive belonged to the generation of Epigoni through his father Mecisteus, the brother of Adrastus; for this reason, he participated in the fight against Thebes. Besides this expedition, he followed the Argonauts in their journey and accompanied Diomedes to the Trojan War, with another of the Epigoni, Sthenelus, the son of Capaneus.

2. Also known by this name is a Trojan warrior who formed a tender bond of friendship with Nisus and accompanied him to Italy under the leadership of Aeneas. He perished during a combat against the Rutuli.

EURYDICE. **1.** The most famous of all the Eurydices is the dryad who married Orpheus. Pursued by the shepherd Aristaeus one day while she was playing in the fields with some companions, she was stung on the foot by a viper and died from the wound. Orpheus descended to the Underworld to bring her back to Earth and life. Eager to feast his eyes on his beloved, and despite the prohibition of Hades, he turned around to look at her before she

Eurydice, center, about to be led to the Underworld by Hermes, bids farewell to Orpheus, whose lyre can be seen. Both exchange a look of desperate tenderness. Greek relief, Louvre, photo Arch. phot.

emerged from the Shadow. She disappeared immediately forever.

2. Legend also tells of others named **Eurydice:** a daughter of Lacedaemon; the mother of Danaë; a daughter of Amphiaraus and Eriphyle; and the wife of Creon, the king of Thebes.

EURYLOCHUS. The husband of Ctimene, the sister of Ulysses, and one of the hero's most loyal comrades, Eurylochus was known for his prudence; hidden behind the window in the palace of Circe, he watched as the sailors of Ulysses were changed into swine, and then alerted the hero to the situation. But at the end of the voyage, famished after several days of fasting, he came up with the idea of killing several sacred cows that belonged to the herd of Helios, despite Ulysses' prohibition. The enraged god had Zeus sink all of the ships and Eurylochus perished. Only Ulysses was spared.

EURYNOME. One of the very first divinities, Eurynome was born of the union of Oceanus and Tethys. She herself had relations with the Titan Ophion and reigned with him over Olympus before the appearance of Cronus and Rhea, who lost no time dethroning the intruders and throwing them into the sea. Zeus fell in love with her and made her the mother of the Charites and the river-god Asopus.

EURYPYLUS. **1.** When Heracles wished to touch land in Cos, he was at first repelled by the natives under the leadership of their king, Eurypylus, who was soon killed by the hero after he had succeeded in entering the city.

2. The son of Telephus and Astyoche, another **Eurypylus** was forced by his mother, who had received a golden vine from her brother Priam, to join forces with the Trojans at the head of a contingent of Mysians. After killing a good number of Greek heroes, among whom was Machaon, the son of Asclepius, he died at the hand of Neoptolemus when, under his leadership, the Trojans were trying to set fire to the Greek ships.

3. Also known by the name of **Eurypylus** is a Greek warrior who fought at the head of a contingent from Thessaly against the Trojans.

4. According to Pindar, **Eurypylus,** the son of Poseidon, is the incarnation of the god Triton.

EURYSTHEUS. The son of Sthenelus, the king of Argos, and of Nicippe, the daughter of Pelops, Eurystheus was the cousin of Amphitryon because Perseus was the ancestor of both. Since Zeus had declared that the first grandson of Perseus would have a royal destiny, Hera arranged that Eurystheus would be born first, before the son of Alcmene, Heracles, whom she knew to be the son of Zeus. Eurystheus thus became the sovereign master of Tiryns, Mycenae and a region of Argolis. But he trembled incessantly before Heracles because he was aware of his divine ancestor; he sought to humiliate Heracles and forced him to perform the famous labors from which the hero always emerged victorious. After the death of Heracles, Eurystheus persecuted his progeny and forced them to leave Mycenae. Then, some time later, he marched on Athens accompanied by the Heraclidae and was killed by Iolaus during a battle. The head of Eurystheus was brought to Alcmene: she gouged out his eyes.

EURYTUS. The king of the city of Oechalia in Thessaly, or in Euboea, or in Messenia, Eurytus was famous for his skill with a bow. His father, who possessed the same talent, claimed to be the son of Apollo, the supreme bowman. He had four sons including Iphitus and a daughter, Iole. He had promised her in marriage to whoever surpassed him with a bow and arrow. Heracles matched skill with the king and was proclaimed the winner; Eurytus refused to keep his promise and even accused the hero of having stolen his cattle. Only Iphitus rose to the

Euterpe. Capitoline Museum, Rome, photo Anderson-Giraudon.

defense of Heracles. But he was scarcely rewarded, since he was killed by the hero, who was overcome by a fit of madness, or else because he did not want to share his booty with him. This murder did not go unpunished. Heracles was condemned to slavery and sold to Omphale. Once freed, he returned to the court of Eurytus, killed him and massacred his sons, sparing only Iole, the price of his victory.

EUTERPE. One of the nine Muses, Euterpe's main power was her flute playing. Crowned with flowers, she presided over festivities and amusements. Equipped with her musical instrument, she also accompanied the procession of Dionysus. Along with the god, she is credited with the invention of the dithyramb, the source of Greek tragedy.

EVANDER. The legends differ on the birth of this Greco-Roman hero. According to the most current version, he is the son of Hermes and the Arcadian nymph Nicostrate (or Telpousa, or Themis, or Tyburtis), whom the Romans called *Carmenta*. Several years before the Trojan War, Evander, at the head of a colony of Arcadians, came to settle in Italy. Thanks to his wisdom and knowledge, he won the esteem of the local population; he taught them new laws, how to write, and how to worship the great gods such as Pan, Poseidon and Demeter. He received Heracles and granted him divine honors. Aeneas also came to see him and sealed an alliance with him against the Rutuli. An altar to Evander was placed at the foot of the Aventine.

F

This faun, a spirit of exuberant nature, with his horns, shaggy hair and tail, seems lost in a spell of madness or drunkenness. Ancient bronze, National Archaeological Museum, Naples, photo Alinari-Giraudon.

FAMA. The Latin divinity that personifies Rumors.

FAME. The messenger of Zeus for the Greeks and particularly for the people of Athens, who had erected a temple in her honor, Fame (in Latin, *Fama*) assumed her ultimate character with the Romans who honored her with respect and fear. A monstrous winged divinity, a daughter of the Earth, Fame possesses many mouths and numerous eyes, which enable her to disclose the most intimate secrets of mortals and proclaim them throughout the Universe. Error, Rumors and many other allegorical divinities freely enter her palace, which buzzes with the echoes of human voices, and bring her valuable information about men.

Fatum. The sacred expression of Destiny among the Romans, Fatum represents the decided will of the gods and the fate accorded to each mortal.

FAUNA. This wife of Faunus, considered by the Latins to be the mother of the god Latinus, one of the legendary kings of Latium, protects women against sterility.

fauns. These Roman divinities of the woods, who may be compared with the Greek satyrs, are, according to legend, descendants of King Faunus, the grandson of Saturn. However, they are only demigods and death is their final lot

Faun following the procession of Dionysus and playing a double flute (a strip of leather holding his cheeks). Taken from an ancient relief, National Archaeological Museum, Naples, photo Alinari-Giraudon.

after a long life. They are portrayed with small horns, a tail and goat's hooves.

FAUNUS. 1. This god is one of the oldest divinities of the Roman religion. The son of Picus and the grandson of Saturn, he was assigned a twofold power. On the one hand, as he is on familiar terms with the woods, cultivated plains and fresh flowing waters, he protects cultivation and watches over herds. On the other hand, much like Zeus of Dodona, he delivers oracles by rustling the branches of the trees. These rural functions have incited Roman artists to portray him as a bearded god, clad in a goat's skin, holding either the club typical of cattle herders or the horn of plenty, because he promotes the fertility of the fields. Furthermore it should come as no surprise that he was often identified with Pan, after the systematic Hellenization of the Roman gods. Eventually he assumed the same features as his Greek counterpart: horns on his forehead and goat's feet.

2. A barbaric king who killed Hercules also went by the name of **Faunus.**

FAUSTULUS. This shepherd, who perhaps watched over the flocks of Amulius, the king of Alba, played an important role in the Roman legend of Romulus and Remus. Indeed, having followed a wolf whose gentleness intrigued him, he found the twins in her lair and took them to his small home, entrusting them to his wife Acca Larentia who raised them. Faustulus told the two brothers of their origin. Romulus, knowing that he belonged to a line of gods and kings, killed Amulius who had usurped power. But when the two brothers began to quarrel, Faustulus, it is said, tried to intervene and was killed in the struggle. Later the Romans, grateful for what he had done, placed him in their Pantheon. The cottage of Faustulus was supposed to have been preserved on the Palatine.

FECUNDITY. The principal goddess of Fecundity, Bona Dea was invoked and worshiped during the mysteries strictly reserved for Roman women. These matrons either thanked the goddess for having granted them numerous children or, if they were sterile, they asked the goddess to make them mothers. The Roman

A Roman relief that is the very image of fecundity and fertility, with the three elements that are indispensable to all life: air, at left, symbolized by a swan; earth, center, with voluptuous contours, suckling two spirits; on her lap, fruits and leaves; at her feet, a cow and a lamb; at right, under a sort of fantastic fish, fertilizing water flows. Detail of a relief, "Ara Pacis" (Altar of Peace), National Museum, Rome, photo Anderson-Giraudon.

empresses, for their part, dedicated a special cult to the allegorical goddess Fecundity, whom they asked for many descendants to ensure the perpetuity of the Roman State. Domestic animals and cattle were also placed under the protection of gods like Faunus or Pales, who ensured their rapid and abundant reproduction.

FELICITAS. This goddess belongs to a group of numerous Roman allegorical divinities. Her image is found on coins. She is portrayed as a corpulent woman holding the caduceus of Hermes and a horn of plenty: one symbolizing health, the other affluence, two indispensable elements of happiness.

FERONIA. Of Etruscan origin, this ancient Italian divinity was venerated at Terracina, near Mount Soracte. Among the divinities of fields and woods, she assured fertility, although her powers are obscure.

fertility. Famines were always a source of fear in Antiquity. Rain and moisture, the abundance of the harvest, were always crucial to the survival of civilization at this era. The Romans in particular, who for quite a long time preferred agriculture to trade, had many gods of Vegetation and Fertility. They worshiped Ceres, goddess of the Harvest; Priapus, god of Gardens and Orchards; Ops and Copia, the divinities of Abundance; Flora, who favored the fertility of flowers; Pomona, who permitted fruits to ripen. They asked all of these divinities for help and protection by placing their statues, symbols or emblems in the fields and dedicating festivals to them on a set date.

FIDES. This personification of fidelity to a promise finds its place among the Roman divinities with abstract characters that grew in number during the course of Antiquity. Fides appeared at Jupiter's side, an old woman with white hair, as the guardian and guarantor of oaths. She bears witness to the fact that all law, all social order, depend on the respect of promises. When sacrifices were made to her the right hand was wrapped in white linen.

FLORA. Adored by the Sabines, Flora was the divinity of Flowers and Springtime. In order to explain these attributes, Ovid connected Flora with a Greek myth and identified her with the nymph Chloris, whom Zephyrus married, granting her all power over springtime blossoming. According to Ovid, she gave Juno a flower that could make a woman fertile simply by being touched by her. Thus Juno, without the help of Jupiter, became the mother of Mars; and it is in memory of this birth, in which Flora had indirectly taken part, that the Romans call the first month of Springtime "March."

flute. Along with the lyre, the flute is the prin-

With a delicate hand, Flora gathers flowers in the field, whose blossoming she promotes, and places the bouquet in a cone-shaped basket resembling the horn of plenty. Fresco from Pompeii, National Archaeological Museum, Naples, photo Anderson-Giraudon.

cipal musical instrument of the Ancients. Unlike the modern flute, it was a reed instrument: "clarinet" or "oboe" would be a more exact designation. The Ancients claimed that it had been invented by Hermes to distract him in his loneliness and boredom. Apollo, charmed by the melodious sounds that emerged from this rustic instrument, traded it for a golden wand, the caduceus, and became a skillful flute player. Marsyas learned it and tried to compete with the god; he was skinned alive. Another type of flute, the syrinx, was held horizontally against the mouth; this had been fashioned by Pan from a reed, the form of which had been assumed by a nymph whom he was pursuing.

FONS (FONTUS). The son of Janus, Fons was generally worshiped as the god of Springs and flowing Waters.

foreign gods. As the Greeks and Romans extended their domination or influence throughout the Mediterranean, their Pantheon welcomed foreign gods in ever-increasing numbers. Certain gods were simply assimilated, like Anubis, the Egyptian god, who took on the characteristics and powers of Hermes; or Dusares, the sun god of the Arabs, who became confused with Dionysus. Certain other gods provided an additional surname to one of the divinities of Olympus, such as Dolichenus, an Asiatic god, whose name was sometimes attached to that of Jupiter. Also known are gods such as Horus, goddesses such as Astargatis, who took on new names for the Greeks and Romans: the first became known as Harpocrates while the second assumed the name of Dea Syria. Sometimes the Romans adored foreign gods under their original names: this was the case for Mithras and Elagabalus. However, in spite of these transformations and assimilations, the Romans exhibited a constant respect for foreign gods, and avoided stripping them of their original powers. Both out of religious concern as well as political conviction, they realized that by adopting the gods of the territories they took over, they would ensure the loyalty of the inhabitants to the laws of Rome.

FORNAX. This Latin name meaning "oven" referred to a divinity that presided over the baking of bread. She was worshiped, in particular, during the festival of the Fornacalia.

FORTUNA. Without a doubt, there has never been a divinity that was so feared by the Romans, who identified her with the Greek goddess Tyche. The goddess of blind Luck and Chance, she offers mortals, according to her whims, wealth or poverty, power or subservience. Presiding over all of life's events, she holds all power over men. Holding a horn of plenty and a rudder, because she guides the affairs of the world, Fortuna, her face veiled, is

One of the numerous Roman allegorical divinities, the goddess Fortuna holds the horn of Amalthea which distributes an abundance of fruits, vegetables and grain, indispensable to the wealth of Rome. Here, however, she does not have the somewhat frightening look of seriousness generally given her in legends. Marble found in Ostia, Vatican Museum, photo Anderson-Giraudon.

invoked by men (*Fortuna virilis*), by women (*Fortuna muliebris*), by travelers, by horsemen, and by all those exercising an activity that is subject to uncertainty or danger: in the most famous sanctuaries, such as Antium or Praeneste, the Ancients, trembling, listened to her deliver her oracles.

FRAUD. Allegorical divinity of the Underworld, the incarnation of perjury, Fraud lived in the waters of the Cocytus where she hid her monstrous body, with its serpent's tail, showing only her face which was hypocritically kindly and gentle. Artists often portrayed her with two heads and the mask of deceit.

FRIENDSHIP. An allegorical divinity honored both in Greece and in Rome, Friendship was represented with the features of a young woman whose robe was half-fastened on the side and who wore a crown of flowers or myrtle branches and held in one hand a vine branch laden with grapes.

FURIES. These demons of the Underworld, inspired by the Etruscan divinities of the Underworld, occupied an important place in the Roman religion, but their origin, name and worship were all borrowed from the three Greek Erinyes.

FURRINA. This very ancient Roman divinity was either a nymph of one of the springs of the Tiber, which bore her name, or was identified with one of the Furies.

G

GAIA. According to the cosmogeny of Hesiod, Gaia personifies the Earth as it was formed. Immediately after Chaos, Gaia one day emerged from the void and gave birth to a son, Uranus. With him, she formed the first divine couple, bringing into the world a generation of gods and monsters: the Titans (she acquired from them the name of Titeia), the Titanids, the Cyclopes, the Hecatoncheiroi, the sea divinities—among whom were Nereus and Thaumas whom she conceived by one of her sons, Pontus, the wave. She helped Cronus castrate his father by providing him with a sickle. Other divinities joined with Gaia, among whom was Tartarus to whom she bore the terrible Typhon. She is also believed to have given birth to the Harpies, Python and Charybdis. Gaia, Mother Earth, fertile origin of everything, lost no time gaining considerable importance in Greek and Roman worship. A Homeric hymn celebrates her as the protective divinity of the Fertility of the soil, because of her many children, the multiplication of human beings. Demeter, the goddess of the Harvest, is often associated with her. Identified with Tellus by the Romans, Gaia became, during the classical era, a Chthonian divinity.

GALATEA. Polyphemus loved Galatea, who was born of Doris and Nereus. But the ugliness of the Cyclops was so repulsive that the Nereid fled whenever he came near her. She preferred Acis, a young Sicilian shepherd. Touching up this legend, a Greek satirist claimed that Galatea's disdain changed to prudent kindness when she learned that the Cyclops was the son of Poseidon. Some people even claim that Galatea yielded to the desires of Polyphemus and bore him three sons—Galus, Celtus and Illyrius.

GALEOTES. Apollo, his father, during one of his voyages to the land of the Hyperboreans, had transmitted to Galeotes the gift of divination. Galeotes, in turn, emigrated to Sicily where he founded in the city of Hybla, which took the name of *Galeotes*, the famous race of soothsayers on the island—the Galeotae.

games. During the Homeric era, the games were only matches, whether poetic or athletic, during which heroes entered into competition for pleasure, to obtain the hand of a woman or possession of a throne, or to honor the memory of warriors or heroes who had died in battle. Thus the *Iliad* tells at length of the funerary games given by Achilles to honor Patroclus, killed in the Trojan War. More recent and quite different were the public games which appeared toward the middle of the 6th century and which took place on a set date. They were not reserved exclusively for the aristocracy, but, marked by a feeling of religious worship, they were always quite popular among the people. Every four years, in fact, in Olympia, in the sacred arena of Altis, the Olympic games were held. These were, without a doubt, the most famous games and were founded by Heracles to commemorate his victory over Augeas. For the duration of the games, all hostilities among Greeks were to be suspended. The Pythian games, held in Delphi, every four years as well, commemorated the victory of Apollo over the serpent Python. As the god was principally the patron of music and the arts, the most popular events were the song and dance competitions. Meanwhile, the Nemean games took place every two years. They were founded either by Heracles, who had just killed the Nemean lion, or by Adrastus, one of the Seven Leaders, in memory of the accidental death of Opheltes, the son of one of the kings of the country. Finally, the Isthmian games, which took place in Corinth every three years, were organized for the first time by Poseidon in honor of Palemon-Melicertes, or by Sisyphus, or else by Poseidon and Helios, who thereby sealed their agree-ment on the possession of the Isthmus by the former and Acrocorinth by the latter. It is also claimed that the true founder of the Isthmian games was Theseus.

Other games, with even more overt political and religious characters, took place regularly in Greece, such as the Panathenaean festivals, which each year assembled all Greeks of Attica to worship the goddess collectively and to permit the city of Athens to reaffirm its power and unity. During the classical era, one of the goals of public games was this awareness, by the pilgrims who assembled in the sanctuaries of a god, of a single, united Greece.

GANYMEDE.   Without a doubt, the legend of Ganymede originated in Asia Minor. The son of Tros and Callirhoë, the young Ganymede was known for his beauty. Zeus fell in love with him and changed himself into an eagle so that he could take him in his claws and carry him up into the heavens. Having been granted immortality, Ganymede sometimes assisted Hebe in her task, pouring ambrosia for the gods.

The young cupbearer, Ganymede, with whom all of the gods are smitten, pours hydromel and the beverages of immortality into the cup that Zeus extends to him, in the midst of the relaxation and general joyfulness of the other divinities, including Athena, who has removed her helmet as a sign of peace. Detail of a cup, National Museum, Tarquinia, photo Alinari-Giraudon.

Geryon. Here, the picture clearly depicts the three helmeted heads of the winged giant along with the three shields and the three arms that brandish spears. To conquer this formidable mass of flesh and bronze, Heracles used only a bow, a weapon that, admittedly, in his hands was deadly. Chalcidian amphora, photo Giraudon.

genius. Portrayed in the form of a serpent, the specific animal of the underworld, Genius symbolizes for the Romans the spiritual and living strength of men, of emperors (the Genius of the Emperor), and of gods (the Genius of Jupiter). Indeed, every living being is accompanied by his Genius, an individual divinity that accompanies him from birth until the end of his days, protecting all his actions, and blessing especially the phenomena of generation and death.

GERYON. A monster with three heads and three bodies, Geryon was the son of Chrysaor and Callirhoë. He reigned over the island of Erythia, doubtless located near the strait of Gibraltar. He possessed magnificent oxen guarded by the shepherd Eurytion and by Orthrus, a ferocious two-headed dog. Upon his arrival at Erythia, Heracles began by strangling the shepherd and the dog, then crushing

Geryon himself to death. He was thus able to take hold of the herd and set out for Sicily with his precious booty.

GIANTS. After having conquered the Titans, Zeus, his brothers and his sisters were obliged to wage another battle against the Giants, born of the blood which flowed from the wounds of Uranus when he was castrated by Cronus. Immense colossi, their bodies ended in a serpent's tail; indomitably brave, they undertook to scale Olympus by piling up mountain upon mountain. In the face of this new danger, the gods enlisted the help of Prometheus, the son of Iapetus, and Heracles, because an oracle had pre-

The artist has tried to express the enormous turbulence of the struggle that pitted the gods of Olympus against the Giants. One of the Giants tries in vain to stop the quadriga of Zeus. Nothing seems to work against the vengeful fury of the gods who are attacking the Giants relentlessly. One of the divinities has seized one of the Giants by the hair and prepares to plunge her dagger into him. Amphora with red figures, originating in Melos, 5th cent. B.C., Louvre, photo Giraudon.

dicted that only a mortal could guarantee total victory for the gods. Heracles pushed away the mountains which tumbled down on top of the Giants, crushing them, while Zeus struck them with a bolt of lightning. Those who survived, such as Enceladus, were imprisoned in the depths of the earth.

GLAUCUS. 1. This sea-god, before becoming immortal, was but a lowly fisherman from Boeotia. One day as he was pulling his catch up onto the shore, he saw, to his great astonishment, that the fish were wriggling about and bounding successively back toward the sea, where they disappeared. Glaucus had placed them on a magic patch of grass that had been sown by Cronus. He swallowed a few blades of grass and felt himself drawn by the sea, into which he plunged. Tethys and the Nereids purified him of his mortal exterior and Glaucus assumed the features of a dignified old man whose beard and hair were the color of the sea and whose body was covered with seaweed and ended with a fish's tail. He delivered oracles which were respectfully heeded by all seamen. He also played a part in the expedition of the Argonauts on whose side he found himself in the struggle against the Tyrrhenians.

2. Another **Glaucus,** the king of Ephyre, the future Corinth, was the son of Sisyphus and the father of Bellerophon. He was known in his kingdom for his equestrian skills. As he wanted to make his horses stronger, he prevented their mating. Aphrodite, vexed at this offense against the laws of nature, received permission from Zeus to punish the king. The goddess made the horses drink from a sacred spring and gave them the power to consume human flesh: thus, during the funerary games given in honor of Pelias, Glaucus was thrown from his chariot, torn apart and devoured by his own carnivorous steeds.

3. The son of Hippolochus, another **Glaucus,** great-grandson of the preceding Glaucus, is

known especially for his exploits during the Trojan War. One day, in combat, he met Diomedes, who was in the opposing camp. But they both realized that they were united by sacred bonds of hospitality since the grandfather of Diomedes had welcomed Bellerophon, the grandfather of Glaucus, to his palace and had given him gifts. The two warriors, on the battlefield, renewed the gesture of their ancestors and exchanged weapons. It is said that Glaucus, killed by Ajax, son of Telamon, was transported by the winds to Lycia where he founded the first generation of kings in that country.

4. It is said that yet another **Glaucus,** the son of Minos and Pasiphaë, was pursuing a mouse when he disappeared. Weary of looking for him, Minos learned from the oracle of Delphi that he who could give an interpretation of the daily metamorphosis of one of the cows of his herd, which changed from white to red and finally to black, would find his son and save him. A certain Polyeidus succeeded: "This fur," he said, "changes like the appearance of a mulberry as it ripens." He immediately discovered the body of little Glaucus who had drowned in a full jar of honey. Minos then locked up the wily soothsayer with the body of his son and ordered him to revive him. Polyeidus rubbed the young child's body with a magical herb brought to him by a serpent and Glaucus returned to life.

gods. Expressions of the force of nature, the gods also personify the qualities and faults of

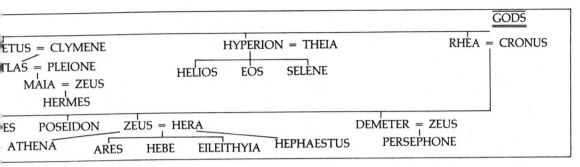

men whose appearance they assume while nonetheless retaining their immortality. The gods were, for the most part, born, under the general name of "Titans," of the cosmic union of two entities of the World, the heavens and the terrestrial crust. Then Cronus, Coeus and Oceanus begat the generation of gods who, after tremendous struggles with the primitive and anarchistic divinities, settled on Olympus. However, certain gods were created in a somewhat strange manner. Hephaestus was born of Hera alone, without the help of Zeus, her husband, while Athena emerged completely armed from the skull of Zeus without having been borne by any woman. What is more, Aphrodite, according to one of the legends, burst forth from the sea, while Dionysus was the product of the union of the mortal Semele and Zeus. Generally speaking, the gods born of nature itself could claim to govern it and direct it at will.

golden fleece. The famous ram with the golden fleece was a gift from Hermes to Nephele, the wife of Athamas, the king of Orchomenus in Boeotia. This ram was blessed with intelligence and reason, was able to speak, and could fly through the air at will. Phrixus, the son of Nephele, persecuted by his stepmother Ino, was able to flee with his sister Helle on the animal's back. When he arrived in Colchis, where Aeetes reigned, he married Chalciope, the king's daughter, and sacrificed the ram to Zeus. The god of gods, therefore, made the ani-

mal's fleece a token of prosperity and power, and Aeetes fastened this precious object to an oak in the wood of Ares. The golden fleece was later stolen by Jason and the Argonauts.

GORDIAS. An oracle had told the Phrygians, who were overwhelmed by domestic struggles and a vacancy on the throne, that they should proclaim as king whoever appeared on an ox-drawn chariot. Gordias appeared thus right before their very eyes: he was immediately proclaimed sovereign of Phrygia. King Gordias, as a sign of his gratitude, founded the city of Gordion, dedicated his chariot to Zeus, and tied a knot around his chariot that was so complicated that people predicted that whoever suc-

Accompanying Jason on his difficult journey to capture the Golden Fleece were many great Greek heroes including Heracles, Orpheus, Castor and Pollux. They were aided by Hera and Medea. Athenian vase, 5th cent. B.C., Metropolitan Museum of Art.

ceeded in undoing the knot would one day be proclaimed sovereign of Asia. During the 4th century B.C. Alexander the Great, while passing through Gordion, drew his sword and cut the "Gordion Knot."

GORGONS. The Gorgons were three sisters: Stheno, Euryale and Medusa, the daughters of Phorcys, whom Pontus had begotten, and Ceto, a daughter of Oceanus. Primitive divinities, they lived not far from the kingdom of Shad-

A grimacing face, turned up lips revealing an enormous tongue, immense eyes, extremely prominent cheekbones, flat nose, all contribute to making the Gorgon one of the most terrifying monsters in Greek mythology. Louvre, photo Giraudon.

ows, in unknown places. They were a terrifying sight. They had enormous heads with serpent hair, teeth as long as boar's snouts, golden wings that enabled them to sail through the air. Their huge eyes turned whoever looked at them to stone. Only Medusa, the most famous Gorgon, was mortal. She perished at the hand of Perseus.

GRAIAE. Their name means "old women" (Gr. *graiai*). Numbering three, Pephredo, Enyo and Dino were born of the union of Phorcys and Ceto, the parents of many other monsters. Decrepit, they had white hair and but one eye and one tooth among them, which they took turns using. Sisters of the Gorgons and responsible for guarding the route that led to their dwelling, the Graiae played a considerable role in the legend of Perseus and Medusa. The hero stripped them of their eye and tooth and, taking advantage of their slumber, managed to pass them unharmed. According to another version, Perseus refused to return their sight unless they told him where the nymphs had hidden the winged sandals and the helmet of Hades which made him invisible. Armed with these objects, he was able to chop off the head of Medusa.

griffins. Fabulous animals with the head of an eagle and the winged body of a lion, the griffins guarded the treasures of Apollo in the legendary country of the Hyperboreans, in Scythia. They often fought with a mythical people, the Arimaspians, who possessed only one eye each and incessantly sought to steal the treasures guarded by the monsters. This legend may have originated with the gold mines that are found in Russia, particularly in the Urals.

GYGES. This historical character, the king of Lydia (685–657 B.C.), was the subject of a certain number of fables. Gyges was but a modest shepherd in Lydia when one day he discovered in the flanks of a bronze horse a golden ring

Its clawed foot raised, with a crested neck, the body disappearing beneath immense wings, the griffin stands erect, ready to attack. Capital from the temple of Apollo in Miletus, Louvre, photo Giraudon.

that had the power to make the one who wore it invisible. An ambitious man, Gyges slipped it on his finger, went to King Candaulus, and brazenly murdered him. He acceded to the throne and married the queen. The king entrusted his riches to the Treasury of the Athenians in Delphi. One of the Hecatoncheiroi also bears the name of Gyges.

H

HADES. The son of Cronus and Rhea, Hades, after the division of the Universe into three parts, gained sovereign possession over the netherworld while his brother Zeus reigned over the heavens and Poseidon ruled the seas. The husband of Persephone, whom he abducted from Earth, stealing her away from her mother Demeter, Hades is a god who was dreaded by the Greeks. A merciless judge, he is seated on a throne in the depths of the Underworld and holds in his hand a scepter with which he governs, showing no pity, the souls of the dead who inhabit his somber and unknown kingdom. He wears on his head a helmet that makes him invisible; the Cyclopes gave it to him as a gift and he would sometimes lend it to legendary heroes to whom he had decided to give his help and protection. Surrounded by divinities of the Underworld, his servants, his messengers, he dictates the terrible law of death to the World. However, like his wife Persephone, the terrible goddess of the Underworld, who is nonetheless gentle with men on Earth, to whom she grants fertility and abundance in their harvests, Hades is sometimes known as *Pluton* ("the Distributor of wealth"). He is invoked by farmers and he is portrayed as a good-tempered god, holding in one hand a horn of plenty and, in the other, farming implements. During his stays on Earth, Hades always commits a few infidelities with mortals or

The god Hades, an inflexible old man, seated on his throne in the Underworld. Attributed to Bryaxis, 4th cent. B.C., Villa Borghese, Rome, photo G.F.N.

nymphs of plants and the woods.

The twofold symbol of Death and Life attributed to Hades is, in mythology, common to almost all of the major divinities of the Underworld.

HAEMON. **1.** This nephew of Jocasta's was one of the very first men devoured by the Sphinx of Thebes. Creon, his father, king of this city, was so heartbroken that he promised his kingdom to whoever killed the monster. In another legend, Haemon, still the son of Creon, was the fiancé of Antigone. When she was condemned to be buried alive, Haemon killed himself before the eyes of his father. A third tradition, followed by Euripides in a lost tragedy, shows Antigone and Haemon fleeing the palace of Creon. They had a son who returned to Thebes and took part in funerary games. Creon, recognizing him as his grandson, had him put to death. Wild with grief, Haemon killed his wife and then himself.

2. The son of Pelasgus, father of Thessalus, this **Haemon** lived in Haemonia, the land that took the name of *Thessaly* at his death.

HALIRRHOTIUS. This son of Poseidon and the nymph Euryte tried to rape Alcippe, the daughter of Ares and Aglauros. To defend her, the god of War killed him. Referred to Poseidon for judgment, Ares was presented to the tribunal of gods sitting on one of the hills in Athens. He was acquitted; the hill on which the trial took place later became the spot where the tribunal of Athens, the Areopagus, met.

HAMADRYADS. Like their sisters the Dryads, the Hamadryads chose the forests as their dwelling places and lived in unison with the tree of their choice, beneath its bark. But they thus surrendered their liberty and the death of the tree spelled the end of their existence as well. Furthermore, the woodsman was obliged to listen to their desperate pleas when he decided to fell a tree and yet was forced to

refrain from imitating Erysichthon who refused to allow himself to be moved and was severely punished by Demeter for his sacrilegious act and his hardness of heart.

HARMONIA. The offspring of the love of Ares and Aphrodite, Harmonia was married to Cadmus, who founded Thebes, and their wedding was celebrated by all the gods of Olympus. As gifts, Harmonia received a mantle woven by Athena and a necklace forged by the god Hephaestus. A curse was attached to these two gifts since those who possessed them perished tragically, especially the generation of Labdacids to whom Oedipus, the grandson of Harmonia, belonged. Eriphyle, Phegeus, Alcmaeon, Arsinoë and Callirhoë were also victims of the two objects. Begun in joy, the marriage of Harmonia and Cadmus was to end unhappily. Their children—Semele, Ino-Leucothea, Agave, Autonoë—and their grandchildren knew various misfortunes. However, when

This Harpy ferociously clasps a woman's body. Detail of a frieze found in the acropolis of Xanthus, Lycia, late 6th cent. B.C., British Museum, photo Mansell.

they died, Harmonia and her spouse were changed into serpents to compensate for their afflicted old age.

HARPIES. These daughters of Thaumas and the Oceanid Electra—Aello and Ocypete who were later joined by Celaeno—were considered by Hesiod to be winged women with beautiful hair; then, gradually, legend gave them the appearance of dreadful monsters. Their bony, vulturelike bodies, their wrinkled faces, their beaks, their hooked nails and the offensive odor they spread were sensitive representations of drought, famine and epidemics, but also the image of impossibly insatiable monsters who abduct children and carry away the dead to the Underworld. The gods did not destroy them

Hecate carries her traditional symbol, the great flame that lights the night. The dog that follows her was consecrated to her. Detail of a relief, 4th cent. B.C., British Museum, photo Boudot-Lamotte.

because they used their wickedness to torment mortals, such as the blind Phineus, whose food they stole and devoured. Pursued by the sons of Boreas, Zetes and Calais, they settled in the Strophades Islands. But their infernal role continued and the Latins identified them mainly with the Furies, the guardians of somber Tartarus.

HEBE. The Romans called this goddess *Juventus*. The daughter of Zeus and Hera, she distributed eternal youth and immortality by pouring nectar for the gods of Olympus. She was replaced in this sacred function by Ganymede. She married Heracles when he was received among the gods, and bore him two sons, Alexiares and Anicetus.

HECATE. The daughter of Perseus and Asteria, Hecate belongs to the first generation of gods. When the children of Cronus reigned under the supreme sovereignty of Zeus, Hecate

Hebe holds in one hand a container filled with nectar; in the other, she holds ambrosia. Detail of a vase, Jatta Museum, Ruvo di Puglia, photo Alinari.

Heavily armed and helmeted, Hector falls to the ground, wounded in the left thigh by Achilles who, naked and armed with only a dagger, prepares to deal the fatal blow to the Trojan hero. Athena, behind the Greek hero, ensures the victory of her protégé. Detail of a hydria, 5th cent. B.C., Vatican Museum, photo Alinari-Giraudon.

retained her former privileges and prerogatives. Considered in remote times to be a kindly goddess, Hecate distributed, in all things, material and spiritual wealth as well as victories both to mortals and to immortals and gods, who respected her and even feared her. Gradually, Hecate acquired a dreaded and evil nature. A messenger of demons and phantoms, followed by a howling mob, she positioned herself at the crossroads and dabbled in various magical operations and divinations. Portrayed as a three-headed divinity, the triple Hecate was sometimes identified with the three divinities Selene, Artemis and Persephone. Her statue was erected at the crossroads; people offered the goddess sacrifices and sought to curry favor by incantations.

HECATONCHEIROI. Giants with one hundred heads and one hundred arms, the Heca-toncheiroi—Cottus, Briareos and Gyes (or Gyges), the sons of Uranus and Gaia—took Zeus's side in the struggle pitting the gods against the Titans. The conquered Titans were thrown into the depths of Tartarus. As a sign of gratitude, the three Giants were entrusted with the care of the Titans.

HECTOR. Homer represents the eldest son of Priam and Hecuba as the most courageous and noblest hero of the Trojan War and depicts him as a model of solicitude toward his wife Andromache, the daughter of the king of Thebes of Mysia, and toward his son Astyanax. An oracle had predicted that Troy would not be defeated as long as Hector remained alive. Thus, the hero basked in the confidence and reverence of his fellow Trojans. Protected by Apollo, he emerged victorious from numerous single combats. But, when Hector had killed

Patroclus, Achilles, overwhelmed with sorrow at the death of his friend, called the hero to a duel. Hecuba and Priam begged their son to avoid the combat. But Hector, yielding to fate and hoping, as usual, for the help of the gods, accepted the challenge of Achilles. The two warriors began their pursuit of one another around the city. Athena, better to trick Hector, took on the form of Deiphobus (one of Hector's favorite brothers) and urged the hero to engage in battle; then she abandoned him to his fate while Apollo also ceased to protect Hector who began to realize that all was lost. He fell, his throat pierced by the sword of Achilles, and, dying, he begged his victorious enemy to grant him a burial. The Greek hero refused this last favor. Hector, therefore, predicted his imminent death. After making a hole in his ankles to pass a strip of leather through them, Achilles attached the body of his unfortunate victim to his chariot and rode thus several times around the city of Troy amidst the laments of all the Trojans. However, on the order of Zeus, who inspired moderation in him, the hero let himself be tempted by the wealth and pleas of Priam and returned the beloved son to his father. For having preferred death to slavery, Hector remained in Antiquity a model of filial and marital piety as well as an example of generosity and courage.

HECUBA. The daughter of Dymas, the king of Phrygia, or the daughter of Cisseus, the king of Thrace, depending on the tradition, Hecuba married Priam, the sovereign of Troas, and gave birth to many children who were all to attain tragic fame in the Trojan War: Hector, Creusa, Paris, Laodicea, Polyxena, Deiphobus, Helenus, Pammon, Polites, Antiphus, Hipponous, Polydorus, Troilus, Cassandra. Since a soothsayer predicted that Paris would bring destruction upon the city of Troy, Hecuba exposed the child; but Paris managed to survive and return to his native city where he was wel-

Hecuba, the wife of Priam, welcomes Helen, who is to marry her son, Paris. Detail of an Attic cup, Louvre, photo Giraudon.

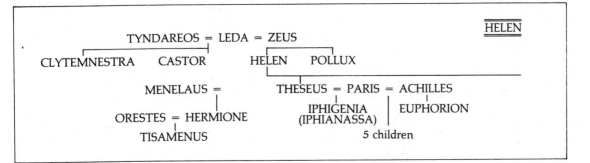

```
                 TYNDAREOS = LEDA = ZEUS                          HELEN
        ┌──────────────┴──────┐        ┌───────┴───────┐
   CLYTEMNESTRA      CASTOR        HELEN      POLLUX
                                    │
        MENELAUS =              THESEUS = PARIS = ACHILLES
              │                   IPHIGENIA   │  EUPHORION
   ORESTES = HERMIONE            (IPHIANASSA) │
              │                              5 children
          TISAMENUS
```

comed with joy by his father Priam. Although Hecuba plays but a modest role in the legend, the unhappiness that overwhelmed her, the massacre of her children, almost right before her eyes, her solitude as well as her firmness of spirit all imbued her with an indisputable grandeur: after the fall of Troy, while she was chosen as a slave by Ulysses, she saw on the shore the body of her son Polydorus whom she had entrusted, along with considerable treasures, to the king of Chersonnesus, Polymestor. Hecuba decided to take revenge; she summoned the traitor king, gouged out his eyes, and killed his two sons. Pursued by the companions of the king who wanted to put her to death, just as she was about to be stoned she was changed into a dog and leaped into the sea in a place called *Cynossema* ("the dog's tomb").

HELEN. The daughter of Zeus, Helen was born of an egg laid by her mother Leda; but her official father was Tyndareos, the king of Sparta, and her brothers were the Dioscuri. However, her destiny was so ill-omened for the Greeks that some traditions consider Nemesis, the goddess of Vengeance, to be her mother. The character of Helen, one of the most famous in Greek mythology, was the subject of so many versions, commentaries and interpretations over the course of Antiquity that it is difficult to distinguish the original characters of the legend.

Helen was endowed with all the gifts that beauty confers and was the object of the desires of many heroes. Theseus took her by force to Attica and, before leaving for the Underworld, he married her. The young woman was rescued, in the absence of her husband, by the Dioscuri and was given in marriage to

The Greek Helen, gently restrained by Paris, who is seen wearing a Phrygian cap, steps into the boat that will take her to Troy. Helen seems perfectly happy and shows barely a sign of terror as would be expected of a woman who was being abducted. Greek relief, Lateran Museum, photo Giraudon.

Menelaus, one of some hundred suitors who vied for her hand and were committed to back up the chosen one if an outrage were committed against him. By this second marriage, she had a daughter, Hermione. But Helen, more beautiful every day, won the heart of Paris who abducted her, not completely against her wishes, and took her to Troy. True to their oath, all of the suitors decided to avenge the affront suffered by the Greeks at the hands of the Trojans. An interminable war began. Later traditions tried to absolve Helen of any guilt for her behavior, and claimed that only her phantom was taken to Troy while she herself stayed out the war in Egypt where Hermes had transported her; it was there that she was reunited with Menelaus. At the death of Paris, she married Deiphobus. But she did not hesitate to betray her husband, and during the sack of Troy she delivered him to Menelaus, with whom she became reconciled. After many adventures, both returned to Sparta and finally reigned over the city in happiness and peace. Helen, whose grace had disarmed many a fearless hero and many an indomitable enemy, had, according to some versions, a worthy end to her exceptional destiny: as Proteus had predicted in the *Odyssey*, the gods granted her immortality and the favor of living eternally in the company of Menelaus in the Elysian Fields. According to another version, after disappearing from Earth, she married Achilles, one of the rare heroes who, because of his youth, was not among her suitors. Their wedding took place on the island of the Blest, White Island, and they were blessed with the birth of a winged son, Euphorion, who several years later disdained the love of Zeus and was thunderstruck. The version of Pausanias was even more dramatic. After the death of Menelaus, Helen took refuge in Rhodes. But Polyxo, who welcomed her to the island, was despairing over the death of her husband Tlepolemus in Troy, blamed Helen for this misfortune, and drove her to commit suicide.

HELENUS. The son of Priam and Hecuba and twin brother of Cassandra, who taught him the art of divination, Helenus fought at the side of his brother Hector against the Greeks. When Priam refused him the hand of Helen, he fled and sought refuge on Mount Ida where he was captured by Ulysses. He thus betrayed his fatherland and revealed to the Greeks the conditions necessary for victory. After the fall of Troy, he became the counselor and soothsayer of Neoptolemus who, assassinated by Orestes, left him the kingdom of Epirus and Andromache, by whom he had one son, Cestrinus.

HELIADES. 1. The daughters of Helios and the nymph Clymene, one of the most beautiful of the Oceanids, the Heliades generally number three: Lampetia, Phaethusa and Phoebe. After the death of Phaethon, their brother, they wept over his remains on the banks of the river Eridanus for four months. The gods, showing compassion at the keenness of their sorrow, changed them into white poplars and changed their tears into drops of amber. This brilliant material, which has the brightness of the sun and the transparency of a tear, found in this fable a mythical justification for its prominence in trade.

2. The seven sons of Helios also bear this name. They were worshiped in Rhodes, the birthplace of their mother, the nymph Rhodos, and they were known for their knowledge of astrology.

HELICON. This famous mountain range in Boeotia, not far from the gulf of Corinth, was the privileged abode of Apollo and his procession of Muses. The Aganippe and Hippocrene springs burst forth there.

HELIOS. The son of Hyperion and Theia, the brother of Eos and Selene, Helios was the divine representation of the Sun, heat and solar light. The husband of Perseis, he had several children who played an important role in legends, namely Aeetes, who was involved in the legend of the Argonauts, and Pasiphaë during the reign of Minos in Crete. Moreover, the nymph Rhodos bore him seven sons and the Oceanid Clymene, seven daughters, the Heliades, and one son, Phaethon.

Never confused with Apollo in early legends, Helios is not one of the great Greek gods. He is, above all, the servant of Zeus. Each day, ensconced in his golden chariot, he completes a course across the skies; in the evening he rests in the West, just north of the Ocean, on the island of the Blest. Strikingly beautiful, his forehead encircled by a crown made of golden rays, Helios is the only god who can take in the entire Earth with a single glance and he informs the gods of Olympus on all that is happening below. He informed Hephaestus of Aphrodite's infidelity with Ares, and alerted Demeter to the abduction of her daughter Core (Persephone) by Hades. He also appears in the legend of Ulysses; when the companions of the hero devoured part of his sacred herd in Sicily, Helios demanded that Zeus avenge him, dealing an exemplary punishment, and the sovereign god mercilessly struck down the impious creatures. In the Greek Pantheon, he occupies a humble place; however, the idea he evokes, namely that of the Sun, in the center of the world, distributing the light and warmth that are essential to life, in opposition to the darkness and death, assumed an important place at the close of the age of Antiquity, to such a point, in fact, that the Sun god, known by various names (Mithras, Sol Santissimus, Sol Invictus, Elagabalus) became the essential, if not unique, god of the paganism that was nearing its end.

HELLE.   The daughter of Athamas and Nephele, Helle managed to flee with her brother

In a quadriga drawn by fiery steeds, Helios takes off for the skies. He wears a crown of luminous rays; his slightly fleshy face expresses both the grandiose nobility and the sovereign strength of light of which he is the most noble representation. Greek relief, Berlin Museum, photo Giraudon.

Phrixus, who had been promised as a sacrifice, on a ram with golden fleece which bore them away through the air. She fell into the sea, near Chersonnesus, in the strait that has since been known as the *Hellespont*. Her brother, however, arrived unharmed in Colchis.

HELLEN.   The son of Deucalion and Pyrrha, Hellen, the king of Phthia, was considered by all Greeks (Hellenes) to be their father. Legend attributes three sons to him, namely Dorus, Aeolus and Xuthus, born of the nymph Orseis, the mythical ancestors of all Greeks. Dorus and Aeolus founded the Dorians and Aeolians, respectively. Furthermore, the two sons of

Xuthus—Achaeus and Ion—gave rise to the Achaeans and the Ionians.

HEPHAESTUS. The son of Zeus and Hera, according to one version, but according to another the son only of Hera, who conceived him alone, without the help of her husband, because she was jealous that Athena was born of Zeus without having spent time in the womb. Hephaestus had a gnomic appearance and was particularly hideous as he was lame in both legs. It is even said, in connection with this, that Zeus threw him down from Olympus for daring to side with Hera in a quarrel; he landed on the island of Lemnos and was lame for the rest of his days because of this incident. It is also said that Hera, disgusted at having given birth to such an ugly son, threw him from the skies into the sea where, for nine years, he was raised by Tethys. He was the spouse of several goddesses but the most famous was Aphrodite who was often unfaithful to him, particularly with Ares. Helios reported this adultery to Hephaestus who, in revenge, surprised the two lovers in the act and imprisoned them in a net, making them appear ridiculous to all the other gods of Olympus.

The god of Fire and the very divine personification of fire, Hephaestus quickly became the god of Metallurgy and the official blacksmith of the gods and heroes. Set up, according to later traditions, in the depths of volcanoes or volcanic islands such as Hiera and Imbros, assisted by the Cyclopes and the Cabeiri, Hephaestus, with consummate and inimitable skill and genius, made the armor of Achilles, the trident of Poseidon, the breastplate of Heracles, the weapons of Peleus, the scepter and aegis of Zeus. He also fashioned a magical throne from which Hera was unable to stand up because he wanted to take revenge on his mother for having abandoned him; but he soon agreed to free the goddess provided she promise that he be reintegrated into the assembly of gods of

In this archaic representation, Hephaestus does not yet appear with the features of a god whose ugliness was later to become legendary. Here he expresses the power and even the radiance of fire which is indispensable to the flourishing of life. Archaic Greek art, Barracco Museum, Rome, photo Alinari-Giraudon.

Olympus. Identified by the Romans with their Italic god Vulcan, Hephaestus was portrayed either as a dwarf, whose statue was placed in front of the hearth to retain the strength of the flame, or, more generally, as a robust old man with a full beard, somewhat wild looking, his head covered with the oval cap of a blacksmith, and holding a hammer.

HERA. The daughter of Cronus and Rhea, Hera was raised by Oceanus and Tethys before becoming the wife of Zeus whose sister she also was. Jealous and vindictive, she is known in legends for the many quarrels that pitted her against her divine husband, whose constant infidelity she deplored. So, to avenge herself, she relentlessly persecuted the children that Zeus had with mortals: Europa, Io, Dionysus, Heracles, just to mention the most famous, were among the victims of her anger. One day, to prevent Zeus from descending to Earth to join one of his paramours, Hera, along with Poseidon and Athena, devised the scheme of chaining up her husband. But Zeus foiled the plan and temporarily hung his wife by the hair from a ring attached to the clouds, after having tied her hands and feet. However, the irascible couple was seen to be reconciled for short periods. Zeus was, therefore, the father of four legitimate children, namely Ares, Hebe, Hephaestus and Eileithyia. Meanwhile, Hera often meddled in the affairs of mortals. She was often seen supporting the Greeks against the Trojans to take revenge on Paris who did not grant her the golden apple, which would have declared her to be the most beautiful of all goddesses, but gave it instead to Aphrodite. She also protected the *Argo* during the expedition of the Argonauts, especially during the dangerous passage through the planktae (the wandering rocks). She was sometimes the object of attention for mortals, such as the Giant Porphyrion and Ixion. Zeus, demonstrating that he was even more jealous than she, struck down the first and snatched Hera away from the second in the form of a wave.

The only married goddess among all the feminine divinities of Olympus, Hera enjoys certain privileges and is treated with constant respect. She thus appears in the eyes of the Greeks as the goddess of legitimate marriages, the protectress of the fertility of the couple and, in particular, with Eileithyia, she protects women in childbirth. In literature as in art, she is depicted with the traditional royal symbols: the scepter and the diadem; her veiled head is the symbol of marriage. Sometimes, she even holds in one of her hands a pomegranate, the symbol of fertility. The peacock is the animal

With the attitude of a submissive wife, Hera approaches her husband Zeus who has grasped her wrist. Here, Hera embodies the married woman rather than the jealous and irascible goddess of the legends. Metope from the temple of Selinus, National Archaeological Museum, Palermo, photo Anderson-Giraudon.

that is sacred to her in memory of Argos, whose one hundred eyes she took, when he was killed, and placed on the bird's plumage. Hera may not, however, claim the title of queen of the gods and men: she is simply the unanimously worshiped spouse of the supreme god.

HERACLES. One of the most famous heroes of Greek mythology, Heracles was the son of Zeus and Alcmene, a descendant of Perseus. The supreme god begat him in the absence of Amphitryon, the legitimate spouse of Alcmene. After nine months, the jealous Hera made Zeus promise that any descendant of Perseus who

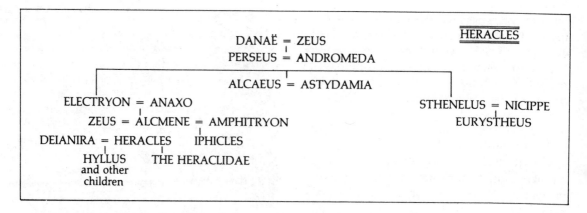

would be born the following night would have immense power over men. The goddess hurried to Mycenae and allowed Nicippe, the wife of Sthenelus, also a descendant of Perseus, to give birth to a son, Eurystheus, before Alcmene gave birth to Heracles. Thus, the latter was deprived of his rights. Hera continued her work of vengeance. She sent two serpents to the cradle of the newborn; but while Iphicles, the twin brother of Heracles and son of Amphitryon, fled horrified, the future hero, without losing his composure, strangled the monsters, thus proving that he was of divine stock. During his infancy, Heracles received a choice education: he learned from Amphitryon the art of driving a chariot; from Eurytus, the way to handle a bow; from Linus, the way to sing and play the lyre. He was then assigned to guard the herds of Amphitryon and began his series of exploits by killing the lion of Cithaeron that was ravaging his father's kingdom and that of King Thespius; as a reward, the latter granted the hero the favors of his fifty daughters. Then Heracles fought and killed Erginus, the king of Orchomenus, who exacted a heavy tribute from the people of Thebes. Creon, the king of Thebes, gave him the hand of his daughter Megara. But Hera, whose wrath was still not appeased, drove Heracles mad and the hero slaughtered his own children. In despair at having committed these involuntary crimes, he sought refuge with Theseus, who purified him. On the advice of Pythia, he went to Tiryns to atone for his crimes and was pressed into the service of Eurystheus who imposed the Twelve Labors upon him. If the twelve labors were accomplished victoriously, and once twelve years had passed, the hero would be able to dream of being granted immortality.

1. *Struggle against the Nemean lion:* This dreadful beast, the product of the love of Echidna and Typhon, was terrorizing the Nemean valley. Heracles, having tried in vain to fell the animal with his arrows and club, finally strangled the animal with his bare hands; he skinned the animal and covered himself with the hide so that arrows could not pierce him.

2. *Struggle against the Hydra of Lerna:* Sent by Hera, this monster with nine poisonous serpents' heads was ravaging the country of Lerna, near Argos; Heracles cut off the heads one by one and buried the one that was immortal under an enormous rock.

3. *Capture of the Erymanthian boar:* Heracles had received orders from Eurystheus not to kill the animal, which lived on Mt. Erymanthus in Arcadia; the hero spent many long months pursuing it. He received the hospitality of the centaur Pholus but, during a discussion, he became involved in a struggle with the centaurs

Fearlessly, the newborn Heracles has seized the serpent sent by Hera to kill him. Compare this calm assurance with the fear of Iphicles, the twin brother of Heracles, at the sight of the same serpent (see p. 146). Heracles already proves himself to be the son of a god. Capitoline Museum, Rome, photo Anderson-Giraudon.

and killed a good number of them. Afterwards, the hero found the tracks of the boar, which he caught in a net. At the sight of the beast, Eurystheus was so frightened that he hid in a barrel.

4. *Capture of the Ceryneian hind:* This magical hind, which had golden horns and hooves of bronze, was pursued for a year by Heracles, but in vain. Finally, the hero managed to wound the animal with one of his arrows and, placing it on his shoulders, brought it back alive to Eurystheus.

5. *Destruction of the Stymphalian birds:* Immense eagles with beaks and claws of bronze, these birds lived on human flesh and spread terror through the Lake Stymphalus region in Arcadia. With the help of Athena, who gave him the cymbals that frightened the birds of prey,

Heracles was able to shoot them down with his arrows.

6. *Cleaning of the Augean stables:* Again on the order of Eurystheus, Heracles cleaned the enormous stables of Augeas, the king of Elis, by diverting the courses of the Alpheus and the Peneus. The king who, beforehand, had promised him a tenth of his cattle, refused to grant him this reward. Heracles was forced to kill him and all his sons, except Phyleus, who had had the courage to testify in his behalf.

7. *Capture of the Cretan bull:* Poseidon had driven mad a white bull that Minos, the king of Crete, had refused to sacrifice to him, and the animal was devastating the crops of the island and threatening the inhabitants with famine. The hero succeeded in capturing it by the horns, overwhelming it, and bringing it back unharmed to Eurystheus in Greece. There, the bull was set loose and was finally captured by Theseus at the gates of Marathon.

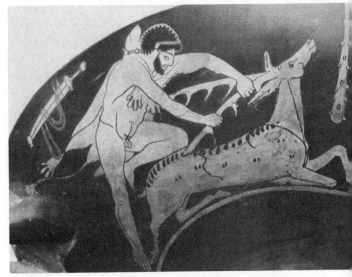

Using only the strength of his wrists, Heracles manages to overwhelm the Ceryneian hind by seizing one of its horns. The attitude of the hero illustrates the power and elegance in strength. Detail from a Greek cup, Louvre, photo Giraudon.

Heracles has laid down his quiver, bow and breastplate to attack the Nemean lion bare-handed. He has lifted the animal up and is plunging his hands into the mane of the beast to strangle it. The half-strangled animal sticks out its tongue while its enormous feet seem paralyzed and hang with no movement whatsoever. Silver platter from the Treasures of Bernay, Bibl. Nat., photo Giraudon.

8. *Capture of the mares of Diomedes in Thrace:* With the help of his companion Abderus, Heracles was instructed to seize the mares of Diomedes, the king of the Bistonians, which fed on human flesh. During one combat, Diomedes was killed by the hero and his remains were thrown to the man-eating animals which had just devoured the unfortunate Abderus. Appeased, the animals were delivered to Eurystheus, who in turn had them destroyed by the ferocious beasts on Mount Olympus.

9. *Seizing of the belt of the Amazon queen:* This magical belt, a gift from Ares, adorned the waist of Hippolyta, queen of the Amazons. Heracles, welcomed warmly at first by the queen, was finally obliged to kill her in order to seize the precious object. Upon his return, the hero delivered Hesione, who was about to be devoured by a sea monster. But, as he did not receive as his reward the two horses of Laomedon, king of Troy and father of the young girl, which had been promised him, Heracles vowed to take revenge.

10. *Capture of the cattle of Geryon:* This giant lived in a country somewhere in the West, beyond the known limits of the Earth. Heracles departed on his expedition, passed through the strait of Gibraltar, erecting two pillars there to leave some trace of his passage. But, overwhelmed by the heat, the hero threatened Helios with his arrows. To appease him, the Sun gave him a golden boat that enabled him to cross the Ocean. Thus Heracles killed Geryon and the guardians of the cattle and took hold of the herd. He then returned by way of Gaul, Italy and Thrace to the territory of Eurystheus, who sacrificed all of the animals to Hera.

11. *The golden apples of the Hesperides:* These marvelous fruits, which Hera had received for her marriage to Zeus, were guarded by nymphs and a dragon in an enchanted garden. After learning from Nereus the route to take, Heracles temporarily took the place of the giant Atlas, who supported the weight of the world, and asked him to bring back the apples. The giant returned some time later with the fruits but refused to take back his load. However, Heracles managed to flee with the apples, thanks to a trick, and the fruits were offered up to Athena.

12. *Abduction of Cerberus from the Underworld:* This was the last and most dangerous of all the missions that Heracles accomplished. With the help of Hermes and Athena, the hero descended into the kingdom of Shadows from which no mortal had ever returned alive. He took advantage of this journey to free Theseus, who had been immobilized for some time on the Chair of Forgetfulness, and managed to take hold of Cerberus and bring him to Argolis. Terrified, Eurystheus had him return the monster to the Underworld immediately.

After these labors, Heracles was able to return to Thebes. He gave Megara, his first wife, to Iolaus; he then defeated King Eurytus at a bow and arrow match but did not receive Iole, the daughter of the king, who had been promised to him if he were the victor. Furious, he killed Iphitus, the son of the king, and was forced, to be totally cleansed of the crime, to work as a slave in the service of Omphale, the queen of Lydia. She humiliated the hero by forcing him, according to a somewhat romanticized version of the legend, to spin yarn at her feet. But it is also said that Heracles had certain freedoms to take part in other activities; thus, he participated in the Calydonian Boar Hunt and in the expedition of the Argonauts. Delivered from the yoke of Omphale, he left for Troy and killed Laomedon as he had vowed he would. He then lent his services to the gods of Olympus in their struggle against the Giants, and afterwards took revenge on Augeas who had refused to pay him his wages; fought King Neleus, who had refused to purify him; undertook an expedition against Sparta, where Hippocoon reigned; and accomplished a host of other exploits. He then went to Calydon where he married Deianira, first being obliged to fight one of her suitors, the river-god Acheloüs. However, having accidentally killed the young Eunomus, one of the pages of his father-in-law Oeneus, he was again forced into exile with Deianira. During this journey, the centaur Nessus tried to rape Deianira and Heracles mortally wounded him with his arrows. The centaur, dying, offered the hero's wife a poisoned potion. Settled in Trachis, Heracles carried out his last act of vengeance by killing King Eurytus and all of his sons and finally taking possession of Iole. At this news, Deianira poured the potion on a tunic, thinking that the hero, if he put it on, would remain forever faithful to her, as Nessus had assured her. But the garment consumed the body of the unfortunate hero.

Deianira, horrified, hanged herself. Hyllus, the eldest son of Heracles, received the last wishes of his father who wanted to be burned on a pyre at the top of Mount Oeta. It is said that Zeus snatched him from the Earth and transported him to Olympus, granting him deification and immortality.

A symbol of strength and energy, and even of heroism, Heracles was revered as both a hero and a god. A great drinker, a large eater, a *bon vivant*, he represents for the Greeks justice fighting evil and perjury, punishing the impious, and he remains a model of courage in the face of the mortal perils that beset man. Finally, through his posterity, the Heraclidae, he is the mythical ancestor of all the Greeks of Peloponnesus.

HERACLIDAE. All the descendants of Heracles are known by this name. At the death of the hero, pursued by the hatred of King Eurystheus, they first took refuge in the kingdom of Ceyx, the king of Trachis, who, for fear of reprisals against his country, sent them away. Then the Heraclidae went to Theseus, the king of Athens, who proved quite helpful to them. The hero agreed to wage war with them against Eurystheus who, during the battle, perished with his sons. The Heraclidae then conquered the Peloponnesus and settled there. But they were soon chased away by a plague sent by the gods who were annoyed that the heroes had not waited for the moment dictated by destiny and the oracles for such an undertaking. During two expeditions, the first under the leadership of Hellus, the second under that of one of his descendants, Aristomachus, the Heraclidae tried to pass the isthmus of Corinth but each time they were repelled by the king of the country because they were unable to interpret the oracle that advised them to pass by way of the straits. Finally, the three sons of Aristomachus—Temenus, Cresphontes and Aristo-

Traveling Hermes, protector of the young Dionysus, with winged feet, his petasus attached to his back, a rather flowing tunic with his doctor's caduceus in his hand. Detail of a krater, Louvre.

demus—having finally understood that "straits" meant the maritime route between continental Greece and the Peloponnesus, ensured relief and resumed the struggle. Aristodemus died, stricken by thunder shortly before entering the Peloponnesus, leaving twin sons and the Heraclidae to begin the last victorious battle during which they killed King Tisamenus, the son of Orestes. When the region was divided, Temenus received Argos; Procles and Eurysthenes, sons of Aristodemus, received Laconia; and Messenia went to Cresphontes. The settling of the Heraclidae in the Peloponnesus corresponds in History to the invasion of the Dorians and the organization of the territories conquered at that time. Subsequently, all ancient royal families, in order to secure power, established genealogies indicating that they were all descendants of Heracles. Thus Croesus claimed to have been a descendant of Heracles through Omphale. King Tarquin of Rome contended that one of his ancestors was Antiochus, the son of Heracles; there were even certain Roman families that invented genealogies pointing to Heracles as one of their ancestors.

HERCULES. A Latin transposition of *Heracles,* Hercules borrowed from his Greek model almost all of his legends. However, Roman writers added a few legends of their own. Thus Hercules felled the giant Cacus and killed King Faunus, who had the dreadful habit of slaying strangers who happened to venture into his kingdom. Finally, Hercules was benevolently welcomed by King Evander who founded a sanctuary in his honor in Rome. Less formidable than Heracles, he bears a lyre as his symbol and often accompanies the procession of Muses and Apollo Musagetes.

HERMAPHRODITUS. The offspring of the union of Hermes and Aphrodite, whose names he took, Hermaphroditus was a young man of

Olympian Hermes, with a wise and philosophical face. His profile is Greek, his hair well tended, the overall representation expressing to perfection nobility and order. Greek art, Louvre.

Hermes "Psychopompos," guide of the dead, has placed a warrior on each tray of a scale. Zeus, both ferocious and vigilant, armed with lightning, prepares to render a sentence. Depending on whether the tray tipped to one side or the other, one of the heroes would be the conqueror, the other the conquered; one living, the other dead. The heroes and their destinies are mere toys in the hands of the gods. Detail of a Greek vase.

extraordinary beauty. One day as he was journeying through Asia Minor, he was bathing in the waters of Salmacis, where a nymph dwelled; the nymph, marveling at his beauty, leaped toward him, embracing him and asking the gods to be united with him forever. The gods obliged and from that point on, they were but a single being with a dual nature. The myth of the androgyne, which resembles that of Hermaphroditus, was evoked by the comic poet Aristophanes in Plato's *Symposium:* he claimed that, in the beginning, men possessed both masculine and feminine natures. The gods, fearing their power, cut them in two, thus creating men and women.

HERMES. The son of Zeus and Maia and grandson of Atlas, Hermes was born in a cave on Mount Cyllene in Arcadia. Immediately he exhibited astonishing precociousness and extraordinary intelligence and cunning. He was barely more than a newborn when he succeeded in leaving his cradle and fleeing to Pieria. There, for both profit and a lark, he stole Apollo's oxen. When he returned to the cave where he had been born, he came across a tortoise shell that was lying on the ground; he picked it up and stretched strings across the shell which was naturally resonant; he thus invented the lyre. During this time, Apollo had managed to seek out Hermes, the thief, but rather than lash out at the young god, he was enchanted by the sounds that emerged from this new musical instrument and immediately befriended Hermes. He offered Hermes his shepherd's wand which was later transformed into the caduceus. Promoted, within a short time, to the position of official herald of the gods, Hermes appears in many legends and his influence on the gods, men and the course of events is far from negligible. The god was seen leading Priam to Achilles to demand the body of Hector; placing the three goddesses, Aphro-

Hermes "Psychopompos" leads a weeping woman to Charon's ferry. Tanagra terra-cotta, private coll., photo Giraudon.

dite, Athena and Hera, in the presence of Paris who was to judge their beauty; killing Argos, the guardian of Io; offering Nephele the golden fleece which saved Phrixus and Helle; going many times to the aid of Ulysses when he was in danger; and giving heroes as famous as Heracles and Perseus their unavoidable weapons. He also had the less pleasant task of leading the souls from the world of the living to the world of the dead; on these sad occasions, he bore the name of Psychopompos. Hermes often wore a winged helmet, a cloak and a traveling hat, with small wings attached to his heels. Thus accoutered, the ambassador of Olympus, the instrument of divine will was able to perform his many tasks quickly and easily. Intelligent, crafty, even a bit deceptive, Hermes is, without a doubt, one of the most colorful gods of Olympus. The Greeks worshiped him as the

patron of orators, as the inventor of the alphabet, music, astronomy, weights and measures (he was, therefore, the god of merchants), and gymnastics. Statues were erected in his honor at crossroads and along the sides of the roads. His presence lent support to voyagers and the difficult tasks of the traveling merchants because the god protected them from the dangers of the highways and bad encounters. Thus, Hermes is the god of all intercourse and exchange, both human and divine.

HERMIONE. The only child born of the union of Menelaus and Helen, Hermione was engaged to Orestes shortly before the Trojan War. But in order to attract Neoptolemus, whose presence was crucial to ensure the capture of Troy, Menelaus gave his daughter in marriage to the son of Achilles. Orestes, dissatisfied, killed Neoptolemus and was able to marry Hermione freely. She bore him a son, Tisamenus.

HERO. A young woman of Abydos for whose love Leander would swim across the Hellespont each night until the day he drowned.

heroes. In mythology, the term "hero" is used to refer to any character who has had such an influence on men and events, who has waged war with such bravura, or accomplished exploits with such temerity that he distinguished himself from his peers, other mortals, and may claim to approach the level of the gods, thus deserving veneration and worship after death. The epic poem, the *Iliad,* in particular, first created the notion of the hero. Thus, tales are told of Achilles, Ajax, Ulysses and many others, displaying great and wondrous ingenuity and courage during the Trojan War. But even from their birth these heroes are already different from other men. Most of the time, they are the sons of a god or goddess from whom they receive help and protection during their lives. Over the years, the notion of the hero gradu-

A group of Greek heroes surrounds Achilles, the warrior, who is armed for combat. The same nobility of behavior, the same submission to Destiny, which made all of these mortals heroes by the distinguishing grace of the gods, is apparent. Greek relief, Louvre, photo Giraudon.

ally changed. Each territory wanted to have its own hero, a true national or regional symbol. Thus, Athenian heroes such as Theseus emerged, Theban heroes such as the Labdicids appeared, Argive or Boeotian heroes were invented along with a host of other eponymous heroes. Certain sacerdotal or noble families later claimed to be descendants of legendary heroes, the soothsayers of Melampus, Caesar of Aeneas and consequently Venus, Marc Antony of Hercules. During the Greek classical era (5th century B.C.), an outstanding Spartan, General Brasidas, was worshiped as a hero at Amphipolis where he died in battle.

HERSE. The youngest of the three daughters of Cecrops, Herse was, with her sisters Pandrosos and Aglauros, one of the heroines of the legend of the cradle of Erichthonius. It is told that Hermes, who was in love with her, paid a sum of gold to enlist the aid of Aglauros in stealing her heart. But Aglauros out of envy did not keep her promise. The god, vexed, turned Aglauros to stone, and did not hesitate to rape Herse, who gave birth to Cephalus and Ceryx.

HERSILIA. This Sabine heroine, who mediated between the Sabines and the Romans, when war broke out between them as a result of the rape of the Sabine women, married Romulus to whom she bore a daughter, Prima, and a son, Aollius, later known as Avilius. She died, stricken by Jupiter, and was transported to the heavens where she took her place among the divinities as *Hora Quirini.* She was, from that point on, invoked by Roman youth as the goddess who promoted courage.

HESIONE. 1. According to Aeschylus, this name was used by one of the Oceanids, the wife of Prometheus.

2. Another **Hesione,** the daughter of Laomedon, was tied to a rock in Troy by her father. Her father wanted to appease Apollo and Poseidon whom he had offended and agreed to sacrifice his daughter as food for a sea monster. Heracles freed the unfortunate girl and went to the king to claim the price of his exploit: the two horses that Zeus had given him in exchange for Ganymede; but Laomedon refused. Several years later, Heracles returned to Troy, invaded the city, killed the king who had gone back on his word, and gave Hesione in marriage to his friend Telamon. Of this union, a son, Teucer, was born.

HESPERIDES. At the Western limits of the Earth lived the three Hesperides—Aegle, Erytheia and Hespera-Arethusa. Beautiful, carefree young women, they, with the help of the

Under the tree that bears the golden apples, two Hesperides who guard the enchanted fruits can be seen, one on each side of Heracles. Olympian metope, Temple of Zeus, Villa Albani, Rome, photo Alinari-Giraudon.

dragon Ladon, guarded the enchanted garden where the famous golden apples grew. These had been given to Hera by Gaia at her marriage to Zeus. Heracles, with the help of Atlas, stole the magical fruits. Dedicated to the goddess Athena, they were returned to the Hesperides some time later.

HESPERUS. The son of Eos and brother of Atlas, according to the most common genealogy, Hesperus disappeared from the world of mortals and it was thought that he had been transformed into the star that shines first at dusk: the Evening Star.

HESTIA. The daughter of Cronus and Rhea, Hestia belonged to the generation of the twelve great divinities of Olympus. When Zeus, her brother, seized supreme power, she obtained the favor of keeping her virginity forever in order to escape the amorous advances of Apollo and Poseidon. The embodiment of the domestic hearth, of the sacred flame that burns continuously in homes and temples, purifying them, Hestia is worshiped as the protectress of families, cities and colonies. Indeed, whenever the Greeks wanted to found a colony, they would carry from the metropolis the fire of Hestia that was intended to light the hearth of the new country. Hestia, always unchangeable and unchanged, thus symbolizes religious perpetuity, the continuity of civilization and its lights in defiance of the emigrations, destructions. revolutions and vicissitudes of time. The Romans identified her with the goddess Vesta. There are no stories told about her.

HILAERA. The daughter of Leucippus and Philodice, Hilaera was a priestess of Artemis. Her sister Phoebe was a priestess of Athena. They were both known by the name of *Leucippides*. They were abducted by the Dioscuri and Hilaera married Castor.

The goddess Hestia survived the revolution of the gods, because fire, which she symbolizes, is the element that is essential to life from the beginning of time until the end of the world. Here she resembles a woman of a ripe age, looking corpulent and Roman. Through these features, she embodies the idea of the family gathered around the comforting and sacred hearth. Greek art, 460 B.C., Palazzo dei Conservatori, Rome, photo Alinari-Giraudon.

HIPPOCOON. Heracles was obliged to battle Hippocoon who had usurped the power in Sparta and had banished Tyndareos, his brother. Aided by his twelve sons, Hippocoon made the country tremble under his tyrannical law. Heracles managed, but not without some difficulty, to kill him as well as his sons and to reestablish Tyndareos on the throne.

HIPPOCRENE. This "horse's fountain" gushed forth on the Helicon under the hoof of the horse Pegasus and was chosen by the Muses as the center of one of their favorite dwelling places.

HIPPODAMEIA. This daughter of Oenomaus, the king of Pisa in Elis, was the prize in a chariot competition between her father and her suitors. Only Pelops, aided by Myrtilus, was able to defeat the king and marry Hippodameia. She bore him many famous children such as Atreus, Pittheus, Alcathous, Plisthenes, Thyestes. Banished from her country for having murdered her brother-in-law Chrysippus, whose ambition she feared, Hippodameia sought refuge in Argolis.

HIPPODAMIA. The wedding celebration of Pirithous and Hippodamia, the daughter of Adrastus, was a pretext for the famous battle between the Centaurs and the Lapiths.

HIPPOLYTUS. The fruit of the love of Theseus and Antiope, the queen of the Amazons, Hippolytus was entrusted at birth to his grandmother Aethra in Troezen, while his father married Phaedra shortly after. Like his mother, Hippolytus was particularly devoted to the goddess Artemis. However, he exhibited such disdain for women that Aphrodite, jealous of his devotion to her divine rival and furious at Hippolytus' attitude toward love, decided to take revenge. She inspired in Phaedra an obsessive passion for her stepson. Hippolytus shunned her love. Fearing that he would tell Theseus of the advances she had made, Phaedra condemned the young man, who was ordered by his father to leave Athens and never return. Then the king prayed to Poseidon to punish his son in an exemplary fashion. Hippolytus, in his chariot, was riding along the coast when he saw a monster emerge from the white foam of the waves and drive his steeds mad; the horses bolted, overturning the chariot, and trampled Hippolytus. According to Ovid and Virgil, Artemis asked Asclepius to revive him and after

Despite the poor state of the sarcophagus, it is easy to see the natural beauty of the young Hippolytus who, banished by his father, bids a sad farewell to his companions and servants. He seems to have the feeling that he is heading towards his death. Fragment of a sarcophagus, Louvre, photo Giraudon.

that, Hippolytus lived in Italy, near Aricia, where he was identified with the god Virbius.

HIPPOMEDON. The son of Aristomachus and the nephew of Adrastus, Hippomedon was killed in the siege of Thebes during the expedition of the Seven Leaders. But he left behind a son, Polydorus, who, to avenge his father's death, joined the Epigoni in a second expedition against Thebes.

HIPPOMENES. The son of Megareus and grandson of Poseidon, Hippomenes was the husband of Atalanta. Atalanta, who was fiercely opposed to marriage, defeated all of her suitors in races and had them all put to death. She was saving herself for whoever succeeded in defeating her. Hippomenes enlisted the aid of Aphrodite, who was angered at the chastity of Atalanta. The goddess gave Hippomenes three golden apples, doubtless gathered in the garden of the Hesperides, and advised him to drop them one at a time in the arena where the race was to take place. Intrigued by the apples, Atalanta stopped three times to pick them up and was not able to defeat Hippomenes, who then married her. Having insulted Zeus (some say Cybele) by indulging in displays of affection in a sanctuary, the couple was changed into lions that Cybele harnessed to her chariot. In Antiquity, it was said that the lion could only mate with the leopard: thus Atalanta and Hippomenes were never again able to have relations.

HIPPOTHOUS. The son of the giant Cercyon, Hippothous was placed on the throne of Arcadia by Theseus, the very murderer of his father. He was accidentally killed by Telephus, his nephew; his son Aepytus succeeded him but died, blinded by Poseidon, for having forced open the doors of one of the god's temples.

HOPE. Known to the Greeks as *Elpis*, this allegorical divinity was the only gift of the gods that did not escape from Pandora's box. The wife of Epimetheus, owing to her curiosity, had imprudently opened the box. Thus, the Ancients revered Hope with a special solemnity. The Romans, who had given her the name of *Spes*, erected several temples in her honor and portrayed her with the features of a gracious young woman, raising the hem of her dress with one hand and holding in the other hand a flower in full bloom.

HORAE. The daughters of Themis and Zeus, the Horae—Thallo, Carpo and Auxo—are, above all, the divinities that preside over the order of nature and the seasons. They represent, therefore, in the most common traditions, spring, summer and winter. At a later era, the Greeks, when they divided the day into twelve hours, increased the number of Horae. They were called the "Twelve Sisters." As the Horae are not included in Greek mythological legends and the concepts that concern these divinities developed or changed during Antiquity, it is difficult to define their respective attributes. At the very least, they are portrayed as happy young girls, dancing in the company of the Muses and the Graces, and bearing the agricultural products of the various seasons—flowers, heads of wheat, branches of the vine and fruits.

HORATII (the). 1. Legend and history have retained the names of three famous brothers of the city of Rome who fought the Curiatii of Alba to determine which of the two cities would dominate the other. During the battle, two of the Horatii were killed but the third, unharmed, managed to massacre the three Curiatii, who were all wounded. Upon his return to Rome, Horatius killed his sister who was mourning the death of her fiancé, one of the Curiatii. Acquitted of this crime, he was nevertheless obliged to live in dishonor, his head veiled.

2. Another hero of Roman legend went by this name, **Horatius the One-Eyed** (*Horatius*

Cocles). With two warriors, he defended a bridge *(Pons Sublicius)* on the Tiber against an Etruscan invasion, thereby preventing the enemy's entry into Rome; he escaped by swimming away and was wounded in the thigh. A statue was erected in his honor and he was rewarded with lands.

3. In another Roman legend, a third **Horatius** appeared. At the end of a battle between Rome and the Etruscans, neither side knew who had won since the battle had been particularly devastating and there were many corpses everywhere. The Roman Horatius therefore cried from a neighboring wood that the Etruscans had lost one warrior more than the Romans. The enemy fled immediately, leaving the Romans victorious.

horn of plenty. A symbol of wealth, the horn of plenty was torn one day by Heracles from the river-god Acheloüs, who had changed himself into a bull in a dispute with the hero over Deianira. Conquered, the god asked the hero to return his horn in exchange for that of Amalthea, the goat of Mount Ida whose horn became the real horn of plenty. According to other versions, the infant Zeus inadvertently broke off one of the horns of his nurse Amalthea. To console the animal, he promised her that in the future the horn would become the symbol of all possible riches.

HUNGER. This divinity, the daughter of Night, whom Virgil places at the gates of the Underworld and who brings sterility to fields, is also described by Ovid as a woman squatting in an arid field where she is uprooting a few measly plants. Erysichthon, the Thessalian hero, was her most tragic victim.

hunt. In a country like Greece, haunted by wild, often ferocious beasts, hunting was placed from its earliest days under the protection of certain divinities. Mythology took over this theme and attributed the invention of hunting to the centaur Chiron who taught his pupils (Heracles, the Dioscuri, and many others) the art of victoriously fighting with animals. Artemis and her brother Apollo became, in legends, formidable and dreaded hunters. Their arrows never missed their mark and they were generally the instrument for the vengeance of the outraged gods. Thus the children of Niobe perished like common animals. This punishment was in store for Marsyas, who boasted of having surpassed Artemis in skill, and Agamemnon who, claiming to have killed a doe with more rapidity than Artemis, saw his fleet immobilized in Aulis. But Artemis also protects humble hunters. She is depicted, like Diana, in hunting gear with a quiver and arrows, surrounded by a pack of dogs. She bears, in this case, the surnames of *Elaphebolus* ("killer of stags"), *Agrotera* ("protectress of fields and wild places"), and *Lagobolus* ("killer of hares").

HYACINTHUS. This beautiful young man, for whose favors the gods competed, was mortally wounded one day by the quoit of Apollo during a game. It is also said that Zephyrus, jealous of the affection that Apollo displayed for Hyacinthus, turned the quoit with his breath and, making it deviate from its course, directed it into the forehead of the young man. Apollo, in the face of this misfortune, was overcome with grief. To perpetuate the memory of his friend, he changed the blood which flowed from his wound onto the ground into a purple flower with a lily-shaped cup and petals on which was inscribed the Greek word *ai*, which means "alas!" or else the initial of the name of Hyacinthus (Y). Like Narcissus and Adonis, Hyacinthus was one of the young beings whose lives were taken away in the springtime and who were changed into flowers.

HYADES. The generic name of the nymphs forming a group of seven stars in the constellation of Taurus. They were the sisters of the Pleiades and the daughters of Atlas and Pleione

Hygieia holds a bowl in which she prepares remedies; with her right hand, she gestures soothingly. Vatican Museum, photo Alinari.

or Aethra, depending on the version. Their number varies. The best known are Ambrosia, Eudora, Coronis, Polyxo, Phaeo, Dione, Aesilae. Zeus, to thank them for having nourished and protected Dionysus, placed them among the heavens' constellations. According to another tradition, the Hyades, overcome with grief at the death of their brother Hyas who had been killed in Lybia by a ferocious beast, moved Zeus with their cries of sorrow. To console them and put an end to their weeping, the god changed them into stars. But their weeping did not cease, hence the name *Hyades* ("the rainy ones"): their appearance at the rising or setting of the sun announces rain.

HYDRA OF LERNA. Born of Typhon and Echidna, this monster lived in a cave near Lake Lerna. He had the body of a dog and nine serpents' heads. Only one of these heads was immortal. Sent by Eurystheus to kill Hydra, Heracles accomplished the second of his twelve labors. First the hero chopped off one head, but two more emerged in its place. With the help of Iolaus, his faithful companion, Heracles burned the heads of the Hydra, chopped off the one that was immortal and buried it under a heavy rock. Then he dipped his arrows in the blood of the monster in order to ensure that the wounds they inflicted would be mortal. It is said that this blood was part of the poisoned potion that the dying Nessus gave to Deianira and which, in turn, caused the death of Heracles. It is also said that the foul odor that the River Anigrus in Elis exuded was caused by the blood of the monster that had been spilled into its waters.

HYGIEIA. The daughter of Asclepius, the god of medicine, a descendant of Apollo, this goddess assisted her father not only in relieving human illnesses but also in curing animals. She advised humans on the diets and medications that would remedy their sicknesses.

HYLAS. The son of Theiodamas, the king of the Dryopians, Hylas, a friend of Heracles, took part in the expedition of the Argonauts and stopped on the shores of Mysia with his companions. On his way to draw water from a spring, he was abducted by the nymphs dwelling there who were smitten with his beauty, and he disappeared forever. Heracles, assisted by the Lapith Polyphemus, wandered through the woods in search of him, calling out to him in vain. During this time, the Argonauts took advantage of a favorable wind and raised anchor without waiting for the return of the two heroes who had gone ashore. Polyphemus remained behind and founded the city of Cios, over which he reigned. Heracles, for his part, promised the Mysians that he would leave them in peace if they continued to search for Hylas. The tradition was perpetuated during the historical ages when, each year, priests could be seen roaming the countryside crying out the name of Hylas.

HYLLUS. One of the favorite sons of Heracles and Deianira, Hyllus was raised by Ceyx, the king of Trachis, in Thessaly, while his father accomplished his exploits. Sent by his mother in search of his father, he found him clad in the tunic of Nessus and dying; he, therefore, transported him to Mount Oeta where he listened to his last wishes and, on his last order, married Iole. He became the leader of the Heraclidae and tried to enter the territory of Peloponnesus from which he had been banished. He challenged King Echemus, the king of Arcadia, to a single combat with the promise that he would obtain the kingdom if he emerged victorious but with the threat that, if he were defeated, all the descendants of Heracles would be banished from Peloponnesus for fifty more years. He was killed and buried in the city of Megara.

HYMENAEUS. This god of marriage, the son of Apollo and a Muse, or of Dionysus and Aphrodite, presided originally over the bridal song itself and was the personification of it. To justify his invocation during wedding ceremonies by the name of "Hymenaeus," many legends were attributed to him. He was supposed to have been a magnificent young man who was to have freed young women who had been abducted by pirates and returned them to their parents on the condition that they grant him the hand of the one whom he loved but who spurned him. According to another tradition, he was supposed to have lost his voice during the wedding of Ariadne and Dionysus. All of the legends recognize that the beauty of Hymenaeus rivaled that of Aphrodite. Artists did not overlook him; subsequently, they attributed to him the very symbols of marriage—the nuptial flame, the flute and the crown of roses.

HYPERBOREANS. This mythical people, who were visited by only a few wandering heroes such as Perseus and Heracles, lived in enchanted regions beyond the land where Boreas, the north wind, made his chilly, snowy presence known. For the Hyperboreans, night did not exist. Eternal day and a fragile warmth inspired perfect happiness in them. Always happy, practicing simple goodness and piety, fearing neither sickness nor death, they spent their days singing and dancing in the sacred fields and woods where choirs of gracious, fragrant nymphs dwelled. They were consecrated to Apollo, who, at the arrival of the first chill in autumn, left Greece; driving a chariot, drawn by white swans, he found incomparable refuge among them. He spent the winter months in their kingdom which basked in the mildness of an endless temperate season.

HYPERION. This Titan, the son of Uranus and Gaia, had relations with his sister Theia, who gave birth to Helios (the Sun), Selene (the Moon) and Eos (the Dawn).

Thanks to the wings attached to his temples, Hypnos can fly quickly to the help of mortals who ask for sleep, of which he is the divine incarnation. Greek art, bronze found near Perugia, photo X.

HYPERMNESTRA. **1.** Danaus, the king of Argos, had ordered his fifty daughters to slaughter their husbands. Only Hypermnestra spared her husband, Lynceus, and bore him a son, Abas. Brought before a tribunal of Argives for having defied her father, she was acquitted.

2. The mother of Amphiaraus was also known by this name.

HYPNOS. The personification of Sleep (Somnus to the Romans), Hypnos was the twin brother of Death, of which he is a more mild image. A winged spirit, "he flutters tranquilly, full of gentleness for mortals," said Hesiod. He is sometimes portrayed on sarcophagi with the features of a sleeping young man. His symbols are the horn and the poppy.

HYPSIPYLE.   The daughter of Thoas, king of the island of Lemnos, Hypsipyle was the granddaughter of Dionysus. For having abandoned the worship of Aphrodite, the Lemnian women incurred the vengeance of the goddess: she overpowered them with an odor that was so strong their husbands could no longer stand them and they preferred concubines, slaves or strangers. Furious at being neglected, the women slew all of the men of Lemnos, except Thoas, whom Hypsipyle managed to save. Chosen as queen, during the stay of the Argonauts, she fell in love with Jason by whom she had two sons, Euneos and Nebrophonus. But later, the Lemnian women learned that Thoas was still alive and Hypsipyle was forced to flee. She was captured shortly after and sold to the king of Nemea, Lycurgus, who instructed her to care for his son Opheltes. Having abandoned the child for an instant to point out the way to the Seven Leaders, she returned to find him dead, strangled by a serpent. Luckily, the heroes interceded, begging Lycurgus and his wife to spare the irresponsible nursemaid whom they wanted put to death. Hypsipyle was able to return to Lemnos with her two sons, safe.

I

IACCHUS. This young god, crowned with myrtle branches, a torch in one hand, leads the procession of the mysteries of Eleusis. According to the most common tradition, Iacchus is the son of Zeus and Demeter, the brother of Core-Persephone and the half-brother of Dionysus. However, according to certain other versions, Iacchus is the son of Dionysus. Later, at the time when the Orphic mysteries came into existence, he was regarded as the son of Zeus and Persephone and the reincarnation of Zagreus.

IAMBE. When Demeter, in search of her daughter, was received kindly in the court of Celeus, the king of Eleusis, the nymph Iambe wanted to console the weeping goddess by reciting comical verse for her. This role is sometimes attributed to Baubo.

IAPETUS. The son of Uranus and Gaia, this Titan, who belonged to the very first generation of gods, is famous for his posterity. The spouse of the Oceanid Clymene, he fathered Atlas, Prometheus, Epimetheus, Menoetius. Having rebelled against the seizing of supreme power by Zeus, he was thrown into the depths of Tartarus with his brother Cronus and the other Titans.

IASION. The son of Zeus and the Pleiad Electra, this Titan, the brother of Dardanus, was loved by the goddess Demeter and had relations with her in a thrice-plowed field. Zeus discovered the lovers and, vexed at this show of audacity, struck Iasion with his thunder. Several months later in Crete, the goddess gave birth to Ploutos who took a place in the Greek Pantheon among the divinities of Fertility and Wealth.

IASUS. Several heroes went by this name: one, the father of Atalanta, reigned over Arcadia; another was the father of Amphion; a third, the king of Argos, is sometimes considered to be the father of Io.

IBYCUS. Although this Greek lyrical poet, born in Rhegion, who lived in the court of the tyrant Polycrates of Samos around 540 B.C., belonged to the literary history of Greece, his death was the subject of a legend: not far from Corinth, a band of thieves mortally wounded Ibycus; he begged the cranes flying above him to avenge him. Shortly afterwards, above the theater in Corinth, where a crowd had assembled to watch a spectacle of games, a flock of cranes appeared; one of the assassins of Ibycus who was in the crowd cried out, crazed: "The cranes of Ibycus, the avengers!" In a moment of panic, the murderer had thus publicly acknowledged his crime. He was put to death with his accomplices.

ICARIUS. **1.** This Athenian one day welcomed Dionysus hospitably; to thank him, the god taught him how to make wine, just as he had given the vine to Oeneus, whose guest he had also been. Icarius, quite proud of his new drink, invited the shepherds to dine with him. But they became intoxicated and were soon frightened by the ailments they were experiencing: believing themselves poisoned, they killed Icarius. His daughter Erigone, happening upon his tomb, killed herself. Dionysus took revenge by driving the young women of Athens mad.

2. There are two versions of the genealogy of another **Icarius;** according to the first, he was the son of Perieres; according to the second, he was only his grandson. Banished with his brother Tyndareos of Lacedaemon by Hippocoon, he lived in Arcanania after Heracles murdered Hippocoon. He married the nymph Peribola by whom he had a certain number of children, including Thoas, Aletes and Penelope. When Penelope was of marrying age, Icarius, who loved her tenderly, tried all imaginable obstacles to prevent her marrying. Finally, he made his daughter the stake in a chariot race, which was won by Ulysses. Icarius thus asked Ulysses to remain with his daughter. Ulysses refused but let Penelope make the choice between him and her father. The young woman blushed and covered her face with a veil indicating that she had chosen Ulysses. Icarius yielded to the decision and even erected a temple to the goddess Modesty on the spot where this scene had taken place.

ICARUS. The son of Daedalus and one of the Cretan slaves of King Minos, Icarus found himself trapped in the Labyrinth with his father. Both were able to escape thanks to the wings that Daedalus fashioned, which they fastened to their shoulders with wax. Before taking flight, Daedalus instructed his son not to fly too near the sun; but Icarus, intoxicated with the power to fly, soared even higher into the air, so high, in fact, that the rays of the sun melted the wax. The wings fell off and the unfortunate young man plunged into the sea which has since borne his name (the sea around the island of Samos).

IDA. In Antiquity, two mountain ranges bore this name. One, in the center of the island of Crete, had been the place of refuge of the newborn Zeus, who was suckled by a nymph, Ida. The other was found not far from Troy and was, during the war that pitted the Greeks against the Trojans, the favorite dwelling place of the gods when they took part in the battles.

IDAS. The son of Aphareus and Arene, Idas took part in various mythical expeditions with his brother Lynceus. He made his mark especially in the Calydonian Boar Hunt and the expedition of the Argonauts. But having wanted to seize the kingdom of Mysia, he was conquered by Telephus. The most famous parts of his legend are his battle against Apollo and his combats with the Dioscuri.

He had abducted Marpessa, the daughter of Evenus, and married her. But Apollo, also in love with the young woman, wanted to steal her away. Zeus put an end to the quarrel by allowing Marpessa to choose the one she loved; she preferred Idas.

Furthermore, a bitter struggle pitted Idas against the Dioscuri, his cousins, involving the division of a herd of cattle. In fact, the hero, through trickery, had stolen the entire herd. He and his brother Lynceus were attacked by the Dioscuri. Castor was killed during the struggle and Pollux was about to meet the same fate when Zeus intervened and struck down Idas. It is also said that this punishment was inflicted upon Idas because he had wanted to quarrel over the daughters of Leucippus—Hilaera and Phoebe.

IDMON. **1.** A dyer from Colophon, the father of Arachne, was known by this name.

2. Another **Idmon,** the son of Apollo and Asteria, or of Cyrene, was officially the son of Abas. A soothsayer responsible for advising the Argonauts in their expedition, he knew in advance that death awaited him there. Having reached the land of the Mariandynians, he was attacked by a ferocious boar. Despite the spear of Idas, which killed the beast, Idmon died of his wounds.

IDOMENEUS. This king of Crete, the son of Deucalion and the grandson of Minos and Pasiphaë, was one of the suitors for Helen. He left Crete with a fleet of twenty-four vessels, manned by a large contingent of Cretans, to take part in the siege of Troy. Later, he was one of the heroes who hid in the famous wooden horse and entered the city. According to the *Odyssey,* his return was a happy one. But other traditions after Homer give his legend a dramatic turn. His fleet having been beset by a storm, Idomeneus promised Poseidon to sacrifice the first person he saw on his return to Crete. His sorrow was keen, however, when, dropping anchor, he saw on the shore his own son who had come to greet him and celebrate his return. Most mythographers contend that he kept his word and sacrificed his son. But, when a plague ravaged their island, the Cretans, already horrified that the king had sacrificed his own son, banished him to appease the gods. Idomeneus, therefore, went to Calabria and founded Salenta, introducing in this city the wise laws of his grandfather Minos. He is also said to have preferred Thetis to Medea in a contest of beauty and thus provoked Medea to say, "All Cretans are liars."

ILIONE. The eldest daughter of Priam and Hecuba, Ilione married Polymestor, the king of Chersonessus in Thrace, to whom she gave a son, Deipylus. The latter was killed by his father who mistakenly thought that he was eliminating an enemy, Polydorus, the very brother

of Ilione. Ilione avenged the death of her child by killing her husband. According to another version of the legend, it was Hecuba herself who ordered the death of Polymestor, after having blinded him.

ILUS. The son of Tros and the nymph Callirhoë, the brother of Cleopatra, Assaracus and Ganymede, the great-grandson of Dardanus, Ilus married Eurydice who bore him a son, Laomedon, the father of Priam. A second wife bore him a daughter, Themiste, the grandmother of Aeneas. After having carried off a victory in the games, he received slaves and a cow as his reward. As an oracle had advised him, Ilus followed the animal which finally stopped on a hill, Ate (infatuation), in Phrygia. He founded a city there, the city of Ilion, later called *Troy.* Zeus confirmed and approved the choice by sending Ilus a statue of Pallas-Athena, the Palladium, intended to protect the new city.

immortality. Generally granted to all the gods, immortality is constantly distributed on Olympus by nectar and ambrosia, the only food of the gods. Sometimes, certain mortals may acquire immortality; some, like the fisherman Glaucus, by eating a magic herb that changed him into a sea-god; others, like most heroes and heroines, because they have divine blood in them and have displayed superhuman courage and bravery. Often too, heroes, like Tydeus, invoked the disdain of the gods through their cruelty and were refused immortality. The chances of nature give certain mortals conditional immortality; thus, King Pterelaus died only when his daughter cut his golden hair, which had ensured his immortality. Finally, it sometimes happens that immortality is exchanged for death: such was the case for Prometheus who agreed to accept the immortality of the centaur Chiron who, wounded and suffering intensely, preferred the comfort of death to eternal suffering.

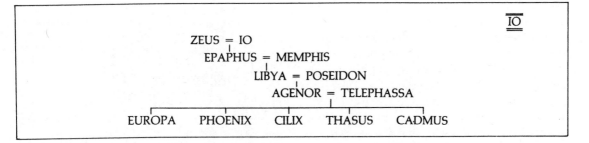

ZEUS = IO
EPAPHUS = MEMPHIS
LIBYA = POSEIDON
AGENOR = TELEPHASSA

EUROPA   PHOENIX   CILIX   THASUS   CADMUS

IO

INACHUS. This river-god of Argolis, the son of Oceanus and Tethys, himself the father of the nymph Io, was one day chosen by Hera and Poseidon as a mediator: they were quarreling over the sovereignty of a country through which he flowed. Inachus ruled in favor of Hera. Vexed, Poseidon dried up his waters. Only the rains return his normal flow.

INO. The daughter of Cadmus and Harmonia, wife of Athamas, the king of Boeotia, Ino was known as *Leucothea* after she was changed into a sea-goddess. She had two sons, Learchus and Melicertes.

IO. This young priestess of Argos, the daughter of King Inachus, or of Iasus, the king of Argos, according to another version, one day seduced the ever-ardent Zeus with her charm; the god had relations with her but was forced to change her into a heifer so that his jealous wife would not discover his infidelity. Hera, who was not tricked by the transformation, asked Zeus to consecrate the animal to her. The god obeyed. Io was entrusted to hundred-eyed Argos who never slept with more than fifty eyes closed. Seized with compassion, Zeus asked Hermes to snatch the prisoner away from her guardian. Once freed, Io did not enjoy her freedom for very long. Hera sent her a gadfly; the insect clung to her flanks, making the false heifer so furious that she spent months wandering through Greece, never stopping to rest. She passed through Bosphorus (or "ford of the Cow") and met Prometheus, attached to his

rock on Mount Caucasus, who, according to Aeschylus, predicted that she would meet with a pleasant fate. From there, Io went to Egypt, where she resumed her original form, and gave birth to Epaphus, one of the Danaids. She was then identified with the goddess Isis. After her death, with the goddess Luna, she was portrayed as a woman with golden horns.

IOBATES. The king of Lycia, Iobates had two daughters, Stheneboea, who married Proetus, and Philonoë, who married Bellerophon. Iobates played an important role in the legends of these two characters.

IOLAUS. The son of Automedusa and Iphicles (the half-brother of Heracles), Iolaus was one of the most faithful companions of his uncle whose chariot he usually drove; he thus helped him to conquer the Hydra of Lerna and to capture the oxen of Geryon; he took part in the Calydonian Boar Hunt with the Argonauts and won the chariot race at the first Olympic games introduced by Heracles. Heracles sent his nephew to Sardinia at the head of the sons whom he had had by the daughters of Thespius. Iolaus died on this island. Later, the Underworld granted him permission to return to Earth to help the children of Heracles when they were in danger: thus he killed Eurystheus and, honored by all, returned to the kingdom of Shadows.

IOLE. King Eurytus of Oechalia promised his daughter to Heracles if the hero succeeded in surpassing him in precision with a bow and arrow; Heracles defeated him easily. But the king went back on his word and Heracles, in order to seize the girl, killed the king and his sons. In view of the murder of her family, Iole wanted to kill herself by throwing herself from atop the ramparts. The wind filled her clothing, however, and she descended to the ground unharmed. Heracles sent her to Deianira. Deianira, believing that her husband preferred the girl to her and wanted to betray her, sent him the tunic that the centaur Nessus had given her. In fact, the poisoned tunic caused the death of Heracles. In this way, Iole was the indirect cause of the demise of one of the greatest heroes of Antiquity.

ION. Of the three sons of Hellen, one, Dorus, emigrated to Mount Parnassus; another, Aeolus, was the eponymous hero of the Aeolians; and the third, Xuthus, fled to Athens where he married Creusa, the daughter of Erechtheus, who bore him two sons, Achaeus and Ion. However, another tradition followed by Euripides claims that Apollo was the real father of Ion. The god had taken his abandoned son to Delphi and made him one of the servants in his temple. Xuthus and Creusa, saddened at having had no children, went to Delphi one day to consult the oracle, who asked them to adopt Ion. But Creusa tried to poison her son whom she did not recognize; at that moment she was brought the basket in which she had abandoned him at birth. After these events, Ion married Helice, the daughter of Selinus, the king of the people of Aegialus, whom he succeeded before becoming the king of Attica at the death of Erechtheus. He governed this kingdom wisely after dividing it into four tribes. At his death, the country took his name and a colony of Athenians, who had set out for Asia Minor, gave the name of Ionia to the country in which they settled.

IPHICLES. The son of Amphitryon and Alcmene, Iphicles was born the night before Hera-

Iphicles, the twin brother of Heracles, raises his hands in fear and folds one of his legs under him to avoid being bitten by the serpent sent by Hera. Ancient bronze, Bibl. Nat., photo Giraudon.

cles, the son of Zeus and Alcmene. Of mortal birth, he had neither the strength nor the courage of his half-brother. One night, to take revenge on her rival, Hera sent two serpents to the home of Alcmene and these were supposed to kill Heracles. At the sight of them, Iphicles fled from his cradle, screaming, while Heracles, without losing his composure, and despite his tender age, strangled the two monsters. Later Iphicles was especially fond of the hero and accompanied him on several expeditions. His first marriage was to Automedusa, by whom he had Iolaus, and his second marriage was to the youngest daughter of Creon. He perished at the side of his brother during the war against the sons of Hippocoon.

IPHIGENIA. The daughter of Agamemnon and Clytemnestra, according to the most common tradition, Iphigenia was destined, on the advice of the soothsayer Calchas, to be sacrificed by her father to the goddess Artemis, who was delaying the Greek fleet in Aulis and preventing their setting sail for Troy. Summoned by her father on the pretext that she was to become the bride of Achilles, she was to perish by the knife of the high priest when Artemis, overcome with pity, substituted a doe for the girl and carried her away in a cloud, taking her to Tauris. There, Iphigenia became the high priestess of Artemis, responsible, above all, for sacrificing strangers to the goddess. One day, her brother Orestes landed on the coast of Tauris along with his friend Pylades. Taken prisoner, he was led to the temple where Iphigenia presided and was recognized by his sister. To save Orestes, the priestess annulled the sacrifice, claiming that the stranger who was guilty of murder could not be sacrificed before being purified. Then, taking the statue of Artemis, she fled with her brother and Pylades and arrived in Greece owing to favorable winds. It is said that Iphigenia died in Megara; but it is also said that Artemis had made the young woman immortal, identifying her with the goddess Hecate. In fact, it seems that Iphigenia had originally been one of the representations of Artemis.

Stripped, Iphigenia, carried by two servants, is brought before the high priest who raises his knife as he prepares to sacrifice her. He seems to hesitate a moment and turns his eyes toward the heavens. The goddess Artemis, mounted on a stag, rushes through a cloud and prepares to snatch the girl away. Here the artist has followed the later version of the legend. Fresco from Pompeii, Museum of Naples, photo X.

IPHIS. 1. A young Cretan woman, Iphis was destined to be exposed by her mother Telethusa because her father, Ligdus, did not want a daughter. On the advice of Isis, she was raised and dressed like a boy, to such a point that Ianthe, another young Cretan woman, was fooled and fell in love with Iphis. Telethusa tried, on several occasions, to prevent the marriage from taking place, not wishing to reveal the truth. Isis finally took pity on the unfortunate mother and changed Iphis into a young man, thus enabling him to marry Ianthe.

2. Also known by this name was the lover of Anaxarete who, out of despair over the disdain of the girl, killed himself.

IPHITUS. 1. The son of Eurytus, the king of Oechalia, Iphitus distinguished himself as a formidable archer among the Argonauts. He was the only one of the king's sons who sided with Heracles, who had just won Iole in a bow and arrow competition, but who quarreled over his prize with Eurytus. However, Iphitus was killed shortly after by Heracles from whom he tried to take back the stolen oxen. Another version claims that he was thrown from atop the walls of Tiryns by the hero who was suddenly overcome by a fit of madness.

2. Also known by the name of **Iphitus** was a semilegendary, semihistorical king who ruled Elis during the 9th century B.C. His kingdom was beset by divisions, famines and epidemics. On the advice of the oracle of Delphi, the sovereign reorganized the Olympic games founded by Heracles and in which the people had lost interest. He, therefore, reached an agreement with Lycurgus, the king of Sparta, and was able to introduce the first union among Greeks whose territories had been parceled up into many enemy States; during the Games, all hostilities were supposed to be suspended.

IRIS. This ancient divinity was the daughter of Thaumas and Electra. Messenger, servant,

Here Iris appears as the messenger of the gods. Her wings, her grace, because she was supposed to be a diplomat, the harmonious complexity of the folds of her robe, everything in this divinity expresses swiftness and charm. Greek drinking vessel (skyphos), 4th cent. B.C., Louvre.

and even the confidante of Hera, she took pains to obey even the most insignificant of orders from her mistress. She symbolizes the rainbow, the bridge between heaven and earth, between the gods and men, that she uses in her travels, in the form of a winged young woman, holding in one hand the wand of a herald. In later poems she is the wife of Zephyrus and the mother of Eros.

IRUS. 1. This beggar of Ithaca tried, to the delight of Penelope's suitors, to chase Ulysses, who had just returned home in disguise, by fighting with him. The hero easily triumphed over him.

2. Legend speaks of another **Irus,** the father of the Argonauts Eurydamas and Eurytion. Having accidentally killed one of his sons, Peleus offered him his cattle to console him. Irus refused to take the cattle and abandoned them, leaving them to be devoured by a wolf. The ferocious beast was changed into a stone statue.

ISIS. An Egyptian goddess, the wife of Osiris and mother of Horus, Isis was adored in late Antiquity by the Greeks who identified her legend with that of Io, then with that of Demeter. Indeed, in the legend, the goddesses left together, one in search of her husband, the other in search of her daughter, to snatch them from the kingdom of Death and Shadows. Isis was also worshiped under the Roman Empire, and a special temple was even erected in her honor on the Campus Martius. Thus she symbolized the Earth and the inexhaustible and fertile rebirth of all things.

ISMENE. Like Antigone, Eteocles and Polynices, Ismene was one of the children born of the marriage of Oedipus and his mother Jocasta. When Oedipus was banished from Thebes after his crimes, Ismene remained behind and did not accompany her sister Antigone and her blind father over the highways of Greece. But she was with Oedipus when he died in Colonus and she returned to Thebes with her sister. She witnessed the struggle that ended in the deaths of her two brothers, Eteocles and Polynices, who killed one another, and did not dare defy the order of Creon denying Polynices burial. However, when Antigone defied the order, Ismene tried to share the fatal lot of her sister by claiming that she too was responsible for the deed; Antigone gently pushed her away and met death alone. Ismene later loved a young Theban and was killed by Tydeus.

ITALUS. According to certain authors, Telegonus, the son of Circe and Ulysses, after having involuntarily killed his father, married Penelope, the widow of his father, and had a son,

Italus. This son gave his name to the country known as *Italy*, which was inhabited by the Siculi. In other legends, however, Italus is regarded as a native king.

ITHACA. One of the seven Iolian islands, Ithaca, not far from the coast of Epirus, was the fatherland and kingdom of Ulysses. It played a part in legends owing to the poems of Homer and its eponymous hero, Ithacus.

IULUS. Ascanius, the son of Aeneas, having led the people of Latium to victory against the Rutuli, was given the name of *Iulus*, a diminutive of *Jovis*, Jupiter, as a sign of grateful veneration. Other mythographers claim that Iulus was the son of Ascanius. He was supposed to have been banished from the kingdom of Latium by his uncle Silvius and was forced to dedicate himself to the priesthood.

IXION. Ixion received the punishment reserved for ingrates in the Underworld. This king of the Lapiths, after having married Dia, the daughter of King Deioneus, refused his father-in-law the riches that he had promised him and then killed him by flinging him into a furnace. The crime was doubly heinous because the perpetrator was guilty not only of perjury but of the murder of a relative as well. Ixion, whom no one would agree to purify, implored Zeus: the sovereign god was touched by his tears and even invited him to his table, where he consumed nectar and ambrosia, ensuring his immortality. However, showing no gratitude for this kindness, Ixion tried to seduce Hera. Zeus, therefore, created a cloud that resembled his wife. Ixion had relations with this apparition. The centaurs were the offspring of this illusory love affair. Hermes was in-

The Roman legend has followed the Greek legend. Mercury, identified by his caduceus, comes to chain up Ixion, at the extreme left, to a flaming wheel that will turn eternally in the Underworld; at the right, Juno, whom the accused criminal tried to seduce, watches the scene with satisfaction. Fresco from Pompeii, House of the Vettii, photo Alinari-Giraudon.

structed to administer the punishment that this ingrate deserved. The god tied Ixion with serpents to a wheel which turned endlessly in the depths of Tartarus.

J K

JANUS. This divinity is doubtless one of the greatest gods of the Roman Pantheon and even possesses a certain preeminence over the supreme god, Jupiter. He was supposed to have arrived in Italy with a fleet and settled in Latium where it is said that he founded a city which took his name, *Janiculum.* He ruled Latium and welcomed Saturn there when he was banished from the heavens. To thank him, Saturn gave Janus the gift of "double knowledge," that of the past and that of the future, a myth that the Romans illustrated by portraying Janus with two faces turned in opposite directions. This two-faced god possessed many other attributes. He is the divinity that watches over doors, because all doors look at both sides (*Janus Bifrons*). Whenever war was declared, the Romans solemnly opened the doors of his sanctuary to indicate that the god had left for war, and closed them in times of peace to show that the god, protector of the city, had returned to his sanctuary. Gradually, the attributes of Janus were extended considerably. He became the god of beginnings, that of the year (*Januarius* means "January"); the god of the Four Seasons: as such, he has four heads instead of two. Ovid claims that Janus possessed a double face because he exercised his power over both Heaven and Earth. He was perhaps not even a cosmogonical god but merely, and exclusively, a Roman god, symbolizing surveillance of the city, where traffic flowed through the Tiber, both upstream and downstream.

The god Janus, whose two faces, looking in opposite directions toward the left and right, toward peace and war, upstream and downstream, are the most significant expression of the ambiguity of human and divine thought and the Manicheism of all religion. Roman silver coin, circa 268 B.C., Bibl. Nat., Cabinet des Médailles, photo Larousse.

JASON. The son of Aeson, the king of Iolcus in Thessaly, Jason was still a child when his uncle Pelias dethroned his father. He was able to escape, however, and was raised by the cen-

Like all the other heroes of mythology, Jason was familiar with the art of medicine. He learned it from his master, the centaur Chiron. Here he can be seen examining the liver of a sick man. The liver is the organ of strength in primitive beliefs. Greek funerary stele, photo B. Guégan.

taur Chiron. When he reached adulthood, he left Mount Pelion for Iolcus in the hope of taking revenge on Pelias and reestablishing Aeson on the throne. On the way, on the banks of a river, he met an old woman who was actually Hera in disguise, and she asked him to carry her to the other side. After rendering this service, which earned him the favors of the god-

dess for a short time, he realized that he had lost one of his sandals. Now an oracle had told Pelias to beware of anyone who came to him barefooted. Thus, when Jason arrived in his court, the king, at the sight of this man with no shoes, was overcome with fear. In order to be rid of him, Pelias instructed Jason to lead an expedition in search of the Golden Fleece, which was guarded by the king of Colchis, Aeetes. Jason agreed and set sail on the *Argo* with the major Greek heroes known as "the Argonauts." With the help of Medea, whom he married, he was able to seize the Golden Fleece and return to Iolcus with it. There he avenged the death of his father, whom Pelias had killed in his absence. But, banished by Acastus, he was forced to flee to Corinth with Medea. There, he fell in love with Creusa, the daughter of Creon, and betrayed Medea, who took revenge by causing the death of her rival and killing her own sons. There are two different versions of the demise of Jason: according to one, the hero killed himself in despair at the news of the death of his children; according to the other, he died, crushed by the prow of the *Argo*.

JOCASTA. The daughter of a prince of the royal family of Thebes, Jocasta, known as *Epicasta* in the poems of Homer, had the sad privilege of being both the mother and wife of Oedipus, the murderer of her first husband Laius. Jocasta bore him four children—Eteocles, Polynices, Antigone and Ismene, also known as the "Labdacidae," whom, as a sign of a curse, mis-

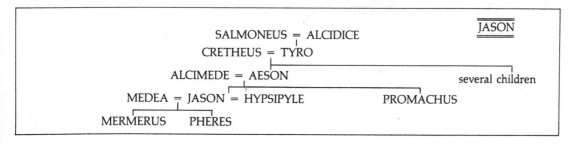

Here Juno poses majestically. However, the goddess of women and fertility has the general appearance of a matron with ample curves and large hips. Ancient sculpture, Vatican Museum, photo Alinari-Giraudon.

fortune was to plague. When she learned of her incestuous act, Jocasta hanged herself in her palace.

JUNO. The name of Juno is most unlikely to have come from the same root as that of Jupiter. As Jupiter is the king of the Heavens and of the gods, Juno was worshiped in Rome as the queen of the Heavens and the wife of Jupiter. Protectress of women, she accompanies them, during life, from birth until death. She plays the part of a sort of double divinity, each woman having her Juno just as each man possesses his own genius. For each decisive stage in a woman's life, she bears a different surname. When she presides over marriage, she is known as *Jugalis*. Women in childbirth ask for her aid, invoking her as *Juno Lucina*. When children are born they are placed under her protection. In fact, more than merely the goddess of Wives, she is the supreme patron of mothers, in whose honor the *Matronalia* was celebrated on March 1. Her political role is not an insignificant one either. In the company of Jupiter and Minerva, she is part of the Trinity of the Capitol which preserves the Roman state and ensures its perpetuity. Less important, but nearer to mortals than the Greek Hera with whom she is identified, the Roman Juno bears witness, above all, to the fertile power of women.

JUPITER. Throughout Roman Antiquity, Jupiter was the greatest of all gods, the sovereign of Heaven and Earth. Worshiped originally as the divinity of the Elements—time, thunder, lightning, light—bearing various surnames, suggestive epithets such as *Fulminator, Fulgurator, Tonitrualis, Pluvius, Tonans,* he gradually absorbed the smaller local deities of Italy, and his attributes as well as his representations took on many novel aspects. The Roman State, centralized to the extreme, needed a god who, on the religious level, ensured and strengthened its unity. Jupiter became, to a certain extent, a political god, guaranteeing laws, treaties and oaths, and supporting Rome in its wars. The spoils of enemy leaders were dedicated to Jupiter Feretrius. Jupiter Stator was invoked to stop an invasion—during the conflict between the Romans and the Sabines, for instance. A temple was erected in his honor on the Capitol where, along with Juno and Minerva, he made up the Capitoline triad that protected the integrity of the city. He bore the name of *Optimus Maximus* and consuls implored his assistance and indulgence as they began the exercise of their office. The preeminence of Jupiter in the Roman State was so strong that it was not overshadowed even by the introduction of Zeus in the Pantheon. Although it may be true that the countless myths of the latter were attributed to the former, Jupiter nonetheless retained his political importance until the end of paganism. He continued to ensure a unique bond among the various cities of the Roman Empire which each possessed its own temples and statues dedicated to Jupiter. Augustus, the architect of the Roman Empire, claimed to be under his special protection; and Caligula adopted the name *Optimus Maximus.*

JUSTITIA. This Roman allegorical divinity, with a severe yet dignified appearance, was identified with the Themis of the Greeks. At one time, she lived on Earth, when men lived in goodness and peace. But when the golden age ended and certain tendencies toward crime and iniquity were born in the hearts of men, Justitia preferred to flee and return to the heavens where she became the constellation of Virgo.

JUTURNA. Originally a nymph of a spring in Latium with the name *Diuturna,* Juturna, the sister of Turnus, king of the Rutuli, was famous in Roman mythology for her beauty. Jupiter, who was in love with her, granted her immortality and the power to reign over the

A colossus with powerful muscles, Jupiter appears here as the sovereign god. The lightning he brandishes adds to the feeling of respectful fear he inspires in men. Ancient sculpture from Smyrna, Louvre, photo Giraudon.

LABDACUS. The name of this king of Thebes, the grandson of Cadmus and Harmonia, father of Laius and grandfather of Oedipus, deserves to be retained, above all, because it was used to designate by the surname *Labdacidae* the famous Theban heroes and heroines, including Oedipus, Polynices, Eteocles, Antigone, Ismene. Little is known about Labdacus except that he reigned in Thebes at a rather late period and that his reign was marked by a war against Pandion, the king of Athens.

labyrinth. The word labyrinth is undoubtedly pre-Greek. The famous labyrinth was designed and constructed by Daedalus, on the order of the Cretan King Minos, to hide from the sight of the living the Minotaur, a monster with the body of a man and the head of a bull. It was built in the open and comprised a series of rooms and overlapping corridors, arranged with scientific disorder. Only Theseus, with the help of Ariadne's thread, succeeded in finding the way, coming upon the Minotaur and killing it. The myth of the labyrinth was taken up in a more original way by another legend, that of King Cocalus. To discover Daedalus, Minos proclaimed that he would offer a reward to anyone who could pass a thread through the inside spiral of a snail's shell. Daedalus succeeded by fastening a thread to the leg of an ant; the insect entered the shell and passed through the turns of the spiral to reach the end of the labyrinth with this thread.

LACEDAEMON. The eponymous king of the territory occupied by the Lacedaemonians, Lacedaemon married Sparte, the daughter of King Eurotas, and he named the capital of his kingdom after his wife. He had a son, Amyclas, who succeeded him on the throne, and a daughter, Eurydice, the wife of Acrisius, son of Abas.

LADON. **1.** River-god of Arcadia, a tributary of the Alpheus, the son of Oceanus and Tethys, the spouse of Stymphalis and the father of Daphne and Metope. On his banks, the god Pan met the nymph Syrinx and began to pursue her. She threw herself into the river, who changed her into a reed.

2. The dragon that guarded the golden apples of the Hesperides also bore the name of **Ladon.**

LAERTES. This king of Ithaca, the son of Acrisius, took part in the expedition of the Argonauts and in the Calydonian Boar Hunt. His wife Anticlea, the daughter of Autolycus, gave birth to Ulysses. He led a sad and withdrawn existence during the long absence of his son. He revived when his son returned, and, according to post-Homeric legend, rejuvenated by Athena, he was able to help Ulysses do away with the relatives of massacred suitors.

LAESTRYGONIANS. Having stopped somewhere after leaving the island of Aeolus, Ulysses and his companions were attacked by the Laestrygonians, man-eating giants, who threw stones at them and sank almost all of their ships. The king of Ithaca was able to escape them but many of the seamen who accompanied him were gathered up in the immense hands of the Laestrygonians and devoured.

LAIUS. The son of Labdacus, king of Thebes, Laius succeeded his father and married Jocasta, according to the tradition of the tragic poets. The oracle of Delphi had predicted that if he had a son by this woman, he would be killed by him; he sent his wife away from his bed, without giving her a reason. Annoyed, Jocasta plied him with liquor, plunging him into a state of semiconsciousness, and conceived a son, Oedipus. Abandoned on a mountain, Oedipus was rescued and raised by Polybus, the king of Corinth. One day, Oedipus met Laius along the way. Unaware of their family bond, they quarreled and Oedipus killed Laius. Later he married the widow of his victim, his own mother. It is also said that Laius was the first homosexual.

LAMIA. Often identified with Empusa, Lamia assumed the appearance of a terrifying phantom to kidnap and devour children. At one time she had been a beautiful young woman, the daughter of King Belus. After having relations with Zeus, she gave birth to several children whom Hera, out of jealousy, caused to perish. Lamia took revenge by changing herself into a monster and devouring nurslings. Hera, therefore, forbade her to sleep. Zeus, to console his beloved who was the victim of such persecution, granted her the power to remove her eyes or put them back at will.

LAMPETIA. The daughter of Helios, Lampetia, with her sister Phaethusa, guarded the sacred herds of her father in Sicily. When the companions of Ulysses devoured some of the cattle, the two sisters went to Helios and informed him of the sacrilege. The enraged god had Zeus strike down the impious creatures.

LAOCOON. According to the best-known version of his legend, Laocoon was the son of the Trojan prince Antenor. Responsible for the cult of Apollo, he committed a sacrilege by marrying, thus violating a vow of celibacy, which incurred the wrath of Apollo. He played a determining role in the fall of Troy, especially in the episode of the famous wooden horse against which he threw his spear to show the Trojans that the flanks of the animal were hollow and concealed weapons. He urged them not to allow this camouflaged fortress into their city. At that moment, two enormous serpents emerged from the sea and lunged at the impious priest and his two sons, lacerating them and strangling them. However, the Trojans thought that his refusal to allow the wooden horse to enter the city had incurred the anger of the gods. Thus they threw open the gates of the ramparts and, with this unfortunate gesture, they set the wheels in motion for the ruin of Troy.

LAODAMEIA. 1. This daughter of Acastus loved her husband Protesilaus passionately. When she learned of his death before the walls of Troy, she begged the gods to grant her the permission to see her husband once more for just three hours. This favor was granted but when the time allotted ran out and Protesilaus prepared to descend to the Underworld for the second time, Laodameia killed herself so that she could remain with him. It is also said that Laodameia would spend the night in the embrace of a wax statue that she had fashioned into a likeness of Protesilaus. Learning of this,

In this masterpiece of Hellenistic art, the artist has powerfully rendered the feeling of impotence of these victims of the anger of the gods. Rebellion, as well as supplication, animates the bodies as well as the faces of Laocoon and his sons, who try to pry themselves loose from the grip of the serpent, a gigantic monster sent by the gods. Marble, circa 50. B.C., Vatican Museum, photo Anderson-Giraudon.

Acastus had the statue thrown into the fire. Laodameia plunged into the flames after it and perished.

2. Also known by this name is a nursemaid who rescued and saved Orestes.

3. A third **Laodameia** was the daughter of Bellerophon. She was loved by Zeus and gave birth to a son, Sarpedon.

LAODICE. **1.** The daughter of Priam and Hecuba, Laodice was, according to some, the wife of Telephus; according to others, the wife of Helicaon, the son of Antenor. She had been the mistress of Acamas, one of the sons of Theseus, when he came to Troy on a mission, and had given birth to a son, Munitus. At the fall of Troy, she fled, but the earth opened up beneath her and swallowed her up.

2. Another **Laodice,** the daughter of Clytemnestra and Agamemnon, is known by the Greek tragic poets as *Electra*.

LAOMEDON. This son of Ilus succeeded his father on the throne of Troy. With the help of Poseidon and Apollo, he had the city surrounded by immense ramparts and constructed a port protected by huge dikes. When the gods had accomplished their respective tasks, Laomedon refused to sacrifice the heads of cattle born during the year as he had promised. To take revenge, Apollo sent his kingdom an epidemic and Poseidon unleashed a monster that ravaged the fields by flooding them with seawater. The oracle consulted announced that the king had to expose his daughter Hesione to the furies of the monster in order to appease the enraged god of the Sea. Laomedon was thus obliged to fasten his daughter to a rock on the shore. But chance decreed that Heracles, along with Telamon, should land on the banks of Troy at that moment and see the girl. The hero broke the chains immediately and offered to slay the monster. As a reward the king promised to give him the two immortal white horses, lighter than air, that had been given to him by Zeus after the abduction of Ganymede. Heracles, therefore, plunged his sword into the throat of the monster. Once again, Laomedon went back on his word. Having decided to take revenge, Heracles left the city of Troy, mobilized an army and returned to the city, declaring an immediate siege. He toppled the walls, killed Laomedon and all of his children, except Priam, whom he placed on the throne, and Hesione, whom he offered to his faithful companion, Telamon.

LAPITHS. A mythical people, the Lapiths lived in the mountains of Thessaly. They played a role in many legends (Argonauts, Calydonian Boar Hunt) and made their mark particularly in the battle that pitted them against the Centaurs, who were claiming their share of their heritage. Indeed, they were governed by Pirithous, the son of Ixion, and, consequently, the half-brother of the Centaurs. To appease them, Pirithous invited them to his wedding. Intoxicated, the Centaurs attacked the Lapiths, trying to rape Hippodamia, the bride of Pirithous, but were finally defeated.

Combat of Lapiths against the Centaurs. Hydria from Cerveteri, Latium, photo Giraudon.

LAR. A Roman god of Etruscan origin, the son of Mercury and Lara (according to Ovid), Lar, in the form of a small statue with the features of an adolescent, embodies the souls of the dead. He protects each Roman dwelling, transmitted from generation to generation. The domestic Lares were joined by the many public Lares who guaranteed the safety of the streets, fields and crossroads, and the Lares of the city who were chosen from among the Roman gods: thus Janus, Diana, Mercury.

LARA. Lara, whose name was originally *Lala* or "tattletale," is the heroine of a legend related by Ovid in his *Fasti*. Nymph of the Almon, a stream that empties into the Tiber, she refused to yield to the orders of Jupiter who had asked divinities of the rivers to help him steal Juturna, his beloved. What is more, Lara went to tell Juno and Juturna of the plans of Jupiter. Furious, the god pulled out her tongue and ordered Mercury to take the gossip to the Underworld. (She was henceforth called *Dea Muta* or *Tacita*.) En route, the god seduced her and made her the mother of the Lares. Lara was considered by the Romans to be the goddess of Scandalmongering as well as one of the divinities of eternal silence, death.

LARVAE. These evil-minded, demoniacal genii were often confused with the Lemures. They also represented the spirits of the dead that had not received burials or had committed unatonable crimes during their lifetimes. The Larvae returned to earth to torment the living and appeared to them in the form of ghosts or skeletons, bringing with them terror, neuroses and even epilepsy.

LATINUS. This legendary king, who gave his name to the Latins, was for the Romans one of the sons of Circe and Ulysses or else a grandson of Ulysses, or else the son of Faunus and the nymph Marica. By his wife Amata he had one daughter, Lavinia, whom Turnus, the king of the Rutuli, desired. But one day, as she was offering a sacrifice, Lavinia burst into flames without experiencing the slightest pain. Asked about this miracle, her grandfather Faunus assured her that she was to await, before marrying, the arrival of a splendid warrior who would glorify the name of the Latins. When Aeneas landed in Latium, the king recognized the hero whose arrival had been foretold and gave him his daughter in marriage. After his death, Latinus was divinized by the name of *Jupiter Latiaris*.

LATIUM. A territory located between Etruria, to the north, and Campania, to the south, Latium is mentioned in many Roman legends prior to the founding of Rome. It was, in fact, governed by a series of legendary kings who, after their death, were granted the honors of deification (Janus, Picus, Faunus, Aeneas). The population of its capital, Alba Longa, emigrated throughout the region and, it is said, founded the city of Rome.

LAVERNA. This Roman divinity of obscure origin frequented infamous places and granted impunity to the bandits who invoked her. Thus she became the goddess of Thieves. The name seems Etruscan.

LAVINIA. The only daughter of King Latinus and Amata, Lavinia was engaged to marry a native leader, Turnus. But Faunus, her grandfather, opposed this marriage through his oracles and requested that she await the arrival of a stranger who would beget a race that would be called upon to rule the world. Aeneas, landing shortly afterwards in Italy, found refuge with Latinus, who, convinced that Aeneas was the incarnation of the prophecy, gave him the hand of his daughter. But Juno, who relentlessly persecuted all members of the Trojan race, provoked, through the intervention of the Fury Alecto, the anger and opposition of Amata and the jealous fury of Turnus, and gave rise to an inexpiable war. Aeneas emerged victorious and married Lavinia. Widowed, Lavinia gave birth, after her husband's death, to Silvius, to whom Ascanius, his half-brother, was forced to yield the city of Lavinium, designating him later as his successor to the throne.

LEANDER. This young man of Abydos would swim across the Hellespont each night to join Hero, a priestess of Aphrodite, who lived on the opposite bank. She guided the way of her beloved with a torch. They left one another in the morning, at dawn. But, one stormy night, a gust of wind blew out the flame of the torch. Leander was lost in the darkness of the waves and, thoroughly exhausted, drowned. The sea threw his body up on the shore where, mad with worry, Hero had spent hours awaiting him. In despair, the unfortunate young woman threw herself into the waves and, in this way, joined her deceased lover.

LEARCHUS. Persephone had entrusted the young Dionysus to King Athamas of Orchomenus and his wife, Ino. Crazed by Hera, the king killed his son Learchus, taking him for a stag, and cut his body into pieces. It is also said that Learchus was inadvertently killed in place of his mother Ino. Athamas wanted to punish his wife for having persecuted Phrixus and Helle, the two children he had had by Nephele.

LEDA. The daughter of Thestius, king of Aetolia, Leda lived in her father's court where she made the acquaintance of Tyndareos, who had been dethroned in Sparta. She married him and bore him an illustrious progeny that came from an egg: Pollux and Helen, children of Zeus, who had had relations with Leda in the form of a swan, and Castor and Clytemnestra, the legitimate children of Tyndareos.

LELEX. The eponymous king of the Leleges in Sparta, Lelex had two sons, Myles and Polycaon. The former was the father of the river-

god Eurotas while the latter gave the territory he governed the name of his spouse *Messene* (Messenia). Also considered to be the grandfather of Teleboas as well, Lelex would thus be the ancestor of the Teleboans, the subjects of King Pterelaus.

LEMNOS. One of the most famous islands of the Aegean Sea, Lemnos is seen in mythology as the territory through which a host of heroes passed, such as the Argonauts and Philoctetes; it is thought that Hephaestus landed there when Zeus threw him out of Olympus. The island was populated by the Thracians. But they were massacred by their wives, who were damned by Aphrodite. This episode gave rise to the phrase "Lemnian Evils." Hypsipyle, one of the Lemnian women, was chosen as queen. Jason landed on Lemnos, and the Argonauts had relations with the Lemnian women, but the race that was born was banished from the island by the Pelasgians.

LEMURES. These were the pernicious, disturbed and disturbing spirits of the dead who sometimes returned to their dwellings to terrorize the living. In order to appease them, or rather to be rid of them, the Romans celebrated the feast called the "Lemuria" on May 9, 11, and 13. During this feast, each pater familias threw black beans behind him while saying nine times, "With these beans I redeem myself and my family." Afterwards, he beat on bronze nine times, saying, "Be gone, ancestral shades." Furthermore, during this period all the temples were closed and marriages were prohibited.

LETHE. The daughter of Eris (Discord) and the mother of the Charites, Lethe is a spring in the Underworld to which the souls of the dead come to drink in order to forget their past sufferings and the circumstances of their previous earthly existence. Under the influence of neo-Platonic doctrine, Lethe became the river in which every soul that returned to Earth had to be immersed to forget the former person it had inhabited and to forget, above all, the related images of the Underworld and Death.

LETO. Known as *Latona* by the Romans, Leto, the daughter of the Titan Coeus and the Titanid Phoebe, was loved by Zeus who begat twins by her. But the god, dreading the wrath of Hera, abandoned his beloved. Hera, having discovered the infidelity of her husband, ordered all lands to refuse to welcome Leto. The poor creature wandered from place to place for months. She finally reached a small bit of land floating in the water that went by the name of Ortygia. This arid, desolate island opened its doors to Leto, who was already experiencing the first pangs of childbirth. Neither Hera nor Eileithyia, the goddess of Childbirth and Birth, would come to the aid of Leto to help her obtain a prompt delivery. Thus the woman suffered for nine days and nine nights: she did not give birth to her divine children, Apollo and Artemis, before the arrival of Eileithyia, who

Under the palms of Delphi where Apollo established his cult, Leto listens to the melody her son draws from his lyre and accompanies him on a sort of crotalum. Greek amphora, Louvre, photo Giraudon.

finally let herself be swayed. Thus Ortygia was fastened to the depths of the sea by four pillars and vegetation and flowers began to break through the arid crust of its soil. It took the name of *Delos,* "the brilliant one," and became one of the most famous and fertile islands of the Cyclades. Leto, as a reward for her steadfastness and courage, was entitled to the affection of her two children who defended her against the giant Tityus, the insults of Niobe and the serpent Python.

LEUCIPPUS. **1.** This son of Oenomaus disguised himself as a woman to draw nearer to Daphne, whom he loved. But his trick was discovered and the nymphs tore him to pieces or, according to another version, he was taken away by the gods.

2. Another **Leucippus** is known, the son of Perieres of Messenia and the husband of Philodice, the daughter of the river-god Inachus. He had three daughters, Phoebe and Hilaera, engaged to Idas and Lynceus and abducted by the Dioscuri, and Arsinoë, who was the lover of Apollo and considered the mother of Asclepius in some regions. This Leucippus gave his name to the city of Leuctra.

LEUCOTHEA. This is the name assumed by Ino after she acceded to the ranks of the sea divinities. She was the daughter of Cadmus and Harmonia and the sister of Semele, mother of Dionysus. Athamas, the king of Thebes, had dishonored Nephele, by whom he had two children, Phrixus and Helle, in order to marry Ino. She bore him two sons, Learchus and Melicertes. Fearing that the children of the first marriage would reign in the place of her own sons, Leucothea caused a terrible famine to plague Thebes. Having then bribed the oracle, she had it proclaimed that the gods demanded the sacrifice of Phrixus. Phrixus had just enough time to flee with his sister. But the curse was to fall upon the couple: to punish them for having raised the young Dionysus, the son born of the

Ino, the daughter of Cadmus, raises the young Dionysus in the woods and quenches his thirst. The scene is brimming with a delicate grace: tender gestures of the woman toward the child; agricultural scenes (Pan with his flute, goats, the animals consecrated to Dionysus, the eagle tearing its prey, the little birds in their nest). Roman relief, Lateran Museum, photo Alinari-Giraudon.

adultery of Zeus, Hera drove both of them mad. Taking him for a wild beast, Athamas killed his own son, Learchus. Leucothea, for her part, flung Melicertes into a cauldron of boiling water and threw herself into the sea with the corpse of her child. Thus the wrath of the gods was appeased. Leucothea became a divinity of the sea and she was colored white, similar to the spray of the sea. She was granted certain

powers to calm storms and was identified by the Romans with the goddess Mater Matuta. Her son was also revered as a god and associated with the Roman god, Portunus, the guardian of ports.

LIBER. This archaic divinity of central Italy, who did not possess his own mythology, and his assistant Libera presided over the cultivation of the vine and the fertility of the fields. Thus they were easily identified with Bacchus or Dionysus, the god of Wine, and Ceres, the goddess of Corn.

LIBERTAS. This allegorical divinity was created for the needs of Roman imperial policy. Associated with Jupiter, she was worshiped mainly on the Aventine; she was given the appearance of a woman wearing a Phrygian cap, a universally recognized symbol of freedom since the French Revolution, and holding laurel branches.

LIBITINA. This very old divinity of the netherworld possesses neither a legend nor a myth. She was assigned to funeral ceremonies, the smooth progress of which she ensured. Thus she was quickly confused with Proserpina, the goddess of Death. As a result of erroneous etymology, she was identified with *Libido* (Passion) and she became part of the entourage of Venus.

LICHAS. A companion of Heracles, Lichas was instructed by Deianira to take the tunic of Nessus to his master who was to put it on as he offered a sacrifice to Zeus. As he put it on, Heracles felt his entire body being consumed. Wild with pain, overturning altars, uprooting trees, he cursed the terrified Lichas who tried to disclaim any responsibility. Heracles did not listen to him, seized him by the foot, twirled him over his head and flung him into the Gulf of Euboea. There, the unfortunate creature was changed into the rocky islands known as the Lichades.

LICYMNIUS. The son of Electryon and a slave, Media, Licymnius, after the death of his father, accompanied Amphitryon and his half-sister Alcmene to Thebes where he married Perimede, the sister of Amphitryon, who bore him three sons, Oenus, Argeius and Melas, all of whom accompanied Heracles on some of his expeditions. The first was killed in Sparta by the sons of Hippocoon; the other two were massacred during a raid in Oechalia against King Eurytus. After the death of his nephew Heracles, Licymnius was pursued, with the Heraclidae, by Eurystheus and tried in vain to settle in Peloponnesus. It is said that Tlepolemus, one of the Heraclidae, wanted to beat one of his slaves with a rod but instead inadvertently struck Licymnius as he tried to intervene, killing him.

LINUS. It seems that originally the Linus was a sort of song of mourning. But, gradually, the Linus was personified. According to a tradition of Argolis, Psamathe, the daughter of King Crotopus, had a son, Linus, by Apollo. Fearing her father's wrath, she exposed him. Shepherds retrieved him, but shortly afterwards he was devoured by dogs. Psamathe was unable to hide her sorrow and thus revealed her deed. Furious, her father had her put to death. This double crime incurred the wrath of Apollo who punished the city of Argos by sending a Harpy, then a plague. The oracle of Delphi instructed the Argives to establish a cult in memory of Linus and Psamathe: the epidemic immediately ceased.

In Boeotia, another legend related that the mother of Linus was a Muse. An excellent musician, he was assigned to teach Heracles. But one day as Linus was reprimanding his disobedient pupil, the hero killed his master. It is also said that Linus was shameless enough to compete with Apollo by claiming that he played the lyre better than the god did. Enraged, the god was supposed to have killed him to punish him for his insolent pride.

LOTIS. This nymph always managed to escape the god Priapus who would try to seduce her by surprise. She was saved by the braying of the ass of Silenus, which enabled her to flee whenever the god came near her. One day as she was about to succumb to Priapus, she changed herself into a bush, the lotus.

LOTOPHAGI. This fantastic people, whom the Ancients identified with the populations of Northeast Africa, had the strange, yet original, custom of eating only a fruit, the lotus with its flavorful taste of honey and crushed flowers. Anyone who landed in their territories, as did Ulysses and his companions one day, would be given this unknown food, the flavor of which was so fine and so delicate that the newcomers, enchanted, would forget their homelands and refuse to leave a country that afforded such euphoria. In the face of this danger for which he had not planned, Ulysses was obliged to use force to get his companions to return to their boats and set sail for their fatherland.

loves. In the Roman Empire, the Loves were described or represented as little winged cherubs, the customary companions of Venus, who acted as her attendants. They played music and, for their own enjoyment, they even took part in violent pleasures, such as hunting or the forging of arms. Soon, they symbolized the seasons and they were depicted in various and typical ways depending on the time of year: as reapers or wine-harvesters, for instance. The paintings of Pompeii multiplied the Loves in the mythological scenes found there. They gave them a part to play, as kindly spirits, in the feelings uniting Helen with Paris, Ariadne with Dionysus, or Mars with Venus.

LUA. The Ancients consecrated to this primitive Italic divinity the booty of war and the

Love, the young son of Venus, is the size of an adolescent. A winged spirit, in order to fly more rapidly towards smitten hearts, he holds a crown for every lover. "L'Amour Farnese," Louvre, photo Giraudon.

weapons captured during battles. Since she came into contact with dead warriors, she was sometimes placed among the divinities of the Underworld and referred to as *Lua Saturni*.

LUCIFER. Star-god of the Romans, identified with Phosphorus of the Greeks, Lucifer ("bearer of light") announced the Dawn, whose son he is. He is known by other names, all of which designate the Evening or the Morning Star: Hesperus, Heosphorus. He is the father of Ceyx and of Daedalion, the father of Chione.

Lucifer is also the epithet assumed by the principal divinities of Light.

LUPERCUS. This ancient Italian god, a friend of shepherds and protector of herds against wolves, was quickly identified by the Romans with Faunus, then, after the conquest of Greece, with the Arcadian Pan. The Lupercalia was celebrated in his honor to prevent feminine sterility.

LYCAON. **1.** The son of Pelasgus, Lycaon, the king of Arcadia, and his fifty sons were known for their impiousness. Zeus decided to visit them one day in the form of a poor peasant. Lycaon, to find out whether this stranger at his table was actually a god, had the effrontery to serve him food mixed with human flesh. Zeus, indignant, pushed the banquet table away and struck down all of the sons of the king except Nyctimus, who acceded to the throne. Zeus changed Lycaon into a wolf. According to one legend, Lycaon was also the father of Callisto, who became the constellation of the Great Bear.

2. Son of Priam, another **Lycaon** was surprised in the garden of his father by Achilles, who made him prisoner. Patroclus sold Lycaon at Lemnos, but Eetion of Imbros ransomed him, and Lycaon returned to Troy in secret, only to be killed by Achilles twelve days later.

LYCOMEDES. The king of the island of Scyros, Lycomedes received Achilles who, dis-

Hidden among the daughters of Lycomedes, Achilles spends his time playing the lyre. His face, through a sort of mimesis, is almost that of a girl whose appearance he has assumed to hide from the Greeks who were looking for him. But Ulysses, to the right, blows into a trumpet and awakens the warrior zeal of the hero who agreed in the end to leave for Troy. Greek relief, Louvre, photo Giraudon.

guised as a woman, tried, on the advice of his mother Thetis, to avoid leaving for Troy. There, Achilles had by Deidameia, the daughter of Lycomedes, a famous son, Neoptolemus. This king is also seen in the Athenian legend of Theseus. When the hero arrived in Scyros, Lycomedes received him with much ostentation. But fearing that his guest would steal his kingdom from him, he had him taken to the top of a cliff and pushed into the void.

LYCURGUS. **1.** When Dionysus arrived in Thrace with his entourage of Bacchantes and faithful followers, he was attacked by Lycurgus, king of the Edonians, who captured the army of the god and forced him to flee and take refuge in the sea, in the depths of the grotto of Thetis. The impiousness of the king brought him a punishment. The gods helped the imprisoned Bacchantes to break their chains and drive Lycurgus mad: the unfortunate king put his son Dryas to death by the blows of an axe, thinking that he was chopping down a vine. In light of the horror of this crime, the ground of Thrace became sterile. Lycurgus was attached to four wild horses, which quartered him and tore him to pieces. The countryside was once again fertile.

2. The king of Nemea, another **Lycurgus,** welcomed the Seven Leaders who were on their way to Thebes, agreed to give them water, and instructed Hypsipyle to guide them.

LYCUS. **1.** The son of Cadmus, the king of Thebes, Lycus was put to death with his wife Dirce by Amphion and Zethus for having treated Antiope so cruelly.

2. Another **Lycus,** the son of Pandion, was banished from the kingdom of Athens by his brother Aegeus and sought refuge in Messenia where, having become the high priest of the goddesses Demeter and Persephone, he introduced their mysteries and received the gift of prophecy. But it is also said that he emigrated to the country in Asia Minor that bears his name, *Lycia.*

3. A third **Lycus,** king of the Mariandynians, received the help of Heracles and, thanks to him, was able to seize control of the kingdom of the Bebryces.

LYNCEUS. **1.** The son of Aegyptus, Lynceus was the only one to escape the massacre of his brothers by the Danaids and was saved through the help of his wife, Hypermnestra. He fled to Argos and, on a neighboring hill, awaited a signal from his wife to return safe and sound. The Argives each year commemorated this legend by a torchlight retreat. It is said that Lynceus became reconciled with his father-in-law Danaus, but other legends indicate that Lynceus later killed the king and reigned in his place. Perhaps he even massacred all of his sisters-in-law to avenge the murder of his brothers.

2. A hero of Messenia, the brother of Idas and son of Aphareus, this **Lynceus** was one of the most famous Argonauts: his sight was so piercing that he saw in the darkness as well as he did in broad daylight. He was killed by Pollux, one of the Dioscuri.

LYNCUS. The king of Scythia, Lyncus received in his court one day Triptolemus whom Demeter had instructed to teach the entire world the art of cultivating corn. Jealous of his powers and his gifts, the king wanted to kill his guest during the night. But Demeter prevented this criminal act and changed Lyncus into a lynx.

lyre. According to some, the Muse Polyhymnia should be credited with the invention of this musical instrument, but others say that it was Hermes who, still a newborn, escaping from his cradle, happened upon a tortoise, which he killed, and stretched seven strings across the hollow of the animal's shell. A symbol of poetry, the lyre is not only the favorite instrument of Apollo but also that of the myth-

The lyre, played with the fingers, without plectrum. Detail of a Greek cup with white background, Louvre, photo Giraudon.

ical poets, such as Orpheus, who could charm the Sirens with its sounds, and Thamyris, who wanted to compete with the Muses: punished for his vanity, he was stricken blind.

M

MACHAON. The son of Asclepius, Machaon reigned with his brother Podalirius over three cities in Thessaly. A suitor for Helen, he took part in the expedition against Troy. Having received from his father the precious gift of healing even the most serious of wounds, he offered his services to the heroes. He cared for Menelaus, wounded by an arrow of Pandarus, and Philoctetes, gnawed at by a wound inflicted ten years before by an arrow of Heracles. He was also one of the warriors who hid in the flanks of the Trojan horse. Machaon was later killed by Eurypylus, the son of Telephus. The sacred ashes of this physician with his miraculous science were taken by Nestor to the sanctuary of Gerenia where the sick went to seek cures.

madness. Mysterious, sometimes sudden, madness often strikes characters in mythology. It is most of the time a manifestation of the wrath of the gods. A particular god usually sends the Erinyes, who torment criminals or murderers until they begin to hallucinate, and sometimes plague even a group of men or women for collective faults. Only purification can put an end to the onset of insanity. Purification is, therefore, a privileged sign of pardon from the gods. Once cleansed of his crime, an insane criminal may once again become a normal being. Certain divinities associated with the cult of Dionysus, such as the Maenads, were suddenly seized by the god and seemed to be possessed by a mysterious force that caused them to lose all reason and drove them on mad and tumultuous flights throughout the countryside. Even epilepsy, the "sacred malady," a short manifestation of a type of insanity, was considered, especially by the Romans, to be a sign of the sometimes benevolent presence of the gods.

MAENADS. This word, which in the plural means "the frenzied ones," refers to the Bacchantes. Indeed, the Bacchantes fell prey to a sort of mad frenzy when they celebrated the mysteries of Dionysus.

MAIA. This Pleiad was loved by Zeus in a grotto of Mount Cylene. She gave birth to Hermes. She was also the nursemaid of Arcas, the son of Zeus and Callisto, which aroused the resentment of Hera. The Romans, who worshiped Maia, even added that, persecuted by Juno, she could not rest until her lover had changed her into a star.

MANES. Originally, the Manes were the tutelary genii of the Roman household just like the Penates and the Lares. They represented the souls of the dead that had once inhabited the house. Later, the Romans gave this name to the souls of the dead whom they had deified, and

A Maenad dancing: her body racked by a feverish delirium, her chest bare, arm thrown back behind her head, wearing an ample garment of a thin veil that does not impede the movement of her legs when she dances. Sculpture by Callimachus, 5th cent. B.C., Palazzo dei Conservatori, Rome, photo Alinari-Giraudon.

they were the divinities of the netherworld with cults dedicated to them to appease their wrath. By calling them *Manes*, that is "Benevolent," the Romans, by this naive flattery, tried to win their favors. Two festivals were consecrated to them: the *Rosaria*, when one put roses on tombs, and the *Parentalia*.

MANIA. Similar to the Erinyes, this divinity had the terrifying power to arouse folly in the souls of the guilty and to urge them to commit rash acts, crimes, murders or sacrileges.

MANTO. Daughter of the soothsayer Tiresias, Manto was captured by the Epigoni during their expedition against Thebes. They sent her, along with the booty pillaged in the city, to Delphi to thank Apollo for his help. There she learned the art of divination and became a sibyl; then she left Greece for Asia Minor where, having become the lover of Apollo, she gave birth to Mopsus. It is also said that Manto was seduced by Alcmaeon, one of the Epigoni, who begat a son, Amphilochus. The Romans contended, for their part, that a Manto, the daughter of Hercules, had given birth to a son, Aucnuus, who, in honor of his mother, later founded a city to which he gave the name Mantua.

MARICA. According to Virgil, this nymph of the ancient Latin religion was considered to be the spouse of Faunus and the mother of Latinus, the king of Latium. She was honored in a sacred wood, on the banks of the Liris, by the inhabitants of Minturnae, an important city in Latium, on the borders of Campania.

MARON. The grandson of Dionysus, the son of Evanthes, and priest of Apollo in Ismaros in Thrace, Maron gave Ulysses a very strong wine with which the hero succeeded in plying the Cyclops Polyphemus so that he plunged into a deep sleep and Ulysses was able to gouge out his eye. Maron, owing to his origin, was part of the entourage of Dionysus and personified Drunkenness, mainly among the Romans.

MARPESSA. The daughter of Evenus, king of Aetolia, and granddaughter of Ares, Marpessa was promised by her father to whoever could defeat him in a chariot race. He stipulated, however, that any suitor whom he defeated would have his head chopped off. Defying the danger, many suitors competed and many perished, decapitated. One day, Idas, smitten with Marpessa, asked his father Poseidon to give him an enchanted chariot. He was thus able to carry Marpessa away. But Apollo, in love with the maiden, challenged the hero to a duel. Zeus, having separated the opponents, asked Marpessa to choose between them. Wisely, she chose a mortal husband, fearing, and with good reason, that the fickle god would abandon her when she began to grow old. Thus, for the Ancients, she came to symbolize rational prudence.

marriage. In Antiquity all marriages were placed under the protection of a certain number of divinities who watched over harmony between spouses and the fertility of their union. Thus, it was customary that the bride-to-be, on the night before her marriage, offer her toys ex-voto to the goddesses Artemis and Aphrodite in order to curry their favor. On the day of the marriage, the Ancients would invoke Juno (Hera), the goddess of Woman, and would eat special cakes that promoted the conception of children.

MARS. The Latin transposition of the Hellenic Ares, Mars is one of the Roman gods about whom mythographers' interpretations are the most controversial. Certainly, he is the god of War: the colleges of Salian priests, who honored him, invoked him by beating on shields, and Augustus erected a temple in his honor, giving him the surname *Ultor* ("the Avenger"). However, the influence of Ares on Mars should

Mars, the god of War, was worshiped particularly by the Romans. Here he is portrayed as a young man resting. He has set down his shield and holds a marmot in one hand while a Love plays at his feet. Roman art, Louvre, photo Anderson-Giraudon.

not conceal the much more complicated character of the original Mars, worshiped primarily by the Sabines and the Oscans. Far from being a god of Destruction, Mars, on the contrary, protected vegetation and ensured that it would thrive. A festival was dedicated to him during the month that bears his name, when the blossoming of the first buds and flowers takes place. Contemporary mythographers have tried to find a plausible connection between the two natures of the god: war and prosperity. They have shown that the festivals of Mars take place at the time when armies cease to hibernate and combat resumes. Mars would be the symbolic figure of the reawakening of force and vigor both in nature and in the hearts of warriors.

MARSYAS. This Silenus, who was considered to be the inventor of Phrygian harmony, one day picked up a flute that Athena had thrown away. She cursed it, claiming that blowing into it distorted her cheeks. Enchanted by the melodious sounds that emerged from this instrument, Marsyas challenged Apollo to a contest. The god agreed on the condition that the loser would abandon himself to the discretion of the winner. The Muses and King Midas were chosen as the judges of the competition. After a close competition, the Muses declared Apollo the winner while Midas, for his part, gave his vote to the Silenus. Apollo punished Midas and then inflicted upon Marsyas the terrible punishment of being skinned alive, hanging from a fir. It is said that Apollo, in repentance for this frightful vengeance, changed Marsyas into a river and consecrated his flute to Dionysus.

MATER MATUTA. This goddess was adored by Roman matrons whose fertility she promoted. The epithet *Matuta*, which has the same root as our "mature," caused her to be confused with the morning light and Dawn. When Greek myths entered Rome, Mater Matuta

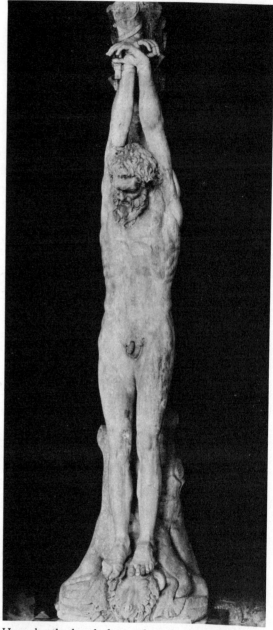

Hung by the hands from a branch, the unfortunate Marsyas will perish, skinned alive by Apollo. Greek art, ancient replica of a figure belonging to a group from the 3rd cent. B.C., Louvre, photo Giraudon.

Medea, torn between her hatred for Jason and her love for her children. Her eyes stare at the horror of the premeditated crime. The heroine clutches the dagger that is to kill her children. Fresco from Pompeii, National Archaeological Museum, Naples, photo Anderson-Giraudon.

was, for obscure reasons, identified with Leucothea who, transformed into a goddess of the sea after her suicide, had come, according to legend, to seek refuge on the coast of Italy.

MEANDRUS. Like all deified rivers, Meandrus was the son of Oceanus and Tethys. He has his source in Phrygia and empties into the Icarian Sea. He is the father of Cyanea, the mother of Caunus. Caunus was loved by his sister Biblis; to escape this unpardonable love, he left for Caria where he founded the city of Caunus.

MEDEA. The story of Medea is connected with the legend of the Argonauts. When the Argonauts landed on the coast of Pontus in Colchis to capture the Golden Fleece, they came up against the hostility of King Aeetes, the guardian of the precious treasure. However, they received the help of Medea, the daughter of the king, who fell in love with Jason. An expert in the art of magic, the young woman gave her lover an ointment with which he was to cover his body to protect him from the flames of the dragon that guarded the Golden Fleece. She also gave him a stone which he threw amid the armed men who had been born from dragon's teeth: immediately, the warriors killed one another and the hero was able to steal the Fleece. To thank Medea, Jason made her his wife. Therefore she fled with him. In order to prevent the pursuing Aeetes from catching them, she killed her brother Absyrtus and chopped him up, scattering his bloody limbs behind them on their way. When they arrived in Iolcus in Thessaly and were received with great ostentation, out of love for Jason, she engaged in all manner of crimes. Thus, she incited the daughters of Pelias, on the pretext of rejuvenating him, to kill their father and cut him into pieces, throwing him into a kettle of boiling water. Then, banished by Acastus, the son of Pelias, the couple took refuge in Corinth, where Medea gave birth to two sons, Pheres and Mermerus. After several years of happiness, Jason abandoned Medea for Creusa, the daughter of Creon, the king of Corinth. Deserted and rejected, Medea tried to think of a way to avenge herself. She gave Creusa a tunic which burned the young girl's body and set the palace ablaze; then she slaughtered her own children. After these crimes, she fled to Athens on a chariot drawn by two winged dragons and married King Aegeus to whom she bore a son. Banished by Theseus, whom she had tried in vain to kill, she finally returned to the palace of her father in Colchis and, according to one tradition, descended to the Elysian Fields where she married Achilles.

Without looking at Medusa for fear of turning to stone, Perseus, after having seized the monster by the hair, chops off her head. The horse Pegasus was born of the blood that flowed from the wound. Selinus metope, 6th cent. B.C., National Archaeological Museum, Palermo, photo Brogi.

MEDUSA. The only one of the three Gorgons that was not immortal, Medusa took advantage of the particular terror she inspired in mortals with her serpent hair, her enormous teeth, the convulsions that contorted her face, and her stare which turned to stone all those upon whom it fell. Myths abound on this subject: they all try to explain her evil spells. According to some, she was supposed to have been a beautiful young woman, who was a bit too proud of her hair. To punish her, Athena changed her hair into a mass of serpents. According to others, the same Athena punished her for having relations with Poseidon by inflicting a hideous form upon her. Her death is also the subject of many tales: the most famous involves the hero Perseus who, on the order of Athena, and with her special assistance, chopped off the head of Medusa, taking care, so as to avoid being turned to stone, not to look at the image of the Gorgon as she appeared in the polished surface of his shield. The blood that flowed gave birth to Pegasus and Chrysaor, the sons of Poseidon, the only god who was not afraid to have relations with the horrible monster. The head of Medusa adorns the aegis of Athena. The goddess, thanks to this magical power, causes all of her adversaries to flee.

MEGAERA. One of the Erinyes, Megaera ("Hatred") has two main functions: she arouses among men armed disputes, anger and crimes of jealousy and envy; in the Underworld, with her sisters Alecto and Tisiphone, she torments the guilty mortals whom she herself drove to murder.

MEGARA. The king of Thebes, Creon, gave his daughter Megara to Heracles, the conqueror of the Minyans of Orchomenus and their king, Erginus, who had taxed the Thebans with a heavy tribute. This union was to end in a tragic way. When Heracles was away one day, having descended to the Underworld to fetch Cerberus, a certain Lycus gained control of Thebes, killed Creon, and wanted to massacre Megara and her children in order to reign in peace. Upon his return, the hero murdered the usurper, but Hera drove him mad and incited him to slaughter his wife and children. Another version claims that Megara escaped the slaughter but that Heracles could not stand the sight of his wife because she reminded him of the death of his children, so he gave her in marriage to his cousin Iolaus.

MELAMPUS. The grandson of Cretheus, Melampus or "Blackfoot" had acquired an unequaled gift of divination by burying the body of a serpent. The offspring of this animal, worshiped by the Ancients, rewarded him for this pious action by licking his ears while he slept. When he awoke, he realized that he understood the language of the birds, the insects and many other animals. He put his talents at the service of his brother Bias, who, to obtain the hand of Pero, daughter of Neleus, had to steal a herd from Phylacus; the herd, in fact, was guarded by a ferocious dog that never slept. The soothsayer went to Phylacus and was held captive for one year. One day, he heard two worms announce the imminent crumbling of the worm-eaten beams that supported the ceiling of his cell. Melampus informed his guards and was transferred to another prison. The prison he left collapsed shortly afterward. Astounded at such foreknowledge, Phylacus asked Melampus to cure his impotent son. He succeeded with magic. To thank him, Phylacus offered him his herd and Bias thus won the hand of Pero.

Melampus subsequently worked other miracles. He was the first to worship Dionysus in Greece. He brought the daughters of Proetus, king of Tiryns, back to their senses. The girls, crazed, thought they were cows and were wandering through the countryside bellowing. In compensation for his care, Melampus asked for two thirds of the kingdom. After refusing and hesitating, the king agreed and even gave two of his daughters, Iphianassa and Lysippe, in marriage to Melampus and his brother.

MELANIPPE. Hippe, the daughter of the centaur Chiron, was seduced by Aeolus, the son of Hellen, on Mount Pelion. She bore him a daughter, Melanippe, and was granted permission from Poseidon to be placed among the stars, where she became the constellation of the Horse. Thus, the centaur Chiron never knew of his daughter's deed. Melanippe was herself seduced by Poseidon and gave birth to two sons, Boetus and Aeolus. Another legend portrays her as the queen of the Amazons. Captured by Heracles, she was brought back by her sister Hippolyta, but was killed shortly after by Telamon in combat because she had broken a truce.

MELANIPPUS. **1.** When Theseus killed the bandit Sinis, he had relations with Perigoune, the daughter of the latter, and had a son Melanippus.

2. The most famous **Melanippus** in legend was the one who fought with Eteocles against the Seven Leaders and killed Mecisteus and Tydeus. Tydeus, on the verge of dying, saw Amphiaraus arrive carrying the head of Melanippus. In his savagery and out of vengeance, Tydeus split open the skull of the enemy and swallowed his brain in one gulp. Then he passed away. Athena, horrified by this act of cruelty, refused to grant Tydeus immortality.

MELANTHIUS. This goatherd betrayed his master Ulysses and sided with the Suitors. When the hero returned to Ithaca, disguised as a beggar, Melanthius insulted him and gave weapons to the suitors attacked by Ulysses. He was taken captive after the victory of Ulysses;

his nose, ears, hands and feet were chopped off and fed to the dogs.

MELANTHO. **1.** The daughter of Deucalion, Melantho, according to the most common version of the legend, had relations with Poseidon and gave birth to a son, Delphus, who was the eponymous hero of Delphi.

2. Legend tells of another **Melantho,** the sister of Melanthius, the goatherd of Ulysses, whom she followed in treason as they sided with the Suitors. Like all unfaithful servants of the hero, she was hanged.

MELEAGER. Two versions of the legend of Meleager are known; one, in the *Iliad,* which

Phoenix recounts to Achilles, the other, later. In the first version, Meleager is the son of Oeneus, the king of Calydon, and Althaea. His father had forgotten to offer a sacrifice to Artemis. The goddess was so outraged by this that she immediately sent a monstrous boar that ravaged the country of Calydon and presented the risk of gradually bringing a famine to the Aetolian kingdom. Meleager offered to hunt the boar and asked for the help of the surrounding cities as well as the help of the Curetes. Once the animal had been slain, Artemis, during the dividing of the remains, gave rise to a quarrel between the Aetolians and the Curetes, which quickly turned to an armed battle.

In the company of Atalanta and two other hunters, Meleager savors his victory over the Calydonian Boar, to which he has dealt the fatal blow. The head of the monster can be seen at his feet. Fresco from Pompeii, National Archaeological Museum, Naples, photo Brogi.

In the general mayhem, Meleager killed his mother's brothers. His mother invoked the curse of the gods and the anger of the Erinyes. Meleager withdrew from the battle, for fear of the wrath of the divine powers. However, as the victorious Curetes were laying siege to the city and setting it ablaze, all the friends of Meleager, along with his mother and his wife Cleopatra, threw themselves at his feet and begged him to resume combat. The hero let himself be moved, donned his splendid armor and repelled the Curetes.

According to another tradition, Althaea received a visit from the Parcae when Meleager was born. They told her that her child would live as long as the firebrand in the hearth existed. Althaea hastened to extinguish the brand and carefully hid it. Meleager grew in strength and courage and with a host of heroes took part in the Calydonian Boar Hunt. Once the ferocious beast was conquered, he wanted to offer its remains to the huntress Atalanta. Annoyed that he preferred a woman to them, the brothers of Althaea threatened him. Irritated, Meleager struck them and killed them. But Althaea, in a burst of desperate fury, took the firebrand from its hiding place, set it on fire, and when it had burned out, Meleager breathed his last breath of life. When she realized what she had done, Althaea hanged herself in despair and the sisters of Meleager wept until Artemis changed them into fowls.

MELIA. An Oceanid, Melia married the river-god Inachus and gave birth to Phoroneus, one of the fabled kings of Argos, Aegialeus and Phegeus, one of the kings of Arcadia.

MELIADES. These nymphs were born of the blood that flowed from Uranus when he was castrated by Cronus. To commemorate this myth, the Greeks assigned them ash trees as their dwelling. With ash wood, they fashioned murderous weapons that resulted in great outpourings of blood. They protected infants

Tragedy, placed under the protection of Melpomene, is symbolized by the mask that the divinity holds in one hand. Her look is inspired, dreamy and serene at one and the same time. Roman statue, Vatican Museum.

abandoned under the branches of the ash, the crown of which served as a natural protection against the elements. Other traditions attribute to the Meliades, for the same reason undoubtedly, the power to protect herds.

MELICERTES. The son of Ino and Athamas, Melicertes was the victim of a murderous fit of frenzy by his parents and was, according to some, thrown into a kettle of boiling water or, according to others, killed by his father with a hunting spear, or thrown into the sea by his mother. However, this tragic destiny merited him a supreme reward: Melicertes was admitted to the ranks of the divinities of the Sea and assumed the name of *Palemon;* the Isthmian games were instituted in his honor by Sisyphus. Melicertes was identified by the Romans with the god Portunus, the protector of the ports of Rome.

MELPOMENE. Tragedy is placed under the protection of this Muse. But, originally, Melpo-

Memnon has been killed by Achilles. Eos, winged Dawn, whose tears turn to dew, lifts her son to transport him to Ethiopia where Zeus granted him immortality. Attic cup by Douris (painter of Greek vases), early 5th cent. B.C., Louvre, photo Giraudon.

mene shared in song and musical harmony. As she was soon associated with Dionysus, the Ancients thought to place tragedy under her protection as well since tragedy was born of the Dionysiac cult. In her right hand was placed the club of Heracles, the hero whose exploits the theater so loved to glorify, and in her left hand, she carried the mask of tragedy. All of these are late developments; originally only Calliope was distinguished among the Muses.

MEMNON. The son of Eos (the Dawn) and of Tithonus, leader of a contingent of Ethiopians in the Trojan War, Memnon was a hero of great valor and fought with courage at the side of the Trojans against the Greeks. Thanks to his armor, which, like that of Achilles, had been forged by Hephaestus, he killed numerous Greek heroes and, in particular, Antilochus, the son of Nestor. Achilles decided to avenge the death of his compatriot and friend and engaged in single combat against Memnon. In the heavens, Zeus weighed the destiny of the two heroes before Thetis and Eos, the weeping mothers. The balance swayed in favor of Achilles and, as a consolation, the god granted Memnon immortality. The body of the hero was buried with great ceremony, while in the sky appeared birds, known as the Memnonides, which each year, it was said, visited the ashes of the hero on the banks of the Hellespont. It is also said that Memnon was buried at Thebes, in Egypt, and that the statue of him that was erected behind the temple emitted a sound similar to that of the lyre when it was caressed by the first rays of the sun at dawn. Only Eos never recovered from the death of her son and each morning she sheds tears that are transformed to dew.

MENELAUS. Like his brother Agamemnon, this son of Atreus was involved in the conflict that pitted his father against Thyestes. When circumstances granted the throne of Atreus to Thyestes, he sought refuge in the court of King Tyndareos of Sparta, who had a stunning daughter, Helen. Menelaus fell instantly in love with her and married her. While Agamemnon succeeded in regaining the throne of Argos, Menelaus established himself on the throne of Sparta which had been handed down to him by his father-in-law when he died. He was to live happily with Helen, who bore him many children, until the day that Paris, son of Priam, king of Troy, who was passing through Sparta, came to seek him out. Menelaus received him hospitably, then was obliged to leave to offer a sacrifice. While he was gone, Paris seduced Helen, abducted her, and took her with him to Troy. Upon learning of the flight of Helen, Menelaus summoned all of Helen's former suitors to avenge this affront. Menelaus and Ulysses were sent on a mission to Troy to claim Helen back peacefully. But in view of the refusal of her abductors, they prepared for war. Most of the Greek States declared their solidarity and mobilized a common army. During the Trojan War, which was to last ten years, Menelaus killed many Trojans and would have killed Paris had Aphrodite not protected him. At the death of Paris, Helen wed Deiphobus and it was to the house of this Trojan that Menelaus hastened when the city was burned and sacked. Deiphobus perished at the hand of Menelaus. The meeting of Helen and Menelaus after so many years of separation was dramatic. But, overwhelmed by her beauty, the hero forgave his young wife and the reconciliation was complete. After an eventful return home, which lasted eight years, because Menelaus, in his delight, had neglected to offer a sacrifice to the gods, he lived in Sparta with his wife for quite a long time, basking in prosperity and happiness; but the gods decreed that Helen would be barren after giving birth to Hermione. At his death, Menelaus was transported by the gods to the faraway lands of eternal happiness, the Elysian fields.

MENESTHEUS. Banished from the kingdom of Athens, Peteus, grandson of Erechtheus, had a son, Menestheus. During the absence of Theseus, who had descended to the Underworld, the Dioscuri invaded Attica and searched for a king. The exiled Menestheus was recalled and acceded to the throne of Athens. As a suitor for Helen, he commanded an Athenian contingent in the Trojan War where he made his mark as a master of military tactics. After the fall of the city, Menestheus, according to one version of the legend, did not return to Athens but settled in Melos, where he was proclaimed king. Another version contends that after the return of Theseus to Athens, Menestheus went to end his days in Scyros.

MENIPPE. This daughter of Orion, along with her sister Metioche, did not hesitate to sacrifice herself to appease the gods who had sent a plague to the country of Orchomenus.

Destined to be handed over to the divinities of the Underworld, their courage and sacrifice moved the gods who changed them into stars. In the legend, they assumed the name *Coronides*.

MENOECEUS. **1.** Grandson of Pentheus, father of Jocasta and Creon, Menoeceus threw himself from the top of the walls of Thebes to try to put an end to the plague that was ravaging the city to punish it for the incest committed by Oedipus.

2. Grandson of the above and son of Creon, he committed suicide, just as his ancestor had, in order to curry favor with Ares, the god of War, during the battle between Thebes and the Seven Leaders. In fact, the Seven Leaders were repelled and six of them were killed.

MENTOR. The son of Alcimus of Ithaca, Mentor won the friendship of Ulysses who, upon his departure for Troy, instructed him to manage his lands and possessions and to oversee the education of Telemachus. In the *Odyssey*, Athena appears several times in the form of Mentor to protect and instruct Ulysses and his son. His name subsequently became proverbial.

MERCURY. After the Hellenization of the Roman gods, Mercury was identified with the Greek Hermes, whose characteristics and legends he borrowed. However, the original character of Mercury is marked, above all, by his very name which is related to the word *merx* ("merchandise") and *mercari* ("to trade"). Originally, therefore, he was most certainly a divinity of Negotiation. However, there is no Roman legend connected with him; he only appears in the *Amphitryon* of Plautus, and he plays the part of the intermediary at the service of Juno in her amorous adventures. Finally, the Romans sometimes consider him to be the father of the Lares, the protectors of roads, and of Evander, the founder of an Arcadian city at the foot of the Palatine Hill.

Mercury was sometimes considered a dreaded god, but he is also remembered as an accomplice for Juno's amorous liaisons. Bargoin Museum, Clermont-Ferrand, photo Lauros-Giraudon.

MEROPE. 1. The daughter of King Cypselus, Merope had married one of the Heraclidae, Cresphontes, king of Messenia; but he and his sons were killed by another one of the Heraclidae, Polyphontes, who seized control of the kingdom and forced Merope to marry him. However, the young woman managed to save one of her sons, Aepytus, and sent him away. Polyphontes was aware of this and did everything in his power to find the child and kill him so that he would not be dethroned by this legitimate heir. One day, Aepytus, who had reached manhood, went to the court of the king using the name of Telephontes and claiming that he had killed Aepytus. Polyphontes did not trust him and kept him in his court in order to verify what he had said. Meanwhile, Merope, who had learned that her son had disappeared, was convinced that the stranger was telling the truth. One night, she went to the bedroom of the false Telephontes with the intention of killing him, but she learned at the last minute from a servant that Telephontes was none other than her son. Then Merope, with the full cooperation of Aepytus, played the role of the weeping mother who had just lost a son and who succumbed to her lot. Polyphontes congratulated the false Telephontes and asked him to preside over a sacrifice. Using the sacrificial knife, Aepytus assassinated his stepfather and was proclaimed king.

2. This Pleiad of the same name, who was the only Pleiad to marry a mortal, Sisyphus, rather than a god, gave birth to Glaucus, father of Bellerophon. Ashamed of this union, she refused to shine in the sky when she was changed into a star by Zeus: she is, in fact, the least shining star of all the Pleiades.

3. Legend tells of another **Merope,** the daughter of King Oenopion.

metamorphosis. A sign of the presence of the gods, metamorphosis appears in mythology as the essential peripeteia or conclusion of a legend. Those whom it affects escape either the amorous pursuits of gods or men or else the wrath of mortal or immortal enemies. They may be granted all imaginable forms—animal, vegetable or even mineral. Thus, Daphne, about to be caught by Apollo, who was smitten with her, was changed into a laurel. Likewise, the nymph Arethusa, for whom the river-god Alpheus felt deep passion, was transformed into a spring with the help of Artemis. It sometimes happens that the gods, the better to trick those they want to seduce, or to thwart a trick, assume the form of an animal: it was by assuming the appearance of a bull that Zeus abducted

Europa and in the form of a swan that he had relations with Leda, who had been changed into a goose. Sometimes, a metamorphosis is the brutal and final expression of the wrath and punishment of the gods: their victims are changed most often into statues and condemned to immobility for the rest of eternity. It also happens that metamorphosis is a gift from the gods, a reward for a praiseworthy act. The best example of this is that of Philemon and Baucis, who were both changed into trees for having extended their hospitality to Jupiter and Mercury. Metamorphosis may also be a sign of the gods' pity: the Heliades, daughters of the Sun, could not be consoled after the death of their brother Phaethon and were changed into poplars. Changing form, changing essence, is in the eyes of mortals doubtless the highest expression of divine power because although the immortality of the gods is not always perceived by the human spirit, metamorphosis is almost always a visible, even tangible miracle.

METANEIRA. The daughter of Amphictyon and the wife of Celeus, king of Eleusis, Metaneira welcomed Demeter hospitably in her city and took her into her service. One night, through her cries of fright, Metaneira was the involuntary cause of the death of her son Demophon, whom the grateful goddess wanted to render immortal by fire: surprised, Demeter dropped the child into the hearth. To soothe the tears of the queen, Demeter promised that she would give birth to a son, Triptolemus, to whom the goddess would grant the most marvelous talents.

METIOCHE. The daughter of Orion and sister of Menippe, Metioche was changed into a star, as her sister was, and took the name *Coronide.*

METIS. The personification of Prudence and Craftiness, the daughter of Oceanus and Tethys, Metis was the first wife of Zeus. A sorceress, she gave him a magic potion which, drunk by Cronus, obliged the Titan to restore his children. The couple's first child was a girl; but an oracle of Gaia revealed that the next son to be born would dethrone Zeus in Olympus. Thus Zeus swallowed Metis but was immediately overwhelmed by a terrible headache. To relieve him, Hephaestus, on the advice of Hermes, split open his head from which emerged Athena, armed and helmeted.

MIDAS. This king of Phrygia entered into popular legends due, above all, to his donkey's ears. Indeed, one day as he was wandering through the woods, he came to Mount Tmolus where Apollo and Marsyas were competing to determine who was the better musician. Chosen as judge, Midas had the unfortunate and foolish idea of declaring Marsyas the winner. Apollo, vexed, immediately gave him a pair of donkey's ears. Mortified, the king hid them beneath a Phrygian cap. Only his barber knew his secret until, one day, unable to keep the secret any longer, he dug a hole in the ground and screamed into it: "King Midas has donkey's ears!" In that very spot, reeds sprang up and, when they rustled, they constantly repeated this impertinent phrase. Soon, the entire kingdom had wind of it and everyone mocked the king.

This legend, a later version, recounted by Ovid, follows another legend that illustrates once more the heedlessness of Midas. Silenus was accompanying the procession of Dionysus and the Satyrs when he went astray. Discovered sleeping by the inhabitants of Phrygia, he was taken, in chains, to Midas who lost no time freeing him and returning him to Dionysus. To reward the obliging king, Dionysus granted him the choice of a favor. Midas, in his foolishness, asked that everything he touch turn to gold. When the wish was granted, he realized at once that all food that he brought to his lips turned to gold bars and all drinks turned to gold as well. In danger of dying of thirst or starvation, he begged Dionysus to put an end to the spell. Dionysus, pleased at having taught Midas a profitable lesson, simply requested that he purify himself in the river Pactolus. Ever since then, the river has had nuggets of gold.

MILETUS.   One of the versions of the legend, recounted by Ovid, says of Miletus that he was the son of Apollo and Deione. Banished by Minos from Crete, he went to Caria and founded a city and kingdom there, known as Miletus. Another tradition claims that he was the son of a daughter of Minos. He was abandoned and raised by shepherds. Minos discovered him and, smitten with him, wanted to rape him, unaware of the family bonds that joined him to the adolescent. On the advice of his uncle Sarpedon, Miletus fled, landed on the coast of Asia Minor, and founded Miletus.

MILON of CROTON.   Like Gyges and many other heroes, Milon of Croton belonged less to mythology than to the tradition of popular legends. Toward the end of the 6th century B.C., he was one of the greatest athletes in all of Greece. The winner in all the Olympic and Pythian games for several years, he also performed unexpected exploits, some of which equal those of Heracles. He carried a live ox in his arms, covering the entire length of the Olympic stadium. Not satisfied with having affirmed his superiority over his competitors, he beat the animal to death with his fists and devoured it whole in the space of a single day. But, in the end, he became presumptuous with respect to his strength. One day, he felled an oak and split it down the middle but his hands remained caught between the two parts of the tree which had joined together and, immobilized, he was devoured by wolves.

MINERVA.   This very ancient Roman divinity, of Etruscan origin, was associated with Juno

Following a widespread ancient custom, the artist has given the face of Minerva rather thick features. On her helmet, the image of Pegasus can be seen; on her breastplate appears the head of Medusa, a present given to her by Perseus. Roman sculpture, National Archaeological Museum, Naples, photo Alinari-Giraudon.

and Jupiter within the Capitoline triad in Rome. She represented elevated thought, literature, the arts and music, wisdom and intelligence, all allegorical images of which many examples are found in the Roman religion. She was identified with the Greek Athena and it was soon impossible to distinguish the solely Roman characteristics and attributes.

MINOS.   The son of Zeus and Europa, Minos succeeded Asterion on the throne of Crete. From the start of his reign, he incurred the wrath and vengeance of Poseidon by refusing to sacrifice a bull to him. Pasiphaë, the wife of the king, fell in love with the animal and gave birth to a monster, the Minotaur. Minos deserted this impious woman and engaged in countless amorous adventures; it is said that, to avenge herself for the repeated infidelity of her husband, Pasiphaë cast a spell on the bed of the king from which emerged serpents and scorpions that killed all of the king's mistresses. His reign was marked mainly by the murder of one of his sons, Androgeus. In order not to let the murderer go unpunished, Minos waged war against the Athenians, and he demanded of them an annual tribute of seven young men and seven maidens who were fed to the Minotaur. Theseus managed to enter the Labyrinth and kill the monster. Then he abducted Ariadne, one of the daughters of the king, who had helped him. From that point on, the misfortune of Minos was multiplied. He learned that Daedalus had undoubtedly promoted the monstrous loves of Pasiphaë and had him imprisoned, but the architect succeeded in escaping. The king, therefore, mobilized an army and began to pursue him. When he arrived in Sicily in the kingdom of King Cocalus, he was thrown into a kettle of boiling water. Despite his tragic existence, Minos was considered by the Ancients to be a wise king and a noteworthy lawmaker. It was said that he conversed frequently with Zeus in a sacred grotto and that he drew from his conversations with the god the best instruction for governing the affairs of his States. Thus, because of his spirit of equity, he was seated at the side of his brother Rhadamanthys and of Aeacus as a judge in the Underworld.

MINOTAUR. A hideous monster, with the body of a man and the head of a bull, the Minotaur was born of the irresistible and unnatural love of the Queen of Crete, Pasiphaë, for a white bull that King Minos, her husband, had refused to sacrifice to Poseidon. Horrified by this birth, the king wanted to hide the news from his subjects so he had Daedalus construct a multicolored palace with overlapping rooms and countless intersections and there he locked up the Minotaur. The monster fed on human flesh, supplied, above all, by the annual tribute of seven young men and seven maidens sent from Athens. Theseus, with the help of Ariadne, killed the Minotaur.

MINYAS. The grandson of Poseidon, Minyas emigrated from Thessaly to Boeotia where he founded the city of Orchomenus and ruled the Minyans, who were the ancestors of some of the Argonauts. Soon, the Minyans extended their domination over Iolcus, in Thessaly. Minyas was a very rich king, one of the first sovereigns who had a "Treasury" built. His offspring were famous: his daughters, the Minyades, Alcithoë, Leucippe and Arsippe, refused to join the entourage of Dionysus; vexed, the god drove them mad before changing them into bats. Minyas had many other famous children

Having immobilized the Minotaur, a man with the head of a bull, Theseus, armed with a long dagger, chops off its head. Attic amphora, Louvre, photo Alinari-Giraudon.

as well: one of his daughters became the mother of Tityus and another, Clymene, was the wife of Phylacus and the grandmother of Jason. As for his son Orchomenus, he succeeded him on the throne of the city of Orchomenus, a rich city of Boeotia.

MNEMOSYNE. The daughter of Uranus and Gaia, this Titan gave birth to the nine Muses, after having spent nine consecutive nights with Zeus. She is, above all, the personification of Memory. The Ancients portrayed her as a woman holding one of her ears with her right hand.

MOIRAE. Identified by the Romans with the Parcae, the Moirae were three sisters: Clotho, Lachesis and Atropos. The daughters of Zeus and Themis, or even of the Night, they were, originally, a single divinity. Their appearance in Greek worship is as ancient as the beginning of religion and myths. They dwell in a palace near Olympus. They oversee the unfolding of every man's life. Clotho spins, and her turning distaff symbolizes the course of existence. Lachesis distributes the lots received for each man. Atropos, never letting herself be moved, cuts the thread of life.

MOLOSSUS. After the fall of Troy, Andromache was taken captive by Neoptolemus and bore him several sons, including Molossus. The newborn was exposed by his mother but was soon recovered and taken in by his father, who, in the meantime, had married Hermione. Hermione, whose marriage was sterile, persecuted Andromache and Molossus and she was about to slaughter them on the altar of Thetis when Peleus succeeded in rescuing them. Thetis therefore ordered Andromache and Molossus to leave for Epirus where Andromache married Helenus, the king of the country. Shortly after, Molossus succeeded Helenus, giving his name to the people of Molossia.

MOMOS. The personification of criticism and sarcasm and the inseparable companion of Comus, the god of Feasts, Momos is first mentioned by Hesiod who contends that she was a daughter of the Night. She is the heroine of several legends, the most famous of which shows her laughing at the human being fashioned by Vulcan who had forgotten to leave in the chest of his creature a small opening so that the creature's secret thoughts could be read.

MONETA. Surname of Juno, "Notifier," for having alerted the Romans of a night attack by the Gauls in 390 B.C. through the geese sacred to her on the Capitoline Hill. During the war with Pyrrhus, Juno advised the Romans that if their wars were conducted justly they would never lack for money. So all money minted at Rome was under her protection.

MOPSUS. **1.** The son of Ampyx and the nymph Chloris, this Lapith, one of the most famous soothsayers of Greek mythology, offered his talents to the Argonauts and the hunters of the Calydonian Boar. In Libya, he was stung by a serpent, born of the blood that flowed from the head of Medusa when it was chopped off; he died almost instantly. The Argonauts buried him with full funerary honors.

2. Legend tells of another **Mopsus,** the son of Apollo and Manto, the daughter of Tiresias. His adoptive father was the Argive Rhacius. The founder of the Colophon, Mopsus entered the city in competition with another soothsayer, Calchas, who had just returned from Troy. Twice, Mopsus surpassed Calchas in their science and Calchas killed himself in shame. After this victory, Mopsus and Amphilochus, who also possessed the gift of prophecy, founded the city of Mallus in Cilicia. Sole sovereign for but a moment, Mopsus witnessed the return of Amphilochus who claimed his share of the kingdom. A single combat ensued between the two heroes and ended in the death of both.

MORPHEUS. One of the many sons of Hypnos, Morpheus is a winged god who constantly wanders around the Earth caressing mortals with a poppy that induces sleep; moreover, he stimulates dreams by assuming the appearance of human beings: in this capacity he is seen in legends, particularly that of Alcyone to whom he appeared in the form of her husband Ceyx who had drowned in a shipwreck.

mountains. The top of the high mountains was generally the place where a divinity dwelled. Through extension and assimilation, the Ancients ended up adoring the mountain itself just as they adored the divinity. This custom, of Semitic and Phoenician origin, developed mainly in the countries of Asia Minor and the Near East, which were colonized by the Greeks. An example of this practice was Mount Argeus, in Cappadocia, which can be found on coins with the features of Zeus and sometimes of Apollo. In his *Theogony*, Hesiod cites a certain number of mountains as sacred and deified places. Among those were Olympus, the dwelling place of the gods, and Ida, the birthplace of Zeus. These mountains were soon personified. They became similar to goddesses or nymphs (Mount Taygetus) or heroes, like the Cithaeron which, in legend, assumes the appearance of a king of Plataea. The same is true of Mount Atlas, the Giant, who, changed into stone, joined the Heavens and Earth. Finally, mention should be made of the mountains sanctified by the oracle of a god (Mount Parnassus).

MUCIUS SCAEVOLA. Having decided to kill the Etruscan king Porsenna, who was laying siege to Rome, the Roman Mucius one day stole into the enemy camp but mistook his target and killed one of the king's officers. Immediately arrested and taken to Porsenna, he placed his right hand on a brazier that had been brought there for a sacrifice and let it be burned without saying anything to prove to the enemy that a Roman fears nothing. Seduced by this act of courage, Porsenna freed Mucius. Before leaving, Mucius warned Porsenna that three hundred other Romans were prepared to assassinate him. Frightened, the king requested peace and ended his siege. Revered as a hero, Mucius, who lost his right hand in the adventure, was given the surname of *Scaevola* ("the left-handed one").

MUSAEUS. The son of Orpheus or Eumolpus and the goddess Selene, Musaeus belongs to the generation of mythical poets of Thrace that played an important role in the founding of the mysteries and the invention of new forms of purification. It is said that Heracles approached him to be included, in Eleusis, among the initiates of the Mysteries.

MUSES. According to Homer, the Muses were the goddesses who inspired song. In the 8th century, however, they still did not possess very precise characteristics. On the other hand, a century later, their characters were, in the *Theogony* of Hesiod, more clearly defined. The daughters of Zeus and Mnemosyne (Memory), nine in number, they presided over the various forms of poetry. Clio was the patroness of History, Euterpe of Lyric Poetry, Thalia of Comedy and Melpomene of Tragedy; Terpsichore inspired Dance, Erato Erotic Poetry, Polyhymnia, Song; Urania was granted Astronomy and Calliope, Epic Poetry. Their procession is led by Apollo who, on these occasions, receives the surname of "Musagetes." Their dwellings are many and correspond most often to places of worship or legend. They live on Olympus and entertain the gods with their songs but they have favorite spots on Earth such as Mount Pierus, in memory of the nine daughters of King Pierus of Macedonia, who wanted to compete with them and were punished by being

The group of nine Muses. From left to right: Clio, Thalia, Erato, Euterpe, Polyhymnia, Calliope, Terpsichore, Urania, Melpomene. Roman sarcophagus, Louvre, photo Giraudon.

changed into magpies by Apollo. The poets were accustomed to speak of their gaining inspiration on Mount Helicon and in the sacred springs of Aganippe and Hippocrene where, according to legend, the Muses often stayed. The Muses were identified by the Romans with the Camenae.

MYRMIDONS. This people of Phthiotis, in Thessaly, was thus named in honor of King Myrmidon whose mother, Eurymedusa, was seduced by Zeus. But another tradition, more famous and much more elaborate, recounts a legend that explains the etymology of the Greek word *myrmidons* (in Greek, *murmêkès* "ants"). At one time, on the island of Aegina, Aeacus, the son of Zeus and Aegina, reigned. Hera, who was not very tolerant of her husband's infidelity, wanted to punish the son born of Zeus's adultery. She sent his kingdom a plague that killed all its inhabitants. Frenzied, Aeacus, seeing himself deprived of his subjects, ran to the temple of Zeus, his father, and begged him to repopulate his island. That very

evening, he dreamed that ants had been changed into human creatures. The following morning, his son Telamon came to awaken him and showed him in the distance, an armed multitude that was approaching his palace. All of the island's ants had, indeed, been changed into warriors. Commanded by Peleus, the son of Aeacus, the Myrmidons emigrated to Thessaly. Under the leadership of Achilles, they fought courageously during the siege of Troy.

MYRRHA. The king of Cyprus, Cinyras, one day claimed that the beauty of his daughter, Myrrha (or Smyrna), surpassed that of Aphrodite. The goddess avenged herself for this insult: Myrrha conceived an incestuous love for her father and, one night, slipped into his bed. Thus Cinyras begat a son, who was also his grandson, the famous Adonis. Realizing his crime, the king banished his daughter from his palace. Reaching the top of a hill, the unfortunate young woman was changed into a myrtle tree by Aphrodite who, taking pity, rescued Adonis.

MYRTILUS. The charioteer for Oenomaus, the king of Pisa in Elis, Myrtilus was a son of Hermes and Phaethusa, one of the Danaids. In order to gain Hippodameia, the daughter of the king, Pelops was obliged to win a chariot race, at any price; he therefore offered Myrtilus a deal: the latter was to betray his master and he would be granted the permission to spend a night with Hippodameia. Having accepted the offer, Myrtilus substituted wax for the axles of the wheels of the royal chariot. During the race, the chariot broke and Oenomaus was killed. Pelops, the victor, stole Hippodameia but refused to honor his promise and threw Myrtilus into the sea. Before dying, Myrtilus cursed Pelops and all of his descendants.

mysteries. In Antiquity, "mysteries" were the series of magic rites celebrated, in the greatest of secrecy, by a certain number of initiates in honor of a god or goddess like Demeter or Dionysus. The most famous mysteries were celebrated in Eleusis. The rites consisted of "things spoken", "things shown", and "things done"; just as those inducted went through the three stages of initiation (*muesis*), perfection (*teleth*), and beholding (*epopteia*). The mysteries of Eleusis not only rendered homage to Demeter, the goddess of Harvest and, more generally, of the Fertility of the Earth, but also celebrated the story of Core-Persephone, the daughter of the goddess, who spent six months each year in the Underworld to be reborn on the Earth and in life for the six other months. Thus, to the homage rendered to the personification of Fertility was added worship for the one who died and was reborn each year. Soon Core came to represent the immortality of the soul which would be attained only by those who, through certain practices, processions and liturgies, were initiates and, therefore, became a select group that would one day know eternal happiness and serenity of the soul.

N

NAIADS. The origin of these nymphs of flowing waters, springs, brooks, rivers and the like differs according to tradition. Homer considered them to be the daughters of Zeus, other mythologists considered Oceanus to be their father. Sometimes it was claimed that they were born of the river where they lived. Young women with delicate faces and dazzling white bodies, they were constantly objects of the desires of gods and mortals. However, they knew how to defend themselves against the advances of those they scorned and were able to drive them mad. They often paralyzed those who unduly bathed in their forbidden sacred waters. But they could also be generous toward those who asked to be cured of an illness and bathed in certain springs and clearly defined rivers that had healing properties.

NARCISSUS. The son of the nymph Liriope and the river Cephissus, in Phocis, Narcissus, an astonishingly beautiful young man, was oblivious to the feelings of love he aroused. The nymph Echo, who experienced a mute adoration for him, was rejected with disdain and plagued with sorrow. His other suitors were indignant and complained to Nemesis about the egotism and indifference of Narcissus. The goddess, therefore, decided to avenge his rejected admirers. The soothsayer Tiresias,

having declared that Narcissus would live as long as he did not see himself, Nemesis, during a hunting outing, drove the young man to quench his thirst in a spring. Smitten with the face he saw reflected in the water, which he could not reach, and incapable of looking away from it, Narcissus forgot to eat and drink. Taking root on the banks of the spring, he was gradually transformed into the flower that bears his name and which, since then, is reflected in water in summer only to wilt and die in autumn. According to another version of the same legend, Narcissus had a sister who resembled him and whom he loved madly. The young woman had just died. So as not to lose the memory of her image, Narcissus looked at himself in a spring, day and night, and died of consumption.

NAUPLIUS. 1. One **Nauplius,** the son of Poseidon, founded the city of Nauplia, not far from Argos.

2. A second **Nauplius,** a descendant of the first and often confused with him, married Clymene, the daughter of King Catreus of Crete, according to the most common version; he had several sons, the most famous of whom was Palamedes. Nauplius was a famous navigator and his services were often enlisted to banish or deport the undesirable elements of a king-

dom. Thus, King Aleus asked Nauplius to drown Auge, his daughter, who had been seduced by Heracles. En route, the unfortunate Auge gave birth to a son, Telephus; Nauplius, overcome with pity, spared them and sold them to merchants of the kingdom of Teuthras in Mysia. But the most famous part of the legend of Nauplius is inseparable from that of Palamedes who, falsely accused of treason by Ulysses, was stoned by the Greeks during the Trojan War. Nauplius thus decided to take revenge. He first incited the wives of the Greek heroes and kings who had left for Troy to betray their husbands, by telling them that their husbands were dead or that they were freely engaging in adultery. Thus Clytemnestra took Aegisthus as her lover; Aegialeia, the wife of Diomedes, became the mistress of Cometes; and Meda, the wife of Idomeneus, became the lover of Leucus. Not satisfied with having sown the seeds of misunderstanding among these couples for the future, Nauplius lit torches, after the fall of Troy, on the dangerous promontory of Caphareus, on the coast of Euboea, and thereby attracted the Greek ships, almost all of which were shipwrecked.

NAUSICAA. The daughter of Alcinous and Arete, rulers of the Phaeacians, Nausicaa one morning went to the banks of the river not far from the sea to wash some clothes. When this task was completed, she played ball with some servants and companions. The ball escaped her and fell into the river. Hearing the cries of the young girls, Ulysses, who, having been shipwrecked had landed there exhausted and naked, appeared, his body covered with branches. The frightened maidens fled; only Nausicaa dared approach the hero, giving him clothes and taking him to her father's palace. Alcinous comforted him and gave him a ship for his return to Ithaca. Nausicaa regretfully watched the shipwrecked hero leave because, though she loved him, she knew she could never marry him as he was already married to Penelope.

NAXOS. One of the Cyclades, Naxos owes its name to an eponymous hero who settled on the island with a Carian colony. It was on Naxos that Ariadne was abandoned by Theseus. She married Dionysus shortly after. There a particularly sumptuous cult was dedicated to Dionysus.

NELEUS. The son of Poseidon and Tyro, Neleus was abandoned with his brother Pelias and saved by peasants. Later, the twins learned the secret of their birth and, having sought out their mother, they killed Tyro's stepmother on the altar of Hera. The enraged goddess gave rise to violent quarrels between the two brothers and Neleus was soon forced to take exile in Messenia, where he founded the city of Pylus and was proclaimed king. The husband of Chloris, a daughter of Amphion, he had one daughter and twelve sons. The sons were all killed by Heracles, except for Nestor, because their father had refused to purify the hero of the murder of Iphitus. Neleus, it is said, was subjected to the same fate as his sons, but it is also said that he died of an illness in Corinth, having escaped the massacre.

NEMESIS. A primitive divinity of Attica, Nemesis was gradually worshiped throughout Greece. Sometimes identified with the Erinyes, she slowly and progressively acquired her own genealogy and legend. A daughter of the Night, she was pursued by Zeus, who was in love with her, and she assumed all sorts of forms to escape him. Thus she changed herself into a goose; but Zeus changed himself into a gander to have relations with her. The goddess laid an egg that was given to Leda and from which emerged Helen and the Dioscuri. Nemesis differed from the Erinyes, however: the revenge she took was not blind. She simply ensured that proud mortals would not try to equal the

Troy having been taken, Neoptolemus has avenged the death of his father Achilles, by flinging Astyanax, the son of Hector, from the top of the citadel of the city. The artist has embellished the legend somewhat. Neoptolemus, at right, has seized the corpse of his victim and prepares to strike King Priam with it. A grandfather killed by the corpse of his grandson—what a powerful symbol of the rage that overwhelmed the Greek warriors when they entered Troy! Detail of a Greek cup by Brygos (Athenian potter), circa 500 B.C., Louvre, photo Giraudon.

gods; she humbled those who had received too many talents and boasted of them. She counseled moderation and discretion: thus she is portrayed holding her index finger over her lips.

NEOPTOLEMUS. The son of Achilles and Deidameia, also bearing the surname of *Pyrrhus* because of his red hair, Neoptolemus was raised in the court of King Lycomedes, the sovereign of the island of Scyros. When he reached manhood, he was obliged to follow the Greeks who had learned from an oracle that the presence of the son of Achilles in their ranks was crucial to a victory over Troy; but he was also needed to fetch Philoctetes from Lemnos. During the final struggle, Neoptolemus conducted himself courageously and showed himself to be the worthy successor of his father: thus he was one of the warriors who hid in the flanks of the wooden horse. Once they had entered the city, Neoptolemus killed old King Priam and his grandson Astyanax. When the Trojan captives were divided up, Neoptolemus received Andromache, who bore him three children—Molossus, Pielus and Pergamus. Upon his return home, he sacrificed Polyxena, one of the daughters of Priam, to the spirit of Achilles. But he did not succeed in reaching Phthia, the land of his ancestors, which had been seized by Acastus in his absence, and he stopped in Epirus where he was proclaimed king. To thank him for his eminent services, Menelaus gave him the hand of his daughter, Hermione, who had been promised to Orestes. The latter avenged himself by killing Neoptolemus in Delphi where Neoptolemus had gone to consult the oracle on the reason for the sterility of his marriage.

NEPHELE. A cloud created by Zeus, Nephele had relations with King Athamas and bore him two children, Phrixus and Helle. But she was soon deserted by her husband who preferred Ino and even wanted to sacrifice Phrixus to Zeus to put an end to a drought. Nephele saved her children by letting them climb up on the back of a ram with golden fleece, which took flight and landed in Colchis. It is also said that Zeus gave her the form of Hera and that, having had relations with Ixion, she gave birth to the dreadful and monstrous centaurs.

NEPTUNE. Identified with Poseidon at a relatively ancient date, Neptune gradually lost his specifically Italian character but benefited, in return, from the myths concerning his Greek counterpart. It is probable that Neptune, in the primitive religion of the peoples of Latium, was not the god of the Sea. This nation, in fact,

Neptune, his feet placed in the rings of a sea serpent, is drawn by four fleet-footed horses with hooves bearing a sort of flipper. He is surrounded by a multitude of small sea creatures: fish, crustaceans, Loves mounted on tritons, and men with the bodies of fish. Mosaic from Ostia, photo Chevallier.

relied heavily on agriculture, contrary to the Greeks, whose economy was based for the most part on maritime commercial traffic. In the eyes of the Latins, Neptune was a divinity of Moisture. The Neptunalia took place in his honor, during the heat of July, in leafy huts that afforded a certain coolness and where the very essence of the god Neptune could be found.

NEREIDS. Divinities of the sea, the daughters of Nereus and Doris, the Nereids were, to some extent, the nymphs of the Mediterranean. They lived in a radiant palace at the bottom of the sea and entertained their father with their songs and dances. But, as each personified a form, a particular aspect of the surface of the water, they often appeared there and, magnificent creatures, half-woman and half-fish, they mingled in the waves and the algae riding Tritons or sea horses. Few legends were attributed to them. However, some of them were famous, such as Amphitrite, the wife of the Poseidon, Oreithyia, Galatea, and Thetis, the wife of Peleus and mother of Achilles.

NEREUS. This very ancient sea-god, more ancient even than Poseidon, was distinguished from the great god of the Sea by his just, wise and peace-loving nature. The son of Pontus and Gaia, the husband of the Oceanid Doris and father of the fifty Nereids, Nereus is portrayed as an old man whose image appears on the sea, in the ripples of the water, among the white bubbling of the foamy waves. His empire extends particularly over the waters of the Aegean Sea. He lives there in the depths of a

There is evidence of intended symmetry in the composition of this group created by a 5th-century A.D. artist. The two Nereids seem to be floating in an aquatic medium, symbolized by the triton bearing a Love. At the top, the head of Helios can be seen. Despite triumphant Christianity, mythology continued to inspire artists, in an admittedly formal manner. Coptic art, fragment of a cornice, Trieste Museum, photo Giraudon.

grotto bursting with light. But he often emerges from his sumptuous refuge to show himself to mortals and predict their futures. Thus he told Heracles which route would lead to the garden of the Hesperides. He also warned Paris of the disasters that threatened his country if Helen were abducted from hers.

NESSUS. This centaur, the son of Ixion and Nephele, became the ferryman of the River Evenus. He tried to rape Deianira, the wife of Heracles, as they crossed the river but he was mortally wounded by one of the hero's arrows. Before breathing his last breath, he gave Deia-

The artist, the better to reveal his talent, has taken liberties with the legend. Here, Nessus is not killed by the arrows of Heracles but is strangled by the giant-hero. This is a fine portrayal of struggle. With an almost rational sureness, Heracles has twisted the arm of Nessus and has immobilized the centaur. The latter seems to beg for mercy. Ancient sculpture, Uffizi Gallery, Florence, photo Alinari-Giraudon.

nira a phial, which contained a mixture of his blood and his seed, and maliciously assured her that if the potion were spread on the garments of Heracles, he would remain forever true to her. When he donned a garment on which the credulous Deianira had poured the potion, Heracles felt his body being gradually consumed and, wild with pain, he asked to be burned on a pyre at the top of Mount Oeta.

NESTOR. One of the twelve sons of Neleus and Chloris, Nestor saw his other brothers perish at the hand of Heracles but was himself spared. The king of Pylos, a wise and just warrior, he took part, in particular, in three main events which, in Greek mythology, occupy a choice place. He sided with the Pylians against the Epians; he took part in the combat of the Lapiths against the Centaurs; and he participated in the Calydonian Boar Hunt along with the Argonauts. Since Apollo had granted him the favor of seeing three generations of men, he was able to leave at the head of ninety vessels that he commanded in the siege of Troy. His eminent role as a moderate element and his constant care to resolve differences between the Greek heroes (such as Achilles and Agamemnon) are attested to by the many laudatory portraits painted by Homer in the *Iliad* and in the *Odyssey*. After the fall of Troy, he was one of the rare Greek warriors to return unharmed to his fatherland where he lived until the end of his days, governing with justice and piety.

NIGHT (NYX). This divinity, whose origin can be traced to very ancient times, represents primitive, distressing darkness, full of somber uncertainty. The daughter of Chaos, she had relations with her brother Erebus and became the mother of Aether ("air") and Hemera ("light"). But she also mothered deified abstractions that were unfavorable for humans, such as Death, the Parcae, Fraud, Old Age, Nemesis

The goddess Night does not have the civilized appearance of the divinities of Olympus. She is the daughter of Chaos, a disordered and mysterious Fury, incessantly combating the forces of light, the somber personification of one of the elements that rules human existence. Detail of the frieze of the altar of Pergamum, Berlin Museum, photo Berlin Museum.

and the Hesperides. She dwelled in Hesperia, beyond the pillars of Hercules (Strait of Gibraltar) in countries where no one has ever dared to venture.

NIKE. This Greek divinity is the personification of Victory and one of the surnames of Athena.

NIOBE. Niobe, the daughter of Tantalus and the wife of Amphion, gave birth to seven sons and seven daughters, the Niobids. Proud like her father, she boasted to whoever would listen about her fertility and the beauty of her children and she ridiculed Leto who had given birth only to Artemis and Apollo. Indignant at such presumptuousness, the two children of Leto killed the children of Niobe with their arrows; one daughter escaped the massacre but was so very frightened that, throughout her life, she retained a deathly pallor and was given the name of Chloris ("pale"). Hearing the cries

This statue of Niobe exhibits all of the grief of a mother who has just seen her children perish. The unfortunate woman has torn her garments. Her body is bent, on the point of collapse, and her eyes seem to be riveted on the heavens as she implores the indulgence of the gods. Her mouth is half open and her arms are twisted in a sign of despair. Ancient statue, late 5th cent. B.C., Museo delle Terme, Rome, photo Anderson-Giraudon.

Apollo raises his bow and prepares to shoot another arrow at one of the children of Niobe. For her part, Artemis, unpardoning, takes an arrow from her quiver and continues the massacre. At the feet of the merciless gods, two of the children lie in agony. Attic krater, Louvre, photo Giraudon.

of her children, Niobe emerged from her palace and, at the terrifying sight of the wounded bodies, she was virtually petrified; taking pity, Zeus changed her into a rock from which her tears flowed in the form of a spring. For nine days, the bodies were not buried. On the tenth day, the gods relented and buried the children of Niobe themselves.

NISUS. **1.** The son of Pandion, the king of Athens, Nisus had three brothers—Aegeus, Pallas and Lycus—who, like him, had been banished from Attica at the death of their father. Soon, the four heroes reestablished their sovereignty over this territory, which they divided among themselves. Nisus obtained the kingdom of Megara with its port, Nisa. During an expedition against Greece, in order to avenge the death of his son Androgeus, killed by Aegeus, the king of Athens, Minos, the king of Crete, beseiged Nisa. Scylla, the daughter of Nisus, in love with Minos, betrayed her fatherland and cut her father's golden hair which protected him aginst death. She thus delivered the city to the enemy in exchange for the promise that the king of Crete would marry her. But Minos was so horrified at this patricide that, it is said, he had Scylla drowned. It is also said that Nisus, changed into an eagle, had his daughter changed into a bird.

2. A companion to Aeneas and a friend to Euryalus, the **Nisus** of Virgil participated with Euryalus in the funerary games celebrated in honor of Anchises. In the foot race, he slipped and fell; however, getting up immediately, he ran into one of his competitors, who happened to be well placed, and thus enabled Euryalus to carry off a victory. Later, during the war against the Rutuli, Nisus and Euryalus left during the night to surprise the sleeping enemies in their camp after numerous libations. They killed one of the leaders, Rhamnes, and many other warriors. As they were preparing to return to their own camp, they were surprised by Rutuli horsemen and were just barely able to escape to the woods. Soon, Euryalus was taken captive. Nisus then attacked the Rutuli single-handedly and together the inseparable friends, fighting a fierce enemy, fell and were united in death as they had been united in life.

NOTUS. This warm, moist wind, the son of Eos, blows from the South.

numen. For the sake of simplicity, the word *Numen* is usually translated as "divinity." Indeed, for the Romans, the Numen corresponded to the divine, mysterious force that guides each of man's actions, renders them effective, and is found in everything—in each plant, in each animal—giving them thus the breath of life and will. Moreover, there are countless *Numina* and it is crucial for men to be

Three nymphs holding hands. Their hair is carefully arranged in buns and their bodies are covered with transparent tunics whose many folds evoke the glistening purity of the waters of the rivers and springs. Archaic Greek art, stele of nymphs, Acropolis Museum, Athens, photo Alinari-Giraudon.

reconciled with them by offering them feasts or sacrifices. It may also be said that the Numen is the primitive expression of the divine, such as the first men conceived of it, well before building myths and legends on the notion of genealogies.

NYCTEUS. When his daughter Antiope fled to Sicyon to the court of King Epopeus, Nycteus, the son of Hyrieus and Clonia, who governed the city of Thebes at the time, mobilized an expedition against the enemy king and lay siege to his kingdom, but was defeated and killed, leaving the power to his brother, Lycus. According to another version of the legend, he was supposed to have killed himself when he learned of his daughter's departure.

NYMPHS. Under this very general name, the Greeks group all the feminine divinities of nature that populate the seas, waters, woods, trees, forests, mountains, fertile valleys, springs, plains, rocks and grottoes. Young women of rare beauty, depicted naked or half-dressed, they were the daughters of Zeus and the Sky. The rain that the god sent to earth gushed forth in springs and gave birth to the Nymphs. Thus the Ancients attributed to the Nymphs a fertilizing and nourishing power that they exercised by mingling with the moisture in the air, the water and the forests. But their beneficent action did not involve only nature. Human beings, for their part, benefited from their tender solicitude. They protected fiancés, who plunged into the water of certain springs to obtain the purification that is essential to fertility. This regenerative character, which was highly valued by the Greeks, was complemented by two other attributes: The Nymphs loved to prophesy and they were capable of inspiring in men who drank the sacred water of their springs noble thoughts and the desire to accomplish great exploits. They also revealed to them the outcome, whether good or bad, of their illnesses. They could even cure them of their ailments with the healing action of their water.

In Greek mythology, the Nymphs were classified and labeled with precision: The Nereids populated the seas; the Naiads, the rivers and, generally speaking, flowing waters; the Dryads dwelled in oak forests; the Alceids, in swamps. The Oreads lived in the mountains and the Hamadryads lived in the woods. Other nymphs lived only in valleys while the Meliads lived only in ash trees. The countless legends involving Nymphs show that they were not only in love with the gods but also with simple mortals. Their unions with mortals gave rise to heroes, demigods, the ancestors of the first human races. Carefree, wandering and singing on the waves and in the trees, they live, although they are mortal, for thousands of years. They are the fairies of Antiquity.

NYSUS. Dionysus entrusted Nysus, his adoptive father, with the kingdom of Thebes before his departure for a long journey to India. But when the god returned, Nysus refused to hand over the power of the city. Dionysus patiently waited for several years, then requested permission to celebrate a feast in Thebes; the king agreed. Disguised as Bacchantes, the warriors of the god dethroned Nysus and reestablished their divine leader on the throne.

O

OCEANIDS. Crowned with flowers, accompanying the train of their mother Tethys, the Oceanids are the nymphs that dwell at the inaccessible bottom of the sea and the ocean, Oceanus their father. In various legends, some of them were prominent, such as Clymene, the wife of the Titan Iapetus, and Dione, the lover of Zeus.

OCEANUS. The original element that appeared even before the world itself and which presided over Creation, Oceanus holds an important place in mythology. The son of Uranus and Gaia, he is the divine personification of water. He surrounds the Earth like an immense river where everything is created and everything returns to die. He is the father of some three thousand rivers which supply men with water and fertilize the Earth. Tethys, his spouse, bore him a multitude of daughters, the Oceanids. Later portrayed in works of art, Oceanus is depicted as an old man with a green beard; he holds the horn of a bull, symbolizing the powerful and nourishing abundance of his waters.

OEAGRUS. This river-god, the king of Thrace, married the Muse Calliope and was, according to one of the versions of the legend, the father of Orpheus. He also had by Calliope another son, Linus, who was also a poet.

OEDIPUS. The king of Thebes, Laius, disturbed at having no heir, went to consult the Oracle at Delphi. The oracle predicted that the son who would be born to him would kill his father. Despite this fatal prediction, a child was born in the court of Thebes. Jocasta, his mother, frightened at the sentence of the oracle, abandoned the child on Mount Cithaeron after piercing his ankles with a needle and binding them together with a strip of leather. Shepherds rescued the infant; they named him Oedipus ("swollen foot"), and presented him to Polybus, the king of Corinth and spouse of Periboea, who, having had no children, adopted him joyfully and raised him as her own son. One day, a drunk Corinthian informed Oedipus that he had been found as an infant. Intrigued by this revelation, Oedipus consulted the Delphic oracle, who doubled the horror of the prediction made to Laius: "You will kill your father and will marry your mother." In a procession, not far from Delphi, he happened upon Laius, not knowing that this was his real father, and, involved in a dispute with him, killed him. He thus fulfilled the first prophecy. He continued along his way and arrived at the gates of Thebes where he met the Sphinx, a terrifying monster that asked a riddle of all travelers and devoured them if they did not produce a response. Oedipus did indeed come up with the correct answer and the

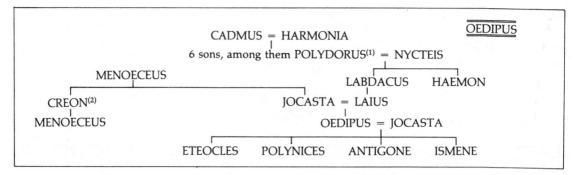

OEDIPUS

```
                    CADMUS = HARMONIA
                            |
           6 sons, among them POLYDORUS⁽¹⁾ = NYCTEIS
     MENOECEUS                     LABDACUS    HAEMON
      |_____|    |
     CREON⁽²⁾              JOCASTA = LAIUS
     MENOECEUS              OEDIPUS = JOCASTA
                            |
           ETEOCLES   POLYNICES   ANTIGONE   ISMENE
```

Sphinx, in despair, threw itself from the top of a rock and killed itself, thus delivering the country from terror. Welcomed in Thebes as a benefactor, Oedipus was proclaimed king and married Jocasta, unaware that she was his mother. Thus the second prophecy was fulfilled. Of this incestuous union four children were born: Eteocles, Polynices, Antigone and Ismene, all of whom were destined for tragedy. Several years later, a plague beset the city and the oracle consulted answered: "The murderer of Laius must be expelled from the city." Against this murderer, namely himself, Oedipus, still unaware of his crime, pronounced a merciless curse. But soon the perplexing revelations of the soothsayer Tiresias enabled the hero to guess the awful truth. In shame, Jocasta hanged herself; Oedipus gouged out his eyes and, banished from Thebes, he wandered through the country begging, accompanied by his daughter Antigone, who alone remained faithful to him. At the end of his days, the unfortunate king found asylum in Attica, with Theseus. In Colonus, a small town not far from Athens, the Erinyes led him to death. However, Theseus granted a burial to the body of the victim of the most terrible fatality of all because he said that the tomb of Oedipus would be a token of victory for the people of Athens.

OENEUS. The king of Calydon in Aetolia, Oeneus first married Althaea, who bore him several children; at her death, he remarried, this time to Periboea, who gave birth to several children including Tydeus, the father of Diomedes. The kingdom of Oeneus was the setting of the Calydonian Boar Hunt, in which Meleager killed the raging boar, and it also set the

A simple traveler with his rod, sandals, cap and tunic, Oedipus has sat down on a stone. In front of him, the dreaded Sphinx, with the body of a lion and the head of a woman, perched on an Ionic column, asks him the famous riddle about man. His legs crossed, indicating composure, the attentive hero, chin in hand, raises his face toward the monster and listens. Attic cup, Vatican Museum, photo Anderson-Giraudon.

stage for numerous exploits by Heracles prior to his marriage to Deianira. Dethroned by the sons of his brother Agrius, who killed him, he was avenged by his grandson, Diomedes.

OENOMAUS. The son of Ares, and of Harpinna or else the Pleiad Sterope, Oenomaus was the king of Pisa in Elis. He decided to grant the hand of his daughter, Hippodameia, to whoever was able to defeat him in a chariot race. Many competitors were therefore put to death by the ever-victorious king who rode in a chariot that was drawn by indomitably fleet-footed horses given to him by his father, Ares. Only Pelops, with the help of Myrtilus, was able to trick the king and defeat him as his chariot broke and the king was trampled by his horses.

OENONE. Daughter of the river-god Cebren, this nymph had received from Apollo the gift of preparing medicinal herbs. The first wife of Paris, she was soon deserted for Helen. Oenone, who could look into the future and knew the unhappy outcome of the Trojan War, tried in vain to dissuade her unfaithful husband from marrying her rival. However, she asked him to come to her if he were wounded; indeed, she alone had the power to heal him. Later, when he was stricken by the arrows of Philoctetes during a battle, Paris sent messengers to beg his wife to come to his aid. But the nymph, forgetting her promise in her jealousy, refused to help and Paris died. Overcome with remorse afterward, the nymph left for Troy where she found her lifeless husband. In despair, she hanged herself or had herself burned on a rock.

OENOPION. The king of the island of Chios, Oenopion, the son of Ariadne and Dionysus, learned from his father the art of making wine. Of his many children, the most famous was his daughter Merope. Orion fell in love with her and, to win her heart, he fought and killed all of the ferocious beasts and game that infested the island. Once this task was accomplished, he asked the king for the hand of Merope. Oenopion refused. But one night, having had too much to drink, Orion tried to seduce the girl. To avenge this offense, the king gouged out the eyes of the impudent Orion and banished him.

OLD AGE. This allegorical divinity, daughter of Erebus and of Night, was venerated as much in Athens as in Rome. With all the traditional attributes of decrepitude and sadness, dressed in black, she leans, heavily bent over, on a staff.

olive tree. The symbol of peace and wealth, the olive was the basic food of the Greeks. The olive tree was introduced in Greece for the first time by Athena during her quarrel with Poseidon over the supremacy of Attica. The goddess caused an olive tree to rise behind the Erechtheion as the finest gift she could offer the Athenians. During the classical era, people still adored the twelve shoots of the original stump that had been planted in the gardens of the Academy. Oars or crowns of olive branches were presented to the winners of the Panathenaean games and to murderers who came to be purified. The olive tree was the tree of civilization, of peace, and of victory over dark, sterilizing, unjust forces.

OLYMPIA. This city of Elis in Greece, on the right bank of the Alpheus, was to acquire in Antiquity immense fame because of the games that were held there every four years in honor of Zeus. The games were founded for the first time by Pelops, the husband of Hippodameia, in honor of Hera, the goddess of Marriage. Later, Heracles, after his victory over Augeas and the city of Elis, resumed the tradition of the games but this time in honor of Zeus, his father, who had afforded him such great protection in his exploits. A sacred arena, Altis, was marked off by Heracles and a temple was dedicated to Pelops, his illustrious predecessor. The

From this photograph it is easy to see why Olympus inspired fear and respect in the Greeks of Antiquity. An unscaled mountain with dense, snow-covered peaks and deep gorges, Olympus is usually veiled in somber, heavy clouds. The gods are enthroned there in solitude, keeping a close watch on the happenings of the earth, concealed from the sight of mortals. Photo Boissonnas.

wood of the white poplar used for sacrifices in Olympia was, it is said, brought back from the Underworld by Heracles. However, the Olympic games did not take on their real importance until they were furthered by legendary heroes such as Oxylus and Iphitus, both kings of Elis. Iphitus wanted, above all, by creating an atmosphere of unity in the games, to put an end to the internal struggles that were ravaging Greece.

OLYMPUS. This famous mountain located between Macedonia and Thessaly was regarded in Antiquity as the dwelling place of the gods. After his victory over the Giants, it was on Olympus that Zeus established himself, in all his majesty, with his many powers and the assistance of the assembly of great divinities. There he deliberated over the destiny of heroes and mortals and, sometimes, that of the gods themselves. Concealed from the sight of mortals by a mantle of clouds, which covered the top of Olympus, the gods reveled in sumptuous banquets, drinking nectar and savoring ambrosia, amidst the singing and dancing of the gracious Muses.

OMPHALE. Having killed, in a fit of anger, one of his best friends, Iphitus, the son of King Eurytus, Heracles went to consult the oracle of Apollo who advised him to sell himself as a slave to the queen of Lydia, Omphale, who would purify him of the murder. The queen subjected the hero to a certain number of tasks, which he performed in a flash. Thus, he rid the region of the two thieving Cercopes, who were known for their cruelty, and of Syleus, who forced transient strangers to cultivate his vineyards before killing them; he waged war on the Lydians of Itona, who were devastating the kingdom of Omphale, recovered their booty, then razed their city. Finally, he killed an enormous serpent that devoured both men and beasts. Seduced by the bravery and beauty of her slave, Omphale freed him and married him. A strange Latin version of the legend relates that the queen of Lydia humiliated Heracles by dressing him as a woman and forcing him to spin yarn at her feet while she donned the Nemean lion's skin and brandished her spouse's club.

omphalos. This sacred conical stone, whose name means "navel," was considered to be the center of the Earth. Two eagles sent by Zeus around the world, one in the direction of the West and one East, happened to meet there. The omphalos was at Delphi and associated with the worship of Apollo.

OPS. Identified with Cybele and Rhea, Ops, the spouse of Saturn and goddess of Wealth, is ranked among the Roman divinities of the Earth. She protects crops and her public festival is celebrated at the time of the harvest and sowing. Introduced, according to legend, by the leader of the Sabines, Titus Tatius, into the Roman Pantheon, she was later portrayed as a matron who extends her right hand to offer help and her left hand to distribute bread.

oracle. Warning, counsel or order of a god, the oracle enabled men to know the will of the Immortals and to make decisions with respect to the answer of the god. It was consulted in a special temple, in a place to which legend had generally granted great credit. The oracles of Zeus and Apollo were the most famous. The oracle of Dodona, in Epirus, expressed the thoughts of Zeus by the rustling of the leaves in a sacred wood. But the servants of the god of gods also queried the flight of the birds and the lapping of springs. The oracle of Apollo was founded in Delphi (there was another one in Didyma), according to Homer, in honor of Apollo Python, by the god himself after his victory over the serpent Python. He thus dethroned the very ancient oracle of Gaia, the Earth. A sort of religious confederation was

The dagger in his hand, the muscles of his arm still swollen from the mortal blows with which he has just stricken his mother, Orestes' face already bears the traces of folly immediately sent to him by the gods. Roman relief, National Archaeological Museum, Naples, photo Giraudon.

formed around the sanctuary and the Pythian games were instituted to seal this new union of all pilgrims who came to hear the Pythia. People came to ask the oracle's advice in political matters as well as personal matters. Murderers, such as Orestes, were also purified there. Men sought the new location of a colony. The oracle was the proof of mortals' submission to divine destinies and, in legends, no hero ever succeeded in escaping them.

OREADS. These nymphs, who frequent the mountains whose steep slopes they enjoy, do not have the gentle, somewhat languorous, natures of their sisters of the valleys and woods. Delighting in vigorous exercise, in the company of Artemis the huntress whom they sometimes choose as their guide, they pursue game in the most dangerous places, on the edge of chasms, apparently oblivious to danger or fatigue.

OREITHYIA. The daughter of Erechtheus, one of the legendary kings of Athens, Oreithyia was abducted by Boreas and transported to Thrace. There, she gave birth to four children, the Boreads, including two sons, Zetes and Calais, who took part in the expedition of the Argonauts along with Jason.

ORESTES. There is not one legend of Orestes, but several, all of which complement one another and to which the tragic poets have given a prominent place. Orestes was but a child when his father Agamemnon was killed by Clytemnestra and Aegisthus. With the help of his sister Electra, he was able to take refuge with his uncle Strophius, in Phocis; there, he formed a bond of friendship with Pylades, his cousin, who remained the faithful companion to his unfortunate relative. When Orestes reached manhood, he decided, on the advice of Apollo, to avenge the death of his father. Accompanied by Pylades, he went secretly to Mycenae and killed Aegisthus and Clytemnestra. His murder, which seemed to be just revenge, horrified the gods. They sent the Erinyes to torment the assassin of his own mother until he was driven mad amid hallucinations and remorse. However, Apollo did not desert the poor creature. He advised him to take refuge in Athens where the Areopagus, owing to the decisive intervention of Athena, acquitted him of the murder. Then the god purified him in Delphi and, through the Pythia, made it known that he would be cured of his madness by going to seek the statue of Artemis in Tauris. In Tauris, therefore, Orestes and Pylades, about to be sacrificed as strangers, were recognized by Iphigenia, the priestess of Artemis, who fled with them, handing over the statue. Upon their return to Peloponnesus, to Mycenae, the hero took possession of the kingdom of his father, Agamemnon, which had been unjustly seized, then abducted and married Hermione. Orestes reigned over Argos from that point on and died a peaceful death at a very ripe old age.

ORION. There are countless legends involving this beautiful giant hunter; some consider him to be the son of a Boeotian peasant who welcomed Zeus, Poseidon and Hermes into his home. The gods, to thank him for this hospitality, presented him with such a son. Other legends claim that he was the son of Poseidon and Euryale; his life and death are also described in many different ways. Having gone to Chios, he fell in love with Merope, the daughter of King Oenopion and granddaughter of Dionysus, and wanted to seduce her. The king, to punish him, deprived him of his sight. To recover his sight, he was obliged to go to the East and expose himself to the rays of the sun. Afterwards, he lived as a hunter in the company of Artemis, but Eos, who loved him, abducted him. Out of jealousy, Artemis killed him with an arrow. According to other mythographers, the goddess killed him at the instigation of her brother who showed her a faraway point in the sea and challenged her to reach it. She drew one of her arrows, which hit the mark, but it was the head of Orion that was passing over the sea. Apollo had been unable to bear the affection that his sister had for the hunter. Horace, for his part, claims that Orion tried to rape Artemis and that the virgin killed him with the sting of a scorpion that she caused to emerge from the ground. Regardless of the version of the legend, they almost all agree that Orion, after his death, was placed among the stars and became the constellation that bears his name.

Portrayed as a god of Asia Minor in accordance with the legend, Orpheus is seen wearing a Phrygian cap. Domestic or wild animals, birds of every kind, encircle him. They listen, suddenly charmed or subdued, to the magical tunes that the musician, seated under a tree, draws from his lyre with one hand. In the other, he holds the stylus with which he inscribes his verses in the wax of the tablets. Roman mosaic, National Archaeological Museum, Palermo, photo Alinari-Giraudon.

ORPHEUS. The son of the king of Thrace, Oeagrus, and the Muse Calliope, Orpheus is the greatest legendary poet of Greece. Blessed with many talents by Apollo, he received as a gift from the god a lyre with seven strings to which he added, it is said, two other strings, in memory of the nine Muses, the sisters of his mother. He drew from this instrument such moving and melodious tunes that the rivers stopped, the rocks followed him, the trees ceased to rustle. He also had the ability to tame ferocious beasts. Horace claims that this trait refers to Orpheus' dissuading men from cannibalism. Through the gentleness and beauty of his voice, he was able to calm the agitated waves, to surpass the seduction of the Sirens, and to lull the dragon of Colchis to sleep. He traveled to Egypt and was initiated into the mysteries of Osiris, from which he drew his inspiration when he founded the mysteries of Eleusis. Upon his return from the expedition of the Argonauts, he settled in Thrace where he married the nymph Eurydice. One day, the young woman, wishing to escape the advances of the shepherd Aristaeus, fled and, stung by a serpent, died immediately. Wild with grief, Orpheus obtained from Zeus the permission to fetch her from the Underworld and bring her back to Earth. With his lyre, he calmed the ferocious Cerberus, soothed the Furies for a moment, and stole his wife away from death, on the condition that he not look at her before reaching the land of the living. Just as they arrived at the gates of the Underworld, he turned his head to see whether Eurydice was following him. She, therefore, vanished right before his eyes forever. When he returned to Thrace, Orpheus wanted to remain faithful to his departed wife and spurned the love of the women of his country who, chagrined, tore the poet to pieces. His head, which was thrown into the Hebrus, was recovered in Lesbos. His lyre was placed by Zeus among the constellations at the request of Apollo and the Muses who, for their part, granted a burial to his scattered limbs at the foot of Mount Olympus.

ORPHISM. The mythical poet Orpheus was, it is said, the founder of this religious sect which, from the beginning of the 6th century B.C., engaged in mysteries, the development and order of which are to this day partially unknown. The success of Orphism among the Greeks as well as the Romans is explained by its tendency to disengage mythology from a complexity that made it almost incomprehensible, and to attempt to reconcile gods, myths and religious doctrines to try to give rise to the idea of a single god who, therefore, bore the name of Zeus or, more commonly, that of *Zagreus*. Indeed, Orphic theogony differed considerably from traditional theogony or that of Hesiod. The world was born on an egg; the upper part of the shell became the sky and the lower part, the Earth. Then came the original gods, and finally Zeus, having had relations with his daughter Persephone, had a son, Zagreus, who was called upon to rule the world. But Zagreus was torn to pieces by his enemies; however, he was revived by his father. According to Orphic doctrine, the soul is immortal; it dwells in a mortal body, marked by sin, soiled by the crimes of many generations. After death, the soul is reincarnated either in another human body or in the body of an animal, and so forth. During successive transformations, it feeds on rich experiences that are provided by its passage in various bodies. In the intervals of its reincarnation, it finds in the Underworld the mortification necessary for its development and its purification. Only the initiates to the Orphic mysteries, namely those who knew the magical formulas for passing from one body to another, from animal life to the blessed life, could hope, one day, for ultimate salvation of their souls. Thus the Orphic mysteries granted the souls of the followers a sort of baptism with goat's milk preparing them for and opening them up to eternal life and happiness, while nonetheless leaving them free to choose between good and evil. Therefore, it can be seen that, through the Orphism that was rather widespread in all layers of Greek and Roman society in the latter years of paganism, hearts were already prepared for the doctrine of Christianity. This doctrine, moreover, in its iconography, did not try to deny all that it owes to Orphism. Very often, on funerary steles at the beginning of the Christian era, Christ has the features and characteristics of Orpheus.

ORTHRUS. A monster born of the union of Echidna and Typhon, Orthrus, the brother of Cerberus, was a two-headed dog. He had relations with his mother and begat the Sphinx of Thebes. He belonged to the king of the island of Erythia, Geryon, whose famous and immense herd he guarded. But he was quickly strangled by Heracles who was thus able to steal the cattle with no difficulty.

OXYLUS. A descendant of Endymion and Aetolus, the king of Elis, who had been banished from his territory and had established a new sovereignty over Aetolia, Oxylus committed a murder and was obliged to spend a year in exile in Elis. During that time, the Heraclidae were seeking a three-eyed creature who, according to the oracle, was the only one who could guide them toward the lands that had been assigned to them by fate. They then saw Oxylus arrive as he was on his way back to Aetolia after his exile had been completed. The hero was atop a one-eyed horse; between them, the animal and the man possessed three eyes. The Heraclidae therefore asked Oxylus to lead them to Peloponnesus. After the division of the territories, Oxylus received, as a promise, the territory of Elis, which had belonged to his ancestors. He introduced a wise government in his kingdom and revived the Olympic games which had once been instituted by Heracles. His son, Laias, whom he had had by Pieria, succeeded him on the throne.

P Q

PACTOLUS. The son of Zeus and Leucothea, Pactolus had a daughter, Euryanassa, the wife of Tantalus. Having committed involuntary incest with his sister Demodice, Pactolus threw himself into the River Chrusorroas ("River that rolls in gold"), the god of which he became and to which he gave his name. The golden sands of the Pactolus soon became legendary. They originated with King Midas who changed everything he touched into gold. Indeed, he bathed in the waters of this river to rid himself of this cumbersome gift.

PALAEMON. Melicertes assumed the surname of *Palaemon* when his mother Ino-Leucothea threw herself into the sea with him. Zeus deified him and sent him to the coast of Corinth, placing him on the back of a dolphin. He was recovered and buried by Sisyphus, who founded the Isthmian games in his honor.

PALAMEDES. When Ulysses received the order to return to the Greek expedition against Troy, he feigned madness. Palamedes, the son of Nauplius, found him working his fields, pretending to understand nothing. Palamedes, to thwart the deception, placed Telemachus, the only son of the hero, in front of the plow. To avoid killing him, Ulysses turned the oxen, proving that indeed he was in control of his senses; he was, therefore, obliged to rejoin the Greek camp. Wishing to take revenge, Ulysses, during the Trojan War, accused Palamedes of treason and supplied well-documented proof, including a letter supposedly written by Priam. Palamedes was tried, convicted and stoned. His father, Nauplius, avenged his death by drawing the Greek fleet, on its return from Troy, against the rocky cliffs of Caphareus where it was shipwrecked. Palamedes, a pupil of the wise and learned centaur Chiron, is often credited with a certain number of inventions including several letters of the Greek alphabet, coins, numbers, the game of knucklebones and dice. It is also said that he invented checkers to while away the hours during the siege of Troy.

PALES. Sometimes considered to be a god, sometimes a goddess, this ancient pastoral divinity, of Latin origin, protects pastures, herds and shepherds; poets often refer to shepherds as the "pupils" or "favorites" of Pales. It is not known whether Pales was a god or a goddess; it was, however, probably a masculine divinity. On April 21, assumed to be the date on which Rome was founded, a festival, the *Parilia*, is celebrated in his honor so that cattle and stables may be purified.

PALICI. Seduced by Zeus, the nymph Thaleia soon carried two infants in her womb. Fearing the effects of the terrible jealousy of Hera, she asked her lover to hide her in the belly of the earth. Zeus granted her wish. Shortly after, not far from Palicea, twins emerged from the Sicilian soil. They were immediately placed in the ranks of the divinities of the Underworld. In honor of these Palici, the Greeks erected a temple not far from a small volcanic lake with bubbling, sulfurous waters, which was considered to have served as the cradle of the divine infants. Tablets were thrown into the water bearing oaths. Depending on whether they floated or sank, the oaths were regarded as true or false.

PALINURUS. This pilot of the ship of Aeneas, overcome by insuperable slumber, fell asleep at the helm during the crossing between Sicily and Italy and was thrown into the sea by a sudden pitch. He managed to swim for several days and reached the coast of Lucania. But he had scarcely touched ground when he was killed by the natives of the country. When Aeneas, guided by the sibyl of Cumae, descended to the netherworld, he found, on the banks of the Styx, Palinurus who, having died without a burial, could not enter the Underworld. The sibyl promised the poor victim that the barbarians who had killed him would hasten to bury his remains when their country was beset by a plague. Cape Palinuro, on the west coast of Lucania, perpetuated his memory from that point on.

PALLADIUM. This small statue of Pallas, three cubits high, whose feet are joined together while the right hand holds a spear and the left hand holds a distaff and spindle, was thrown from Olympus by Zeus, it is said, and fell at the feet of Ilus, the founder of the city of Troy. The hero saw in this miracle a sign of the benevolence of the gods and, with the greatest honors, placed the effigy in the temple of Athena. An oracle then assured him that Troy would exist as long as the Palladium remained within the city. During the Trojan War, the Greeks, alerted to this prediction, attempted to steal the Palladium. Ulysses and Diomedes succeeded by entering the underground portion of the temple during the night. But certain versions claim that, fearing this possibility, the Trojans had had a second Palladium sculpted. Although the first had been stolen by the Greeks, the second was carried by Aeneas to Italy and placed in the temple of Vesta in Rome: thus, the prophecy was fulfilled that Troy would be reborn from its ashes through Rome.

PALLAS. 1. To explain this surname of Athena, it was said that Pallas was a daughter of Triton and that she had been accidentally killed by Athena. The latter, stricken with sorrow, assumed the name of her victim to honor her and sculpted the Palladium.

2. According to certain traditions, **Pallas** was the name of a Giant, the father of Athena. He wanted to violate his daughter and she skinned him alive and donned his skin.

3. **Pallas,** the son of Lycaon, king of Arcadia, gave the Palladium to Dardanus, his son-in-law, when he left to found a colony in Troy. This Pallas is also known as the grandfather to Evander.

4. The eponymous hero of Palatine, another **Pallas** is the son of Evander and the ally of Aeneas in the combats against the Rutuli of Turnus.

5. There was yet another **Pallas,** the son of Pandion, king of Athens; he had fifty sons, the Pallantids, with whom he fought against Theseus, considered to be a usurper. But he and his sons were defeated by the hero of Athens.

PAN. Worshiped particularly in Arcadia, this god, whose name was thought to mean "everything," originally protected herds, goats and shepherds. Deformed, monstrous with his ram's head and feet, his hairy man's body, he

The god Pan, a sort of small ram with a human torso, can be seen tenderly teaching the art of playing the syrinx to Daphnis, a young demigod of the woods. The somewhat feminine beauty of Daphnis excites the hearts of all bucolic divinities in legends. Ancient group, Museo delle Terme, Rome, photo Anderson-Giraudon.

was the laughingstock of all the gods of Olympus when his father, Hermes, introduced him to them. God of Fertility and sexual power, both brutal in his desires and terrifying in his appearances (people speak of a "panic" fear), Pan's worship spread very quickly after he was said to have helped the Athenians at Marathon. He acquired new powers and was associated with a multiplicity of legends. Physician, healer, prophet, inventor of the syrinx, the pastoral flute, expressing, through his rather bestial appearance and his unsated love, the unconquered and diffuse force of all nature, Pan was associated, under the influence of neo-Pla-

tonic philosophy, with the idea of fertility. This idea of a total god was to inspire the highly curious story related by Plutarch. In the reign of Tiberius, a ship was suddenly immobilized on the waters of the Aegean Sea and a voice was heard asking the navigator to scream as he approached the coast: "The great Pan is dead." The pilot, after much hesitation, decided to announce the death of Pan and immediately there was wailing and cries of sorrow as though the earth had gone into mourning. According to Christian authors, the death of Pan marked the death of paganism which was replaced by Christianity.

PANACEA. The daughter of Asclepius and Lampetia, she belongs to the group of divinities that heal all illnesses using medicinal herbs.

PANDAREOS. The son of the soothsayer Merops, Pandareos, born in Miletus, one day stole a golden dog which had been the guardian of the infant Zeus in Crete, and gave it to Tantalus. Then, some time later, he went to claim back his booty. Tantalus pretended to ignore him. Zeus, therefore, punished the two culprits: he turned Pandareos to stone and buried Tantalus under Mount Sipylos. It is also said that Pandareos and his wife Harmothoë were able to flee to Athens and, from there, went to Sicily; but they did not escape the wrath of the god for long and were soon killed. Their three orphan daughters were raised by Hera, Aphrodite, Artemis and Athena until they were seized by the Harpies and taken to the depths of the Underworld.

PANDARUS. This hero commanded a regiment of Lycians during the Trojan War in which he made his mark as a skillful archer, instructed in this difficult art by Apollo himself. When a truce was declared between the two warring camps to enable Menelaus and Paris to compete in a duel, Athena incited Pandarus to fire an arrow at Menelaus. The Greeks, in the face of this provocation, immediately resumed battle and Pandarus was killed by Diomedes.

PANDION. Two kings of Athens are known by this name. One, the son of Erichthonius, had two sons—Erechtheus and Boutes—and two daughters—Procne and Philomela. He arranged a marriage between Procne and Tereus, the king of Thrace.

The other **Pandion** is the great-grandson of the preceding. Orestes was purified of the murder of his mother by this king. It is said that Pandion, banished from Athens, fled to Megara and married the daughter of Pylas, the king of the city, whom he succeeded. Of this union, four children were born—Aegeus, Pallas, Nisus and Lycus.

PANDORA. 1. During the struggle between Athens and Eleusis, King Erechtheus, to obtain final victory, was obliged to sacrifice to the gods his youngest daughter, Chthonia. Her two sisters, Protogenia and Pandora, killed themselves immediately, having vowed that if one of them died the others would also die.

2. When Prometheus stole fire from heaven to give it to men, the gods of Olympus, in order to punish this too powerful race of mortals, created a young woman. She was given beauty, grace, trickery, audacity, strength. After naming her **Pandora** ("she who has all gifts"), she was sent to Earth to seduce mortals and drive them to ruin. Epimetheus, the brother of Prometheus, chose her as his wife. One day, out of curiosity, Pandora raised the cover of a jar that she was supposed to keep closed and all evils escaped, spreading across the Earth. Only Hope remained at the bottom of the container. Later, it was said that this jar contained divine gifts which, set free by Pandora, returned to Olympus, abandoning man with no recourse.

PANDROSOS. The daughter of Cecrops, the founder of Athens, sister of Aglauros and Herse, Pandrosos was driven mad and threw herself from the top of the Acropolis after opening the cradle of little Erichthonius who had been entrusted to her by Athena.

PARCAE. The three Parcae, who assumed the appearance of spinners, presided, in the ancient Roman religion, over birth (the first), marriage (the second) and death (the third). Surnamed *Tria Fata*, "the three fates," the dreaded images of Fate, of Destiny to which all life is bound, they were logically identified by the Romans with the severe Greek Moirae. Their Latin names were Nona, Decima and Morta.

PARIS. Also called *Alexander*, Paris was the youngest son of Priam, king of Troy, and Hecuba. Before his birth, his mother dreamed that she gave birth to a flaming brand that set the city ablaze, a harbinger of the ruin of Troy. Fearing this bad omen, Hecuba abandoned Paris on Mount Ida where he was rescued by a shepherd, Agelaus. After discovering his origin, the hero returned to the court of Priam, was recognized during the funerary games by his brother Deiphobus and his sister Cassandra, the prophetess, and was welcomed immediately by his rejoicing father who had believed him dead. Paris is connected with the story of a famous judgment. When Peleus and Thetis celebrated their wedding, all the gods were invited except Eris, Discord. Furious over this voluntary omission, the goddess threw a golden apple among the guests, with the following inscription: "To the most beautiful." Immediately, Aphrodite, Athena and Hera claimed this laudatory epithet. To decide among them, Zeus asked Paris to be the judge. The three goddesses paraded before him, nude. Hera promised him sovereignty over Asia, Athena the glory of warriors, and Aphrodite, the most beautiful of all women. Paris gave the apple to Aphrodite. In order to honor her prophecy, the goddess protected him and enabled him to abduct Helen, the wife of Menelaus, king of Sparta; this was the origin of the Trojan War.

Holding the famous apple of Discord in one hand and the crown in the other, Paris is about to grant Aphrodite the title of "the most beautiful of all goddesses." Coptic art, bronze from the 4th to 5th cent. A.D., Louvre, photo Giraudon.

Athena and Hera, jealous at not having been chosen, bore savage hatred toward the Trojan Paris and protected the Greeks during the Trojan War. Paris managed to escape the blows of Menelaus, who had challenged him to single combat. Aphrodite hid him in a cloud. He killed many warriors and, most notably, mortally wounded Achilles by shooting an arrow into his heel. Wounded himself by an arrow of Philoctetes', Paris died shortly after as his first wife, Oenone, refused to care for him.

PARNASSUS. This mountain range, located several kilometers from Delphi, was regarded as a dwelling place of the Muses, Apollo and Dionysus, a privileged place where musicians and poets went to seek inspiration. The sides of Parnassus were dotted with many caves, inhabited, according to legends, by agrarian divinities. In one of these caverns was the famous spring, Castalia. At the foot of Parnassus was the valley of Plistus and the road to Delphi on which Laius was killed by his son Oedipus.

PARTHENOPAEUS. The illegitimate son of Meleager, this hero was abandoned by his mother Atalanta on Mount Parthenion, on the borders of Argolis and Arcadia. A shepherd discovered him and took him to King Corythus, who adopted him as he had adopted Telephus, abandoned by his mother Auge. Thus he received the name *Parthenopaeus,* meaning "son of a chaste girl," because it is said that, despite the fact that she gave birth, Atalanta retained her virginity. This hero was one of the Seven Leaders who marched on Thebes where he perished, leaving behind a child, Promachus, who ten years later joined the Epigoni to avenge his father's death by destroying Thebes.

PASIPHAË. The daughter of Helios, Pasiphaë, the wife of Minos, was the mother of Ariadne, Phaedra, Glaucus and Androgeus. But the couple did not remain united. Minos had refused to sacrifice a white bull that Poseidon had sent him: irritated at this impiety, Poseidon inspired in the wife of the king a monstrous love for the bull. Wishing to satisfy her passion, Pasiphaë asked Daedalus to fashion her a wooden cow and she closed herself up in the body of the animal. The bull mistook the wooden animal and had relations with Pasiphaë, who gave birth to a horrible monster that was half bull and half man, the Minotaur.

PATROCLUS. Born in Locris, in the kingdom of his father Menoetius, the husband of Sthenele, Patroclus, still young, killed one of his playmates in a fit of anger. He was forced to leave Locris. Taken in by Peleus, king of the Myrmidons, in Phthiotis in Thessaly, he received the purification necessary to atone for his murder and be absolved of it. But, as he had formed a strong bond of friendship with Achilles, the son of this generous monarch, he did not return home. When the Trojan War broke

Wounded in the left arm during a battle, Patroclus has his wound attended to by his war companion Achilles. Patroclus turns his head but his face shows the signs and creases of suffering. Greek cup by Sosias (Athenian potter), circa 500 B.C., Berlin Museum, photo Giraudon.

out, he followed his friend to battle, at the head of a contingent of Myrmidons, and accomplished valiant exploits under the city's walls. He followed Achilles to his tent when the latter quarreled with Agamemnon. Like his companion, he refused to take part in the battle. However, as the trend of the war was not to the advantage of the Greeks, he agreed to resume combat and Achilles even lent him his weapons and armor. He succeeded in repelling the Trojans, but during single combat he was killed by Hector. Furious that his friend had been killed, Achilles was seized by such a desire for vengeance that he came out of his retirement, took up his weapons once again, and killed Hector. He honored the memory of his friend with solemn funerary games. The two inseparable friends were to meet again later on White Island, the mythical and blissful dwelling place of heroes, where they continued an eternally heroic existence even after death.

PAX (PEACE). This Roman allegorical divinity, whose cult appeared only later, was identified with *Eirene*, the Greek goddess of Peace, and one of the three Horae. She generally assumes the appearance of a woman with a kind face, carrying a horn of plenty and an olive branch.

PEGASUS. This magical winged horse, which was as swift as the wind, was born of the blood of Medusa when her head was chopped off by Perseus. He lived, always, in search of springs. With a thrust of his hoof on the Helicon, it is said that he gave birth to the fountain Hippocrene. One day, as he was drinking from the spring of Pirene, on the Acrocorinth, he was broken in by Bellerophon. The latter, mounted on this miraculous steed, accomplished great exploits. In particular, he slew the Chimaera. But his pride was his downfall. Carried by Pegasus, he wanted to ascend into the heavens, but Zeus unseated him. Alone, the winged

With his immense, spread wings, his fine legs perfectly suited to running, Pegasus can be compared with today's finest race horses with respect to the strength of his neck and the thoroughbred character of his body. Corinthian coin, Bibl. Nat., Cabinet des Médailles, photo Larousse.

horse reached the dwelling place of the gods, who placed him among the constellations.

PELASGUS. The Pelasgi, the first legendary inhabitants of Greece, claimed to be descendants of Pelasgus, that mythical hero who was born in Arcadia, of the love of Niobe and Zeus. The spouse of the nymph Cyllene, he had one son, Lycaon, and one daughter, Callisto, the mother of Arcas, the eponymous hero of Arcadia. In another version of the legend, he is the son of Triopas and Sosis and the brother of Iasus and Agenor; he had one daughter, Larissa. Other traditions claim, however, that Larissa was his mother and Poseidon, his father. With his two brothers, Achaeus and Phthius, he shared sovereignty over Thessaly and Peloponessus, dividing the territory into three regions: Achaea, Phthiotis and Pelasgiotis.

PELEUS. The son of Aeacus, king of the Myrmidons, Peleus committed a murder: during his adolescence, he assassinated Phocus, his half-brother, with the help of his brother Telamon. Banished from the city, Telamon and Peleus split up to pursue different destinies. Eurytion, the king of Phthia, granted Peleus the necessary purification to cleanse him of his murder and even gave him his daughter Antigone in marriage. However, the happiness of the hero was short-lived; during the Calydonian Boar Hunt, Peleus accidentally killed his father-in-law and was banished. Taking refuge in the court of Acastus in Iolcus, he refused to yield to the advances of Queen Astydamia, who twice slandered him. First, she sent a letter to Antigone saying that Peleus had been unfaithful to her; Antigone, believing herself dishonored, hanged herself. Second, Astydamia told her husband that Peleus had tried to seduce her. The king abandoned Peleus on Mount Pelion. But the hero managed to escape with the aid of the centaur Chiron and ferocious beasts, and he returned to Iolcus where he killed Acastus and stoned Astydamia. The nymph, Thetis, the daughter of Nereus, was the second wife of Peleus. Refusing to marry a mortal, despite the order of the gods, she assumed all manner of forms when Peleus tried to approach her, from the smallest to the largest, from the most monstrous to the most intangible. But Peleus did not lose heart, nor was he frightened, and he did succeed in winning her heart. The wedding was held with much ado and was attended by all the gods who gave them an abundance of

Seated alongside his wife, Thetis, who does not seem particularly overjoyed by the wedding, as confirmed by legends, Peleus receives the homage and gifts of divinities and mortals. Roman sarcophagus, Villa Albani, Rome, photo Alinari-Giraudon.

Oenomaus falls from his chariot with its broken wheel. Pelops, his opponent, gallops toward victory—the hand of Hippodameia is at stake. Ancient sarcophagus, Vatican Museum, photo Alinari-Giraudon.

presents; above all, Peleus received an invincible armor and two immortal horses, which were later used by Achilles. Peleus lived a long life, but while his son was in Troy, he was banished from his kingdom by the sons of Acastus and ended his days on the island of Cos, not far from the coast of Caria.

PELIAS. The son of Poseidon and Tyro, Pelias was exposed at birth with his brother Neleus and rescued by shepherds. Both learned later that they were of divine origin and went to Iolcus to free their mother who was persecuted by her stepmother Sidero. Pelias killed the latter in the temple of Hera and, after expelling his brother, he seized the throne. His union with Anaxibia gave birth to one son, Acastus, and four daughters, Pisidice, Pelopia, Hippothoë and Alcestis. After ruling for several years, Jason, the son of his half-brother Aeson, arrived to claim the kingdom. To rid himself of this burdensome relative, Pelias sent him to fetch the Golden Fleece in Colchis. He took advantage of Jason's absence to drive Aeson and Alcimede, the mother of Jason, to commit suicide and to kill his cousin Promachus, a possible pretender to the throne. When Jason returned, his wife Medea urged the daughters of Pelias to cut their father to bits and boil him on the pretext of restoring his youth. Only Alcestis refused to be a party to the crime. When he became king, Acastus banished his criminal sisters along with Jason and Medea and celebrated funerary games in honor of his father whose memory was glorified by the participation of several great legendary heroes.

PELION. A mountain in Thessaly which the Giants piled on top of Ossa to lay siege to Olympus, Pelion was also the dwelling place of the centaur Chiron. A famous temple, dedicated to Zeus, graced its peak.

PELOPIA. 1. The daughter of Thyestes, Pelopia lived in Sicyon in the court of King Thesprotus where she exercised the duties of priestess. Of her incestuous union with her father a son, Aegisthus, was born and she exposed him at birth. She was expecting this child when she married her uncle Atreus and killed herself when Aegisthus grew up and learned the secret of his birth.

2. Another **Pelopia** is the daughter of Pelias.

PELOPS. Tantalus, the king of Lydia, one day received the gods at his table and served them his son Pelops, claiming that the dish was one of the finest. Demeter ate a shoulder but the other gods, immediately realizing the sacrifice and the crime, would not touch a morsel and hastened to revive Pelops; the missing shoulder was replaced by an ivory one. Pelops emigrated to Greece and was received by Oenomaus, the king of Pisa: he married his daughter Hippodameia after a chariot race in which she was the prize and thus Pelops, even before Heracles, was the first founder of the Olympic Games. To carry off this victory, he was assisted by Poseidon, who cared very much for him. His life was happy but he had by his wife several children, at least two of whom surpassed one another in cruelty, Atreus and Thyestes.

PENATES.   According to some, the worship of these gods was supposed to have been imported from Phrygia by Tarquin the Ancient. In the Roman religion, they form with Lara and Vesta a triad protecting homes and families. A place for worship and offerings is reserved for them in each home so that they might ensure, above all, supplies. This private worship was supplemented by public worship of the Penates, in humble villages and large cities alike. In Rome, the Penates of the city, portrayed by two seated youths, had, according to legend, been brought from Troy to Italy by Aeneas.

PENELOPE.   The daughter of the nymph Periboea and of Icarius, the brother of Tyndareos, king of Sparta, Penelope was given in marriage to Ulysses, who was the winner of games in which the many suitors of the beautiful young woman competed. She gave birth to a son, Telemachus, who was still but a child when Ulysses was forced to leave his kingdom of Ithaca for Troy. During the twenty years' absence of her husband, Penelope was forced to thwart the advances of her suitors who, claiming that Ulysses was dead, urged her to choose another husband. She declared that she would finish weaving the shroud of her father-in-law Laertes before making a choice. At night, she would undo the work that she had accomplished during the day. This strategy was revealed by one of her servants. At the point when, increasingly pursued by her suitors, she was about to end her many years of marital fidelity despite her-

self, Ulysses returned to Ithaca. After being recognized by his wife, he massacred all the men who had invaded his home. Then he returned to Penelope, and Athena, it is said, prolonged the night for them. Not all post-Homeric traditions followed this version of the tale. Some contend that Penelope succumbed to her suitors and mothered the god Pan. Others add that Ulysses repudiated her upon his return and that she went to end her days in Mantinea. Finally, some say that Telegonus, the son of Ulysses and Circe, after inadvertently killing his father, married her. However, Penelope remains the symbol of marital fidelity which is especially rare among the wives of the heroes who left to wage war on Troy.

PENEUS.   The principal river of Thessaly, the Peneus has its source on Mount Pindus and flows through the valley of Tempe between Mount Ossa and the sea. Deified, regarded as the son of Oceanus and Tethys, he was consecrated mainly to Apollo because his daughter, Daphne, had been changed into a laurel tree for having spurned the love of this god.

PENTHESILEA.   This queen of the Amazons, the daughter of Otrera and Ares, was forced to leave her native land after accidentally killing her sister Hippolyta; purified of this murder by Priam, she lent her aid to the Trojans who had lost heart after the death of Hector. During a combat, Achilles mortally wounded her but, seeing her fall, he found her so beautiful and so proud that he fell in love with her and wept over her corpse for quite some time. Thersites, the son of the Aetolian Agrius, the most talkative and deformed warrior of the entire Greek army, ridiculed the grief of his leader. Achilles killed him. To avenge him, Diomedes, a relative of Thersites, threw the body of Penthesilea into the river Scamander. Achilles managed to retrieve it and bury it with full funerary honors.

Her left breast pierced by the dagger of Achilles, Penthesilea, the queen of the Amazons, gives the hero a look of love and final supplication, but already her legs are buckling beneath the weight of death. Achilles was moved by this last thought of the royal victim and he granted her full funerary honors. Greek cup, 5th cent. B.C., State Collections of Classical Art, Munich, photo Giraudon.

PENTHEUS. The son of Echion and Agave, Pentheus succeeded Cadmus on the throne of Thebes. When Dionysus, upon his return from Lydia, entered his kingdom, Pentheus tried to stop the introduction of the cult of the god's mysteries, whereupon the god decided to seek revenge. Having been invited by the god to witness, on Mount Cithaeron, the Bacchic delirium with which the women of Thebes had been stricken, Pentheus was discovered by the frenzied women who mistook him for a wild beast and tore him to pieces. His mother, Agave, herself driven mad, chopped off his head and realized too late that she had committed a horrible crime.

PERDIX. One of the apprentices of Daedalus, whose nephew he was, Perdix invented the saw, the compass and the potter's wheel. Jealous of so much skill and ingenuity, his uncle threw him from the top of the temple of Athena on the Acropolis. The Areopagus convened to judge this murder and condemned Daedalus to exile. A variation of this legend about the death of Perdix is known. He was also known as Talos and it is said that the goddess Athena changed him into a partridge (*Perdix*) just as his body was about to hit the rocks.

PERGAMUM. Known by this name is the historical city of Asia Minor, the eponymous hero of which is Pergamus, the son of Neoptolemus and Andromache. But the Greek poets also used the name Pergamum to refer to the citadel of Troy and sometimes even to the city itself.

PERIBOEA. 1. The wife of Telamon, Periboea was the mother of Ajax the Greater. She was one of the young women destined for the Minotaur when Theseus went to conquer the monster. King Minos, seeing the girl, fell in love with her and even tried to seduce her; Theseus prevented him.

2. Legend tells of another **Periboea,** the wife of Polybus, king of Sicyon or Corinth, who rescued Oedipus who in this version was abandoned in a basket in the sea. The two sovereigns adopted the infant. Later, after learning that he was destined to kill his father and marry his mother, Oedipus fled and, after killing Laius, went to Thebes. In the city, he married the widow Jocasta. Soon, he learned from Periboea that neither she nor Polybus were his real parents and he understood that he had killed his father and married his mother without realizing or willing it.

3. A third **Periboea** was the wife of Icarius and mother of Penelope.

4. A fourth gave birth to Nausithous, founder of the kingdom of the Phaeacians.

5. A fifth **Periboea** was sent to Troy by the

Locrians to become the servant of Athena, in order to appease the goddess who was enraged that Ajax had tried to seduce Cassandra in one of her temples.

6. Yet another **Periboea** was the wife of Oeneus and the mother of Tydeus.

PERICLYMENUS. 1. The son of Poseidon and Chloris, Periclymenus is, in legend, the ally of Eteocles against Polynices and, more generally speaking, against the Seven Leaders. During the struggle, he killed one of them, Parthenopaeus. After the victory of the Thebans, Periclymenus pursued Amphiaraus, whom Zeus finally swallowed up into the earth.

2. Legend speaks of another **Periclymenus,** the youngest son of Neleus; he took part in the expedition of the Argonauts. But he made his

The goddess Persephone appears as the submissive, even fearful, wife of the god Hades. Greek amphora, Louvre, photo Giraudon.

mark, particularly, for his ability to assume all sorts of forms. When Heracles mounted an expedition against Pylos, Periclymenus tried to attack the hero and changed himself into a bee. Warned by Athena, Heracles was not tricked by this metamorphosis and killed Periclymenus. It is also said that the latter had time to change himself into an eagle but was felled by one of Heracles' arrows.

PERIPHETES. A lame giant, Periphetes, the son of Hephaestus and Anticlea, used, when walking, a bronze crutch with which he was in the habit of bashing travelers. Theseus met him one day along his way, tore the improvised weapon away from him, and struck him with it, killing him.

PERSEPHONE. The daughter of Demeter and Zeus, Persephone also bears the surname *Core.* Unbeknownst to Demeter, Zeus had promised Core to his brother Hades. One day while the girl was gathering flowers in the country with some companions and carefree nymphs, she saw a beautiful narcissus which she proceeded to pluck. At that moment, the earth opened up. Hades appeared and carried his niece away on his chariot. Demeter, wild with grief, because she did not know who had abducted her daughter, left in search of her and roamed the earth for nine days and nine nights. After this time, Helios the Sun, moved, told her the name of her daughter's abductor. To take revenge, Demeter left Olympus and ceased to fertilize the earth. Disturbed about the fate of mortals, Zeus sent Hermes to the Underworld to fetch Persephone and bring her back to her mother, on the condition that, during her stay in the Underworld, she eat nothing. Hades, realizing Zeus's trick, gave his wife some pomegranate seeds. He thought that this would enable him to keep Persephone. However, the god was forced to accept a compromise. Persephone was to stay with him only six months of the year and would spend the rest of the

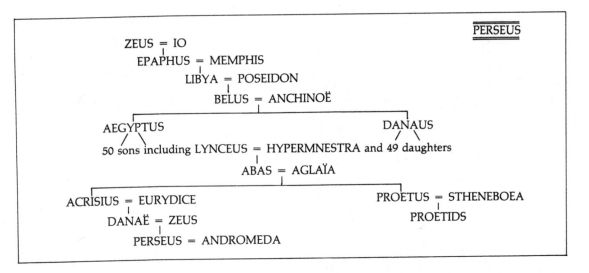

PERSEUS

ZEUS = IO
|
EPAPHUS = MEMPHIS
|
LIBYA = POSEIDON
|
BELUS = ANCHINOË
|
AEGYPTUS   DANAUS
/ \   / \
50 sons including LYNCEUS = HYPERMNESTRA and 49 daughters
|
ABAS = AGLAÏA
|
ACRISIUS = EURYDICE   PROETUS = STHENEBOEA
| |
DANAË = ZEUS   PROETIDS
|
PERSEUS = ANDROMEDA

year with Demeter. The legend of this divinity is easy to interpret: Persephone, imprisoned in the Underworld, is none other than the grains of wheat, locked into the earth during autumn and winter. Upon the arrival of spring, and during the summer, Persephone's return to her mother corresponds to the germination of plants. In fact, the mysteries of Eleusis symbolize the sacred character. Generally speaking, Persephone remained, above all, the wife of Hades, the majestic queen of the Shadows, the mother of the terrible Erinyes. In works of art, she bears witness to this dreadful nature given to her by Greek writers. Severe and great, seated on a throne at her husband's side, she holds a flame and sometimes a poppy, the soporific virtues of which symbolize the annual slumber—so close to death—of the earth.

PERSEUS. An offspring of the love of Zeus and Danaë, this famous hero of Argolis was, at birth, placed in a chest with his mother, by his grandfather Acrisius, and abandoned in the sea. The waves tossed them up on the island of Seriphos where Polydectes reigned. Wishing to seduce Danaë, the king sought to be rid of Perseus, who had since reached adulthood, and

asked him to bring back the head of the Gorgon. With the help of Hermes and Athena, the hero forced the three Graiae, after stealing their eye and tooth, to show him the road of the Nymphs. There he received the helmet of Hades, which made him invisible, while Hermes and Athena gave him marvelous weapons.

After killing Medusa, Perseus, himself frightened by his feat, flees and prepares to jump into his chariot to which four horses are harnessed. Detail of a Greek vase, Louvre, photo Giraudon.

Though the archaism of this image gives Perseus a disturbing appearance, the legend takes on greater meaning. Here, Medusa possesses the body of a woman ending in the rump of an animal. Perseus looks away while he kills the monster, whom he has seized by the hair. Perseus has the accouterments of a traveler: light sandals, a small double sack, and a quiver filled with arrows to defend himself against ferocious beasts. Bronze krater, archaic era, Louvre, photo Giraudon.

Thus he was able to chop off the head of Medusa without being seen by the other Gorgons. On his way back, he freed Andromeda and married her, despite a plot devised by Phineus. Then, before returning to Seriphos, he made a detour through Africa; the welcome he received from the giant Atlas was far from hospitable because he was the son of Zeus. Perseus, by showing him the head of Medusa, turned him into the mountain that henceforth bore his name. When he finally reached Seriphos, the head of the monster enabled him to free his mother Danaë who, pursued by the relentless advances of Polydectes, had sought refuge in a temple; Polydectes and his companions were, in turn, changed into stone. However, Perseus was anxious to know his grandfather; he also wanted to claim his rights to the kingdom of Argos. Upon his arrival, Acrisius remembered the prediction of the oracle, which had said that he would be killed by his grandson, and fled to Larissa, the homeland of the Pelasgi. Also passing through the city, Perseus took part in the funerary games. While throwing a discus, he accidentally struck one of the spectators and killed him: this was Acrisius. When he learned the identity of the victim, Perseus granted his grandfather funerary honors, then, not daring to return to Argos, he yielded the kingdom to Megapanthes, the son of Proetus, and received the kingdom of Tiryns in return. Worshiped as a demigod, he was, after his death, placed in the heavens among the constellations.

PERSUASION. An allegorical divinity, Persuasion was worshiped by the Greeks, particularly in Attica, by the name of *Peitho*. Her cult was connected with that of Aphrodite. The Romans had given her the name of *Suada*. They sometimes even used the diminutive *Suadela* to refer to her. Associated with Venus, she aroused a desire for marriage among lovers and incited them to declare their fondness.

PHAEACIANS. It was believed for quite some time, even during Antiquity, that the Phaeacians were an historical people. But contemporary mythographers have shown the absurdity of such an assertion: the Phaeacians fully belong to the realm of mythology. They lived on the island of Scheria and were considered to be peaceloving seafarers who engaged in commerce in the Mediterranean basin and enjoyed their wealth by organizing numerous festivals. Their king, Alcinous, received Ulysses. Under their auspices, Jason and Medea were wed.

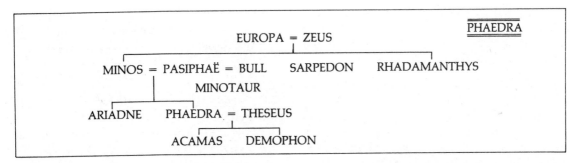

EUROPA = ZEUS   __PHAEDRA__

MINOS = PASIPHAË = BULL   SARPEDON   RHADAMANTHYS

MINOTAUR

ARIADNE   PHAEDRA = THESEUS

ACAMAS   DEMOPHON

PHAEDRA. The daughter of Minos, the king of Crete, and Pasiphaë, Phaedra was the sister of Ariadne. Both were chosen as spouses by Theseus. As the latter had left his royal house, Phaedra developed for Hippolytus, her stepson, an unpardonable love. Theseus took her to Troezen, where Hippolytus was staying, so that he might purify himself of the murder of the Pallantids. Having reached the final degree of anguish, she was forced by her nurse to reveal the secret of her despair. The nurse told Hippolytus, who, horrified, threatened to tell Theseus. Phaedra, in her frenzy, wrote a letter to Theseus accusing Hippolytus of having raped her; she then hanged herself.

PHAETHON. The Greek word *Phaethon* signifies "he who shines." This son of Helios the Sun and the Oceanid Clymene loved to boast to his companions about his divine origin. Each day he would proudly show them the course of his father's chariot in the sky. One of them, however, challenged him to prove his paternity. Cut to the quick, Phaethon went to his father to ask him for a sign of his birth. The Sun swore by the Styx to grant him anything he wished. Phaethon requested his chariot and the right to drive it for an entire day. Horrified, because no mortal was strong enough to break in the horses which drew the chariot, the Sun tried to dissuade his son. But nothing could change his mind: swollen with pride, Phaethon did not heed the pleas of his father. Bound by his oath, the Sun was forced to submit to the

wish of his son. The fiery steeds lurched forward, but as the Sun had predicted Phaethon was quickly overwhelmed by his task. The steeds paid no attention to his commands and the chariot began to follow a reckless course. First he rose too high and was in danger of burning the celestial route or colliding with the constellations, then he went down too low and set the mountains ablaze as the rivers turned to vapor and the earth crackled under the heat. To

Tormented by love and remorse, Phaedra looks away from her stepson, Hippolytus, who wishes to bid her farewell. All the characters in the scene, including Eros at Phaedra's feet, wear the mask of sadness. Sarcophagus, San Clemente Basilica, Rome, photo Boudot-Lamotte.

avoid the destruction of the universe, Zeus struck Phaethon down with his thunder and reduced his chariot to bits. The son of the Sun was thrown into the river Eridanus.

PHEGEUS. The king of a city in Arcadia, Phegeus purified Alcmaeon of the murder of his mother Eriphyle and gave him his daughter Arsinoë in marriage. As a sign of gratitude, Arsinoë received the necklace and mantle of Harmonia. But the presents were taken back by Alcmaeon who wanted to give them to his second wife, Callirhoë, the daughter of the river-god Acheloüs. When he learned of his son-in-law's betrayal, Phegeus ordered his two sons, Pronous and Agenor, to kill him. Widowed, Arsinoë cursed her father and her two brothers. This curse was to bear fruit because the two children of Callirhoë avenged their father Alcmaeon by killing Phegeus and his two sons.

PHERES. 1. The founder and eponymous king of the city of Pheres in Thessaly, Pheres was the son of Cretheus and Tyro. Among his sons, Lycurgus reigned in Nemea and Admetus married Alcestis.

2. Also known by this name was one of the sons of Jason and Medea. With his brother Mermerus, he was killed by his mother in Corinth.

PHILAMMON. In a single night, Chione, the granddaughter of Lucifer, had relations with the god Apollo, who begat Philammon, and with the god Hermes, who made her the mother of Autolycus. Smitten with the nymph Argiope, Philammon had by her a son, Thamyris. Both father and son were, according to legend, musicians of renown. The former invented the choirs of girls and introduced the mysteries of Demeter in Lerna while the latter conceived new forms of music; he was, however, stripped of his talents for having tried to compete with the Muses.

PHILEMON. The legend of Philemon and Baucis is related by Ovid in his *Metamorphoses*. Baucis, a poor and time-worn woman, lived with her husband Philemon in a village of Phrygia. Zeus, traveling in the country as a

The chariot of the sun has been brutally stopped by an envoy of Zeus. The harnesses have been broken; the horses of Helios exhibit the greatest agitation. Phaethon is thrown head first from his chariot and falls dead into the river Eridanus, symbolized by a bearded old man holding a palm. Ancient sarcophagus, Uffizi Gallery, Florence, photo Alinari-Giraudon.

into a superb oak while the latter was changed into a rustling linden.

PHILOCTETES. It was to this witness of his final moments that Heracles entrusted his bow and arrow before succumbing to the flames of a pyre on Mount Oeta. But Philoctetes, despite his promise never to reveal to anyone the place where the ashes of the hero could be found, went back on his word and was punished. Like all of Helen's suitors, he left for the Trojan War armed with the precious poisoned arrows. When the Greeks touched ground on the island of Tenedos, he was bitten by a serpent or, according to other traditions, wounded by the iron of one of his own arrows. The wound that resulted would not heal. It emitted such a putrid odor that the Greeks, ill at ease, were forced to abandon Philoctetes on the island of Lemnos. He stayed there ten years, suffering incessantly from the wound and from loneliness. As Troy remained ever impregnable, the Greeks consulted the oracle. The oracle revealed that the arrows of Philoctetes were indispensable to victory. Ulysses, therefore, left for Lemnos and forced Philoctetes, both through coercion as well as patriotic persuasion, to go to Troy with him. His wound closed up. He took part in numerous battles and killed Paris, the most famous Trojan. When he returned from Troy, Philoctetes settled, it is said, in the south of Italy where he founded several cities.

PHILOETIUS. Guardian of the herds of Ulysses, Philoetius fought with the swineherd Eumaeus on the side of his master against the goatherd Melanthius and the suitors. After the massacre of the suitors, he was instructed, along with Eumaeus, to punish Melanthius for his treason and to chop off all of his limbs.

PHILOMELA. The daughter of Pandion, the king of Athens, Philomela had a sister, Procne, who was married to Tereus, the king of Thrace.

En route to Troy, Philoctetes has just been bitten by a serpent on the island of Tenedos. He was to remain on Lemnos for ten years. Greek vase, Louvre, photo Giraudon.

simple mortal, in the company of Hermes, decided to stop in the village and request hospitality for the night. The two gods knocked on every door, but all remained closed. The only door to open was that of the humble abode of Philemon and Baucis who, despite their old age and fatigue, welcomed the divine travelers. Zeus and Hermes invited the couple to climb a neighboring mountain with them. When they reached the peak, the couple saw the entire village which had just been engulfed by water. But in the place of their house, a small temple arose. When asked to express a wish, Philemon and Baucis told Zeus that they would like to become the ministers of the temple and would like to remain together forever. Their wish was fulfilled. When they reached the end of their days and were on the verge of death, Philemon and Baucis underwent a metamorphosis on the steps of the temple: the former was changed

But Tereus fell in love with his sister-in-law. He locked up his wife and declared her to be dead, and forced Philomela to succumb to him. When Philomela learned the truth, the king cut out her tongue to prevent her revealing this crime. However, the poor creature was able to communicate with Procne by sending her a tapestry in which she had embroidered the main images of her tragic adventure. Pursued by Tereus, she was changed into a swallow, Procne into a nightingale, and Tereus into a hoopoe. The Roman poets had a different account, according to which Philomela was the wife of Tereus, and she became a nightingale and Procne, a swallow.

PHILYRA. The daughter of Oceanus, Philyra was loved by Cronus who, fearing the jealousy of his wife Rhea, changed himself into a horse to have relations with her. Other versions claim that it was Philyra who was changed into a mare in order to escape, in vain, the advances of the god. A child was born of this union, the centaur Chiron, whom she raised in a grotto on Mount Pelion. Later, she attended to the education of some of the major legendary heroes along with her son who was half-man and half-horse.

PHINEUS. 1. The son of Agenor and king of Salmydessus in Thrace, Phineus was blinded by the gods for several reasons. Indeed, he exercised his gift of prophecy with a bit too much zeal, particularly in revealing to Phrixus the return route to Greece. Or else he was blinded for having himself blinded his two sons Plexippus and Pandion, falsely accused of rape by their mother Idaea. Or then again, he might have preferred a long life to eyesight. He was tormented by the Harpies, who stole his food or soiled his plates. The Boreads, Calais and Zetes, delivered him from these monsters during the expedition of the Argonauts. To thank them, Phineus revealed the route to follow to reach Colchis by way of Bosphorus, and the dangers to be avoided.

2. Another **Phineus** tried in vain to eliminate Perseus who had married his niece Andromeda.

PHLEGETHON. In the Underworld, this tributary of the Acheron rolled flames instead of water. For this reason it is sometimes known as Pyriphlegethon, "Phlegethon of fire."

PHLEGYAS. The son of Ares and Chryse, according to one of the versions, Phlegyas was the eponymous hero of the Phlegyans and one of the kings of Orchomenus. His son Ixion was king of the Lapiths and his daughter, Coronis, seduced by Apollo, gave birth to a famous son, Asclepius. Angry with the god, Phlegyas set fire to his temple and was, according to Virgil, punished for this sacrilegious act with a strenuous punishment in the Underworld.

PHOBUS. Born of the goddess Aphrodite, Phobus, the personification of fear, accompanied his father Ares to the battlefields. He inspired cowardice in the hearts of the warring sides and drove them to flee. He was known to have a brother, Deimus, Terror.

PHOCUS. 1. As Dionysus wanted to avenge the death of Dirce, he drove Antiope mad. The poor creature roamed through Greece until Phocus, a grandson of Sisyphus, cured her of her illness and married her in Phocis. He was buried by the Phocians in Tithorea because an oracle had predicted that this act of piety would bring fertility to the entire country.

2. Another **Phocus** was the son of Aeacus and the nymph Psamathe while his half-brothers, Telamon and Peleus, were the sons of Aeacus and Endeis. Having left his fatherland, Phocus conquered the country which took the name of *Phocis*, married Asteria, by whom he had two sons, Crisus and Panopeus. When he returned to his native land, he was killed by his

brothers who were jealous of his power and his glory.

3. Also known by the name of **Phocus** was a Boeotian who had decided to give his daughter, Callirhoë, in marriage to whoever was the winner of a joust. The suitors of the young woman killed her overly demanding father while Callirhoë managed to flee and hide. Some time after, the Boeotians had wind of the murder and succeeded in tracking down the assassins. The guilty ones were soon captured and stoned.

PHOEBE. **1.** The daughter of Leucippus, Phoebe was the priestess of Athena. Promised to Idas, her cousin, she was abducted by Pollux, who married her.

2. The Titanid **Phoebe,** the daughter of Uranus and Gaia, is one of the primitive divinities. A consort of Coeus, she became the mother of Leto and Asteria and subsequently the grandmother of Apollo.

PHOENIX. **1.** Like his brothers Cadmus and Cilix, Phoenix was dispatched by his father Agenor in search of his sister Europa who had been abducted by Zeus. Unable to find her, he passed first through Libya, then went to settle in a country on the coast of the Mediterranean Near East which, in his honor, took the name of Phoenicia.

2. A son of Amyntor and Cleobule, or of Hippodamia, also bears the name of **Phoenix.** At the instigation of his mother, he seduced Phthia, one of his father's concubines, but was damned and banished by his father after having his eyes gouged out. Cared for by the centaur Chiron, Phoenix recovered his sight and was later welcomed by Peleus who made him king of the Dolopians and entrusted him with the care of Achilles. Phoenix was to remain deeply attached to the great hero whom he accompanied to Troy. He even tried to lessen the bitterness of Achilles after his quarrel with Agamemnon. At the death of his friend, Phoenix was part of the contingent that went to search for Neoptolemus so that he might continue the work of his father in the Trojan War; he died during the return trip.

Phoenix. This fabulous bird, the legend of which originated in Egypt, was described at length by certain authors of Antiquity. Similar to a royal eagle with a plumage bursting with iridescent colors, with a slow and majestic flight, the phoenix lived, it is said, in Ethiopia for five hundred, 1,460, or even 12,954 years. Unable to perpetuate its race because there was no female in the species, it was, however, able to ensure its progeny: when it felt that death was imminent, it built a nest of aromatic plants and magical herbs in the center of which it settled after setting it on fire. From its ashes another phoenix was born and the newborn bird hastened to take its father's remains to Heliopolis in Egypt, where the Sun was adored, as the eagle was the incarnation of the Sun. For the Ancients, the phoenix was the symbol of the immortality of the soul or even of the year which is reborn immediately after it terminates its course.

PHOLUS. One day as he was passing through Epirus, Heracles asked for the hospitality of Pholus, a wise and benevolent centaur, the son of Silenus and one of the Hamadryads. Pholus received the hero with all due respect, serving him a sumptuous meal. However, Heracles took it upon himself to ask him to open a bottle of wine reserved for the centaurs. When the centaurs sniffed the intoxicating odor that spread through the countryside, they were furious and besieged the cave of Pholus, attacking Heracles, who killed a great number of them and caused the others to flee. Pholus did not take part in the combat, but while burying his kin he was mortally wounded in the foot with one of the poisoned arrows of Heracles. The hero granted funerary honors to his involuntary victim and buried him under a mountain which took the name of *Pholoë*.

PHORCYS. A divinity of the sea belonging to the first generation of gods, Phorcys is the son of Pontus and Gaia, the brother of Nereus, Thaumas and Ceto, whom he married. This union gave birth to most of the monsters that haunt Greek legends: Scylla, the Gorgons, Echidna, the Hesperides.

PHORONEUS. According to several legends, Phoroneus was the son of the river-god Inachus and the nymph Melia. The first king of Argos, he was also the first to unite men into cities and teach his subjects how to make use of fire. He married the nymph Cerdo, enlarged his kingdom, and conquered the Peloponnesus. At his death, his sons, Pelasgus, Iasus and Agenor, shared Peloponnesus and Car founded the city of Megara.

PHRIXUS. The country of Orchomenus was devastated by drought and famine. The king of the country, Athamas, decided to send some deputies to Delphi to consult the oracle of the god Apollo. Ino, the second wife of Athamas, who hated the children of the first marriage, Phrixus and Helle, bribed the envoys who declared that the gods would only be appeased if Phrixus were sacrificed. The unfortunate victim was able to flee with his sister on the winged ram with the golden fleece that Zeus had sent them, but, since his sister drowned en route, he arrived alone in Colchis. There, King Aeetes welcomed him hospitably and even gave him his daughter Chalciope in marriage.

PHYLLIS. This daughter of a king of Thrace one day saw the arrival in her father's kingdom of Demophon, or his brother Acamas, the sons of Theseus, who was returning from the expedition against the Trojans. Demophon became her lover. He soon left her to return home. Upon his departure, Phyllis gave him a casket which contained, she said, rich presents intended for the cult of Rhea. She enjoined him, however, not to open it as long as he had not lost all hope of ever seeing his mistress again, even for a moment. Demophon settled in Cyprus. He proceeded to forget Phyllis. On the date which he had set for his return to Thrace, Phyllis descended to the seashore nine times to look out on the horizon. No sails appeared. She hanged herself in sorrow. The same day, Demophon opened the casket. A phantom emerged. Horrified, the young man slipped from the horse which he was riding and fell on his sword, which pierced him. According to another version of the same legend, Phyllis, after her death, was changed into a sterile almond tree. Only the embrace of a passionate and repentent Demophon could bring the tree to bear fruit.

PICUS. According to ancient mythographers, this king of Latium, the son of Saturn and the spouse of the nymph Canens, was able to deliver oracles with the help of a woodpecker. Disdaining the amorous advances of Circe, he was supposed to have fallen in love with Pomona. Out of spite, the enchantress changed him into a woodpecker. However, he retained his gift of prophecy even in this form and was especially known for his power to predict rain. Thus, the Roman peasants granted him the prestige of an agricultural divinity who protected fields against drought and ensured the pastures for the herds.

PIERIA. A region situated to the south of Macedonia, Pieria was famous in Antiquity for the worship it rendered to Orpheus and the Muses, to whom the surname of *Pierides* was accorded. On this subject, there is a legend contending that the nine Pierides were the daughters of Pierus, the king of Macedonia, and Evippe. They dared to compare their musical talent to that of the Muses and were defeated by the latter in a song competition. As a punishment for their pride, they were changed into magpies.

PIETY. Honored principally in Rome, this allegorical divinity symbolized the affection that man should bear for his peers, his parents, his friends, the gods and later the genius of the emperor, of whom Piety became the powerful symbol. This divinity bore the attributes of opulence (the horn of plenty) and fidelity (the stork).

pillars of Hercules. This mountainous cape, which belongs to Mount Calpe in Spain and marks off the entrance to the Strait of Gibraltar, possesses its own legend. Indeed, it is said that Heracles, en route to his expedition against Geryon, passed through the strait and erected two pillars there, one at Gibraltar, the other at Ceuta, to perpetuate the memory of his presence.

PILUMNUS. An ancient Roman divinity, about whom there are very few legends, Pilumnus presided over birth. He was accorded various symbols such as a broom, a pestle and an axe. Pilumnus was later worshiped as a god of Cultivation and his cult was sometimes associated with that of his brother **Picumnus.** The pestle, therefore, represented the corn that was milled and the axe was a symbol of lands that were cleared.

PIRENE. This famous spring in Corinth, one of the legendary high places in Greece, was inhabited by the nymph Pirene, daughter of the river-god Asopus. She was changed into a spring because she shed so many tears at the death of one of her sons. According to another legend, the source of this spring which gushed forth from the rock of Acrocorinth had been given to Sisyphus by Asopus when he had learned from this king the name of the abductor of his daughter Aegina.

PIRITHOUS. This king of the Lapiths in Thessaly is the subject of two different legends. In the first, he is the son of Zeus; in the second, he is the son of Dia and Ixion. Listening to tales of the exploits of Theseus, whose feats were proclaimed throughout Greece, he was overcome by a violent jealousy and wanted to see whether this glory was exaggerated. He stole part of the herd of Theseus in an attempt to provoke him. Theseus prepared to fight Pirithous. But the latter, charmed by the hero, laid down his arms and declared himself to be the slave of Theseus. Theseus befriended him. Together, they descended to the Underworld with the farfetched intention of seducing Persephone and stealing her away from her husband Hades. Punished for this impious act, Pirithous was never again to return to Earth.

PITTHEUS. The king of Troezen and the son of Pelops and Hippodameia, Pittheus was known for his knowledge, his wisdom and his gifts of prophecy. Thus he had learned from an oracle that the son that would be begotten by Aegeus would bask in glory. So after plying his guest, the king of Athens, with liquor, he placed him in the bed of his daughter Aethra. Theseus was born of this involuntary union and Pittheus thus had the pride and joy of becoming the grandfather of the hero. Later, Hippolytus, the son of Theseus, was entrusted to the care of his grandfather and succeeded him on the throne of Troezen.

PLEIADES. Various accounts relate the myth of the seven sisters—Maia, Electra, Taygete, Asterope, Merope, Alcyone, Celaeno—the daughters of Atlas and Pleione, who made up the constellation known as the Pleiades. According to a Boeotian tradition, Zeus placed them among the stars after changing them into doves to protect them from Orion who was pursuing them. However, the most common tradition contends that, despairing over the punishment that Zeus had inflicted on their father, they killed themselves and were changed

A face showing no leniency, a mouth that is almost cruel, framed by a thick, curly beard: this is Pluto, the Roman god of the Dead. Roman bust, Museo delle Terme, photo Alinari-Giraudon.

into stars. Their appearance in the spring, in May (the Latins called them Vergiliae from the word *ver*, springtime) indicates to the seaman who tries to chart his route by the heavens the propitious season for navigation (*Pleiades*, whatever its true etymology, was sensed to be cognate with the Greek word for "sail"), and their disappearance in November signals the beginning of heavy weather, which poses a constant threat for ships.

PLEIONE. The daughter of Oceanus and Tethys, Pleione had relations with the giant Atlas and became the mother of the Seven Pleiades. Pursued for five years by Orion, she was finally changed into a star.

PLISTHENES. The son of Pelops and Hippodameia, according to the most common version of the legend. According to other versions, Plisthenes was the son of Atreus and the spouse of Aërope, as well as the father of Agamemnon and Menelaus. Another tradition claims that he was killed by his father. Hardly anything else is known about his life.

PLOUTOS. Having met at the wedding of Cadmus and Harmonia, Iasion and Demeter made love in a thrice-plowed field. A son, Ploutos, was born of this union and he was the personification of wealth. Zeus, it is said, stripped this god of his sight so that he would distribute his wealth, without regard for the merits of either, to the good and the bad alike.

PLUTO. This god, whose name was derived from the Greek word *ploutos* meaning "wealth," was the divine personification of the fertility of the earth, the guarantor of the abundance of harvests; he was also given the name of *Dis Pater*, "father of wealth," and he was frequently associated with the god Ploutos. A divinity of the Underworld, Pluto soon became one of the surnames of *Hades*, the ruler of the Underworld, and he assumed a formidable nature, especially among the Romans. The ancients would sacrifice to him animals with dark coats, black sheep or swine, and those condemned to death were destined to be the victims of his unbending wrath.

PODALIRIUS. This son of Asclepius left for Troy with his brother Machaon at the head of a contingent of Thessalians. As skillful as his father in the art of medicine, he offered his talents to the Greeks for the entire duration of the war and was the only physician, along with Machaon, who was able to heal the frightful wound of Philoctetes. After the victory of his compatriots, Podalirius left Troy with Calchas, Amphilochus and a few other heroes. They reached Colophon on foot, and there Calchas died. Podalirius later consulted the Delphic oracle and was advised to settle in a land where the sky fell to earth. After a great deal of reflection, Podalirius settled in Caria in Syrnus, where he married Syrna, the daughter of the king: the territory of the king was, in fact, surrounded by mountains such that their peaks seemed to be supporting the sky.

PODARCES. 1. When Heracles killed Laomedon, the king of Troy, and all of his sons, he did spare one of them, Podarces, who had sided with him. The young man was subsequently ransomed by Hesione and he took the name of *Priam:* then he acceded to the throne of Troy.

2. Also known by this name is the son of Iphiclus and the grandson of Phylacus, the king of Phylacaea in Thessaly; he commanded a contingent of Thessalians during the siege of Troy where he was killed by Penthesilea, the queen of the Amazons.

POLIAS. This name refers to Athena as the divine protectress of a city (*polis*, in Greek). Athena was adored in Athens by this name, as the protectress of the Acropolis, the center of the city. The corresponding name for Zeus as the protector of a city is *Polieus.*

POLLUX. One of the Dioscuri, the son of Leda and Zeus, the brother of Castor.

POLYBOTES. With the other giants, his brothers, Polybotes took part in the war against the gods of Olympus. With his trident, Poseidon broke off a piece of the island of Cos and threw it at Polybotes, who was crushed under the weight of the rocks. Thus a new island was born, the island of Nisyros.

POLYBUS. 1. This king of Corinth welcomed the abandoned Oedipus and raised him as a

Poseidon has knocked Polybotes over with his trident. He is dropping a piece of the island of Cos on the giant in order to crush him. Bottom of a Greek cup, Bibl. Nat., photo Giraudon.

son. Oedipus grew and learned of the frightful fatality attached to his life, which weighed on his mother and father: in effect, he was to kill one and marry the other. Thinking that Polybus and his wife Periboea were his real parents, the unhappy adopted son left them immediately. After killing Laius and marrying Jocasta, Oedipus learned from a Corinthian messenger of both the death of Polybus and the circumstances surrounding his adoption.

2. Also known by the name of **Polybus** was a king of Egypt who sheltered Helen and Menelaus.

3. Polybus was a king of Sicyon whom Adrastus succeeded before acceding to the throne of Argos.

POLYDAMAS. A son of the Trojan Panthoos and of Phrontis, Polydamas was the brother of Euphorbus. He formed a bond of friendship with the hero Hector, whose strategic advisor he was, in a sense, and whom he helped many times during the war.

POLYDECTES. This king of Seriphos welcomed Danaë and Perseus. But he tried to seduce Danaë. Perseus, to punish him for this outrage, showed him the head of Medusa and turned him to stone. At his death, his kingdom went to his brother Dictys.

POLYDORUS. 1. The son of Cadmus and Harmonia, Polydorus succeeded his father on the throne of Thebes. The spouse of Nycteis, he had one son, Labdacus, the grandfather of Oedipus.

2. Legend tells of another **Polydorus,** the son of Priam and Laothoë. He was killed by Achilles during the Trojan War. However, later versions claim that Polydorus was the son of Priam and Hecuba. When still young, he was entrusted to the king of Thrace, Polymestor, who was also asked to guard the treasures of the city of Troy. After the sack of the city, the king, wanting to steal the treasures, slaughtered Polydorus and threw his body into the sea. The waves tossed his corpse up on the shores of Troas where he was discovered and recognized by Hecuba.

Another tradition, related by the tragic poets, recounts that Polydorus was entrusted to his sister Ilione, the wife of Polymestor. The queen raised her brother, pretending that her son Deipylus was actually Polydorus. Polymestor, on the order of the Greeks, killed his own son thinking that he was killing Polydorus. Then, the latter urged his sister to avenge the death of her son by slaying her husband.

POLYHYMNIA. This Muse, who is ordinarily without precise attributes, is given the title of "she who inspires heroic and divine hymns." However, she is sometimes said to be the Muse of geometry or even of history.

POLYMESTOR. King of Chersonnesus in Thrace, Polymestor was married to Ilione, a daughter of King Priam. During the Trojan War, the couple was entrusted with the treasures of Troy and was instructed to care for little Polydorus, one of the sons of Priam and Hecuba; they raised him as their own child. When Troy fell to the Greeks, Polymestor wanted to kill Polydorus, but he was mistaken and killed his own son Deipylus. Ilione, in revenge, killed her husband, the murderer. It is also said that Polymestor, coveting the gold that had been entrusted to him, obtained from the Greeks, in return for the murder of Polydorus, the right to keep the riches. The body of the youth, which had been thrown into the sea, was tossed up on the shore of Troas and was found by Hecuba. She, therefore, summoned Polymestor on a false pretext and gouged out

Polyhymnia, "she who inspires heroic and divine hymns." Her hand, with its fingers clasping her tunic, seems ready to mark the rhythm of her verses, while her face makes her seem lost in deep reverie. Greek art, Louvre, photo Giraudon.

his eyes. It is further said that, having been taken captive by the Greeks, Polydorus was destined to be exchanged for Helen. But, when the Trojans refused to bargain, Polydorus was supposed to have been stoned.

POLYNICES. This character, who belongs to the Theban legends, was born of the incestuous union of Jocasta and Oedipus. After banishing his father, he agreed to share the regency with his brother Eteocles, with each one reigning for one year alternately. But as Eteocles refused to step down, Polynices fled Thebes and took refuge in the court of Adrastus, the king of Argos, and married his daughter Argeia. He had not, however, abandoned his claim to the throne of Thebes, and he mobilized an expedition against his brother who had gone back on his word. The Argives, under the leadership of Polynices, Tydeus, Capaneus, Parthenopaeus, Hippomedon, Adrastus and Amphiaraus, arrived at the walls of Thebes. The two brothers, burning with an inexpiable hatred, met in single combat and both perished, as their father Oedipus had predicted in his curse. Eteocles was entitled to funerary honors, but the body of Polynices, who was guilty of having borne arms against his fatherland, was abandoned without a burial. Antigone incurred the wrath of Creon, the new tyrant of Thebes, because she had wanted to bury her brother. Thus, the incestuous race of Oedipus knew nothing but hatred and unhappiness until it finally disappeared.

POLYPHEMUS. 1. The son of Elatus and Hippe, this Lapith took part in the expedition of the Argonauts. He settled in Mysia where he built the city of Cios, which he ruled until his death. He was killed in a battle against the Chalybes, one of the people of Pontus.

2. Legend tells of another **Polyphemus,** one who was much more famous. The son of Poseidon and the nymph Thousa, this Cyclops was a gigantic monster who had but one eye in the center of his forehead and fed on human flesh. He lived in a cave, not far from Mount Aetna, and had his enormous flock of sheep graze on the mountain. He had experienced an unrequited love for Galatea, the lover of Acis, and took cruel revenge on the two young lovers. But he is better known for his struggle with Ulysses. The hero approached his territory with a few companions and requested his hospitality. Polyphemus reacted by seizing two of Ulysses' companions. After killing them, he devoured them, chomping on the bones of his

The giant Polyphemus, who is blind in both eyes, bears his only living eye on his forehead. He is seated on an old oak. At his feet, there is a sheep with an abundance of curly wool. In the Homeric tradition, Polyphemus drew his sustenance from the sheep he raised. Like all gods of the woods and fields such as Pan and his famous flute, he filled his lonely hours playing a musical instrument. Here it is the lyre, following the inspiration of the winged genius behind his back. Roman relief, Villa Albani, Rome, photo Alinari-Giraudon.

Polyphemus has devoured one of the companions of Ulysses. He holds the two legs of his victim, the only remains of his horrible meal. Ulysses offers the Cyclops a cup of wine to intoxicate him. With the help of his remaining companions who have managed to escape, Ulysses pierces the only eye of the cannibalistic monster with a post. The serpent, an animal of the darkness of the netherworld, symbolizes the night into which the blind Cyclops has plunged. The fish, doubtless a dolphin, is the symbol of Poseidon, the father of Polyphemus, who was to take cruel revenge on the hero who had mutilated his son. It should be pointed out that, in order to relate the most famous episode of the legend in a single image, the artist has combined the various mishaps. Greek cup from Cyrene, Louvre, photo Giraudon.

unfortunate victims with his enormous jaw; then, he locked up the other seafarers in a cave and blocked the entrance with an enormous rock. The next morning, he ate two other prisoners and, in the evening, two more. Then he drank the wine that Ulysses offered him and, intoxicated, fell asleep. The hero immediately set fire to the enormous end of a tree trunk and, with the help of the remaining companions, pushed it into the eye of the Cyclops.

Then the Cyclops enlisted the aid of his brothers against "No one": This was the name that Ulysses had prudently chosen for the adventure. Believing him insane, the other Cyclopes abandoned him. To leave the cave, Ulysses and his comrades concealed themselves beneath the bellies of the sheep and were able to steal away unharmed despite the vigilance of Polyphemus who was stroking the backs of the animals to make sure that none of them carried his guests on their backs. When they set sail for the open sea, Ulysses, despite his companions' urgent entreaties, addressed insults to Polyphemus who, enraged, threw huge rocks at their ship. Polyphemus then invoked the vengeance of his father Poseidon. The god unleashed a storm to beset Ulysses when he left Calypso.

POLYPOETES. 1. The son of Pirithous and Hippodamia, Polypoetes succeeded his father as king of the Lapiths in Thessaly. A suitor for Helen, he took part as such in the Trojan War and made his mark through his bravery in combat by putting numerous Trojan heroes to death. Finally, he was among the Greek heroes who hid in the flanks of the famous Trojan horse.

2. Also known by the name of **Polypoetes** was a son of Ulysses and Callidice whom he succeeded on the throne of the kingdom of the Thesproti in Epirus.

POLYXENA. The youngest daughter of Priam and Hecuba, Polyxena was involved in certain episodes of the Trojan War recounted by traditions that followed the *Iliad*. Achilles fell madly in love with her when she came to him, with Priam and Hecuba, to claim the body of her brother Hector. It is said that, to obtain her hand, Achilles was prepared to betray his compatriots either by returning to Greece immediately or by joining the ranks of the Trojans. But Paris was standing by and killed the hero. During the sack of Troy, the shadow of Achilles

The goddess Pomona carries in the folds of her tunic the fruits of the orchards. The entire statue expresses the serene certainty of a divinity who will assure the continued fertility of plants and trees. Roman statue, Uffizi Gallery, Florence, photo Brogi.

to whom she bore a daughter, Antiope.

3. The most famous **Polyxo** was the widow of Tlepolemus, the son of Heracles, who, at the head of a contingent of Rhodians, perished at the hands of the Trojans. Wild with grief, Polyxo wanted to avenge the death of her husband. When Helen, the wife of Menelaus, was banished from Sparta and requested her hospitality, she welcomed her as a friend. Blaming Helen for the Trojan War, Polyxo disguised her servants as the Erinyes. Incessantly tormented, Helen was driven mad and finally hanged herself.

POMONA. This nymph of fruits and flowers, who had an official priest assigned to her, was described by the Poets who related her numerous love affairs with agrarian and rustic divinities, particularly Picus, Silvanus and Vertumnus. Ovid contended that she was the spouse of the latter and that their immortal fidelity enabled them to grow old and be rejuvenated eternally, like the cycle of the seasons and the ripening of plants and fruits. Seated on an enormous basket of flowers and fruit, Pomona holds apples and an oar. The poets portray her with a crown of vine branches and grapes, while she distributes the fruits from a horn of plenty.

PONTUS. Mentioned by Hesiod, Pontus is the personification of the sea, its waves and its depths alike. He was mothered by Gaia, later had relations with his mother who then gave birth to the myriad forces of Oceanus, Nereus, Phorcys, Ceto and Thaumas. Pontus is not portrayed in any works of art and there is no legend that deals with him alone.

PORPHYRION. This giant took part in the war against the gods of Olympus, piling rock upon rock right up to the sky. Then he tried to strangle Hera and to rape her. To punish the impudent creature, Zeus struck him down with

appeared to the Greeks and requested that they sacrifice Polyxena. On his tomb, Achilles' own son Neoptolemus carried out this order to appease the tormented spirit of his father.

POLYXO. **1.** Legend tells of a Polyxo of Lemnos, who advised Queen Hypsipyle, whose nursemaid she was, to welcome the Argonauts so that the race of Lemnians would be perpetuated.

2. Another **Polyxo** was the wife of Nycteus,

Just as his brother Zeus brandishes lightning to express supremacy over gods and men, Poseidon holds a trident, a formidable symbol of his domination over the waters and the living species that populate the oceans and the seas. With one hand, he holds back his tunic, which is rolled below his waist, as if to give him freedom of movement and the appearance of near-nakedness, showing him to be admirably proportioned in the eyes of his dazzled subjects. With sovereign nobility of bearing, his sight is directed toward the endless horizon of his kingdom. Poseidon of Milo, National Archaeological Museum of Athens, photo Boissonnas.

a thunderbolt and Heracles finished him off with an arrow.

PORTUNUS. Like the god Janus, this archaic Roman divinity originally protected doors, passages and grain storehouses. Later, he watched over ports and, especially the port of Rome on the Tiber. Identified by the Romans with the Greek god Palaemon, Portunus was the son of Mater Matuta, herself identified with the goddess Leucothea, the mother of Palaemon.

POSEIDON. The son of Cronus and Rhea, Poseidon, the god of the Mediterranean, was raised by the Telchines. Famous, like all the gods of Olympus, for his love affairs with immortals, such as Demeter or Amphitrite, his legitimate spouse, or even with monsters like Medusa, most of his offspring were nefarious creatures such as the Cercopes, the Aloads, Chrysaor or the Cyclops Polyphemus. He often meddled in the affairs of mortals; with Apollo, he took part in the construction of the walls of Troy. He tried in vain to steal the regency of Attica away from Athena. Furious at having been beaten, he struck the rock of the Acropolis of Athens with his trident, and the rock bore the trace of this even during the historical epoch. He quarreled unsuccessfully with Helios over Corinth and with Hera over Argos. During the Trojan War, he sided with the Greeks to spite the Trojans who did not give him his due when he had finished building their wall. He agreed to protect Aeneas, however, by concealing him from Achilles as he prepared to kill him.

The god of Earthquakes and the Liquid Element, the most impressive representation of which is the sea with its vastness and savage power, Poseidon dwelled at the depths of the sea. Sometimes he leaves his palace in a chariot drawn by horses the colors of algae and foam, so that he may direct the movements of the waves, calm or arouse storms, by striking the

In keeping with the legend that portrays Priam as an old man with white hair and a beard, leaning on a cane, he is seen accompanied by two slaves bearing jars and caskets filled with gifts, requesting that Achilles return the body of his son Hector. Achilles pretends not to hear him. He is still holding the dagger that mortally wounded Hector, whose body can be seen, riddled with wounds, under the very bed of his murderer. Greek skyphos, Museum of Art History, Vienna.

sea with his trident or crying out his orders with his deep booming voice. Seamen worshiped him and invoked him to grant them a safe crossing. His power extends not only over the sea element, but also over fresh water (except rivers) and the nymphs.

POTHOS. The son of Aphrodite, Pothos personifies, along with Eros with whom he is often identified, amorous desire. He does not possess any legend of his own.

POVERTY. Known to the Greeks by the name of *Penia,* poverty united with Porus, the expedient, son of Metis, to give birth to Eros, Love.

PRAENESTE. This very ancient Latin city was founded by Caeculus, the son of Vulcan. The origin of Praeneste is also attributed to Telegonus, the son of Ulysses and Circe. This Latin city acquired great renown owing to the temple dedicated to the goddess Fortuna, before whom the ancients would toss dice in order to question the fates.

PRIAM. This king of the Minyans was originally called *Podarces,* which means "light-footed." He was the son of Laomedon who was killed by Heracles for refusing to give him the prize agreed upon in return for delivering his daughter Hesione. Spared because he was the

Under a great vinestock, the god Priapus, the Roman protector of gardens, plays the flute while two women approach him with offerings. Roman cameo, Bibl. Nat., Cabinet des Médailles, photo Giraudon.

only one to side with Heracles against his father, he was ransomed by his sister and then took the name of *Priam*, "he who has been sold." He acceded to the throne of Troy, married Arisbe, then, in a second marriage, Hecuba. According to Homer, he was the father of numerous children—Hector, Paris, Deiphobus, Cassandra, Creusa, Laodice, Helenus—almost all of whom perished during the Trojan War. While still a youth, Priam supported the Phrygians in a battle against the Amazons. He was already getting on in years when the Trojan War broke out and the *Iliad* recounts that he did not take an active part in the war. He agreed to act as an advisor; but Hector alone decided on the progress of the operations.

At the end of the *Iliad*, he plays a rather tragic role when he goes to beg Achilles to return the body of his son Hector. The grief of a father and the emotion of the enemy conqueror, both intermingled in the same fatal unhappiness of the war, give the text of the *Iliad*

and the character of Priam a striking aspect. When Troy was invaded by the Greeks, the king took refuge with Hecuba in the darkest corner of his palace and hid behind the altar of Zeus. But the supreme god could do nothing to help the unfortunate sovereign, who was slain by Neoptolemus.

PRIAPUS. This ithyphallic god is, according to the most common tradition, the son of Dionysus and Aphrodite. Hera, who was jealous of his mother, made him deformed at birth. Fearing ridicule, Aphrodite abandoned her son along the riverside of the Hellespont where her cult was mainly located in Lampsacus. A divinity of Fertility, owing to both his symbol, the phallus, and his ancestry, Priapus ensured the reproduction of flocks of sheep and goats, the birth of bees and the growth of grapes, and he was adored by the rustic shepherds on the banks of the Hellespont. His cult spread throughout Italy where he was much in favor. Priapus was identified with a certain number of agrarian divinities, particularly the god Pan. The ancients would place in orchards and gardens a phallic stone to promote blossoming and fructification.

PROCNE. The legend of this daughter of Pandion, the king of Athens, goes hand in hand with that of Philomela, her sister. Married to Tereus, the king of Thrace, who went to the aid of his father during a war, she had one son, Itys, by him. When Tereus seduced Philomela, Procne decided to take revenge and make an example of him. She killed her son, chopped off his limbs, boiled him in a pot and then served him to her husband as a meal. When he had finished eating, she told him the truth. She had just enough time to flee with her sister; but Tereus, wild with grief, set out in pursuit of them and, just as he was about to catch them, the sisters begged the gods to spare them; they were both changed into birds: Procne thus be-

This sarcophagus illustrates two of the main episodes in the legend of Prometheus. At the extreme left, the god fashions the first man under the benevolent eye of Athena. At the extreme right, Prometheus leaves the sky, from which he has just stolen fire, portrayed here by a large torch. Sarcophagus, Louvre, photo Giraudon.

came a beautiful nightingale and Philomela a gracious swallow.

PROCRIS. One of the daughters of Erechtheus, the king of Athens, Procris was accidentally killed by her husband Cephalus.

PROCRUSTES. "He who stretches": this was the surname of the bandit Damastes or Polypemon. Procrustes possessed two beds. He forced large travelers to lie on the smaller bed and small travelers to stretch out on the larger bed. He cut off the limbs of the former and stretched the arms and legs of the latter. Theseus put an end to these ferocious exploits of Procrustes and subjected him to the same fate.

PROETIDS. The daughters of Proetus, the king of Tiryns, Iphianassa, Iphinoë and Lysippe bore the patronymic name of Proetids. Hera drove them mad because they had compared their beauty to that of the goddess, even daring to contend that they were more beautiful. Believing that they were cows, they wandered through the countryside bellowing. It is also said that this punishment was inflicted on them by Dionysus because they had spurned his cult. The soothsayer Melampus succeeded in curing the Proetids and became king of half of the territory governed by Proetus.

PROETUS. The son of Abas, Proetus quarreled over the kingdom of Argos with his twin brother Acrisius. He was banished from Argos and sought refuge in the court of Iobates, the king of Lycia. He married one of the king's daughters, Stheneboea, who bore him three daughters generally known as the *Proetids*. Then he mobilized an army and pressured his

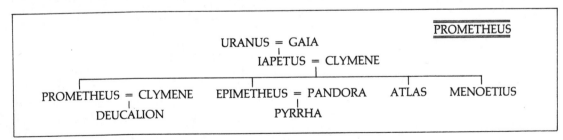

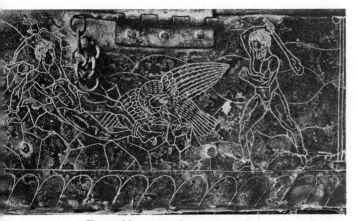

Chained by rings of iron to a rock on Mount Caucasus, Prometheus prepares to endure once again his daily torture: the eagle approaches to gnaw at his constantly regenerated liver. But Heracles brandishes his club that will crush the predator. Greek cist from Praeneste, line engraving, Louvre, photo Giraudon.

brother Acrisius until he agreed to hand over part of his territory, Tiryns. There, Proetus played a role in the legend of Bellerophon. In fact, he purified the hero of a murder. However, on a false accusation by his wife, he sent his guest to the court of his father-in-law, Iobates, to have him put to death. Iobates refused to kill Bellerophon, but subjected him to the most dangerous of trials.

PROMETHEUS. The son of the Titan Iapetus and of Clymene, the brother of Atlas, Menoetius and Epimetheus, Prometheus was a giant whose power Zeus always dreaded. A prophet, an inventor, he created the first man from a lump of clay mixed with water. Not wishing to leave his creature completely defenseless, he stole from the Sun a spark which he hid in the stem of a fennel; when he returned to Earth, he gave this source of divine fire to men who, in his absence, had quickly multiplied. Not satisfied with this first exploit and this insult to the sovereign power of Zeus, he thought up a sec-

ond exploit. He killed and skinned a bull. On one side, he stretched the skin, the marrow and the entrails which he covered with the animal's hide; on the other side, he put down the bones on which he placed the animal's fat. Prometheus told Zeus to choose one of the two parts; the other part was to go to men. Zeus, attracted by the whiteness of the fat, chose the portion that contained only the bones. Having been thus tricked, Zeus decided to take revenge on mortals and on Prometheus. To the mortals, he sent Pandora, a beautiful maiden created by Hephaestus, who spread all imaginable unhappiness through the world by opening the famous box. To Prometheus, he dispatched Hephaestus: the god placed Prometheus in chains on the highest peak of the Caucasus where each day for centuries an eagle came to gnaw at the constantly regenerated liver of the unfortunate victim. Because he warned Zeus not to marry Thetis if the god wished to avoid having a son who would dethrone him, Prometheus was entitled to the clemency of his master. Heracles killed the predator with one of his arrows and freed the giant. However, Zeus forced him to wear an iron ring attached to a small bit of rock. Subsequently, Prometheus was granted immortality, which was given to him by the centaur Chiron.

PROSERPINA. A Roman divinity, Proserpina originally extended her very special protection over the germination of plants. Soon identified with the Greek Persephone, she became the wife of Pluto and queen of the Underworld.

PROTESILAUS. Protesilaus belongs to the legends of Thessaly, the country in which he was born of the marriage of Iphiclus, king of Thessaly, and of Astyoche. A suitor for Helen, he left for Troy at the head of forty vessels after marrying Laodameia, the daughter of Acastus, of the family of Jason. Since an oracle had predicted that the first Greek warrior to touch Asian soil would be killed immediately, no one dared disembark. Protesilaus volunteered and perished at the hand of Hector. His unconsolable wife was granted permission to have him return from the land of the dead for a short time; when he returned, she followed him.

PROTEUS. The son of Poseidon and Tethys, Proteus is a secondary divinity of the sea, responsible for watching over the herds of seals that belonged to his father. According to Homer, he lived on the island of Pharos not far from the River Aegyptus. Virgil claimed that he lived on the island of Karpathos, between Crete and Rhodes. He was famous, above all, for his extraordinary powers of divination. His father had granted him this power in return for the services that he received. He could indicate perfectly what was, what is, and what was to be. But this "Old Man of the Sea," who was far from amiable, refused to share his predictions. However, if someone wanted to have him look into the future, he needed only seek him out at noon, while he was taking his siesta, and to place him in chains. Surprised and furious, Proteus would change into a series of monsters, one more terrifying than the next. He would even assume the elusive appearance of fire and water. However, if the seeker held his own and did not succumb to fear, he would once again assume his original form and would agree to speak. Thus Proteus told Menelaus which means he should employ to return to his native land. Thanks to his advice, Aristaeus was able to repopulate his beehives which had been destroyed by the Dryads.

PRUDENCE. As is the case for all the Roman allegorical divinities, the characteristics and attributes of Prudence are ill-defined. She is generally portrayed with the features of a two-faced woman, one face turning toward the past, the other toward the future. At a later era, she was identified with Metis, the first wife of Zeus.

PSYCHE. In the *Metamorphoses*, Apuleius relates that Psyche (the Greek word for soul) was

A Roman illustration of the Greek legend of Persephone. Pluto, in the center, bursts forth from the Earth on his chariot and, with one arm encircling the waist of Core, the daughter of Demeter, he abducts her. The poor creature, bending backward, exhibits both surprise and fright. The young, carefree Core has become, at this moment, the severe Proserpina, the wife of the god of the Underworld. Roman relief, Vatican Museum, photo Alinari-Giraudon.

The legend of Cupid and Psyche. The delicacy and precision of the gestures of this statue illustrate the traditional yet eternal image of ecstatic lovers. Ancient sculpture, Capitoline Museum, Rome, photo Anderson-Viollet.

the youngest and most beautiful of the three daughters of a king. All the subjects of the kingdom crowded around her to admire her, and they even dedicated a cult to her, forgetting the marks of devotion that were due Venus. The goddess of Love conceived a vengeful jealousy and enlisted the services of her son Cupid, asking him to inspire in Psyche a love for the ugliest, most despicable man on earth. Cupid gathered up his bow and flew off to accomplish his task. But he was so stricken by the beauty of the maiden that he fell in love with her and did not carry out his mother's orders. While the two sisters of Psyche married rich men, the beautiful maiden could not decide on one of her suitors. Rather disturbed by this, her father, the king, went to consult the oracle of Apollo, who ordered him to dress his daughter in black and take her to the top of a hill where a hideous serpent would have relations with her. Despite his despair, the king carried out the orders of the gods and abandoned his daughter Psyche. Then a gentle breeze began to blow and the breath of Zephyrus carried the girl through the air, depositing her safe and sound in a lush, fragrant valley where she fell asleep. The next morning, when she opened her eyes, she found herself in the enchanted garden of a gold and silver palace that was adorned by precious stones. Disturbed yet curious, she approached the unknown dwelling and heard the sound of a voice, which was inviting her to enter the luxurious palace; she pushed the door open and found in splendid rooms a bath that was all ready for her, dinner and a sumptuous bed where she reclined when night fell. Shortly after, she perceived a presence at her side and believed that this was the husband promised by the oracle. This amorous yet tender spouse asked Psyche not to try to look at him. Furthermore, the maiden received permission to return home for a few days to visit her family. Her sisters, seeing her so happy, tried to arouse doubt in her heart and told her that, in the shadows of the Night, she would surely have relations with a monster.

Upset, Psyche, during the night that followed her return to the palace, approached her sleeping husband and illuminated his face with a lamp. Instead of a monster, she found Cupid, the most beautiful and lovable of all the gods. Dazzled, she brought the lamp even closer and a drop of burning oil fell on the shoulder of her divine spouse. Cupid awoke with a start, scolded Psyche for her lack of trust, and disappeared. Wild with grief, the poor maiden wandered about in search of him and finally went to invoke the help of Venus. The goddess, only too happy to take revenge, took Psyche into her service as a slave and imposed brutal and humiliating tasks. But nothing seemed impossible for the young woman as her love gave her the courage and perseverance necessary for these labors. With the help of ants, she sorted the many types of grain that Venus had mixed up. She brought back the golden wool of ferocious sheep. With the help of an eagle, she was able to draw water from the Styx, considered to be inaccessible; to soften Cerberus and to reach the throne of Proserpina, in the very depths of the Underworld, to bring back to Venus a bit of the beauty of the queen of Shadows. However, curiosity was to be her downfall yet another time. She opened a box that Proserpina had given her and plunged into deep slumber. During this time, Cupid, locked up in the palace of his mother, was dying of love for the magnificent Psyche. One day he succeeded in flying through one of the windows of the palace; when he found his sleeping spouse, he awakened her with a slight prick of his arrow. In the face of such love, Venus was unable to remain insensitive. Mercury carried Psyche away from the Earth and deposited her in the palace of the gods where she drank ambrosia and nectar, which granted her immortality. Thus she was forever united to Cupid. The story seems to owe something to the Platonic account of the relation between soul and love.

PTERELAUS. Electryon, the king of the Mycenae, one day received a visit from the sons of King Pterelaus who claimed the throne of the city because it had once belonged to their ancestor Mestor. Electryon refused to submit to this request and, at his death, his nephew Amphitryon was instructed to lead an expedition against Pterelaus. But Poseidon, the father of Pterelaus, had placed on the head of his son a golden hair which made him immortal. However, his daughter Comaetho fell in love with Amphitryon and decided to betray her country: she cut her father's hair and he died immediately. Horrified by this crime, which had nonetheless worked to his advantage, Amphitryon condemned Comaetho to death for this parricide.

purification. Unknown to Homer, this religious practice was introduced, it is said, by Apollo when the god killed the serpent Python. Indeed, every murder, even that of a monster or criminal, accounted for an impurity requiring purification. Apollo, therefore, went to Thessaly and bathed in the waters of the River Tempe. Likewise, in mythology, heroes guilty of assassinations or sacrileges were obliged to take exile and to seek purification by any means in order to appease the divinities of the Underworld. Purification was generally granted to them by a king of a neighboring country. If the murderer repented, he was immediately pardoned by the gods.

PYGMALION. 1. King of Tyre, who sometimes is listed in the genealogy of Dido.

2. A legendary king of Cyprus and renowned sculptor, **Pygmalion** had taken a vow of celibacy and acted out his frustrated love with the statue he had fashioned of a young

woman. He begged Aphrodite to find him a wife who resembled his work of art. The goddess breathed life into the statue and Pygmalion was able to marry Galatea whom he had, in a certain sense, created. This union gave birth to Paphos, founder of the Cypriot city that bears his name, where a famous sanctuary of Aphrodite was to be erected.

PYGMIES. The *Iliad* describes the Pygmies as miniature human beings who lived in the south of Egypt, undoubtedly in the region known today as Ethiopia. One day, a pygmy was changed into a crane by Hera: he had neglected the duties of her cult. Having been changed into a bird, he tried several times to abduct his son. The Pygmies drove him away. From that time on, cranes became their relentless enemies. Another legend connected with the Pygmies involves Heracles. Always ready to fight with those who were bigger than they, they one day attacked Heracles, who had fallen asleep after his struggle with Antaeus. But the hero awoke and gathered them up in a single stroke in his lion's skin and, having rendered them powerless, he carried them to the palace of Eurystheus.

PYLADES. Taken in by Strophius, the king of Phocis, after the murder of his father Agamemnon, Orestes was raised with his cousin Pylades. The friendship that grew between the two heroes was marked by such loyalty that indeed it became proverbial. Pylades was one of the instigators of the murder of Clytemnestra; but he did not abandon Orestes when, after his crime, he was driven mad and tormented by the Erinyes. He was rewarded for his devotion; when Orestes became the king of Argos, he granted Pylades the hand of his sister Electra. Their marriage gave birth to two sons, Medon and Strophius.

PYRAMUS. According to Ovid, Pyramus and Thisbe were two young Babylonians who loved each other dearly. They lived in neighboring houses and could gaze at one another through the slit in the wall that separated them. However, their parents refused to let them marry. One day, they made plans to meet under a white mulberry tree. Thisbe arrived early and was surprised by a lioness; she managed to flee, but she lost her veil, which the animal stained with blood. When Pyramus arrived to meet his beloved, he found the blood-soaked veil and believed that Thisbe had been devoured. Not able to bear this thought, he plunged a sword into himself at the foot of the white tree, the fruit of which turned blood red. When Thisbe returned and discovered the inanimate body of her lover, she killed herself in despair.

According to another version of the story, which is more ancient and less embellished, Thisbe, who was pregnant by Pyramus before their marriage, was unable to bear such shame. She killed herself and her beloved followed her in death.

PYRRHA. The daughter of Epimetheus and Pandora, Pyrrha was the wife of Deucalion, one of mythology's very first heroes. Owing to her great piety, she, along with her husband, escaped a universal deluge and became the mother of a new human race by throwing stones behind her, as did Deucalion, and the stones were transformed into women and men respectively.

PYRRHUS. The name Pyrrhus, "the Red," is sometimes used to refer to *Neoptolemus*, the son of Achilles and Deidameia, undoubtedly because this hero of the Trojan War had red hair.

pythia. Exclusively connected with the Delphic oracle, the pythia was originally selected from among the most beautiful and chaste girls of the city. This function was subsequently reserved for mature women. Seated in the temple on a tripod, above a crevice emitting vapors laden, in a sense, with the spirit of Apollo, the pythia entered a sort of hysterical trance and then pronounced incoherent words, which expressed the thoughts of the god. Interpreted by the priests, the responses of the pythia were transmitted to those who consulted the oracle, who could thus learn what the future and fate held in store for them.

PYTHON. When Hera learned that Leto was pregnant by Zeus, she asked Earth to create a monster, Python, to pursue Leto without stop. Thanks to Poseidon, Leto succeeded in hiding to give birth to Artemis and Apollo. Apollo reached adult size in four days and went to Delphi. There, at the foot of Mount Parnassus, he encountered the serpent (or dragon) Python who had tormented his mother. He chased the Python into the temple of the oracle of the Earth Mother and there pierced it with his arrows. According to another legend, the Hyperborean priests, Pasasos and Agyiæos, established the supremacy of the oracle of Apollo over that of the Earth Mother. In remembrance of his victory, Apollo founded the Pythian Games and took for himself the surname "Pythian."

QUIRINUS. Associated with Mars and Jupiter, this ancient Sabine god bore warrior's symbols, namely a spear, and, for this reason, he was often identified with Mars or with Romulus, the son of Mars and founder of Rome. In memory of this legend, Virgil gave the emperor Augustus the surname *Quirinus*. However, a Latin grammarian, Servius, in a commentary on Virgil, affirmed that Quirinus was a "tranquil Mars."

R

REA SILVIA. A descendant of Aeneas and the daughter of Numitor, the king of Alba, Rea Silvia was condemned by her uncle Amulius, who had usurped the throne, to living as a vestal virgin so that she could not give birth to children who might make legitimate claims to the throne. However, seduced by Mars, she gave birth to Remus and Romulus, who were to reestablish Numitor on the throne. She died shortly afterward. It is also said that the River Tiber, where her body had been thrown, married her.

REMUS. The legend of this founder of Rome goes hand in hand with that of his twin brother Romulus. The two brothers quarreled over the conditions for the founding of Rome. Thus, Romulus, who had marked off a fictitious area to indicate the boundaries of the city, forbade Remus to cross this line. Remus did not heed this warning and was killed by his brother, who was furious over this sacrilegious gesture. Remus was buried with full honors on the Aventine by Romulus who regretted his criminal act, committed in a fit of anger.

resurrection. This myth, which developed especially after the appearance of Orphism, has no more than the importance of an anecdote in legends. Certain characters, such as Persephone, are permitted to return to Earth temporarily. Other mortals, such as Asclepius, the physician, or Circe, the enchantress, are empowered to revive the dead through their knowledge of magical plants capable of overcoming death.

RHADAMANTHYS. The union of Zeus and Europa gave birth to three sons: Minos, Sarpedon and Rhadamanthys. They were adopted by Asterius, the king of Crete, when he married the abandoned mistress of the king of the gods. At the death of this prince, Minos acceded to power, while Rhadamanthys organized the judicial customs of the island and drew up the code of Crete. Another tradition related that Rhadamanthys was forced to flee and went to Boeotia, where he wed the widow of Amphitryon, Alcmene. As he promulgated the laws which governed the Cyclades, and since he was, it is said, the originator of the *lex talionis*, Rhadamanthys acquired a great reputation for justice and wisdom. This is why the gods, wishing to reward him, granted him the third seat on the tribunal of the Underworld, at the side of Aeacus and Minos. He was responsible, in particular, for judging the souls of the dead that hailed from Africa and Asia.

RHEA. The daughter of Gaia and Uranus, this Titanid gave birth to Hestia, Demeter, Hera, Hades, Poseidon and Zeus. As Cronus, her hus-

The goddess Rhea brings her husband a stone wrapped in swaddling clothes. Not realizing the ruse, Cronus swallowed it, believing that he had just done away with his son Zeus, whose ambition he rightfully feared. Detail of an ancient krater, Louvre, photo Giraudon.

band, was devouring all the children she bore, since he had learned that one of them would dethrone him, Rhea took refuge in Crete just as she was about to deliver. There she gave birth to Zeus. She then gave Cronus a stone, wrapped in swaddling clothes like a newborn babe. Cronus, tricked by this ruse, swallowed the inert object. Thus, Rhea became the mother of the supreme god who, seizing sovereignty from his father, brought stability and justice to the world. In the Greek religion, Rhea was worshiped with unfailing devotion. The peoples of Asia Minor identified her with Cybele, the Great Mother of the gods, and she was then adored throughout the West and the Near East by many names and in many forms.

RHESUS. The son of Eïoneus, the king of Thrace, according to the Homeric tradition, Rhesus possessed two fleet-footed steeds whiter than snow, which he placed at the service of Troy during the final year in their struggle against the Greeks. According to a tradition that appeared after the *Iliad,* an oracle had predicted that, if the horses of the hero drank from the waters of the River Scamander, Troy would remain invulnerable. Alerted by Athena, Ulysses and Diomedes stole into the Trojan camp during the night, slaughtered Rhesus in his tent, and stole the precious horses.

RHOECUS. **1.** This centaur, the son of Ixion, wanted to compromise the honor of Atalanta. The chaste young woman shot him with an arrow.

2. Legend tells of another **Rhoecus,** who, having had the pious idea of propping up an oak that was about to fall, saved the lives of the Hamadryads who dwelled there. As a reward, he was entitled to their favors provided he remain faithful to them. But one day he was stung by a bee, their messenger, and stricken blind either because he had not welcomed the insect or because he had been unfaithful to these tree nymphs.

river. The liquid element, water and, above all, the river, marked by perpetual and mysterious motion, played an important part in ancient civilizations because it was a determining factor of fertility and, consequently, economic progress. In addition, the river afforded freshness; it purified the guilty and cleansed them of their crimes; it was the witness of successive generations, of civilizations and of the past. The major rivers of Greece and Asia Minor often appear in mythology in the form of gods with human features. Three thousand strong, they are the sons of Oceanus and Tethys, the brothers of the nymphs and sometimes the fathers of legendary heroes. In addition, they often take part in mortals' struggles against one another. Thus, during the Trojan War, Scamander took the Trojans' side and entered into conversation with Achilles. The most famous river was the Acheloüs who had the greatest flow in Greece and was the senior member in the genealogy of rivers. He was the very symbol, owing to his power and majesty, of the perpetuity of Greece. His strength was indomitable, and only Heracles, from whom he tried to steal Deianira, was able to defeat him after a ferocious struggle.

ROBIGUS. With his female assistant Robiga, Robigus formed, in the Roman religion, a couple of agrarian divinities who protected grain. A cult was dedicated to them with the idea of protecting grain from "blight," a troublesome parasite.

ROME. Several eponymous heroes were associated with Rome. When Ulysses spent some time in the company of Circe, certain legends, subsequent to Homer, claim that he begat a number of children, including Romus, who was

Portrayed as a warrior, the goddess Roma, sporting the helmet of the legionaries and a soldier's tunic, leads the Romans in the conquests that were to account for the grandeur of Rome. Her index finger points the way to victory to those who follow her. This relief is a concrete example of mythology at the service of Roman politics and imperialism. Roman relief, Vatican Museum, photo Anderson-Giraudon.

to give his name to the city of Rome. However, among the many traditions, the most famous is the one that attributes the founding of Rome to the descendants of Aeneas, the son of Aphrodite. The Trojan hero, the king of Latium, had a son Iulus, who founded Alba Longa, the cradle of the future Rome. Later, Rea Silvia, a descendant of Aeneas, became, by Mars, the mother of Romulus and Remus, the first founders of Rome. Thus the city, created by heroes of divine origin, was able to claim domination of the world and later reconcile the Trojans and Greeks. Under the Empire, the Romans adored a goddess Roma who, according to legend, had been one of the captives of Ulysses and Aeneas and who had advised the heroes to settle on the Palatine. As a sign of their thanks, they dedicated a cult to her. In any event, this worship grew as the power of Rome spread beyond the borders of Italy. She was ordinarily portrayed as a woman with a winged helmet. Sometimes, she held in one hand a horn of plenty which bestowed upon the world, which was subject to her rule, both prosperity and peace.

ROMULUS. At his death, Silius Procus, the king of Alba Longa, and a descendant of the Trojan hero Aeneas, left behind two sons: Numitor, the legitimate heir to the throne, and Amulius. Ambitious and completely without scruples, Amulius had Numitor thrown into prison, seized power, killed his nephew Lausus during a hunt, and forced his niece Rea Silvia to dedicate herself to the cult of Vesta so as to avoid the possibility of her bearing a pretender to the throne. The gods, however, decided otherwise. In a sacred wood where she had gone to draw water from a spring, Rea Silvia was one day seduced by Mars who made her the mother of Romulus and Remus. Amulius had Rea Silvia put to death for having violated her vow of chastity and he exposed the twins on the Tiber in a wicker basket; the Tiber was overflowing its banks at the time. But fate dic-

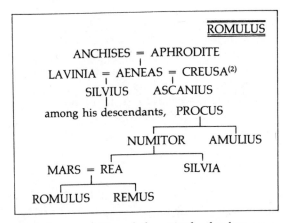

ROMULUS

ANCHISES = APHRODITE

LAVINIA = AENEAS = CREUSA[2]

SILVIUS   ASCANIUS

among his descendants, PROCUS

NUMITOR   AMULIUS

MARS = REA   SILVIA

ROMULUS   REMUS

tated that a whirlpool deposit the basket on a bank at the foot of one of the hills of the future Rome. A wolf, having lost her young, discovered the infants and, transferring her frustrated maternal instinct to the two, she suckled them. Later, a shepherd, Faustulus, and his wife, Acca Larentia, raised them and educated them. When they reached manhood, Remus and Romulus, with the neighborhood ruffians, engaged in highway robbery and stole some head of cattle from the herd of Amulius. Remus was arrested by the king's guards and thrown into prison. Romulus, who had learned of his origins from Faustulus, then went to Alba, killed the usurping king, freed his brother, and reestablished his grandfather Numitor on the throne. Then, the twins left Alba and decided to found a city on the banks of the Tiber, on the very spot where they had been thrown up by the waves, in order to thank the river for not having swallowed them up. But the harmony of the two brothers was but short-lived. A dispute arose as to the location of the city: to resolve the argument, they consulted the oracles; Remus saw six vultures on the Aventine; Romulus saw twelve on the Palatine and declared that the auspices favored him. Remus acquiesced; but when Romulus ploughed a furrow around the future location of Rome, forbidding anyone to cross it, Remus, as a sign of derision,

bounded over the border and perished at his brother's hand.

Finding himself to be the only master of the territory, Romulus undertook the construction of Rome, and seeing that the population was too numerous, he created on Capitoline hill an asylum where the scoundrels of the surrounding region and even fugitive slaves took refuge. Romulus declared himself king of these good-for-nothings. However, there was a dearth of women and the population of the city dwindled; Romulus concocted a scheme; he announced throughout the country that games were to be held in Rome in honor of the god Consus, and he invited the neighboring Sabines to the festivities. During the ceremonies, the men of Romulus carried off the Sabine women. This act of violence gave rise to a war

On this coin with its expressive engraving, an enormous wild wolf with its ruffled mane can be seen suckling the twins Remus and Romulus with its many udders. It is easy to see the tenderness the wolf exhibits for the twins by licking them and warming them with its breath. Roman coin, Photo Larousse.

between the two nations; it was a bloody war with unexpected repercussions, during which the episode of the treason of Tarpeia occurred. With the winds of war against him, Romulus enlisted the aid of Jupiter and promised to build him a temple. The god immediately granted him victory; the Sabines and the Romans joined together in a confederation governed by two kings, Romulus and the leader of the Sabines, Tatius, who, it is believed, was treacherously killed in the end. As for the death of the founder of Rome, there are two known versions, one glorious, the other less so. According to one, after reigning for thirty-three years, Romulus, during a storm accompanied by a solar eclipse, was carried off into the heavens by Mars, his father, and he appeared in a dream to a certain Julius Proculus whom he ordered to proclaim him a god by the name of *Quirinus*. According to another tradition, Romulus was supposed to have been a merciless tyrant. The senators, weary of his power, tore him to pieces and hid the bloody remains of his body under their robes.

RUTULI. The Rutuli inhabited a territory located to the south of the Tiber on the coast of Latium. At the instigation of Turnus, their leader, they fought against the Trojans and Aeneas to prevent the hero's marrying Lavinia. But when Turnus, a legendary hero, perished in single combat, they were rapidly conquered by the Romans and disappeared from history.

S

SABAZIUS. A Phrygian god, Sabazius was worshiped as a divinity with attributes identical to those of Dionysus, with whom he was later identified. He was the son of Persephone and Zeus, but there is no legend attached specifically to him.

sacred animals. In Greek and Roman mythology, certain animals held a privileged place in the legends of the heroes and gods. In this respect, a distinction was generally made between sacrificial animals and animals that symbolized the gods in some way and were associated with them. Among the sacrificial animals are lambs, ewes, oxen and pigs. Among the symbolic animals, which are too numerous to mention, the most famous are the eagle, the majestic symbol of supreme power always associated with Zeus, the god of gods; the serpent, dedicated to the chthonic divinities; the owl, the prophetic bird of the goddess Athena; the dove, as white as the goddess Aphrodite when she emerged from the sea's foam; the lizard is the animal of Apollo; the fish, the animal of Artemis; and the dog, the animal associated with Hecate. The cock is consecrated to the god Asclepius; the peacock, to Hera. Certain animals pull the chariots of divinities, such as the lions of Cybele or the horses of Poseidon and Hades. However, there was no adoration of animals themselves as there was in Egyptian religion. Rather, the gods were adored through them. They are not themselves divinities, but simply sacred symbols.

sacred stones. Often designated by the name of *baetyls,* the stones or aeroliths were originally considered to be the dwelling place of a god or his representation. A stone of a particular shape was dedicated to each god. It was a cubic stone for Cybele, a rectangular stone for Hermes, a cone-shaped column for Apollo Agyiaeos. The sacred stone also recalled in mythology certain actions of the gods or men. Hence, the resounding stone in Megara on which Apollo placed his lyre, the stone whose appearance Anarexete assumed, or the famous stone that Cronus swallowed in place of his son Zeus. In Troezen, people pointed for quite some time to the stone on which sat the nine judges who were responsible for purifying Orestes.

sacred wood. A symbol of the power of plants, the sacred wood, with its tree tops reaching upward, enabled men to know the teachings of the heavens and the counsels of the divinities. Therefore, places of worship were set aside in the sacred woods where certain gods delivered their oracles. Sometimes a temple was even erected in a clearing. Entry into the sacred wood, forbidden to the public, was accessible only to the priests or a limited number of initiates. Clearing of the land was prohibited under penalty of sacrifice. Among the most famous sacred woods are the woods of Ares in Colchis where the Argonauts seized the Golden Fleece; that of Zeus in Dodona; that of the Eumenides in Colonus, where Oedipus died; that of Pan in Arcadia; that of Zeus in Olympia; that of Aphrodite in Paphos, on the island of Cyprus. Among the Romans, countless woods were consecrated to the gods by the great heroes of Latium, such as Aeneas and Romulus.

sacrifice. In mythology, this practice is an offering intended to curry divine favor or to thank a god for some favor granted a hero. Most often reduced to the simple slaughter of an animal, sacrifices involved human beings in cases of great distress or fear. Thus legend tells of Iphigenia who was about to be sacrificed to the goddess Artemis so that the Greek fleet would be propelled by favorable winds; Polyxena was to be sacrificed on the tomb of Achilles to appease the spirit of the hero. Sometimes the hero or heroine even offered himself or herself to the sacrificial knife, such as the Coronides who, through their death, put an end to a plague.

SALMACIS. This Phrygian nymph obtained from Zeus the privilege of being forever joined to Hermaphroditus, with whom she was in love.

SALMONEUS. The son or grandson of Aeolus, the brother of Sisyphus and father of Tyro, Salmoneus emigrated from Thessaly to Elis where he became the eponymous king of a city he founded. He was detested by his subjects because he claimed that he was Zeus's equal and demanded that his subjects establish a cult in his honor. He rode through the streets of his city in a chariot dragging chains to imitate the sound of thunder. From time to time he threw flaming torches to simulate flashes of lightning and these burned passersby to death. Zeus, enraged by such presumptuousness, struck him down along with his subjects and burned the city of Salmone.

SALUS. The personification of Health, Prosperity and Public Well-Being, this Roman divinity, with no particular legend, was soon associated with the Hellenic goddess Hygieia, Health, the daughter of Asclepius and Lampetia. She was portrayed as a young person accompanied by a serpent, the symbol par excellence of the netherworld. She was invoked by the sick and even by the Roman state when grave circumstances so required.

SANCUS. One of the most ancient gods of the Roman religion, Semo Sancus, doubtless of Sabine origin and later identified with Dius Fidius, possessed a temple on the Quirinal and presided over oaths to which he gave a sacred nature.

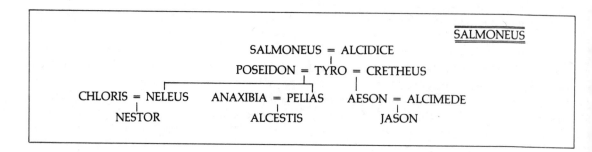

SALMONEUS

SALMONEUS = ALCIDICE

POSEIDON = TYRO = CRETHEUS

CHLORIS = NELEUS   ANAXIBIA = PELIAS   AESON = ALCIMEDE

NESTOR   ALCESTIS   JASON

SARON. This tutelary divinity of the sea, adored by seamen, was at one time a mortal, the king of Troezen, who had dedicated a temple to Artemis and, like the goddess, was passionately fond of hunting. One day he followed a doe down to the seashore. The animal leaped into the waves, drawing Saron out to sea where, exhausted, he drowned. His body was thrown up on a bank, not far from where he had dedicated the temple to Artemis. The Saronic Gulf near Athens was named after him.

SARPEDON. Legend speaks of at least two Sarpedons. One, the son of Zeus and Europa, had several differences with his brother Minos. He took refuge in the country bordering on Miletus and there he was proclaimed king.

The other **Sarpedon** is more famous. The son of Zeus and Laodameia, he headed a Lycian contingent on the side of the Trojans, supporting them in their struggle against the Greeks. Gigantic in size, unequaled in bravery, he was to perish at the hand of Patroclus.

SATURN. Very quickly identified with the Greek god Cronus, for reasons that to this day are obscure, Saturn consequently lost his purely Italic attributes and character. The god of Sowing and Grain, he is portrayed with the sickle of a harvester and the pruning knife of a vine grower. Virgil and Dionysius of Halicarnassus built a legend around Saturn: the god, banished from Olympus, took refuge in Italy; after the reign of Janus, he perpetuated the benefits of the golden age and taught men agriculture.

SATYRS. Greek divinities of the Woods and Mountains, the Satyrs, sometimes called Sileni, sometimes even Fauns by the Romans, symbolize the expansive, unlimited force of living beings, whether vegetable or animal. The Satyrs have the appearance of little men with bushy hair and ears similar to those of wild animals. They have two horns on their foreheads and

A malicious and sometimes evil-minded divinity of the Woods and Fields, the satyr is portrayed here with the features of a dwarf with a thick-set, muscular body and an extremely ugly face: protruding eyes, deformed nose, bushy beard and hair. An obdurate hunter, the satyr holds a dagger in one hand while in the other is a small piece of a bow. His muscles bulging, squatting and ready to leap, he seems to be eyeing his prey. Etruscan art, Wittelsbach, Munich, photo Giraudon.

sometimes have the tail of a horse or goat. Incessantly roaming the countryside, they seek to satisfy their appetites and are, for this reason, dreaded by mortals who fear in them, above all, the nefarious and uncontrolled excesses of nature.

SCAMANDER. This river of the plain of Troy was revered as a god by the name of Xanthus: he was born, in a sense, of the hands of Heracles, who, thirsty, dug into the earth and caused a spring to gush forth. It is a river with red waters, in which Aphrodite dipped her hair to give it a golden tint before participating in all her splendor in the judgment of Paris. Scamander had by a nymph a son, Teucer, the first branch of the royal family of Troy. Thus united with the family of Priam, Scamander fought against the Greeks in his own fashion, trying to drown Achilles by overflowing his banks. But Hephaestus, armed with a flaming torch, immediately sent him scurrying back to his bed.

SCIRON. This scoundrel, who reveled in mischief in Megara, was the son of Pelops or, perhaps, according to other versions, Poseidon. He had the habit of forcing travelers to wash his feet and then, as his way of thanking them, he would throw them from a rock into the sea where a giant tortoise would devour the bodies of the unfortunate victims. Theseus refused to submit to the demands of the bandit and threw him into the sea; then, to atone for his crime, the hero founded the Isthmian games.

SCYLLA. **1.** Traditions vary on the genealogy of Scylla. However, they all agree that unrequited love and vengeful jealousy were the causes of the metamorphosis and death of the monster. Scylla, the daughter of Phorcys and Hecate, or of Typhon and Echidna according to another version, was a nymph of radiant beauty. But she proved to be too proud of her charms to give them to the first suitor who came along. The sea-god Glaucus had eyes only for Scylla. Madly in love with her, he pursued her, enduring day after day the disdainful refusal of this haughty nymph. Not knowing how to win her heart, Glaucus enlisted the aid of the enchantress Circe. Circe proceeded to fall in love with Glaucus and directed her jealousy against Scylla. She prepared an herbal poison which she poured into the spring where the nymph usually bathed. When she immersed herself in the water, her body, with its beautifully perfect form, was changed into a monster with six clawed paws and six dog heads which, when they opened their enormous mouths, howled like lions and revealed three rows of pointed teeth. Devastated by her sudden ugliness, Scylla threw herself into the water. She settled on a rock on the bank of the Strait of Messina, facing Charybdis. Savoring a boundless rancor, she frightened sailors; the latter abandoning control of their ships, felt themselves drawn by the monster who wasted no time devouring them. Six of the companions of Ulysses perished this way. But Jason and Aeneas, with the help of the gods and soothsayers, met a less tragic fate. They succeeded in avoiding the gaping mouths of the monster.

According to Virgil, Heracles tried to put a stop to the deadly exploits of Scylla. As she had eaten some of the oxen of Geryon, the demigod killed her. But, of divine blood, she could not perish this way. Phorcys, it is said, or Glaucus, resuscitated her and she resumed her evil doings.

2. Also known by this name is a daughter of Nisus, king of Megara. Out of love for Minos, who had nonetheless invaded the kingdom, she did not hesitate to kill her sleeping father by cutting the golden hair that made him immortal. Thus she delivered her country to the enemy. But Minos, who had promised to marry her, was so horrified by this crime that he had the parricide put to death.

SELENE. The daughter of Hyperion and Theia, sister of Helios, Selene personified the goddess Luna who, in the Greek sky, shone radiantly. She has the features of a young woman with an astonishingly white face which makes all the stars seem pale in comparison when she journeys through the heavens on a silver

Carrying the torch of the night, the moon-goddess Selene is depicted in the center of this sarcophagus. She lovingly gazes at the young shepherd Endymion who is sleeping, through her influence, for eternity. Roman sarcophagus, Louvre, photo Giraudon.

chariot. Her love affairs are countless, some with Zeus, others with Pan, who seduced her and drew her into the forests, giving her luminously white fleece. But her most famous passion was the one she experienced for the shepherd Endymion. Selene asked the gods to grant him immortality, though he remained plunged in an endless slumber. Each night, Selene visited her immobile lover and caressed him with her silver rays.

SEMELE. The daughter of Cadmus, the founder of Thebes, and Harmonia, Semele was one of the lovers of Zeus. The jealous Hera assumed the features of Beroea, the nursemaid of Semele, and advised her rival to ask Zeus to appear to her in all his splendor. Horrified, but not daring to refuse, because he had promised to grant her everything she desired, Zeus presented himself to her with his thunder and lightning: in an instant, the unfortunate creature was consumed. The god had, however, just enough time to extract from the womb of Semele Dionysus, the son she had conceived. Later, Dionysus was to descend to the Underworld to take his mother from the kingdom of Shadows and transport her to Olympus where she be-

came immortal and assumed the name of *Thyone.*

SEMIRAMIS. The legend of this Assyrian heroine spread throughout Greece and Italy. Derceto, the goddess of Ascalon in Syria, with a harmonious face and a body similar to that of a fish, had felt a violent passion for a young Syrian; she conceived a daughter, the future Semiramis. Abandoned in a forest, the newborn was destined to die when the doves took responsibility for raising her, taking from the neighboring sheepfolds the milk and cheese needed to feed her. Soon discovered by Simius, the main guard of the herds of Ninus, she was adopted by the shepherds. When she grew up, she attracted general attention because of her beauty, grace and intelligence which stirred up the love of Onnes, the young general of Ninus, who married her. Shortly after their wedding, Onnes accompanied his king (who reigned in approximately 2500 B.C.) on an expedition against the Bactrians. During the siege of the city of Bactra, which was apparently impregnable, Onnes called his wife to his side. Semiramis, without hesitating and with unusual judgment and valiant determination, devised a plan of attack on the city. At the head of a Syrian contingent, she mounted an attack on the city and led her warriors to victory. Seduced by such audacity, Ninus wanted to steal Semiramis from her husband, whom he even threatened to kill. In despair, Onnes hanged himself. Thus Semiramis married the king and gave birth to a son, Ninyas. At the death of Ninus, Semiramis succeeded him on the throne of Nineveh. Thus her legend began. Tales of her exploits, her heroism, her spirit of enterprise abound. She had Babylon built, the model city of the East, with its impregnable walls, the unusual layout of its streets and its hanging gardens, of whose charm all of Antiquity boasted. People even credited her with the founding of all cities and all structures the origin of which was unknown. Finally, not content with enriching the heritage of her empire, Semiramis embarked on wars of conquest in faraway places. She conquered several nations in Asia, and subjugated Egypt where the oracle of Ammon predicted that she would perish when her son plotted against her. Then she conquered Ethiopia. In addition, she bore arms against the inhabitants of India. But repelled and wounded she learned, at the very moment of defeat, that her son sought to usurp her power. Without a moment's delay, she handed over to her son the destinies of the empire she was responsible for and disappeared. Certain authors contend that she was changed into a dove and deified.

SERIPHOS. It was on the shores of this island of the Cyclades that Danaë and her son Perseus landed after being abandoned in a chest by Acrisius. Perseus was raised in Seriphos and then left to accomplish his brilliant feats. During his absence, his mother was obliged to resist the advances of Polydectes, the king of the island, who wanted to seduce her. Upon his return, Perseus, irritated, showed the king and his companions the head of the Gorgon and they were immediately changed into stone.

SEVEN AGAINST THEBES. The title of a tragedy by Aeschylus, the *Seven against Thebes* relates the story of the battle which pitted the two brothers Eteocles and Polynices against one another after the death of their father for possession of the kingdom of Thebes. It explains how Polynices, banished from the city by his brother, joined forces with Adrastus, the king of Argos, and five other leaders—Amphiaraus, Capaneus, Hippomedon, Tydeus and Parthenopaeus—and then marched on Thebes. The two warring brothers ended up killing one another during single combat. The magistrates of the city decided to grant a burial to Eteocles but to leave Polynices, a traitor to his country, for the vultures to feed on. But while Ismene was burying Eteocles with full honors, Antigone granted her brother Polynices the decent burial which the city had refused him.

sibyl. A personification of Divination, the sibyl is a priestess of Apollo who emits prophecies and gradually tends, especially among the Romans, to be a substitute for the oracles of the gods. The Ancients recognized, among others, four sibyls of particular fame: the Marpessian sibyl, who lived in a grotto on Mount Ida, in the Troad; that of Erythrae; that of Tibur; and finally, the most famous of all, the sibyl of Cumae, who appears in many legends, particularly that of Aeneas—he consulted her before descending to the Underworld—and that of King Tarquinius who purchased the sibylline Books, the sacred texts of the Roman state.

SICYON. The genealogies of this king are very confused. He is sometimes the son of Erechtheus, the king of Athens; sometimes the son of Pelops; sometimes even the son of Marathon, the son of Epopeus. Most often, however, he is the grandson of the king of Athens, Erechtheus. He succeeded Lamedon on the throne of the city of Sicyon, of which he became the eponymous hero.

A divinity included in the procession of Dionysus, Silenus, always in a state of drunkenness, a towel knotted around his waist, a crown of grapes and leaves around his forehead, has some difficulty holding his body upright. Roman bronze, photo Giraudon.

SIDERO. Salmoneus, the king of Salmone in Elis, had married Alcidice, by whom he had a daughter Tyro. When his first wife died, the king married Sidero, who treated her stepdaughter terribly. Tyro one day had relations with Poseidon and gave birth to twins, Pelias and Neleus, whom she exposed so as not to incur the wrath of Sidero. When they grew up and learned of the persecution their mother was enduring, the twins decided to take revenge on the mother's stepmother. Sidero, nearly driven mad, took refuge in the temple of Hera. But Pelias did not hesitate to slaughter her on the very altar of the goddess.

SILENI. This name referred to the old Satyrs, who were the brothers of the god Silenus. They loved wine, love and sleep. Covered with grapes, they blithely followed the procession of Dionysus.

SILENUS. The son of Hermes or Pan, Silenus is said to have educated the young Dionysus: indeed he was regarded as a sage, a philosopher and a prophet. But, most of the time, he refused to use his various talents and he would have to be forced to, as King Midas did one day. A jovial, voluptuous old man, he was repulsively ugly with a snub nose and an enormous belly. In a constant state of drunkenness, Silenus followed the procession of Dionysus and, atop a donkey, he sang and laughed incessantly.

SILVANUS. The Roman divinity of Groves, Orchards and Thickets, Silvanus was first venerated in the form of a tree, then assumed a human appearance and was identified either with Pan or with Faunus. His mischievous character, which gave him a great tendency to tease, made travelers fear him as they journeyed through the woods, and parents threatened their children with the wrath of Silvanus when they broke branches from trees. This genius had no official cult but was very popular in Rome's rural communities as a tutelary and pastoral divinity. Fruits and young animals from the cowshed were sacrificed to him. He was ordinarily portrayed as a joyous old man who was crowned with ivy and held a billhook in his hand.

SINIS. This rogue, killed by Theseus, had the habit of fastening the limbs of his victims to the branches of two pines, the crowns of which he would draw together beforehand; he then separated the trees which, snapping apart, would tear the unfortunate victims to pieces. Theseus overcame Sinis and then had relations with Perigoune, the bandit's daughter, who had

On their island in the Mediterranean, the three Sirens that Ulysses is forced to confront are depicted here as the Greeks imagined them: amiable feminine faces, long wings and bird's feet. From right to left, according to tradition, the first holds a lyre, the second sings and the third plays a flute. Seafarers who heard the trio with its smooth, enchanting sounds were lost forever. Greek art, Myrina terra-cotta, Louvre, photo Giraudon.

hidden in a field of asparagus. She bore him a son, Melanippus.

SIRENS.   Neither Greek authors nor Latin writers are in agreement on these divinities that haunt the seas or on their origins. Numbering two or three, bearing various names including Parthenope, Leucosia and Ligia, they were the daughters of Acheloüs and Terpsichore, Melpomene or Phorcys. They resembled enormous birds with the heads of women. Living to the west of Sicily, they were regarded as incomparable musicians whose magical song drew to the reefs the seafarers they fed on. However, two heroes resisted their fatal charm. Orpheus, drawing from his lyre melodious tunes that drowned out the music of the Sirens, succeeded in steering the sailors on the *Argo* with him and Jason away from the reefs. Ulysses used wax to plug up the ears of his companions and tied himself to the mast of his ship so that he might satisfy his curiosity without succumbing to the charms of the dreaded songstresses. As a soothsayer had predicted that they would cease to live should someone listen to their song without being victimized by it, the Sirens threw themselves into the sea where they were changed into rocks.

SISYPHUS.   This king of Corinth, the son of Aeolus, married the Pleiad Merope; he had a son, Glaucus, and Bellerophon was his grandson. He is known in legend, above all, for the pain that was inflicted upon him in the Underworld: condemned to roll a rock up to the peak of a mountain, he was never to reach his goal and the rock continually fell back down. The unfortunate creature was obliged to begin his labor again and again for all eternity. Ancient mythographers do not agree on the motives for this punishment. According to some, he was an ambitious and hypocritical king who devastated Attica and was finally killed by Theseus; according to others, he was merely an informer who was supposed to have revealed to the river-god Asopus that his daughter Aegina had been abducted by Zeus. At the very least, others contend, he had committed a sacrilege in instructing men in the divine mysteries. Vexed by these many misdeeds, Zeus sent Thanatos, Death, to the king of Corinth but Sisyphus managed to chain him up. The empire of the Dead was gradually depopulated until Zeus himself forced the hero to free Thanatos. Transported to Hades, Sisyphus succeeded in escaping and lived for many long years afterward before being punished at long last for his crimes. By according him an enormous, endless labor in the Underworld, the gods thus deprived Sisyphus of any free time during which

SISYPHUS

SISYPHUS = MEROPE
|
GLAUCUS(2) = EURYNOME
|
BELLEROPHON

he might devise new ways of escape or yet other crimes.

SOL. Bearing the surname of *Sol Indiges,* Sol was an old Sabine divinity that personified the Light of Day and the Heat of the Sun, without which no earth became fertile. He was always associated with the goddess Luna, who symbolized the cycle of the seasons, and he was represented in her company on the temple of Jupiter Capitoline. Sol was identified only later with Helios. His cult spread extensively under the Roman Empire when, in an attempt at syncretism, the cult of the Sun was established.

SORANUS. Adored on Mount Soracte in Etruria, Soranus, whose cult was associated with that of the wolf, was soon identified with *Apollo-Lycian* (Apollo-Wolf).

SPARTA. This city, the capital of Laconia, in Peloponnesus, owes its name to the daughter of Eurotas, Sparte, who married Lacedaemon, the son of Zeus and Taygete. For this reason, the city of Sparta is very often called "Lacedaemon" by the Greek poets. In Homer, Menelaus ruled Sparta while his brother Agamemnon ruled Argos. But the first of the cities was subordinate to the second. The marriage of Orestes, the son of Agamemnon, to Hermione, put an end to this subjugation. Sparta was later governed by the Heraclidae, Eurysthenus and Procles. One of their descendants, Lycurgus, became its legendary lawmaker.

SPERCHEIOS. River-god of a river in the south of Thessaly, Spercheios was the son of Oceanus and Tethys. He married Polydora, the daughter of Peleus and Thetis, and thus became the brother-in-law of Achilles.

SPHINX. This monster, who ranks among the divinities of the Underworld, possessed all the characteristics of the race of which she was a descendant. From her mother Echidna, she inherited the face and chest of a woman; from her father Typhon (she is also said to be the daughter of Orthrus, the dog of Geryon), she inherited a dragon's tail; from her sister Chimaera, she inherited the body of a lion. Her wings were like those of the Harpies, her other sisters. The Sphinx had been sent to Boeotia, not far from Thebes, to punish the city for the crime of King Laius, the father of Oedipus, whose love for Chrysippus was the first homo-

Very similar to the Sphinx that Oedipus met along his way, this sphinx of Naxos is a monster with the head of a woman with curly, braided hair and the winged body of a lion. Archaic Greek art.

sexual passion. Perched on a rock, the monster asked a question of the travelers who passed her. Those who did not succeed in solving her enigmas were immediately killed and devoured. Oedipus' decided to confront the Sphinx, who asked him to solve the following enigma: "Which animal has four feet in the morning, two at noon and three in the evening?" "Man," answered Oedipus. "As an infant, he crawls around on his hands and knees; as an adult, he walks upright; and in his old age, he walks with the help of a cane." Seeing herself tricked, the Sphinx leaped from the rock and killed herself.

STAPHYLUS ("Grape-cluster"). 1. Abandoned by Theseus, Ariadne was rescued by Dionysus who married her. She was to give birth to a certain number of children, including Staphylus. The latter married Chrysothemis and, it is said, received from Rhadamanthys a small island in the Aegean Sea located not far from the coast of Thessaly.

2. Also known by this name is a shepherd of King Oeneus , who invented wine, by pressing clusters of grapes.

statue. Originally, the divinities were not personified but were simply represented by a stone roughly hewn in a symbolic form. Later, when they acquired an anthropomorphic aspect, sacred statues increased in temples and even, like those of Hermes or Hecate, at crossroads and, generally speaking, in places that such or such a god was supposed to protect. Furthermore, each city possessed its own statue which was considered to protect the city. Thus, Troy remained impregnable as long as the Palladium, the statue of Pallas Athena, stayed within its walls. Mythology also describes people who were changed into stone statues because they had irritated the gods or aroused their pity. Finally, the myth of Pygmalion revolved around the statue of a woman. This king of Cyprus was in love with a statue he had fashioned. Aphrodite agreed to breathe life into the statue, so that Pygmalion might marry it.

STENTOR. This proverbial Greek hero of the Trojan War was famous for the volume of his voice which, according to Homer, was as strong as the combined voices of fifty men.

sterility. A punishment of the gods, sterility strikes the earth and men alike. It is generally sent to punish a country for a crime or sacrilege that has been committed by one of its inhabitants. Dionysus, who did not receive a hospitable welcome from King Lycurgus of Thrace, rendered his kingdom sterile. The rivers dried up in their beds. The earth cracked open. All vegetation disappeared. In order to appease the god, Lycurgus was executed. It may also happen that mortals are made impotent or unable to procreate. In mythology, two famous marriages remained childless: that of Neoptolemus and Hermione and that of Aegeus and his first two wives. The couples were obliged to ask oracles the reasons for the wrath of the gods, the ways to appease the curse, and the necessary steps to ensure their posterity.

STHENEBOEA. Also known as *Anteia* in the *Iliad*, Stheneboea was the daughter of Iobates, the king of Lycia, and the wife of Proetus, the king of Tiryns. When her husband granted hospitality and friendship to Bellerophon, the murderer of a certain Bellerus, she fell in love with the hero. But the hero spurned the seductive advances of Stheneboea indignantly. Vexed at this refusal, she accused Bellerophon of trying to rape her. Proetus banished the hero whom he believed to be an ingrate, but Stheneboea, in shame, killed herself when the hero, after many adventures, returned to Tiryns to avenge himself. Other traditions claim the woman tried to flee on Pegasus: unhorsed, she was supposed to have fallen into the sea, where she was killed.

STHENELUS. 1. The son of Perseus and Andromeda, Sthenelus, the king of Mycenae, was the husband of Nicippe, who bore him four children who were famous in mythology: Alcinoë, Medusa, Eurystheus and Iphis.

2. Legend tells of a **Sthenelus,** the son of Androgeus, who in the company of his brother Alcaeus, accompanied Heracles on his expedition against the Amazons. To thank him, Heracles granted him sovereignty over the island of Thasos.

3. One of the Epigoni, this **Sthenelus** was the son of Capaneus and Evadne. He took part in the siege of Thebes; he later took part in the Trojan War along with Diomedes and the Argives.

STRIGES. These women with the body of a bird and clawed feet of a vulture were believed, in Antiquity, to suck the blood of small children. The goddess Carna, who protected the hinges of doors, was also supposed to watch over children and chase away these monsters with her magical incantations.

STROPHIUS. The son of Crisus and Antiphatia, this king of Phocis was the brother-in-law of Agamemnon whose sister, Anaxabia, he had married. He welcomed to his court young Orestes, whom Electra shielded from the murderous hatred of their mother Clytemnestra after the assassination of Agamemnon. The young fugitive formed a strong bond of friendship with Pylades, the king's son.

STYMPHALUS. The son of Elatus and Laodice, Stymphalus governed the city of Stymphalus in Arcadia. One of his daughters, Parthenope, had relations with Heracles and became the mother of a son, Everes. Other traditions claim that Stymphalus was the father of the Stymphalids who were killed by Heracles. Pelops, who wanted to conquer Peloponnesus but could not succeed in defeating the king, invited Stymphalus to a banquet, killed him, and scattered his limbs which he had torn to shreds.

STYX. The principal river of the Underworld, the Styx with its muddy, glacial waters flowed in the very depths of Hades. It encircled the kingdom of the Dead in its meanderings. Originally, Styx was a nymph who lived in a grotto on the banks of a spring in Arcadia. A daughter of Oceanus and Tethys, she married Pallas, bearing him four children with somewhat meaningful names: Zelus ("zeal"), Nike ("victory"), Bia ("force") and Cratus ("strength"). When Zeus waged his battle against the Giants, Styx rallied her children and made her way to Olympus where she joined forces with the celestial gods in their cause. To reward them, Zeus granted this valiant assistant the right to remain with him forever, aiding him in his undertakings. He endowed Styx with the privilege of being invoked by the gods, which gave an oath absolute value when affirmed this way. When a god prepared to swear by Styx, Iris went to fetch a cup full of water from the river and the god extended his hand over the cup. Any immortal being who went back on his word was punished severely: for an entire year, he would be denied both nectar and ambrosia. Then, for nine years, he would be banished from the circle of gods.

suicide. Considered a crime by Greek and Roman law, suicide, so common in mythology, was not always condemned. One sees heroes commit suicide with their souls full of vengeance to torment the consciences of their enemies. Certain inconsolable lovers ended their lives to join a loved one in death, and the gods pardoned these fatal acts. Such a suicide took on the value of a sacrifice, an act of love of supreme proportions to the honor of Aphrodite. The gods often compensated such a sacrifice by metamorphosis into a star or a constellation.

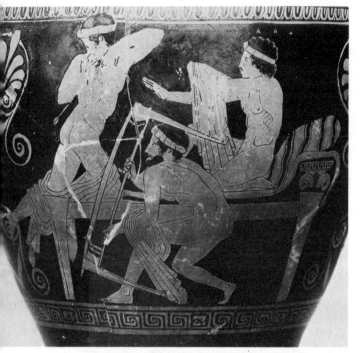

Around one of the beds where they spend their days and nights carousing, some of the suitors of Penelope try to dodge the arrows shot by Ulysses, here invisible. They have been surprised in their nakedness and they are unable to counter effectively without their weapons. One of them has already been stricken by an arrow; another, on the bed, holds his tunic up in front of his body as if to protect himself, while a third suitor, half crouching, uses a table as a shield. Krater from Corneto, Berlin Museum.

suitors. In mythology, the suitors were the heroes who sought to win the hand of a maiden, often of royal birth. The suitors were often obliged to compete either in games, chariot races or archery contests before one was chosen as the spouse. This was the case of the suit-ors of Hippodameia, the daughter of King Oenomaus, all of whom had their heads chopped off when they were defeated. Only Pelops, owing to a ruse, was able to marry the girl. However, in the *Iliad,* the suitors for Helen were not obliged to engage in such dangerous activities. Numbering one hundred, they were some of the most famous heroes of Antiquity. On the advice of Ulysses, Tyndareos forced the suitors to swear that, regardless of who was chosen, all would rush to the aid of Helen's future husband if an outrage were committed against him. Thus, when Paris abducted Helen, all of the suitors headed for Troy to punish the Trojans.

In the legend recounted in the *Odyssey,* the suitors for Penelope tried to convince her that Ulysses was dead and urged her to choose a new husband from among them. They invaded the palace of the king of Ithaca, robbed his treasures, and reveled in festivities and orgies. Upon his return from the Trojan War, Ulysses, unrecognized by all, suggested that Penelope be united with the one who was able to draw his bow. Not one of the suitors was able to do it. Ulysses, with the help of Telemachus, killed all of his rivals.

SYRINX. This nymph of Arcadia, pursued by Pan, threw herself into the waters of the Ladon and was changed into a reed just as the god was about to capture her. Pan cut the reed and fashioned a flute to perpetuate the memory of his beloved. He deposited the instrument in a cave where, later, young girls were imprisoned: if they were virgins, they would leave the cave accompanied by the tender sound of the Syrinx: if they were not, despite their affirmations to the contrary, they would disappear forever.

T

TAGES. One day, in Etruria, near Tarquinii, a laborer saw a newborn emerge from the furrow he was ploughing. The infant told him that he was the son of the Genius Jovialis and that his name was Tages. Soon, the Etruscans and King Tarchon hastened to see him, to admire his profound and astonishing wisdom, equal to that of an old man versed in the experiences of life. Before disappearing, Tages taught them divination and the art of interpreting predictions. All of this precious advice was recorded in sacred books.

TALOS. **1.** Linked by birth to Hephaestus or Daedalus, Talos was either a human being or, more commonly, a bronze robot. He guarded Crete, ruled by King Minos, with formidable vigilance and zeal and prevented travelers from approaching the coasts of the island: he stoned them or burned them by clasping them in his arms, first setting his body on fire. One day, Medea, through her charms, succeeded in driving him mad, and Talos tore a vein in his foot, the only vulnerable point on his body. It is also said that Poeas, the father of Philoctetes, pierced him with one of his arrows.

2. Legend speaks of another **Talos** (or Perdix), the son of Polycastes, the nephew and apprentice of the architect Daedalus. Talos surpassed his master in ingenuity and skill; he

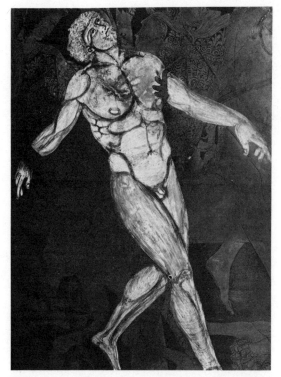

The artist has been able to portray the formidable strength of the robot Talos perfectly by making his muscles bulge. Held firmly by two sorcerers, undoubtedly ministers of Medea, the monster dies due to a torn vein in his foot. Detail of a Greek krater, Jatta Museum, Ruvo di Puglia, photo Anderson-Giraudon.

invented, for instance, the saw from the jaw of a serpent; he designed the potter's wheel and the compass and acquired great renown throughout Attica. Daedalus, jealous of Talos, threw him from the top of the Acropolis and then tried to conceal his crime but, soon confronted by discovery, he was judged by the tribunal of the Areopagus. Convicted of murder, he was banished from the city of Athens. During this time, Polycastes, learning of his son's death, hanged himself. According to certain versions, the soul of Talos was changed into a partridge.

TANTALUS. This king of Lydia or Phrygia was the son of Zeus and the nymph Pluto, and the father of Niobe and Pelops. According to the most commonly accepted version, he revealed to mortals the mysteries of the cult of the gods; but other traditions claim that he stole nectar and ambrosia from the gods to offer his subjects their immortal essence. It is also said that, wishing to test the gods' skill at divination, he served them his own son as a meal. The crime was detected by Zeus, and Pelops was revived by Hermes. It is said further that he incurred eternal punishment for failing to take care of a golden dog that had been entrusted to him to guard a temple dedicated to Zeus. As for the punishment that was inflicted for these alleged crimes, it was considered to be particularly dreadful in Antiquity: either that a rock perpetually threatened to crush him or, consumed by hunger and thirst, he was unable to find relief and to eat the fruit of a tree which disappeared as he was about to gather it. Indeed, Tantalus endured the worst of all punishments: the inability to grasp what he desired.

TARPEIA. During the war against the Sabines, King Romulus instructed Sempronius Tarpeius to guard the citadel of Rome. One day the daughter of Tarpeius saw Tatius, the king of the Sabines, in the enemy camp and fell in love with him. On the promise that the king would marry her, Tarpeia did not hesitate to open the gates of the citadel. But the king did not keep his word and the king's warriors smothered the girl beneath their shields. The Romans, who later placed Tarpeia in the ranks of their heroines, tried to absolve her of any responsibility and added other anecdotes to the original legend, all of which were favorable to her. Thus it was claimed that Tarpeia was the daughter of Tatius and that, abducted by Romulus, she avenged this affront by opening the gates of Rome to the Sabines, her compatriots. It is also said that Tarpeia died because she had refused to give the Sabines the war plans drawn up by Romulus. Finally, it is said that she promised the Sabines that she would open the gates of the citadel but asked them to first drop everything they held in their left hands, as though she coveted their jewels; what she wanted, above all, was their shields without which they were at the mercy of the Romans. Unfortunately, this ruse was discovered and Tatius ordered the Sabines to smother Tarpeia beneath their shields. The heroic young woman gave her name to the Tarpeian Rock from which criminals were thrown.

TARTARUS. In the *Iliad*, Tartarus is the underground spot, in the depths of the Underworld, which is separated from the surface of the earth by a distance equal to the distance between Heaven and Earth. A dark, bottomless abyss, surrounded by a triple bronze rampart, it is the prison of the first generation gods, whom Zeus conquered, namely the Titans, the Giants, and all other divinities who did not submit to the laws of Olympus. Gods caught in the act were constantly threatened with being thrown into Tartarus. Tartarus represented the depths of everything, beyond which nothing existed. Latin poets regarded it as the very expression of the Underworld: a stifling place, located at the bottom of a pit so that the guilty who had been sentenced to eternal punishment had no means of escape.

TATIUS. When Romulus had his men abduct the Sabine women, the king of the Sabines, Titus Tatius, immediately declared war on Rome to avenge this affront to his people. The struggle was long, punctuated by numerous mishaps, one of which enabled the Sabine army to enter the city of Rome, namely the treason of Tarpeia. Soon, the two peoples reconciled and formed a single State, governed by a sort of dyarchy, with Romulus and Tatius as kings. However, after several years, the disputes resumed. Sabines killed Laurentines and the parents of the victims, in retaliation, assassinated King Tatius during a festival in Lavinium. The king was buried with great pomp by his colleague Romulus who, nevertheless, did nothing to punish the assassins and henceforth was the sole ruler of the Romans and Sabines.

TAYGETE. This Pleiad, pursued by Zeus, was rescued by Artemis who changed her into a doe. Later restored to her original form, she consecrated to the goddess the doe with the golden horns that Heracles was called upon to capture. It is also said that she yielded to the supreme god and gave birth to Lacedaemon, the ancestor of the Lacedaemonians, the people of Sparta. In shame, she hid at the top of Mount Amyclas, later called *Taygetus*, in Laconia.

TELAMON. Like his brother Peleus, the father of Achilles, Telamon, the father of Ajax the Greater, was honored by legend. The son of Aeacus, he participated in the murder of his half-brother Phocus. Banished from Aegina, his native land, he went to Salamis where King Cychreus purified him of the murder and granted him the hand of his daughter Glauce. When his wife and father-in-law died, he became king and took as his second wife Peri-

boea, who bore him a son, Ajax. He participated in the Calydonian Boar Hunt and the expedition of the Argonauts. A companion to Heracles in Troy, he assisted the hero in his battle against Laomedon and as a reward received in marriage the daughter of this king, Hesione. A son, Teucer, was born of this union. Teucer and Ajax left for Troy. But only Teucer returned from the expedition and his father banished him from his kingdom because he had not been able to avenge his brother's death.

TELCHINES. These genii, most often evil-minded, were regarded as descendants of Poseidon and assumed a form which resembled that of a man as well as a sea creature because they had fish's tails and webbed feet. Sometimes, they took on the appearance of a serpent. They lived on the island of Rhodes, which was famous for its earthquakes and volcanic eruptions. For this reason, most of the island's calamities were attributed to them: frost, snow, rain; they were even accused of mixing sulfur with the water of the Styx to make the earth sterile and cause animals to perish. It is easy to understand why these genii of the netherworld and spirits of fire were identified with the Cabeiri because, like them, they possessed to an even rarer degree the art of forging metals and fashioning the statues and symbols of the gods, like the harp of Cronus and the trident of Poseidon. However, despite their artistic talents, their evil-mindedness incited the gods to punish them. Zeus threw them into the sea where they were changed into rocks; another version claims that they perished at the hand of Apollo, who pierced them with his arrows.

TELEGONUS. This hero was born of the union of Circe and Ulysses when the latter, returning to his homeland, stopped in the territory of the enchantress. Raised by his mother and told of the circumstances of his birth, Telegonus left for Ithaca with some companions to confront his father. When he arrived in the kingdom of Ulysses, he stole the king's herds. The people of Ithaca joined their leader in fighting the plunderers. Telegonus, without realizing who his victim was, pierced his father with a thorny javelin, thus fulfilling the prophecy that Ulysses would perish at the hand of his son. Realizing his mistake and his involuntary crime, Telegonus cried bitterly over the body of his father. Then he took the remains of Ulysses to Circe who granted them funerary honors. Later, he married Penelope, who bore him Italus, the eponymous king of Italy.

TELEMACHUS. When his father Ulysses left for Troy, Telemachus remained alone in Ithaca with his mother Penelope. But as the absence of his father continued, Penelope's suitors invaded the palace, plundering extensively. Telemachus, repulsed, but fortunately advised by Mentor, and above all by the goddess Athena, left home in search of Ulysses. He was received by Nestor who instructed his own son to lead him from Pylos to Sparta where he was welcomed by Menelaus. But he learned nothing from his hosts and, with a heavy heart, decided to return to Ithaca. There, to his great joy, he found his father, who had returned several days before him, at the abode of the shepherd Eumaeus. Together they prepared to massacre all of Penelope's suitors. Traditions attribute various spouses to Telemachus, namely Cassiphone, the daughter of Ulysses and Circe, Circe herself or Nausicaa, the daughter of Alcinous, the king of the Phaeacians.

TELEPHUS. The son of Heracles and Auge, Telephus was abandoned on a mountain and rescued by shepherds who gave him to King Corythus. When he reached manhood, he asked the Delphic oracle who his parents were. He was advised to go to Teuthras, the king of Mysia, who had married his mother. Telephus succeeded the king several years later. Related by marriage to the royal family of Troy, he opposed the disembarking of the Greeks on the coast of Mysia, and killed at that time a certain number of heroes, including Thersander, the son of Polynices. But Dionysus struck Telephus with terror and made him fall among the vines where he was wounded by Achilles. The wound did not heal. However, on the advice of the soothsayers, who declared that Troy could not be taken without the help of Telephus, Achilles went back to fetch him and closed the purulent wound by touching it with his spear that was coated with rust. The grateful Telephus showed the Greeks the road to take to approach and conquer Troy.

TELLUS. A Roman divinity that personified the principle of fertility, Tellus promoted the development of the human species and protected harvests. She is portrayed as a woman with numerous breasts and a cult is dedicated to her by the name of *Terra Mater*. As a divinity of Wealth, she is frequently placed in the ranks of the divinities of the Underworld. Later identified with the Greek goddess Gaia, Tellus lost her particular attributes, which were replaced by those of Ceres and Demeter or Cybele. Her male counterpart is Tellumo.

TEMENUS. 1. The son of Pelasgus, it is said that Temenus welcomed the goddess Hera when she was born on the island of Samos and raised her in Arcadia. He then had three temples built in Stymphalus in honor of the goddess. In the first, the goddess was worshiped as a divine infant; in the second, as the wife of Zeus; and in the third, as a widow when she was temporarily separated from the supreme god.

2. Also known by this name is a descendant of Heracles. With his brothers Cresphontes and Aristodemus, and, at the death of the latter, with his nephews Procles and Eurysthenes, he

Paestum, South Italy. Temple of "Neptune" (actually Hera), left, early or middle 5th cent. B.C. "Basilica" (also dedicated to Hera), right, middle 6th cent. B.C. Photo Alison Frantz.

wanted to seize control of the Peloponnesus. But when one of the Heraclidae, Hippotes, killed Carnus, the poet of Acarnania, who had stolen into the Greek camp to sing prophetic verses, the angered gods destroyed the fleet of the Heraclidae in a storm and unleashed a famine on the army. The murderer was banished. On the advice of the Delphic oracle, the Heraclidae chose as the leader of their expedition "a three-eyed being," Oxylus, a man mounted on a one-eyed horse. Temenus was able to disembark on the coast of Elis and shared in the division of the Peloponnesus; he received Argos as his share.

temple. Originally a temple was no more than a cave or grotto in which people worshiped a god who, according to legends, was supposed to have been born there or dwelled there. Later temples were constructed of stones and bricks, and these were used to shelter the treasures of the cities. Finally, and much later, they became the dwelling places of the gods on Earth. The temple comprised two parts: one, the *hieron*, was the sanctuary reserved for worship and sacrifices; the other, the *naos*, was the sacred building where, in darkness and secrecy, the image or statue of the god was kept. This area of the temple was not open to the public because it was feared that the god might be disturbed by sacrilege. Only the priests or priestesses of the gods or goddesses were allowed to enter this enclosed area.

TEREUS. The king of Thrace, this son of Ares dared to use dishonest subterfuges to seduce Philomela, the sister of his wife Procne. He was changed into a vulture while Philomela and Procne were changed into a swallow and a nightingale respectively.

TERMINUS. The antiquity of the cult of this god is emphasized by the fact that the Sabines, the Ligurians and the Etruscans all recognize him as one of their divinities. He marks off the

In a harmoniously folded robe that barely conceals her perfect beauty, Terpsichore, the Muse of dance, plays the lyre. Her face expresses the inspired reflection common to all musicians. Notice the admirable truth of her hands whose fingers seem to dance on the strings of the harp. Greek amphora, British Museum.

boundaries of the fields in a permanent way and, by extension, he also marks off the borders of a State. As Jupiter divides the areas in the heavens, Terminus divides earthly spaces, territory and property. He is, therefore, represented by a single boundary stone. Later, he was given a human head placed on a pyramid-shaped stone; with no arms and legs, he was unable to change places and guaranteed the integrity of the area whose boundaries he marked off.

TERPSICHORE. This muse, portrayed as a vivacious young woman, used her lyre to beat the rhythm of songs and choral dances. Thus, certain Greek authors considered her to be the mother of the Sirens who had, like her, the power to charm those who heard their song.

TETHYS. The daughter of Uranus and Gaia, Tethys occupies one of the very first places among the original divinities of Greece. Her name means "foster mother." She is a symbol of the fertility of the waters. United with Oceanus, she gave birth to the Oceanids and to a multitude of springs which, in a sense, ensured nature of the beneficial moisture it needed to thrive.

TEUCER. **1.** The son of the Phrygian river-god Scamander and the nymph Idaea, this hero left Crete where he was born and headed for the coasts of Asia Minor. He was one of the first mythical kings of Troy, the father of Erichthonius and grandfather of Tros.

2. A second **Teucer** is, according to Homer, the most famous archer among the Greek warriors who took part in the Trojan War. The nephew of Priam by his mother Hesione, he was the half-brother of Ajax the Greater by his father Telamon, and he fought against the Trojans. He challenged the Trojans during numerous combats and played an active role in the capture of Troy by hiding in the wooden horse with other Greek heroes. Upon his return to the territory of his father, the king of Salamis, he was keenly reproached for having failed to prevent Ajax from committing suicide. He was banished and took refuge with Belus, in Syria. With the protection of his host, he settled in Cyprus, where he married Eune, the daughter of Cyprus. Other traditions describe his return to Salamis where he tried in vain to claim the throne to which he was an heir. He later went to Spain where he founded the city of Cartagena.

THALIA.   The Muse of comedy and joyful poetry, Thalia is portrayed as a vivacious young woman, crowned with ivy, clasping a shepherd's crook or a garland in one hand and the grimacing mask of comedy in the other hand.

THAMYRIS.   Hailing from Thrace, the son of Philammon and the nymph Argiope, Thamyris was famous for his vocal and lyrical inventions and was considered, with Orpheus, to be one of the most famous mythical poets of Greece. He had learned music from Linus and, it is said, taught his art to Homer. Several legends are attached to his character. It is said that Thamyris was in love with Hyacinthus and was, therefore, a rival of Apollo's. To eliminate him, the god went to the Muses and told them that the poet had boasted that he was more talented than they. Vexed, the nine divinities stripped Thamyris of his sight and the ability to sing. The unfortunate creature, in despair, broke his lyre and threw it into the waters of the River Balyra (taken to mean, "throw-away-lyre").

THANATOS.   In his tragedy *Alcestis*, Euripides describes this god as the god of Death. It is true that Thanatos lived in the Underworld where he was born of the Night at the same time as his twin brother Hypnos, sleep. Like Orcus, his counterpart in the Roman religion, no particular myth is attributed to him. He is more the messenger of death rather than death itself.

Thalia, the Muse of comedy. According to tradition, she was born in the fields among the shepherds and agrarian divinities. She holds the mask of the theater and a shepherd's crook and wears a crown of ivy. The latter are two symbols that recall the rustic origins of comedy. Vatican Museum, photo Alinari-Giraudon.

THAUMAS.   Like all the primitive divinities, this son of Pontus and Gaia possesses no legend but, owing to his genealogy, belongs to the important branch of divinities of the Sea. He had relations with an Oceanid, Electra, a daughter of Oceanus, who gave birth to the

Harpies and Iris, the beloved messenger of the gods.

THEANO. The daughter of Cisseus, the king of Thrace, Theano was, according to one of the well-known genealogies of the heroes, the sister of Hecuba, the wife of Priam. Married to Antenor, she was placed in charge of the cult of Athena in Troy. Since she received Ulysses and Menelaus kindly when they came to claim Helen, who had been abducted by Paris, she and her husband and children were spared by the Greeks during the massacre that followed the fall of Troy. She later lived in Illyria. However, another legend claims that she was saved because she betrayed her country by handing over to the Greeks the Palladium, the statue of Athena that guaranteed the safety of the city.

THEBES. The capital of Boeotia, Thebes, the most famous city in mythology, was founded by the mythical hero Cadmus. The citadel that was built there was called *Cadmea* in his honor. Later, Zethus and Amphion ruled the city and built new walls: the first transported the stones while the second played the lyre with such skill that he was able to charm the building materials: indeed they arranged themselves according to the plans. According to certain legends, Heracles and Dionysus were born in Thebes. The city later became the scene of two great mythical epics, the expeditions of the Seven Leaders and that of the Epigoni. But it was made famous, above all, by the tragic poets who related the misfortunes of its kings as they submitted to fate: such was the case for Labdacus, Laius, Oedipus, Eteocles and Polynices.

THEIA. One of the very first divinities, Theia is the daughter of Uranus and Gaia. United with Hyperion, she was to give birth to three children of light: Helios, the Sun; Eos, the Dawn; and Selene, the Moon.

THEMIS. The daughter of Uranus and Gaia,

This statue of Themis perfectly expresses the order and justice that this ancient divinity embodies in the world of gods and men: a purely oval face, carefully coiffed hair. Right down to the fold of the robe gathered over her forearm, everything about her recalls the familiar attitude of the orator and lawyer, the champions of law. Colossal statue discovered in Rhamnos, Attica, 3rd cent. B.C., National Archaeological Museum, Athens, photo Ass. Guillaume Bude.

Themis belongs to the generation of primitive gods. She is one of the spouses of Zeus and is the mother of the Horae, the Moirae, the Nymphs of the Eridanus and, according to certain authors, the Hesperides. According to Homer, she is the personification of established order and the ruling laws of justice. Respected by all the gods of Olympus, she attends the deliberations of the gods and men and guarantees, at all times, the equity of decisions. Sometimes defined as a divinity blessed with the gift of prophecy, she established her oracle in Delphi where it succeeded that of Gaia. But Apollo replaced her oracle with his own. She is portrayed with scales and a sword (the two symbols of justice). But, above all, her covered eyes remain the symbol of the impartiality of the sentences she renders.

THERSANDER. By his father Polynices, Thersander was the grandson of Oedipus; he took part in the victorious expedition of the Epigoni against Thebes and the first expedition to Troy. But his ship landed in Mysia and the Greeks took advantage of this to ravage the territory of King Telephus who succeeded in killing Thersander. He married Demonassa, the daughter of Amphiaraus, one of the Seven Leaders. This union gave birth to a son, Tisamenus, who ruled Thebes for a time.

THERSITES. A Greek warrior in the Trojan War, Thersites was known for his ugliness, his cowardice and his evilness. Two versions of his death are known and neither is very favorable. According to the first, he was supposed to have tried to stir up a mutiny and was killed by Ulysses; according to the second, he used his spear to gouge out the eyes of Penthesilea, the queen of the Amazons, who had been mortally wounded by Achilles. Achilles, aghast at such cruelty, shattered the skull of Thersites with his fists.

THESEUS. One of the greatest heroes of Attica, Theseus was considered by the Athenians to be an historical character. It is a fact that he plays a role in most legends, and a laconic proverb circulated in the city of Athens: "Nothing without Theseus." According to the most universally accepted tradition, he was simply the son of Aethra and Aegeus, the king of Athens; but it was also said that his prodigious strength could only have been conferred upon him by a god and that Poseidon was actually his father.

Raised by his mother in the court of his grandfather Pittheus, in Troezen, he knew nothing about the circumstances surrounding his birth. Indeed Aegeus had left Aethra, instructing her to reveal nothing to the child that she was carrying until the child was able to raise a rock under which he had placed his sandals and sword. Theseus, therefore, grew up unaware that he was the son of a king but exhibiting, from a very early age, remarkable courage and presence: when Heracles stopped to rest in the court of Pittheus, he negligently threw the lion's skin he was wearing on the ground; immediately, the servants and entou-

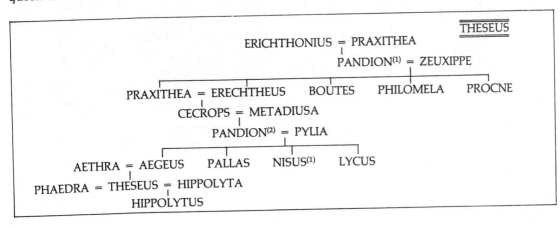

Drawing inspiration from one version of the legend, the artist has portrayed Theseus as the son of Poseidon. The hero has come to greet his father at the bottom of the sea. Greek vase, Bibl. Nat., photo Giraudon.

rage of the king were terrified; only Theseus remained calm and, drawing his sword, he prepared to split the lion in two. When he was sixteen, Aethra took him to the rock; the young hero lifted it up and discovered the two objects hidden there by Aegeus. He decided to join his father immediately. But as the region through which he was obliged to journey was infested with monsters and bandits, his mother and grandfather recommended that he travel by sea. Theseus disregarded this prudent advice and headed to Athens on foot, having decided to prove to all the inhabitants of Attica that he was truly the son of a king. He successively killed Periphetes, Sciron, Sinis, an enormous sow that was ravaging the countryside, Procrustes, Cercyon and, before entering Athens, he was purified of these murders in the waters of the Cephisus. At that time, Athens was still governed by Aegeus but, in fact, the real power was entirely in the hands of the sorceress Me-

dea, who had married the king and inspired his decisions. Medea immediately realized who Theseus was and convinced Aegeus to poison the stranger who threatened to usurp the throne. Welcomed with hypocritical honors, Theseus was able, during a meal, to reveal himself to his father by drawing his sword to cut a piece of meat. Once again a king in all his splendor, because he felt that the perpetuity of power was finally ensured, Aegeus dishonored Medea and banished her from his palace.

However, the Pallantids, the sons of Pallas,

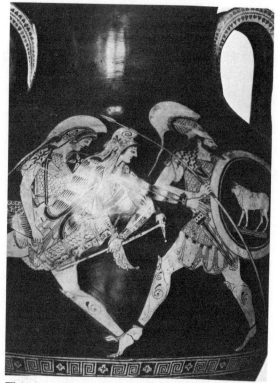

Theseus, recognized by the Cretan bull which he at one time overwhelmed and which adorns his shield, comes with his inseparable companion, Pirithous, to abduct the queen of the Amazons, Antiope. The latter was to marry the hero and bear him a son, the famous Hippolytus. Greek amphora, Louvre, photo Giraudon.

the brother of Aegeus, who had believed that the king would never have any offspring and who hoped to rule Athens one day, conspired to do away with Theseus. The hero succeeded in defeating them and killing all of them. He was banished from the city for these crimes for one year. But Athens was too much in need of Theseus to deliver it from the frightful tribute imposed upon it by King Minos of Crete: seven youths and seven maidens were to be sent, every seven years, to the island to be devoured by the Minotaur. Theseus immediately proposed

Moving in his youth and strength, Theseus crushes the Minotaur by seizing one of his horns and striking him with a club. Roman art, Villa Albani, Rome, photo Anderson-Giraudon.

Theseus carrying off Antiope, Queen of the Amazons. Marble sculpture from the Temple of Apollo at Eretria, Euboea. Late 6th cent. B.C., Archaeological Museum, Chalkis, photo Alison Frantz.

that he deliver his fatherland from this bloody tax and he embarked with the victims. When they arrived in Crete, he seduced Ariadne, one of the daughters of Minos, and the young woman gave him a spool of thread thanks to which the hero was able to find his way in the Labyrinth, where the Minotaur was imprisoned. He beat the sleeping monster to death with his fists. After accomplishing this feat, which brought him the gratitude of all the people of Athens, Theseus abducted Ariadne and headed back to Athens. On his way back, he abandoned her on the island of Naxos, doubtless on the order of Dionysus who wanted to marry the young woman. Saddened by this separation, but proud of his exploits, Theseus forgot to hoist up the white sail as his father had instructed him upon his departure. Scanning the horizon, Aegeus saw the ship's black sails and believed that his son had perished; in despair, he threw himself into the sea.

When he became king, Theseus played an enormous and benevolent political role. By consolidating the various villages, he ensured the unity of the city. He inaugurated great festivals: the Panathenaea and the Isthmian games in honor of Poseidon. He established a stable government and promulgated social laws that did not further the interests of the rich and the nobility. But his days of valor were not over yet. In the company of Pirithous, the king of the Lapiths, one of his most faithful friends, he accompanied the Argonauts in the search for the Golden Fleece, took part in the Calydonian Boar Hunt, and offered his ingenuity to the Seven Leaders, helping Adrastus recover the bodies of the heroes who died in Thebes. This humanity of the hero is seen in the benevolent hospitality he granted Oedipus when he was banished from his country. But, of all his adventures, the most famous is the one in which he was pitted against the Amazons. He succeeded in abducting their queen, Antiope (Hippolyta), despite the attack on Athens that was mounted by those cruel women warriors. His union with Antiope gave birth to Hippolytus. After the death of Antiope, Theseus married Phaedra, who bore him two sons, Acamas and Demophon.

With Pirithous, he headed for the kingdom of Shadows in order to abduct Persephone. Meanwhile on Earth, in the city that was abandoned by its king, intrigues abounded; the nobility was irritated by the democratic reforms that Theseus had instituted in the city; they enlisted the services of the Dioscuri, who hastened to free their sister Helen, abducted by Theseus and held captive by Aethra, and then placed Menestheus on the throne of Athens. During this time, Theseus and Pirithous were welcomed in the Underworld by Hades and Persephone with feigned hospitality and they were invited to feast at the table of the rulers of the Underworld. They were unable to rise from their seat, known as the "Chair of Forgetfulness," because they had lost their memories. Pirithous was to remain there eternally while Theseus, after many long months of waiting, was freed by Heracles. But the state in which he found his kingdom after such a long absence drove him into exile and he retired to Scyros to the court of King Lycomedes who, after feigning friendship, betrayed him and assassinated him. Once, however, Theseus left the realm of mythology to enter that of history: the Athenians contended that they had seen him during the battle of Marathon (490 B.C.). After their victory the Athenians were ordered to give Theseus a proper burial in Athens: the Athenian general Cimon conquered the island of Scyros and observed an eagle scratching at the soil; buried under this spot were the ashes of Theseus, which were thus returned to Athens.

THESPIUS. The son of Erechtheus and the eponymous sovereign of the Thespians in Boeotia, Thespius welcomed Heracles to his court after the hero killed the lion of Cithaeron. This king had fifty daughters. With his help, Heracles had relations for fifty nights, or in a single night, with each of these daughters and begat numerous children. Seven of them stayed in Thespia, two were sent to Thebes, and the others, under the leadership of Iolaus, went to Sardinia where they founded a colony.

THETIS. The daughter of Nereus and Doris, Thetis is without a doubt the most famous Nereid. She was known from a very early age for her gentleness and her sense of hospitality. She welcomed Hephaestus when he was thrown from the top of Olympus by the angered Zeus. She would not agree to marry Zeus because she did not want to hurt Hera who had been her foster mother. But it is also said in connection with this that Poseidon and Zeus abandoned Thetis when they learned from Themis that the Nereid would give birth to a son who would be more powerful than his father. Peleus, a mortal, was thus able to marry the sea divinity who, to escape him, had assumed all possible forms but had finally submitted to him. The wedding of Thetis and Peleus was graced by the presence of all the gods who came bearing gifts. But the goddess Discord, who had not been invited, threw into the gathering the famous apple which gave rise to numerous evils. The union of Peleus and Thetis gave birth to the great Achilles whom Thetis raised lovingly. To make him invulnerable to all wounds, she dipped him into the River Styx. As she held him by the heel, that was his only vulnerable spot. She sought to protect him from the Trojan War and hid him in the court of Lycomedes, the king of Scyros. She also wanted to protect him from mortal blows by giving him armor forged by Hephaestus. She advised him not to fight, but in vain. When her son died, she showered all of her affection on Neoptolemus, her grandson, and saved his life by requesting that he not return home immediately after the fall of Troy. Thus, Neoptolemus escaped the great storm that destroyed the Greek fleet.

THISBE. A beautiful Babylonian maiden, Thisbe was loved by Pyramus. She killed herself in despair at the death of her lover.

THOAS. **1.** This son of Dionysus and Ariadne was the king of the island of Lemnos and was married to Myrina who bore him a daughter, Hypsipyle. When the Lemnian women decided to kill all the Lemnian men, who had deserted them because of a curse from

Thetis, who fears so for the life of her son Achilles, goes to Vulcan to check the quality of the weapons she is to give the hero. At left, one of the Cyclopes finishes the helmet while Vulcan holds up the shield that is polished so perfectly that Thetis can see her reflection. Fresco from Pompeii, National Archaeological Museum, Naples, photo Anderson-Giraudon.

Aphrodite, Thoas was saved by his daughter and was able to flee, depending on the version, to Sikinos in the Cyclades or to Tauris. In the latter case, his legend is often identified with that of Thoas, the king of Tauris, where Iphigenia, the main priestess, sacrificed to the goddess Artemis all strangers who ventured into the country. Thanks to Iphigenia, Orestes and Pylades were not sacrificed and were able to flee and Thoas, who had set out to pursue them, was killed.

2. Another **Thoas** was the son of Jason and Hypsipyle and the grandson of the preceding.

3. The legend of the Trojan War has retained the name of a **Thoas**, the king of Calydon, who went to Troy with forty vessels and was part of the contingent of heroes that hid in the wooden horse.

4. Legend speaks of yet another **Thoas**, a king of Corinth and grandson of Sisyphus, who succeeded his father Ornytion, while his brother Phocus emigrated to the country that was subsequently known as *Phocis*.

thunder. The basic symbol of Zeus, thunder, represented by three parallel rays, was considered to be one of the sacred manifestations of the god. It was his word and his will of presence. The place where it had fallen became a place of worship and thunderstruck corpses were merely covered with earth. It was almost as though they were marked, henceforth, with a mysterious sign that the priests, who specialized in the art of "lightning," were to interpret for the majority of mortals.

THYESTES. The son of Pelops and Hippodameia, Thyestes made his mark in legend owing to the hatred that pitted him against his brother Atreus. Both assassinated their half-brother Chrysippus and were banished by their father for this crime. Having found asylum in the court of Sthenelus, the king of Mycenae, they fought fiercely over power. Thyestes seduced Aërope, the wife of Atreus. When Atreus was proclaimed king, he feigned reconciliation and invited Thyestes to a banquet: he served him his two children. Horrified, Thyestes damned his brother and all his descendants.

THYIA. The daughter of Castalius, the priest of Dionysus, or of the river-god Cephisus, Thyia was, it is said, loved by Apollo and gave birth to Delphus, the eponymous hero of Delphi. It is also said that she was the first woman to offer a sacrifice to the cult of Dionysus, and she introduced the festival which, each year on Mount Parnassus, was celebrated by the Maenads, who were called, on this occasion, the "Thyiades."

THYONE. This name was given to Semele when her son Dionysus descended to the Underworld to fetch her and transport her to Olympus, where she was included in the ranks of the immortals.

TIBER. A river in Italy that crosses Rome, the Tiber at one time was called Albula. He acquired his name in memory of Tiberinus, the king of Alba Longa, who drowned in his waters. A river-god with a green beard and the features of a good-natured old man, he was worshiped especially among the inhabitants of Rome since he had once saved the lives of Romulus and Remus when they were abandoned in a basket in his waters. The Tiber also appears in the legend of Aeneas. He revealed himself in a dream to the Trojan hero and advised him to sail upstream to the court of King Evander who was governing the modest city of Rome. Finally, the Tiber had by the prophetess Manto a son, Bianor, who founded the city of Mantua, where he became the first king.

TIRESIAS. With Calchas, Tiresias is one of the most famous soothsayers in Greek mythology. Born of the nymph Chariclo, he acquired his gift of prophecy in extraordinary circumstances. One day, he met two serpents that were mating and killed them. He was immediately changed into a woman. Seven years later, he again met two entwined serpents and recovered his original form. Since he had been both a man and a woman during his lifetime, he was chosen as a valuable mediator by Zeus and Hera who were arguing over who, male or female, obtained more pleasure from sexual intercourse. As his response did not please the goddess (he said the female received ten times more than the male), Tiresias was stricken blind; in compensation, Zeus granted him a life that was seven times longer than the normal life span and gave him the ability to predict the future. An advisor to the people of Thebes, Tiresias revealed to Oedipus his involuntary in-

The Tiber is portrayed with the features of a kindly old man. In one hand he holds an oar, the symbol of the seafarers who pass through his waters and trade on his banks; in the other hand, he clasps the traditional horn of plenty, a symbol of the fertile power of his waters. Against his side can be seen the wolf that suckled Romulus and Remus, the twin founders of Rome whom the Tiber refused to drown. Roman art, Louvre, photo Giraudon.

cest; predicted the war of the Seven Leaders; declared that Thebes would obtain victory if Menoeceus, the son of Creon, agreed to be sacrificed; finally, he advised the Epigoni to conclude an armistice and to flee the city; he left with them. En route, he stopped to quench his thirst in the Tephusa and, as the waters of the spring were frozen, he died. He left behind a daughter, the prophetess Manto. However, Tiresias did not lose his talents in the Underworld; he advised Ulysses as to the best ways to return to his fatherland safe and sound. His long life enabled him to be part of numerous legends, many of which were quite far removed from one another in mythical time.

TISAMENUS. 1. The son of Orestes and Hermione, Tisamenus, the king of Sparta, was banished from his home by the Heraclidae and killed, it is said, during the struggles that ensued. However, other traditions contend that he escaped safely and that he was able to leave his kingdom and find refuge on the Ionian coast. But his sons seized the territory in which he perished and named it Achaia. Cometes, his eldest son, emigrated to Asia.

2. Also known by the name of **Tisamenus** was the son of Thersander and Demonassa. When his father was killed by Telephus, Tisamenus was still too young to take control of the Boeotians in Mysia during the Trojan War and

Protected in vain by his foster mother, the Earth, the giant Tityus, who tried to rape Leto, is felled by the arrows of Apollo, who is avenging his mother. Notice the contrast between the god and the giant, one sovereign and carefully clad, the other with his bushy beard and his back covered with the hide of an animal: this contrast is a constant symbol in mythology of the struggle between the forces of light and the somber forces created by the Earth. Greek krater, Louvre, photo Giraudon.

he temporarily yielded his position to Peneleus, another Boeotian hero. When he reached manhood, Tisamenus acceded to the throne of Thebes.

TITANIDS. This name is used to designate the daughters of Uranus and Gaia: Tethys, Theia, Themis, Mnemosyne, Rhea and Phoebe. United with their brothers, they gave birth to myriad divinities.

TITANS. The sons and daughters of Uranus and Gaia dwelled in the heavens. They numbered twelve: six sons, Oceanus, Coeus, Crius, Hyperion, Iapetus, Cronus; and six daughters, Tethys, Theia, Themis, Mnemosyne, Phoebe and Rhea, who were referred to as the *Titanids.* Indignant that Uranus wanted to throw them into Tartarus, they revolted, mutilating their father and seizing power. The last of them, Cronus, devoured his children because he feared they would dethrone him. But his youngest son, Zeus, miraculously escaped this series of infanticides, and gave him a drink that made him vomit up his brothers and sisters. With their help, Zeus waged war on the Titans who were armed with gigantic rocks that had been torn from the mountains and were positioned on Mount Othrys, while the children of Cronus set up their line on Mount Olympus. The struggle, known as the Titanomachia, was frightful. But Zeus managed to ensure victory with the help of the Cyclopes, who fashioned lightning, and the Hecatoncheiroi; the vanquished Titans were thrown into the depths of Tartarus. However, victory was not complete. Some of the Titans, such as Mnemosyne and Iapetus, had rallied to the cause of Zeus; but other monsters, such as the Giants and Typhon, prepared to mount an attack on Olympus.

Various interpretations are given to this combat. It seems that Thessaly had, in a very remote time, been subjected to geological upset, the terrible effects of which were related by surviving witnesses. Tradition subsequently took over these tales and constructed myths around them.

TITHONUS. The son of Laomedon, legendary king of Troy, and older brother of Priam, Tithonus was also the son of Strymo, the daughter of the river-god Scamander. His beauty was noticed by Eos, the Dawn, who was smitten with him and abducted him. Of this union, two sons were born, Memnon and Emathion. Now, while Eos retained an eternal freshness, Tithonus, the mortal, began to age and gradually his hair grew white. Eos requested that Zeus grant her husband immortality: however, she inadvertently neglected to request that his youth be restored as well. Tithonus did not die but old age continued to weigh on him. He dried up and begun to shrink: the grieving Eos changed her husband into a cicada. He remains the symbol of decrepitude.

TITYUS. This giant, the son of Zeus and Elara (the daughter of the king of Orchomenus), was born in the belly of the earth where the god had hidden his lover to shield her from the jealousy of Hera. Because he pursued Leto and tried to rape her, Tityus was stricken down by Zeus or, according to another version, was killed by the arrows of Apollo and Artemis, who thus avenged their mother. The gods threw him into Tartarus: there his body covered nine acres and two vultures gnawed constantly at his liver, the organ considered by the Ancients to be the center of brutal desires and the will to power.

TLEPOLEMUS. The son of Heracles and Astyoche, Tlepolemus took part in the expedition that was to ensure the Heraclidae sovereignty over all of Peloponnesus. Argos went to Tlepolemus in the division; but the hero one day inadvertently killed his great-uncle Licymnius by striking him with a stick that was intended for one of his slaves; he was banished from the city of Argos. He took refuge on the island of Rhodes, where he became king, and married Polyxo. Then, as he had been one of the suitors for Helen, he mobilized a small fleet of nine vessels and headed for Troy. He was killed in a battle against Sarpedon; his companions, at the end of the struggle, settled in the Iberian islands while Polyxo took revenge on Helen for the death of her husband.

trees. The symbol of vegetation, of which it is the most powerful and majestic representation, the tree played a role of primary importance in legends. It provides a home for the Hamadryads who, in a sort of symbiosis, live and die with it. Trees are the incarnation and representation of certain gods; thus Zeus resides in the oaks of Dodona and breathes life into the leaves that deliver his oracles. The laurel tree is the tree of Apollo; the myrrh, the tree of Aphrodite; the olive tree, the tree of Athena. Finally, countless divinities or heroes and heroines in myths and legends were changed into trees because the gods took pity on them or because they incurred the gods' wrath.

TRIPTOLEMUS. The son of Celeus, the king of Eleusis, and of Metaneira, or, according to

The divine incarnation of grains of wheat, so necessary to the survival of ancient civilizations, the young Triptolemus is protected, at left, by Core-Persephone, the goddess of Shadows where wheat germinates and, at right, by Demeter, the goddess of Harvests. Low relief from Eleusis, 5th cent. B.C., National Archaeological Museum, Athens, photo Alinari-Giraudon.

other traditions, the son of Oceanus and Gaia, Triptolemus was a favorite of Demeter's because the goddess had received the hospitality of Celeus when she left Olympus after the abduction of her daughter Core-Persephone. As a sign of her gratitude, she had first wanted to grant immortality to Demophon, the younger brother of Triptolemus, but Metaneira was frightened by her mysterious practices and startled Demeter, causing her to drop the child into the purifying fire. In compensation, Demeter bestowed her affection on Triptolemus; she taught him agriculture and gave him a chariot drawn by dragons in which Triptolemus roamed the earth, sowing grain. He sometimes encountered difficulties in his mission: King Lyncus, of Scythia, to whom he wanted to teach the art of cultivation, tried to take his life. In Patras, the son of King Eumelus stole the hero's chariot but was killed.

Associated with Demeter and Persephone in a sort of trinity of fertility, Triptolemus was also considered to have founded the mysteries of Eleusis and introduced the cult of Demeter in the city. Artists have portrayed him with the features of a young man wearing a petasus, with a scepter in one hand and a head of wheat

Among the dolphins that represent the aquatic medium, Triton appears as an enormous fish with the upper torso of a man and the head of an old man. Tyrrhenian amphora, Berlin Museum, photo Larousse.

in the other, two symbols of his sovereignty over the fertility of Nature.

TRITON. This god, not native to Greece originally, was adored by seamen and subsequently received a cult and a legend. The entire sea was his abode because he had been born of the union of the Nereid Amphitrite and of the god of all oceans, Poseidon. He has various appearances but is generally portrayed as a man whose body ends in two enormous fish tails. Both kindly and terrible, he blows into an enormous sea conch which bellows during storms. Seafarers worshiped him especially as a god who calms the raging waves and as an intermediary between them and Poseidon. He showed the Argonauts the proper route, called the waters of the Deluge back to him, and calmed the storm unleashed by Juno against the Trojan Aeneas.

TROILUS. The son of Priam and Hecuba, Troilus was considered to have been begotten by Apollo. As an oracle had predicted that Troy would not fall to the Greeks if Troilus reached the age of twenty, Achilles killed the Trojan hero to thwart the prediction. However, the circumstances of his death differ according to the various versions. The best-known version contends that Achilles, in love, requested that Troilus succumb to his advances. Troilus fled and took refuge in the sanctuary of Thymbraean Apollo. The angered Achilles transgressed sacred laws and was supposed to have killed the Trojan on the altar of the god.

Trojan horse. After ten years of battle, the Greeks had still not succeeded in seizing Troy. The seer Prylis, or Calchas according to another version, and perhaps even Ulysses, advised Agamemnon to build a wooden horse. The king assigned the task to Epeius and Panopeus. They fashioned a hollow horse where Demophon, Menelaus, Ulysses and many other warriors hid, completely armed. The Greeks aban-

The Greeks have brought the famous wooden horse into Troy. Warriors are jumping from the doors and vanquishing the Trojans. Drawing from a painting on a Greek vase, photo Giraudon.

doned this ploy on the beach in Troy and pretended they were lifting the siege. In the city, the Trojans tried to decide on a course of action. Some, like the prophetess Cassandra, condemned by the gods never to be believed, contended that the horse was a stratagem and that under no circumstances should it be allowed in the city under the pretext of offering it to the gods. The priest Laocoon adopted the same point of view and even went so far as to hurl a spear at the imitation animal to prove from the sound that it was hollow. As it happened, shortly afterwards Laocoon was strangled by serpents, so the Trojans thought that they had committed a sacrilege and brought the wooden horse into the city. Under cover of darkness, the Greek warriors jumped from the horse and invaded the city, which they eventually captured.

TROPHONIUS. Born of the love of Apollo and Epicaste, the architect Trophonius was swallowed up into the belly of the earth after killing his father-in-law Agamedes. However, honored after his death, he was entitled to an oracle in Boeotia. The inquirers purified themselves in the waters of the River Hercyne and offered sacrifices to the genius of Trophonius, represented by the Chthonian symbol par excellence, the serpent, and to Demeter, his foster mother.

TROS. The grandson of Dardanus and son of Erichthonius and Astyoche, Tros was one of the founders of the city of Troy, to which he gave his name; subsequently, he acquired sovereignty over all of the Troad. The husband of Callirhoë, daughter of the river-god Scamander, he became the father of a daughter, Cleopatra, and of three sons, Ilus, Assaracus and Ganymede, the youngest, whom he offered to Zeus in exchange for two fleet-footed steeds given to him by the god.

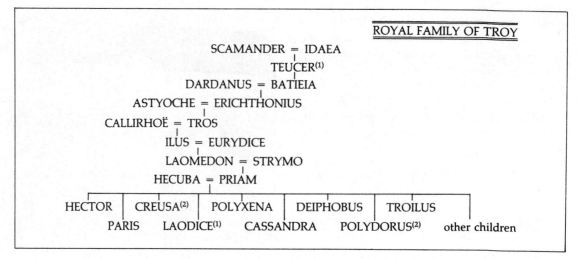

ROYAL FAMILY OF TROY

SCAMANDER = IDAEA
|
TEUCER[1]
|
DARDANUS = BATIEIA
|
ASTYOCHE = ERICHTHONIUS
|
CALLIRHOË = TROS
|
ILUS = EURYDICE
|
LAOMEDON = STRYMO
|
HECUBA = PRIAM
|
| HECTOR | CREUSA[2] | POLYXENA | DEIPHOBUS | TROILUS |
| PARIS | LAODICE[1] | CASSANDRA | POLYDORUS[2] | other children |

TROY. The capital of the Troad, a territory located at the entrance to the Hellespont on the coast of Asia Minor, Troy is extolled by Homer throughout the *Iliad*. There are various versions of its legendary origin. However, the most common tradition contends that the city was founded by Ilus, the son of Tros, and that, in honor of the two heroes, it took the name of Ilion and later Troy. The last king of the city was Priam, the son of Laomedon. It was during his reign that the Greeks besieged the city for ten years, burning and pillaging it until it was totally destroyed. From the 19th century on, scholars and archaeologists have been engaged in digs on the hill of Hissarlik in an attempt to prove the historical reality of the existence of Troy. Also found were the superimposed remains of nine cities. Layer VII A was thought to correspond to the city of Priam where traces of fire were detected. Today, people no longer contest the fact that, at the end of the 13th century B.C., a conflict took place between Greek invaders and the natives of the Troad. The city was supposed to have been ultimately destroyed by an earthquake.

TURNUS. King of the Rutuli, son of Daunus and the nymph Venilia, Turnus bore arms against Aeneas; indeed he quarreled with him over the hand of Lavinia, the daughter of King Latinus. He perished at the hand of the Trojan hero.

TYCHE. The divinity Tyche may be compared with the Roman Fortuna. Like Fortuna, Tyche symbolizes the benevolent or malevolent chance of human destinies. To attract her protection, all cities constructed a temple in her honor and erected a statue which generally depicted her as an imposing woman wearing a mural crown and surrounded by various symbols (horn of plenty, wheel or rudder) which all turned toward uncertain destinies, both favorable and unfavorable. In Roman Imperial times a combined figure of Isis and Tyche developed, called Isityche.

TYDEUS. The son of Oeneus, the king of Calydon in Aetolia, and half-brother of Meleager, Tydeus committed a murder during his youth and was banished from his homeland. He went to King Adrastus in Argos who purified him and gave him the hand of his daughter Deipyle, while he gave the hand of another daughter to Polynices, who had been banished from Thebes. The two sons-in-law of Adrastus headed for Thebes and together they took part in the famous battle of the Seven Leaders. To show his strength, Tydeus decided to challenge the most valiant Thebans to single combat; he always had the advantage. However, after many conquests, he was mortally wounded by Melanippus, who also succumbed. Athena, who had protected Tydeus, decided to grant him immortality when Amphiaraus presented the dying Tydeus with the skull of Melanippus: Tydeus opened it and swallowed the brain. Revolted by this show of savagery, Athena abandoned the hero to death.

TYNDAREOS. According to the most common tradition, Tyndareos was the son of Oebalus and Gorgophone; the latter was born of the union of Perseus and Andromeda. At the death of his father, Hippocoon seized control of the kingdom of Sparta and banished his brothers Icarius and Tyndareos. Tyndareos took refuge with King Thestius in Aetolia, whose daughter Leda he married. He was subsequently able to recover his kingdom with the help of Heracles. The fame of Tyndareos is due to his progeny, the Tyndarids, among whom were the Dioscuri, Helen, Clytemnestra, and mention may also be made of his connection with Zeus who had relations with Leda in the form of a swan. Menelaus became his son-in-law by marrying Helen, and he succeeded Tyndareos on the throne of Sparta. The king's demise remains a mystery. It is said that he was one of the Greeks who were revived by Asclepius and deified.

TYPHON. In order to avenge her grandchildren, the Titans, who were imprisoned in the Underworld on the order of Zeus, their conqueror, Gaia gave birth to a frightful monster, whose body was covered with scales, and whose one hundred mouths vomited flames. There followed the ultimate battle between the heavens and Earth, between the gods of Light

An episode in the war of the Seven Leaders: Tydeus, one of the allies of Polynices, kills Ismene, the sister of Eteocles, who is lying in the company of her lover, Theoclymenus. Photo Giraudon.

and the dark elements created in the belly of the Earth. Finally vanquished, Typhon, the last anarchical force that arose against the law and order of Zeus and the Olympians, was thrown into the depths of the Underworld: there he joined the Titans. However, he had had just enough time to have relations with Echidna. She immediately gave birth to a series of monsters, one more frightful than the next: Cerberus, the Hydra of Lerna, Chimaera, the Sphinx, the Harpies and most of the evil-minded divinities of the nether regions. Another tradition contends that Hera, and not Gaia, was his mother, and that Hera had wanted to take revenge on Zeus who, without her help, had begotten Athena. After many turbulent pursuits, Typhon was finally stricken down by Zeus and buried under Mount Aetna, through whose crater he continues to spit up his flames.

TYRO. The daughter of Salmoneus and Alcidice, Tyro was abducted by her uncle Cre-

U

ULYSSES (ODYSSEUS).

ULYSSES (ODYSSEUS). The most famous Greek hero of Antiquity, along with Heracles, Ulysses was born on the island of Ithaca, where his father Laertes, the spouse of Anticlea, was king. Later traditions claim that Sisyphus, who was visiting the island, had relations with Anticlea, the fiancée of Laertes, and thus begat Ulysses. Through his mother, Ulysses was a descendant of Autolycus, the son of Hermes. The hero was, therefore, of divine blood. In his infancy and in his youth, Ulysses took numerous trips and, in particular, went to the kingdom of his ancestor Autolycus, who invited him to take part in a boar hunt on Mount Parnassus. Wounded by one of the animal's tusks, Ulysses had on one of his knees a scar which, years later, enabled his former nurse to recognize him. Later received in the court of Iphitus, he acquired the precious bow of Eurytus, which shot unstoppable arrows. When he reached adulthood, he replaced his aged father on the throne of Ithaca and began to seek a wife. Like many other Greek heroes, he set his heart on Helen, the daughter of King Tyndareos, whose beauty and grace were well known throughout the country. He skillfully made all the suitors swear to avenge any outrage that might one day be committed against Helen's future spouse or Helen herself, thinking that he would win the favor of Tyndareos this way.

When the young woman chose Menelaus, the king of Sparta, Ulysses received in consolation Penelope, the daughter of King Icarius. This union gave birth to a single son, Telemachus.

Shortly after the birth of Telemachus, Helen was abducted by Paris, the son of Priam, the king of Troy. Menelaus immediately rallied his wife's former suitors and reminded them of their oath, beseeching them to honor it; the heroes agreed to keep their promise and joined together to mobilize an army so that they might send an expedition to punish Troy. Ulysses, a peace-loving soul, feigned madness to avoid joining the ranks of the Greek army. He worked the sand of the sea and sowed salt. But Palamedes, who came to fetch him to try to persuade him to leave with him, placed the young Telemachus in front of the plow. Ulysses immediately raised the blade of the tool and turned his oxen, showing that he was indeed in control of his senses; he was thus obliged to leave the fatherland that was so very dear to him. He was sent to Troy by Menelaus as part of a delegation whose task it was to claim Helen back peaceably. But his mission proved fruitless. However, he did succeed in persuading Achilles, who had taken refuge among the daughters of King Lycomedes in Scyros, to joint the Greeks because an oracle had predicted that the help of this hero was indispens-

Looking fierce and resolved, Ulysses holds the dagger and spear which helped him to emerge safely from many dangerous adventures. He wears a short tunic and the hat of a traveler, the symbols of his destiny which dictated that he would wander for twenty years. Greek vase, Louvre, photo Giraudon.

able if the Greeks were to be assured of victory. At the head of a fleet of twelve vessels, Ulysses landed in Troy and exhibited remarkable courage, killing numerous Trojan heroes. However, under all circumstances he was able to keep his wits about him. In the course of the war, Ulysses proved himself to be a wise and able diplomat, seeking to maintain unity among the Greeks at any price, using persuasion, speeches, secret missions, espionage and trickery. Thus, with his inseparable companion Diomedes, he was able to steal into the city and seize the Palladium, the statue that protected the city. Another time, he succeeded in stealing the steeds of Rhesus before they had drunk from the Xanthus (Scamander), which, according to a prophecy, would have given them the

supernatural force necessary to assure a Trojan victory. He was also able, with the intended silence of Hecuba, to enter the palace of the king of Troy and incite Helen to betray the Trojans. However, even with time, Ulysses never forgave Palamedes who had forced him to leave his homeland, Penelope and his son. Therefore, he accused Palamedes of treason, contending that the hero was corresponding secretly with the Trojans and receiving money in return. Indeed money and letters were found which had been forged by Ulysses and placed in the tent of Palamedes to bring about his destruction. Palamedes was stoned to death by the angered Greeks. Ulysses later took part in many other episodes of the Trojan War; at the death of Achilles, he was awarded the weapons of the hero after having quarreled over them with Ajax, and he was one of the Greeks who hid in the hollow flanks of the Trojan horse. Once the city was taken and sacked, Ulysses

This low relief reproduces the most famous episode of the Odyssey. While his companions, with their ears plugged up with wax, row in rhythm, Ulysses, attached to the ship's mast, listens to the song of the Sirens. His face reflects an almost mad passion; one of his fists is clenched, his body is bent forward as though drawn by the smooth melodies of the enchanting monsters. He tries in vain to break his bonds. Terra-cotta from Myrina, Louvre, photo Giraudon.

```
                                                                    ULYSSES
AEOLUS⁽²⁾
    |
  DEION = DIOMEDES
       |
     CEPHALUS
          |
        ACRISIUS = CHALCOMEDUSA        HERMES = CHIONE
                |                              |
            LAERTES = ANTICLEA ———————— AUTOLYCUS = AMPHITHEA
                   |
        CIRCE = ULYSSES = PENELOPE
            |              |
      several children  TELEMACHUS
    including TELEGONUS
```

received Hecuba, the widow of Priam, and was said to have thrown the first stone when the poor woman was stoned for having killed King Polymestor.

After the *Iliad,* Homer describes in the *Odyssey* the long and turbulent return of Ulysses to his homeland and the adventures and perils the hero encountered. He left ruined Troy and sacked the land of the Ciconi for their alliance with the Trojans, then, constantly assailed by conflicting winds and capricious waves, he landed in Libya among the Lotophagi who fed on lotus, the plant that stimulated complete forgetfulness. Ulysses had great difficulty tearing his companions away from this land of perdition and finally set sail for Sicily, the land of the Cyclopes. One of these one-eyed monsters, Polyphemus, devoured six of his companions but the hero succeeded in gouging out his eye and escaping, with great difficulty, with the rest of his seafaring companions. Poseidon, who was the father of Polyphemus, decided to avenge his son and unleashed monstrous storms to lead the ships of Ulysses to ruin. When he landed in the north of Sicily, Ulysses was welcomed hospitably by King Aeolus, who gave him a goatskin bottle that contained all the winds for which he was responsible. The companions of Ulysses thought they contained treasures; they opened them and let loose the most dreadful storm that man had ever seen. The ship of the unfortunate seamen landed not far from the island of the Laestrygonians, a group of cannibals whom Ulysses was able to escape but not before the king of this people, Antiphates, had devoured one of his companions and destroyed all but one of his ships. The hero finally dropped anchor on the island of Aeaea, where he was received by Circe, who changed all of the sailors into swine; but soon the enchantress restored their original form. Ulysses remained for a few months in the company of Circe, who bore him a son, Telegonus. The hero later landed in the land of the Cimmerians, in the regions where the Ocean flows, marking off the limits of the Earth, and entered Hades in order to consult the soothsayer Tiresias on the best route back to Ithaca. The soothsayer predicted that he would arrive home alone and stripped of everything; he also foretold that he would kill all of Penelope's suitors. After having encountered the souls of the great heroes who had died as well as the shadow of his mother Anticlea, Ulysses left the Underworld and set sail once again. He avoided the Sirens by plugging up the ears of his companions with wax and fastening himself to the mainmast. Then his vessel was able to pass by

Charybdis and Scylla. Approaching the coasts of the island of Trinacria (Sicily), the famished sailors made the mistake of devouring the sacred oxen of Helios. Zeus struck down the impious creatures and destroyed the ships in a storm. Only Ulysses was spared and managed to land on a float of logs on the island of Ogygia, where the smitten nymph Calypso held him captive for eight years until, on the order of the gods, she freed Ulysses. He left on the sea, again assailed by storms, and the sea finally threw him up, naked and exhausted, on the shores of the island of the Phaeacians. Nausicaa, the daughter of Alcinous, the king of the island, discovered him. Washed, revived, he was finally able to set sail, for the last time, in a ship that had been lent to him by his host. He finally dropped anchor on the coast of the island of Ithaca, after twenty years' absence. Disguised as a beggar, he went to Eumaeus, his swineherd, and identified himself, then found his son, Telemachus, and went to his palace, which had been occupied by the suitors who were saying that Ulysses was dead and were urging Penelope to choose one of them as her husband. He had a quarrel with Irus, a beggar who sided with the suitors, and felled him; then he went to find Penelope and, without identifying himself, joyfully welcomed her suggestion that she marry the one who was able to draw the bow of Ulysses. Not one of the men succeeded; only Ulysses could bend the bow. With the help of Telemachus, he massacred the suitors and the servants who had prostituted themselves. Then he revealed his identity to Penelope. Thanks to Athena, the parents of the massacred suitors, who had taken up arms and had wanted to avenge these deaths, were appeased and tranquility was finally restored to the kingdom of Ithaca. According to other versions, Ulysses was supposed to have been killed some time after by Telegonus, who was unaware that Ulysses was his father. He pierced him with a spear that was made of the barb of a stingray, thus fulfilling a prophecy that the hero would perish at the hand of his son and by the sea. Wily, skilled and ingenious, capable of avoiding all danger through his courage and eloquence, a marvelous tamer of stormy seas, Ulysses was the typical hero in which all Greeks loved to see themselves.

Underworld. In Antiquity, this name referred to the place where souls went to dwell after death. However, over the centuries, the idea of the Underworld developed along with philosophical doctrines on the immortality of the soul and on the punishments or rewards granted in the hereafter. Originally, souls dwelled in Erebus, in a sort of obscure world where everything began and everything ended. However, certain privileged heroes found a new life on the bounds of the Earth, particularly in Thrace or in the land of Scythia among the Hyperboreans, or else on the island of Leuce, the White Island where Achilles went after his death with his companions to bask in eternal happiness, enjoying his favorite pleasures. Sometimes these unknown countries, that no one ever reached, are described as somber, foggy places that are cold and lonely and where the Cimmerians lived.

Literary descriptions of the Underworld became even more numerous and more precise and soon the ancients divided the Underworld into the dwelling place of the good and the dwelling place of the evil. In the latter region, which was guarded by Cerberus, flowed the poisoned rivers Acheron, Pyriphlegethon, Cocytus and Styx. It was the domain of Tartarus where souls, led by the ferryman Charon, came to bear indescribable suffering in punishment for their crimes committed on Earth: among the most famous of the damned were Tityus, Tantalus and Sisyphus. On the other hand, the Elysian Fields welcomed the souls of the just in bliss, harmony and peace amidst festivities, dancing, perfumes and enchanted countrysides. The kingdom of the population of souls, the Underworld was governed by Hades and his wife Persephone (Pluto and Proserpina for the Latins). These two divinities were surrounded by a certain number of servants, among whom were the Erinyes, the Furies, the Gorgons, the Harpies, Thanatos and the three judges of the Tribunal—Minos, Aeacus and Rhadamanthys—who assigned to each soul, on the basis of its merits or faults, the damned abode of Tartarus or the blest abode of Elysium.

URANIA. The muse of astronomy, Urania ordinarily holds in her left hand a celestial sphere on which she indicates, with the help of a compass, the respective positions and revolutions of the stars.

URANUS. This god, who was both the son and the spouse of Gaia, is the most ancient of the Greek divinities. He had numerous children (the Titans, the Cyclopes, the Hecatoncheiroi), but he detested his children so much that at their birth he had them imprisoned in the depths of the Underworld in Tartarus. He reaped the hatred he had sown: his young son, Cronus, with the help of his siblings and his mother, Gaia, who provided him with a sickle, castrated him and dethroned him.

Urania, the Muse of astronomy, uses a compass to inscribe the course of the stars on a celestial globe. Ancient statue, Vatican Museum, photo Anderson-Giraudon.

V

VEIOVIS. This ancient Italic divinity is considered to be the opposite of Jupiter, god of the sky; this god is, therefore, invoked, at the same time as Pluto, as one of the masters of the Underworld. He presides over earthquakes and volcanic eruptions. At a later era, after the Hellenization of the Roman Pantheon, he was identified with Apollo and portrayed as a young god, armed with arrows.

VENUS. An ancient Italic divinity of little importance, Venus originally protected kitchen gardens, ensuring the fertility of the flowers and the ripening of plants. From the 2nd century B.C. on, she was identified with the Greek goddess Aphrodite, whose characteristics, legends and attributes she assumed: she acquired noteworthy authority in Roman worship. During the 1st century, Caesar, who claimed that his family, the Julia family, was part of the family of Aeneas, the son of Anchises and Venus, established the cult of his "ancestor." The Romans consecrated to the goddess the month of April, the period during which the world sees the rebirth of love in all of nature.

VERTUMNUS. A divinity of Etruscan origin, Vertumnus symbolized above all the changes that take place in nature, and especially the passing from bloom to fructification. Since the root of his name is the Latin word *vertere* meaning "to change," Ovid concocted a legend about Vertumnus showing the young god to be in love with the nymph Pomona. To seduce her, he assumed various forms, representing the various seasons of the year. He changed himself into a laborer, then into a harvester, then into a vine grower, and finally had relations with the goddess of Gardens in the form

In the basin of a fountain, Venus, the goddess of Beauty, known for the astonishing whiteness of her skin, bathes with the help of a little Cupid. Ancient cameo, photo Giraudon.

The sea, from which Venus emerges, is symbolized here by an immense scallop shell, the first abode of the goddess and her son Cupid. Roman low relief, Villa Borghese, Rome, photo Anderson-Giraudon.

of a young man in the flower of his beauty. Gardeners dedicated a special cult to Vertumnus, offering him the first buds and the first fruit.

VESTA. Vesta is one of the greatest Roman divinities, whose cult undoubtedly goes back to very ancient times since she was identified with the goddess Hestia and was adored by both the Greeks and the Trojans. Vesta is, above all, the divinity of the Hearth. She is represented not only by a statue but also by fire, her living symbol. Every city has its own hearth and its sacred fire maintained by priestesses, the Vestal Virgins, who are buried alive if they break their oath of chastity. If the fire dies, it can only be reignited by the rays of the sun focused in a mirror. According to legend, Romulus and Remus were born of the Vestal Virgin Rea Silvia, and Numa Pompilius, the second king of Rome, was supposed to have instituted a service in her honor.

VICTORIA. The daughter of Pallas and Styx, the sister of Zelus ("zeal"), Cratus ("strength") and Bia ("force"), Victoria (known as Nike to the Greeks) belongs to the first generation of gods. She possessed a famous temple on the Acropolis of Athens. She was always associated with the goddess Athena *(Athena Nike)*. Ordinarily, artists depict her as a winged woman, carrying a palm and wearing a crown, guiding the gods and heroes during their exploits. The Romans, for their part, claimed that the effigy

The goddess Vesta, the incarnation of the hearth, appears as a simple Roman woman, her head covered, as was customary, with a sort of shawl. Roman coin, photo Larousse.

With her two wings, the goddess Victoria hastens towards the victor to whom she will award the crown she is holding in one hand. Notice the skill and inventiveness of the engraver who has imagined a third wing formed by the lower part of the divinity's tunic. Greek coin, Bibl. Nat., Cabinet des Médailles, photo Giraudon.

of Victoria had been erected by Palans, the eponymous hero of the Palatine, where a temple had been built in his honor.

vine. According to the most common legend, the vine was offered by Dionysus to thank King Oeneus for having agreed to lend him his wife. But it is also said that Staphylus ("cluster" in Greek), a shepherd of Oeneus', one day noticed that one of his goats, while eating grapes, became increasingly lively. He, therefore, thought to press the fruit and collect the juice, which became wine. The vine and wine appear in many other legends: that of Ampelus (the "vinestock"), who killed himself trying to grasp a cluster of grapes; that of Polyphemus, intoxicated by Ulysses, who succeeded in blinding him; that of Oenopion, who introduced into his kingdom on the island of Chios the use of wine just as the Roman Saturn had taught the inhabitants of Italy how to cultivate the vine. The Ancients saw in the vine and in Dionysus, the god of Wine with his entourage of merry, inebriated divinities, the symbolic image of the strength of nature full of sap, just as wine flows from the grape. With the cultivation of wheat, the cultivation of the vine is one of the first indications of an agricultural civilization.

VIRBIUS. Revived by Asclepius, Hippolytus was, according to one legend, transported by Artemis to the sacred wood of Aricia, in Italy. Then, when the hero died, he was deified and his name was changed to Virbius, the Roman god associated with the cult of Diana. The horses that brought about the death of Hippolytus were not permitted to enter the sacred wood.

VIRTUS. A Roman allegorical divinity and symbol of virile courage, Virtus is often represented with Honor. The Romans associated the two divinities by erecting two sanctuaries in their honor. Virtus is generally portrayed as a

Assisted by three Cyclopes who strike the anvil with long hammers, Vulcan, the blacksmith god, works fire to fashion the weapons of the heroes. The shield and helmet, at left, and the armor, at right, are under the watchful eye of Athena and Hera. Ancient sculpture, Palazzo dei Conservatori, Rome, photo Alinari-Giraudon.

proud austere woman, bearing a sword in one hand and a spear in the other.

VOLTURNUS. This old Roman divinity, about whose cult little is known, is doubtless the *numen* of a river. His roots may perhaps be traced to the religion of the Etruscans who adored the river-god Volturnus in Campania.

VOLUPTAS. The personification of pleasure in all its forms, Voluptas is portrayed as a beautiful, bright young woman exuding softness and sensuality. She was worshiped in Rome where a temple was erected in her honor under the Empire.

VULCAN. Like most primitive Roman gods, Vulcan lost his native character when the Greek gods invaded the Roman Pantheon. Of very remote origins, without a doubt Etruscan, having a place in certain legends, such as those of Romulus and Titus Tatius, the Sabine, Vulcan or Volcanus was originally worshiped as a great god. The god of Fire, the fire that all mythologies consider to be the primordial element of the world, Vulcan was identified with the Greek Hephaestus and reduced to the simple state of the blacksmith god, forging and fashioning the weapons of the gods in the hollows of volcanoes in the south of Italy.

W

winds. The sons of Eos and Astraeus, the winds are, among the manifestations of nature, divinized powers rather than gods. The master of these powers and winds is Aeolus; in fact, his power is modest; it is delegated by Zeus and it is from Zeus that he receives his orders to unleash the winds imprisoned in caves or goatskin bottles. Pernicious winds destroy everything in their paths and sow calamity everywhere. However, ordinary winds were originally benevolent. The winds number four: Boreas, the north wind (*Septentrio* in Latin), Eurus, the southwest wind *(Volturnus)*, Notus, the south wind *(Auster)*, and Zephyrus, the west wind *(Favonius)*. Although the Latins worshiped only these four winds, the Athenians, during the classical era, added four others to their cult and constructed an octagonal temple on which, on each angle, could be seen the image of one of the winds corresponding to the point on the horizon from which it usually blew. This multiplication of the winds and the sincere adoration with which they were honored is easily understood in a country in which agriculture and navigation were extremely important from an economic point of view and depended in part on the weather brought by the winds.

WISDOM. This allegorical divinity was for quite some time personified by the goddess Athena herself who represented, in the eyes of the Greeks, reason and peace, symbolized respectively by the owl and the olive branch.

Z

ZAGREUS. Zeus in the form of a serpent had relations with Persephone and begat a son, Zagreus, whom he gave to the Curetes to protect him from the jealous wrath of Hera. But Hera succeeded in finding the child and instructed the Titans to administer her vengeance. Seeing himself threatened, Zagreus assumed all manner of forms, both human and animal, and finally changed himself into a bull. The Titans, therefore, took the animal by the horns and, after tearing him to shreds, they devoured him. The remains of their victim were buried in Delphi by Apollo. But Pallas-Athena managed to save the still beating heart of Zagreus and handed it over to Zeus. Semele, or according to other versions, the supreme god himself, swallowed the child's heart, thus conceiving a new god, Dionysus. This myth of the resurrection of Zagreus formed the basis of a special cult during the celebration of the Orphic mysteries.

ZEPHYRUS. Known by the Romans as *Favonius*, Zephyrus, the divine personification of the west wind, brings freshness and bountiful rain to the foggy climates of Italy. A winged young man, he glides softly through the air and heralds the moisture of springtime. He had relations with Chloris, the goddess of new Growth, who gave birth to a son Carpus, Fruit. Like all the gods, Zephyrus sometimes displays anger.

On this subject it is said that, jealous of Apollo's love for Hyacinthus, one of his companions, Zephyrus turned a discus with his breath and the metal plate crashed into the forehead of Hyacinthus, killing him instantly.

ZETES. This Boread, the son of Boreas and Oreithyia, participated with his brother Calais in the expedition of the Argonauts, freed his nephews who were persecuted by their mother-in-law Idaea, and delivered Phineus from the Harpies who were tormenting him. Like his brother, he was killed either by the Harpies, whom he had pursued, or by Heracles.

ZETHUS. The son of Zeus and Antiope, Zethus, whose legend is inseparable from that of his twin brother Amphion, was abandoned on Mount Cithaeron and subsequently succeeded in avenging his mother who was persecuted by Dirce, the wife of Lycus. While Amphion married Niobe, Zethus married Thebe, the eponymous heroine of Thebes. But all their children, except two, were killed by Apollo and Artemis whose mother, Leto, they had insulted.

ZEUS. The god who ensured himself control of all the gods of mythology was originally nothing more than a god who was just a bit more formidable than the others. His glorification as the god of gods came only after centu-

The body of Zeus is both slender and robust, is ready for combat, with no clothing to impede his movement. His right hand prepares to throw lightning, with a harmonious gesture of the forearm and a forward movement of the body identical to that of a javelin thrower. Lekythos, Bibl. Nat., photo Giraudon.

ries of history, myths and various traditions. Adoring many gods, often overlooking one god or another, the peoples of the various Greek cities, separated not only by geographical destinies but by the uncertainties of history as well, acquired only later a sense of divine unity that was so crucial to the development of a hierarchy among the gods, at the top of which Zeus was ultimately to be placed.

Originally Zeus was the god of atmospheric phenomena, the god who illuminated the sky, covered it with clouds, distributed rain and snow, sent forth flashes of lightning, and gave rise to rolling thunder. It was even a common saying, in somewhat significant shortened form: "Zeus is raining or Zeus is thundering." However, in a country like Greece, where agriculture predominated, this exclusive power of a god over uncontrolled elements, dealing scourges or fertility, already indicated the preeminence of Zeus. With Homer, and later Hesiod, Zeus gradually acquired his ultimate personality. Homer defined him as the primary god and the supreme sovereign of mortals in whose activities he meddles. Hesiod, for his part, added to the predominance of Zeus by attributing a genealogy and myths to him. The son of Cronus and Rhea, Zeus was saved from the gluttonous infanticide of his father by his mother, who entrusted him to the Corybantes, the Curetes and the goat Amalthea. When he reached adulthood, he made his father restore his brothers and sisters who had been devoured: Poseidon, Hades, Hestia, Demeter, Hera. After he freed the Cyclopes and the Hecantoncheiroi, he dethroned Cronus, but not without waging a frightful battle against the rebellious Giants to assure ultimate sovereignty over the gods. Zeus then thought to ensure his posterity: he married, successively, Metis, Reason, who conceived Athena; Themis, the mother of the Moirae; Demeter, his sister, the mother of Persephone; Mnemosyne, mother of the Muses; Aphrodite, mother of the Graces; Leto, who gave birth to Apollo and Artemis; and finally Hera, who was his legitimate wife and gave birth to Hebe, Ares and Hephaestus. In addition, Zeus had countless adventures with mortals who brought into the world the race of heroes and demigods. He thus ensured between the gods and men a sort of hierarchy from which his power benefited. Thus, after the fluctuations and transformations of a world in the process of being created, after struggles among the primordial gods and the ensuring anarchy, Zeus appears as the image of appeasement, order, wisdom and justice. Indeed, the rules that Zeus formulated for the gods and the heavens were also established in earthly societies. Henceforth, the kings governed the cities and the peoples. Everyone was answerable to Zeus. Zeus was able to claim the two enviable titles of "father of the gods" and "father of men." He was consecrated as the universal god, the holder of all earthly and heavenly goods. Everything proceeded from him; he bore countless epithets and surnames, all of which indicated his functions or the areas in which he was honored. He reigns majestically, surrounded by everyday symbols and sovereign attributes alike. The eagle, lightning and victory are the representations of Zeus according to the statue of Olympian Zeus by Phidias, which affords him for all eternity the supreme grandeur that he alone, among both gods and men, possesses.

Zodiac. The series of celestial houses visited during the year by the Sun, the Zodiac is divided into twelve parts or signs, each symbolizing a myth, a legend or a figure of the constellation. Aries is the sign which, in mythology, bore the Golden Fleece. Taurus is the animal that abducted Europa. Gemini immortalizes the memory of the Dioscuri: Castor and Pollux. Cancer, a gigantic crayfish, was sent by Hera to bite Heracles. Leo is none other than the beast killed by Heracles in Nemea. Virgo symbolizes, for some, Astraea, for others, Erigone. Libra is the perfect symbol of Justitia. Scorpio is the animal that was dispatched by Artemis to sting Orion. Sagittarius is the image of the centaur Chiron. Capricorn is the symbol of the goat Amalthea, the nursemaid of Zeus. Aquarius is

An ominous head of Zeus dominates a terrace filled with remains of other gods including Mithras and Apollo. Nemrud Dagh, Turkey, photo Theresa Goell.

identified with Ganymede and Pisces commemorates those fish which carried Cupid and Aphrodite on their backs when they were pursued by Typhon.

MAJOR LITERARY SOURCES OF MYTHOLOGY

Circa 750 B.C.	HOMER	Iliad. Odyssey.
Circa 725	HESIOD	Theogony. Works and Days.
Circa 525–456	AESCHYLUS	The Suppliants. The Persians. Seven against Thebes. Prometheus Bound. Agamemnon. Choephoroe. Eumenides.
518–438	PINDAR	Epinicia: Olympic, Pythian, Nemean, Isthmian Odes.
496–405	SOPHOCLES	Ajax. Antigone. Oedipus Rex. Electra. Trachiniae. Philoctetes. Oedipus at Colonus.
Circa 484–circa 420	HERODOTUS	Histories.
485–406	EURIPIDES	Alcestis. Medea. Hippolytus. Heraclidae. Andromache. Hecuba. Heracles. The Suppliants. Ion. The Trojan Women. Iphigenia in Tauris. Electra. Helen. Phoenissae. Orestes. Iphigenia in Aulis. Bacchae. Cyclops.
Circa 295–circa 230	APOLLONIUS OF RHODES	Argonautica.
Circa 305–circa 240	CALLIMACHUS	Hymns to Zeus, to Apollo, to Artemis, to Delos. Baths of Pallas. Argonautica.
Circa 310–circa 250	THEOCRITUS	Idylls.
Circa 180	APOLLODORUS	On the gods. Library.
Circa 90–20	DIODORUS SICULUS	Historical library.
Circa 84–circa 54	CATULLUS	Odes, Elegies, including Attis; Peleus and Thetis; Berenice's Hair.
71–19	VIRGIL	Eclogues. Georgics. Aeneid.
Circa 50–circa 15	PROPERTIUS	Elegies.
59 B.C.–A.D. 17	LIVY	The Annals of the Roman People.
43 B.C.–A.D. 17	OVID	Metamorphoses. Fasti.
4 B.C.–A.D. 65	SENECA	Troades. Phoenissae. Medea. Phaedra. Oedipus. Agamemnon. Thyestes. Hercules Oetaeus. Hercules Furens.
Circa 40–96 A.D.	STATIUS	Thebaid. Achilleid.
Circa 50–circa 125	PLUTARCH	Parallel Lives.
Circa 125–circa 180	APULEIUS	Metamorphoses.
Late 2nd cent.	PAUSANIAS	Periegesis or Description of Greece.

INDEX

References to the left column of each text page are indicated by the letter "a" following the page number, thus: 153a. References to the right column are indicated by the letter "b" following the page number, thus: 233b.

When a person, place or concept is important enough to have an individual entry, that entry is printed in boldface type; for Athena, thus: **41b.**

Illustration pages are shown this way: illus 97b.

The pages of the genealogical tables are indicated this way: gen 13. Some characters (Achilles, Phaedra) are listed in more than one table. If one genealogy is special for that character, the page number of that one is printed in boldface type; for Achilles, thus: **gen 5** ; for Phaedra, thus: **gen 217.** The genealogy of Troy is considered special for its king, Priam; the genealogy of the gods is considered special for the king of the gods, Zeus.